THE ASIATIC HIVE BEE: APICULTURE, BIOLOGY, AND ROLE IN SUSTAINABLE DEVELOPMENT IN TROPICAL AND SUBTROPICAL ASIA

Edited by: PETER G. KEVAN
University of Guelph
Guelph, Ontario, Canada

Enviroquest, Ltd.
Cambridge, Ontario, Canada
1995

ISBN 0-9680123-0-2

The Asiatic Hive Bee: Apiculture, Biology, and Role
in Sustainable Development in Tropical and Subtropical Asia

First Published 1995

Printed in Malaysia by Malindo Printers Sdn Bhd. Lot 3, Jalan Ragum 15/17, Seksyen 15, 40000 Shah Alam. Selangor Darul Ehsan. Malaysia. Tel: 03-5505066. Fax: 03-5504066.

Enviroquest, Ltd., 352 River Road, Cambridge, Ontario, N3C 2B7, Canada

Cover art from the class of 1988, School of Arts and Design, Institut Teknologi Mara, Shah Alam, Malaysia.

DEDICATION

This book is dedicated to the Memory of The Late Professor Gordon F. Townsend whose pioneering devotion to apicultural development with indigenous bees and appropriate technology has been an inspiration to so many.

PREFACE

Beekeeping with *Apis cerana*, the Asiatic hive bee, has long and venerable traditions. Nevertheless, the amount of scientific information on this bee pales by comparison with that on the various races of European honeybees (*A. mellifera*). That is both a blessing and a curse for the apicultural community interested in the biology and potential for beekeeping of the Asiatic hive bee. It is a blessing because there is so much information from which to draw comparisons and so many practical lessons to be learned. It is a curse because it has been assumed that the Asiatic hive bee is not practical for modern beekeeping in Asia. The curse stems from the relatively small size of the Asiatic hive bees, their lower potential for producing honey, their propensity to abscond, and especially from the attitudes of apiculturalists who fail to take into account the long period of domestication, selective breeding, and scientific study which have allowed the European races of honeybees to become such an important and managed part of agriculture in Europe, the Americas, and the South Pacific. This book seeks to promote the Asiatic hive bee as an interesting species with great potential for apiculture and development throughout tropical and subtropical Asia.

This book does not draw comparisons between the two species of cavity-nesting honeybees (*A. cerana* and *A. mellifera*). It is intended to bring together what is known about the Asiatic hive bee from a practical viewpoint, and to point up the extent of knowledge and areas where much more needs to be learned. The authors of the chapters of this book all have profound knowledge about the biology and management of both species of bees so their insights are especially valuable as to the potential for the development of apiculture with the Asiatic hive bee.

I have arranged the chapters of this book into seven sections which start from basic information, proceed through practical concerns of apiculture *per se*, and end with promotion and sustainable development. Because this book is principally aimed at the practicality of bee biology and beekeeping with the Asiatic hive bee, the first chapter by Eva Crane is historical and the second on the natural history of bees in the tropics and subtropics.

Section II starts with Nikolaus Koeniger's introduction to its biology which is followed by L. Verma's discussion of its biodiversity and taxonomy throughout its range while noting the potential for selection and breeding. Thus, the stage is set for some more specific information on the Japanese race in chapters 5 and 6.

The general biology and value for beekeeping with the Asiatic hive bee leads to its potential for improvement for management by genetic selection and genetic engineering in Section III, chapters 7 and 8. Queen rearing and mating manipulation is central to any successful programme of improvement. This aspect of practical bee biology is covered in Sirawat Wongsiri's detailed chapter 9. That is followed by the special example of the Japanese race (chapter 10).

The next section (IV) of nine chapters concerns "bee botany" pollination, foraging, floral calenders (chapter 11) and the specific example of Malaysia being used to illustrate the principles in chapter 12. Pollination is very much a part of apicultural science because honeybees are the most tractable of managed pollinators. The principles of the technology of managing bees for pollination are introduced in chapter 13. This chapter is followed by a brief review of insect-pollinated economically important crops of the region (chapter 14). The use of the Asiatic hive bee in pollination is covered in general by R.C. Sihag (chapter 15) and specific examples are described for apples in northern India (chapter 16) and cruciferous crops in Pakistan (chapters 17 and 18). The final chapter in this section deals with foraging and honey production and illustrates the importance of understanding both botanical and apidological sides of the equation and, using the example of Bangladesh, provides insight into issues raised in Section VI.

The next set of chapters (Section V) concern the protection of bees from diseases, mites, pesticides, and exotic problems. Viruses are the most important cause of colony death for the Asiatic hive bee. Viral afflictions are discussed by Denis Anderson in chapter 20. Mites are also a problem and the biology and control of *Varroa jacobsoni* and *Acarapis woodi* are discussed with examples from the eastern (in Japan, chapter 21) and western extremities (in Pakistan, chapters 22 and 23) of the range of the Asiatic hive bee. More general accounts of diseases are given for Malaysia (chapter 24) and China (chapter 25).

Chapter 26 by R.C. Sihag, on pesticides and beekeeping, has been placed after the discussions on bee botany (Section IV) because bees are poisoned mostly while foraging at the crops they pollinate and while returning nectar to the hive to cure to honey. This chapter brings together management issues which transcend just beekeeping and the protection of bees, and places them in the context of the management of agricultural systems.

The final chapter 27 is presented to illustrate the importance for international co-operation about the importation of honeybees. It behooves the importing country to exercise great caution when introducing any exotic species. The problems caused by the introduction of African stocks of honeybees into South America, by tracheal mites into Mexico, and *Varroa* mites into the U.S.A. should serve as vivid lessons.

Thus, the multiplicity of lessons illustrated in Section V must be kept in mind in the deliberations presented in Section VI.

Although, by now the book has carried the reader from basic bee biology to the principles and practice of apiculture, there remain some rather important practical issues to cover. Section VI is about management at all levels, from bees to apiaries, to business and economics. Chapter 28 by C.C. Reddy brings much of the foregoing into focus in its discussion of the general management practices for stationary and migratory beekeeping with the Asiatic hive bee. Chapter 29 places the above into the realities of management of both bees and beekeeping. The constraints of honey production, foraging range, and nectar resources are brought home in considerations about apiary size and management in chapter 30. From the natural economics of bees and honey production, chapter 31 introduces the human aspects of economics in beekeeping. The fermentation problem of honeys with high water content, as from humid tropical and subtropical climates, can be solved by dehydration as described in chapter 32. Once honey is produced, it must be traded if the beekeeper is to benefit materially as discussed in chapter 33.

The basis for beekeeping with the Asiatic hive bee is well documented above (Sections I - V). Also, its economic and practical potential and actual value in agriculture and for honey production is established (Sections IV - V). There remains the issue of promoting beekeeping industries in tropical and subtropical Asia by using the indigenous hive bee. In Section VII, chapter 34 presents a general model for an holistic approach to the development of beekeeping and chapters 35 and 36 use specifically Bangladesh and the Philippines to illustrate the potential for the approach. Successful projects embrace all aspects of apiculture from basic bee biology to economics and education. Chapters 37 and 38 address opportunities for funding and inter-institutional co-operation, and provide examples of accomplishments.

There remains one crucial and unexplored area for apicultural development in the tropics and subtropics. That is hive design. It is unfortunate that more attention has not been paid to this aspect of apicultural research. Although various hive designs have been ventured, the over-riding thought behind them has been cost. Clearly that is important, but it is more important that the primary goal in hive design is to maintain bees easily and to keep absconding to a minimum. It is my feeling that many of the hives used in modern beekeeping in the tropics and subtropics suffer from their hampering the resident colonies from thermoregulating properly and efficiently under hot and humid conditions. Thus, I think that hives should be designed with all the standard concerns in mind (bee space, moveable frames, ease of inspection, etc.) but to allow the bees to regulate the climate within the artificial cavities. This, I believe, is especially important where shade is wanting. I suggest that hive bodies made of material that can attenuate daily and seasonal temperature fluctuations within, especially as brought about by insolation, be used to test my idea. Such materials are thick coconut wood (as in Malaysian and Indonesian gelodok hives) and concrete and clay (as used in Sri Lanka).

ACKNOWLEDGEMENTS

I would like to thank most sincerely all the contributors to this book for the patience over a series of set-backs in its preparation. The book is the outcome of "The Advanced Course in Beekeeping with *Apis cerana* in Tropical and Subtropical Asia" held from 7 - 14 February, 1988 at the Universiti Pertanian Malaysia, Serdang, Selangor, Malaysia. I thank the members of the Beekeeping Team there for their assistance, and especially wish to thank Makhdzir Mardan for his part in the organization. Dr. Abd. Rahman Razak, Dean of the Fakulti Pertanian and Dr. Syed Jalaluddin, Vice Chancellor for their active interest and assistance in the administration of the Course. Without the enthusiasm of the 69 participants in the course, this book would not have come about. I thank them all. I also thank those who were involved in some initial planning for the original "workshop" with various venues which were removed from consideration by extenuating circumstances (e.g. Sri Lanka, Bangladesh, and Indonesia). The project as a whole would not have been possible without grants from the Canadian International Aid Agency and from the International Development Research Centre. To both agencies and their many personnel who were so encouraging over the years of planning, I am grateful. The Center for International Programs at the University of Guelph has also been most helpful and maintained the flame of interest throughout the long period of difficulties. I am highly indebted to Sue Willis for her assistance with editing at the onset of the preparation of this book. I also give posthumous thanks to Carl Schmidt of Johanns Graphics, Waterloo, Canada. His sudden and untimely death was a major set-back resulting in the loss of a respected colleague and unfinished work. Jan Lupson has been a pillar of strength and perseverance in her crucial role in technical editing and organization as the book has been brought into fruition at the University of Guelph. Habsah Marjuni of CP Business Publishers Sdn Bhd in Kuala Lumpur has kindly and patiently brought the book to press. There are so many people to thank for all their efforts and even though you are not mentioned by name, please accept my heartfelt thanks.

CONTENTS

SECTION VI: MANAGEMENT, ECONOMICS, AND HONEY PRODUCTION

SECTION VII: DEVELOPMENT

SECTION I: HISTORY

SECTION 1: HISTORY

CHAPTER 1

HISTORY OF BEEKEEPING WITH *APIS CERANA* IN ASIA

EVA CRANE

INTRODUCTION

I have been asked to trace the general history of beekeeping with *Apis cerana*. This chapter represents the first attempt to do so, and there are still many gaps in the story which I hope readers will try to fill in.

I have divided the development of beekeeping in Asia into six possible stages, which are set out in Table I.

Stage 1 is the collection of honey from wild nests of bees, and I believe that this stage has occurred almost everywhere in the world where there are honey-storing bees, except where religious ordinance prohibited it. The earliest direct evidence is provided by rock paintings (Table II). These have been found during the present century in all continents except the Americas (Crane 1983); the most recent finds in Asia have been by Mathpal (1984), but these show *A. dorsata* not *A. cerana*.

Stage 2 is the ownership of wild nests in trees or rocks. In the forests of northern Europe tree beekeeping occurred from 2000 or 1000 BC to AD 1700 or later (Crane 1983). A beekeeper owned certain trees that contained a wild nest of *A. mellifera*. He looked after the colonies to a certain extent, and in later centuries fitted a door to get at the

honey. The total amount of honey obtained was large - in the 1100s it was over 6000 tonnes a year in Russia alone (Galton 1971). Vestiges have recently been found of a similar practice among native peoples of northwest Australia, with nests of stingless bees in trees (Dollin and Dollin 1986). *A. cerana* nests have been similarly owned and tended in this way in Laos in southeast Asia. *A. dorsata* nests were certainly owned, for instance in Sri Lanka. Seligmann and Seligmann (1911) devote a chapter to the subject, and quote several cases where a bride's parents gave their new son-in-law a hill or cave containing a number of nests.

Stage 3 is beekeeping proper - the keeping of colonies of bees in hives, i.e. in receptacles that are specially designated or constructed for the purpose; this is essentially an activity of settled agricultural people, in neolithic times or later. I confine Stage 3 to the use of fixed-comb (traditional) hives. Many early writings mention honey, and some from Ancient India and China are several thousand years old. But I would emphasize strongly that a written reference to honey or beeswax does not provide evidence of beekeeping using hives (Stage 3), and neither does a graphic or ornamental representation of a bee. Much honey and wax came from wild colonies, and unless man-made hives are mentioned, or there is

TABLE I. Possible stages in beekeeping in different parts of Asia.

Stage	Dates	Activity
1	early man to present	collecting honey from wild nests: order of importance = *A. dorsata* (including *laboriosa*), *A. cerana* (including *A. koschevnikovi*), *A. florea* (including *A. andreniformis*), Meliponinae (stingless bees)
2	?	ownership of wild *A. cerana* nests in trees or rocks (e.g. tree beekeeping)
3	? AD 500 to present	keeping *A. cerana* in purpose-built traditional (fixed-comb) hives
4	1930s or earlier to present	keeping *A. cerana* in movable-comb hives
5	1876 (or early 1900s) to present	keeping *A. cerana* in modern (movable-frame) hives
6	1880s (or early 1900s) to present	keeping introduced *A. mellifera* in modern hives

TABLE II. Rock paintings that provide early evidence of honey hunting.

Species of bee	Country	Number	Earliest date known
European *A. mellifera*	Spain	several	Mesolithic (6000 BC)
tropical African *A. mellifera*	Africa	very many	various
A. dorsata	India	several	Mesolithic
	Sri Lanka	several	recent
A. cerana		none known	-
A. florea		none known	-
Meliponinae (stingless bees)	Australia (Queensland)	one known	recent

some equivalent evidence, we cannot be sure how they were obtained.

I believe that man has generally obtained honey in the <u>least</u> <u>difficult</u> <u>way</u> available to him - the least hazardous, and involving the least number of stings - although honey was so highly prized that he was willing to face both danger and stings to get it. Stage 3, which in most of Asia was beekeeping with *A. cerana*, is therefore likely to have developed earliest where there was no other, more effective, way of getting honey. A wild nest of *A. dorsata* gave a much higher honey yield, so on this basis early beekeeping with *A. cerana* is most likely to have occurred in the parts of Asia that were without *A. dorsata*, including the ecotype *laboriosa*.

Stage 4 is the use of movable-comb top-bar hives, such as Sir George Wheler found being used for *A. mellifera* in Greece in 1682 (Crane 1983). In Asia, Toumanoff (1933) and Toumanoff and Nanta (1933) described top-bar hives used for *A. cerana* by some beekeepers in Tonkin in north Vietnam (Fig. 1). An upright hollow log was set up with top-bars placed across the top, from which the bees built their combs, and photographs show individual combs being lifted out of the hives - the combs were truly movable. I have not been able to find out when or where this type of hive in Vietnam originated, but Mulder (1988) searched for and found some of the hives still in use in the north. Logs had been hollowed out so that the upper half had a larger internal diameter than the lower half, and the top-bars rested on the resultant ledge half-way up the hive. The brood chamber thus had movable combs; in the (upper) honey chamber, the bees attached their combs to a board that covered the hive.

Stage 5 is modern beekeeping with movable-frame hives (Langstroth 1853), which had its basis in the Greek top-bar hives found by Sir George Wheler

in 1682. As far as I know, beekeepers in Asia learned movable-frame beekeeping from North America and Europe, where the system was used for *A. mellifera*. I cannot find any evidence that it was developed independently in Asia.

There is one other surprise in southeast Asia in addition to the top-bar hives, and this seems to be unique to *A. cerana* beekeeping: tethering the queen, with a hair or a fine thread, in a place where the beekeeper wants a natural or artificial swarm of bees to cluster. The thread is looped around the queen between her thorax and abdomen, using a tie that can finally be pulled undone without touching the queen. I met this practice in Samui Island, Thailand,

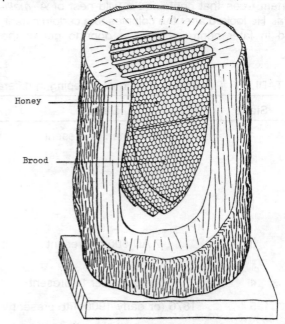

FIGURE 1. Movable-comb log hive used in Vietnam (Toumanoff and Nanta 1933).

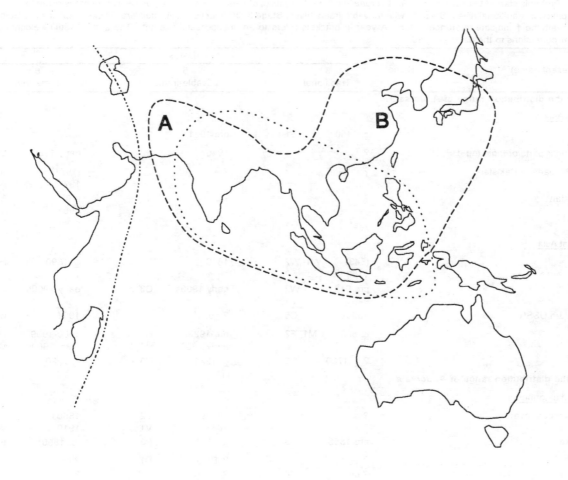

FIGURE 2. Natural boundaries of *Apis mellifera* (-·-··-), *A. cerana* (- - - -), and *A. dorsata* (·· · ··), based on data from Ruttner (1988). The two regions where *A. cerana* is native, but not *A. dorsata*, are marked A and B.

and it is described from Burma (Maung 1984), and from Vietnam (Toumanoff and Nanta 1933).

In some parts of Asia, the use of frame hives for *A. cerana* (Stage 5) came after the introduction of *A. mellifera* in frame hives, which I have called **Stage 6**. In many countries, *A. cerana* and *A. mellifera* beekeeping tends to occur in different regions and, in some, *A. cerana* is still at Stage 3.

Table III gives, for each country where *A. cerana* is native, the earliest date so far found when beekeeping with *A. cerana* was first recorded: with traditional hives (Stage 3), with movable-comb hives (Stage 4) and with movable-frame hives (Stage 5); also when - if at all - *A. mellifera* was introduced (Stage 6). I divided the countries into two groups, the first group without *A. dorsata*, and the second group with *A. dorsata*, on the grounds that there

would have been an early incentive to develop beekeeping (Stage 3) only where *A. cerana* was present, but not *A. dorsata*. Many countries with *A. dorsata* still obtain the greater part of their honey harvest from this bee.

REGIONS WHERE BEEKEEPING WITH *APIS CERANA* IS LIKELY TO HAVE STARTED EARLY

The northwest: Kashmir, northern India, Pakistan, Afghanistan

This region includes parts of the great Indus valley, and especially of the mountain lands that form its upper catchment area (A in Fig. 2).

TABLE III. Probable start of beekeeping with *Apis cerana* in different countries of Asia. The year (AD) of the first record is given for: Stage 3, beekeeping with traditional hives; Stage 5, with movable-frame hives; Stage 6, introduction of *A. mellifera*; Table I explains the Stages. Codes beneath the † indicate references cited. A year in brackets refers to an unsuccessful attempt. The author would welcome any additions or corrections to the dates entered.

Area (present name) Stage:	Dates					
	3 Traditional		5 Movable-frames		6 *A. mellifera*	
Outside the distribution range of *A. dorsata*						
Western Asia		†		†		†
Kashmir	c. 1450	S1	pre-1931	N1		
neighbouring parts of India (eg. HP, UP)	?		1940	S2	early 1960s	S2
W. and N. parts of Pakistan	?		?		(1927)	A1
					1977	A1
Afghanistan	?		?		(1955)	W4
					1961	W4
E. Iran	yes*	G1	?		?	
Northeast Asia						
Japan	(643)	W1, W2	1876	?	c. 1890	H2
	1160	?				
Korea	pre-643	W2	early 1900s	C3	early 1900s	C3
	940	L1				
Far Eastern USSR	1800s	C5	? no		1904	C5
China**	c. 500	M1, F2	pre-1923	H1	1900-1909	H1
			early 1900s	M1	early 1900s	M1
Taiwan	? c. 1700	C2	c. 1920	H3	c. 1920	H3
Within the distribution range of *A. dorsata*						
India and neighbours						
India (except above)	?		1880s	J2	1880s	J2
			1883	V1	1910	M4
Sri Lanka	pre-1855	P3	c. 1875	P3	(c. 1890)	P3
Nepal	?		? 1968	D1	? no	
Tibet	? no	C4	? no		? no	
Bhutan	? no		1980	J1	1988	B1
Southeast Asia						
Bangladesh	1947	A3	1965	A3	? no	
Burma	?		? 1979	D1	? no	
			1982	M3		
Malaysia	?		1950s	P2	1930s	P2, S4
Singapore	?		?		1929	L2
Indonesia***	1864	P1	1918	P1	1877	P1
			1920s	S3	pre-1924	B2
					1972	S5
Thailand	?		1950s	A2	(c. 1940)	W3
					1950s	A2
					1970	W3
Kampuchea	? 1950s		? 1950s		?	
Laos	? 1950s		?		?	
Vietnam	?		pre-1933	T2	1947	M2
			(also Stage 3)			
Philippines	1978	C1	1978	C1	1913	C1

*   Introduced from Pakistan some centuries ago (G1).
**   *A. dorsata* in extreme south.
***   Outside Asia: in 1985, *A. cerana* was found to have been introduced to Irian Jaya (Indonesia) in the island of New Guinea.

FIGURE 3. Two views of a red pottery hive for *Apis cerana* in Kashmir (1980), with flight holes in the rounded end (compare with Fig. 4).

Kashmir

In Kashmir in 1980, I found clear links between beekeeping with *A. cerana* there and beekeeping with *A. mellifera* in the Ancient World of the eastern Mediterranean. Horizontal clay hives were used as shown in Figure 3; they were tapered and rounded at one end and were almost identical to hives of which remnants have been excavated at 26 different sites in Greece, the earliest (Fig. 4) dated to 400 BC (Crane and Graham 1985). Also, I was quite astonished to find that present-day beekeepers in Kashmir pack and sell comb honey in a pair of shallow clay vessels, one inverted on the other to form a lid, as in Figure 5.

FIGURE 4. Red pottery hive from about 400 BC, found in the Agora in Athens, Greece (photo American School of Classical Studies at Athens: Agora Excavations).

I had seen such vessels portrayed in a tomb in Egypt dated to 1450 BC. In the tomb painting (reproduced in Crane 1983), pairs of vessels are being sealed together with mud, and this is done in Kashmir today, 3500 years later.

Crane and Graham (1985) give further information about finds in the eastern Mediterranean, and Shah (1984) has suggested that the diffusion of knowledge about beekeeping and honey handling from that region reached Kashmir, where it was applied to *A. cerana*. He points out that in very early times, the ruler and the people of Kashmir were Hindus, and followers of the Hindu religion are not traditionally beekeepers. Between 1420 and 1470, however, Kashmir was ruled by Zain-ul-Abidin, a Muslim who introduced craftsmen from the Middle East, including Egypt, probably via the Indus valley. A first-hand account from 1819-25 by Moorcroft and Trebeck may well indicamomote what beekeeping in Kashmir was like soon after its introduction, and his account differs little from traditional beekeeping there today.

In Ancient times in both Egypt and Greece, more or less cylindrical hives were placed horizontally, stacked in piles in the open, or embedded in specially built walls. Kashmir has a much more severe winter climate, and traditional hives are laid on shelves in the thickness of house walls (Fig. 6), any one house having up to twenty or more; a flight hole is provided for each hive through the wall, and honey is harvested from inside the house.

FIGURE 5. Pair of red pottery vessels used as a container for honey combs, Kashmir, 1980.

FIGURE 6. Hive entrances in a house wall in Kashmir (one above each of the two upper windows, one to the right of the boys, and one midway up, at the side of the house), 1980.

Neighbouring regions

The practice of siting horizontal hives in the thickness of house walls is also well developed in other areas at the head of the Indus valley. In parts of northern India, Singh (1983) describes rectangular wall cavities (jalas), with a wooden closure plastered on the inner side, as common in parts of Uttar Pradesh, hollowed logs (dhandas) being used to provide wall cavities in the higher hills. In the valley of Swat, high above Peshawar in Pakistan, cavities are also left in the house wall (Verhagen 1971); the wooden closure of the hive forms part of the room wall, and honey is harvested from inside the room by removing the closure, as in Kashmir. A variant in Nepal is described below. Something similar is done in Ladakh above the vale of Kashmir; outdoor hives there are square, of wood, and honey is harvested from the top of them. In Afghanistan, a hollowed log (Fig. 7) is sometimes placed inside the length of the house wall. To the west of the Afghanistan border, in Nuristan and in Paktia farther south, cavities in the mud house walls are lined with a wooden framework (Schneider and Djalal 1970; see also Kloft and Kloft 1971; Nogge 1974), or a cooking pot may be laid on its side in the cavity to serve as a hive. The areas mentioned are up to 2000 m above sea level (Melkania *et al.* 1983). In parts of Uttar Pradesh, annual honey yields per hive (presumably modern) are quoted as 6-10 kg at 1000-1700 m, 10-15 kg at 1700-2100 m, and 12-16 kg at 2100-2700 m. In Turkey, I have seen wall cavities, such as those described, near sea level by the Sea of Marmora, where they are used as hives for *A. mellifera*.

The western boundary of *A. cerana* is separated from *A. mellifera* territory farther west by a belt of desert, shown in Figure 2. According to Gassparian (1977), *A. cerana* bees have been kept in clay pots and gourds for some centuries in Baluchistan (in Pakistan, west of the line joining Quetta and Karachi); hives of these bees were taken from Baluchistan to Iran by man. *A. cerana* has also been recorded in the mountains of north Khorassan (Pourasghar 1986). More information is needed on this foreign introduction of *A. cerana* into Iran.

The northeast: Japan, Korea, Russian Far East, China

A. cerana is native farther north in the east of Asia (45°N) than in the west (35°N) (Fig. 2). In Europe and Africa, where beekeeping with *A. mellifera* developed, most traditional hives were laid horizontally like their prototype in Ancient Egypt (which is known from 2500 BC), except in the north of Europe. There, hives stood upright, following the pattern of a log from a tree containing a wild colony,

as in tree beekeeping. The dividing line between horizontal and upright hives was roughly the chain of mountains running from the Pyrenees in the west, along the Alps, to the Caucasus and beyond in the east. However, there have been many enclaves of upright hives to the south of this line, and of horizontal hives to the north of it.

Traditional hives for *A. cerana* in Asia seem to follow a somewhat similar pattern - horizontal in the south and upright in the north. At present, perhaps because of our less complete knowledge, the pattern appears to be more confused.

Japan

According to Ko Watanabe (1984), the earliest record of beekeeping in Japan is dated to the year AD 643, when Prince Yoha of Kudora in Korea tried to keep bees 'in 4 combs [hives?] at a holy mountain, Miwayama', but he failed.

Traditional hives in Japan are of various shapes, but mostly with only one chamber (Fig. 8). Many are of wood, with an outer protection against the weather such as is shown in Figure 9. Ochi (1985) described a variety in use on Shikoku Island. Tsushima Island, which lies between Korea and Japan, is an important stronghold of traditional beekeeping with *A. cerana*. Figure 10 shows an upright log hive.

One type of hive used in Kumano, and illustrated in 1795 (Fig. 11), was different. It was made up of a tier of shallow square boxes (without frames), stacked one above another. The boxes were secured together by a wide cross-bar across the top and the bottom of the hive, and by an upright on each side of it. The combs were continuous from top to bottom of the hive, and honey was harvested by slicing through combs between boxes; the top boxes thus served as honey supers. I have seen these tiered hives in museums in Japan.

Ko Watanabe (1984) told me that the first experimental *A. mellifera* colonies in Japan were brought by his father, Hiroshi Watanabe, to Gifu in 1901; the first colonies used for practical beekeeping came from Hawaii in 1910.

Korea

There is a reference to bees in the Kingdom of Koguryo dated to c. 30 BC (Choi 1984), but not to beekeeping. A manuscript from AD 300 refers to the harvesting of honey from wild nests: wood honey came from old tree trunks, and stone honey from rocks (Lee 1981). However, the record from AD 643, of an attempt by a Korean Prince to keep bees in Japan, suggests that beekeeping in Korea had an early origin, and there is an AD 940 record of Buddhist monks starting to keep bees (Lee 1981). Traditional Korean hives are upright logs, fairly similar to

FIGURE 7. Afghan beekeeper showing a hive newly hollowed out from a log, to be incorporated (horizontally) in his house wall, Agru, Nuristan, 1970 (photo: R. Verhagen).

FIGURE 8. Harvesting honey from traditional hives in Japan, from 'Remarks on useful products' by Okhura (1859).

FIGURE 9. Traditional, well protected wooden hives in a garden near Fukuoka, Kyushu, Japan, 1983 (photo: I. Okada).

FIGURE 10. Traditional log hive in Shikoku, Japan, 1957 (photo: I. Okada).

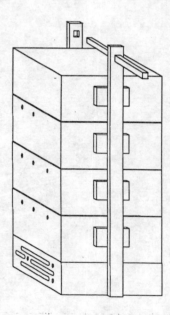

FIGURE 11. Contemporary drawing of the traditional tiered hive described in text, used in Izumo, Japan, in the Edo era (1700s).

that in Figure 10. Sangyō-Yōhō (1934) published photographs of them, and Takata (1937) indicated their dimensions and the method of construction. He also mentioned the use (in Zanra-nando Province) of hives built up from sections of hollow log, each 15-18 cm high; they were piled in a tier, and added to as the colony grew. It has been said that this type of hive 'had been brought there some hundreds of years ago by the resident priest', but I do not know the evidence.

Russian Far East

The native distribution of *A. cerana* extends north of Korea into the Primor'e (Far Eastern) Province of the USSR. As far as I know, beekeeping did not begin there until the 1800s when peasants were emigrated to this coastal region from southern Russia. The beekeepers among them tried to keep *A. cerana* in log hives, such as they had used at home for *A. mellifera*, but were not successful. Then, in 1904, the first Trans-Siberian railway was completed and subsequent emigrants from the Ukraine were able to take with them their own hives of Ukrainian *A. mellifera* and, in due course, modern beekeeping in the region developed successfully.

The *A. cerana* population has since declined and, as a result of mite infestation and insecticide poisoning, there are now only a few colonies in the woods (Bilash 1987).

China

Beekeeping is said to have begun about AD 500 (Ma De-Feng 1984). Books written after about AD 1000 show that the bees were kept in wooden tubs and bamboo cages (baskets?), and that honey and wax were harvested in late autumn and/or early spring. Gong (1983) says that by the 1300s, many households were keeping bees. Various types of traditional hives have been used for *A. cerana* (Ma De-Feng 1984). Hollow logs (30-60 cm in diameter and 1 m long) were positioned horizontally or, in the north, stood upright. Wooden tubs - used also in Japan and Korea - were 40-50 cm in diameter at the bottom and 30-40 cm at the top, and one tub might be 'supered' with another. Long rectangular hives of boards were used, sometimes with a honey chamber below. Bamboo and wicker baskets were coated with slurry (probably cow dung and mud) to make them weather-tight.

As in the upper reaches of the Indus valley, a cavity for bees might be built into house walls; dimensions could be about 20-30 cm deep, 40-50 cm wide (along the wall), and 30 cm high.

Frame hives were used for *A. cerana* in Manchuria before 1922 (Hanson 1923) and in Guangdong, Fujian from the 1930s. Meanwhile, in the early 1900s, Caucasian *A. mellifera* in movable-frame hives had been introduced from Russia in Xinjiang (Sinkiang) and other regions. Then in 1910, Italian *A. mellifera* were imported from Japan, and their use spread rapidly in Beijing, Shanghai, and Hopei Provinces.

REGIONS WHERE BEEKEEPING IS LIKELY TO HAVE STARTED LATE

The rest of India, and neighbouring countries

We shall consider first the whole of India (except for the parts adjacent to Kashmir and other areas that drain into the river Indus), together with Sri Lanka, Nepal, Tibet, and Bhutan.

Muttoo (1944) commented on the surprising absence of references to beekeeping in the vast literature of Ancient India, which contains so many mentions of honey. The most likely explanation seems to be that wild nests of *A. dorsata* were the main source of honey then, as they are today.

Movable-frame beekeeping was introduced in India during the 1880s (Joshi *et al.* 1983), but

developments were very slow. The All-India Beekeepers' Association was founded in 1937, and the Indian Bee Journal in 1939. Since 1949, the Khadi and Village Industries Commission has organized *A. cerana* beekeeping, first on a local, and then on a national level (Thakar 1976). The use of *A. mellifera* is confined to the Punjab and some areas farther north.

Sri Lanka

To the south of India is Sri Lanka, where pot hives were used at least as early as the 1850s, and frame hives in 1875. *A. mellifera* has been introduced several times, but has not succeeded. According to Lanerolle (1984), 65% of the honey still comes from honey hunting, of both *A. dorsata* and *A. cerana*.

Nepal

In Nepal, *A. cerana* colonies are kept in horizontal log hives, hung or otherwise supported under the eaves of the mud houses. This sheltered domestic location is well suited to bees that are gentle; similar hives are placed there, for instance, in Bali in Indonesia for *A. cerana* (Fig. 12) and in Central America by Maya Indians for *Melipona beecheii*, one of the stingless bees. Near Pokhara, in western Nepal, I have seen a cavity left for bees in the east gable wall of houses; one climbs up into the roof space of the house to reach the hive, and a wooden shutter is removed to gain access to the combs. It seems likely that this system is derived from the developments at the head of the Indus valley. Some tribes, such as the Gurung, collect honey from *A. dorsata* (and *laboriosa*) on rock faces north of Pokhara, but where honey collectors and beekeepers lived in the same area, I found little or no interconnection between them.

Modern movable-comb hives with top-bars but no frames are also used in Nepal, especially through Gordon Temple's enterprise, and there are a few frame hives.

Tibet and Bhutan

Tibetans were officially forbidden to take honey from bees' nests, since their Buddhist religion does not allow them to deprive animals of their food (Harrer 1954). Honey harvesting from *A. dorsata* nests in Tibet has been done by Tibetan people from Nepal. Modern beekeeping with *A. cerana* may by now have been introduced by the Chinese.

In Bhutan, a large part of the population are also Buddhist, and there is very little beekeeping. Frame hives of *A. cerana* were brought in from India about 1980 (Jørgensen 1983).

Southeast Asia

Lastly, we come to the countries of southeast Asia: Bangladesh, Burma, Malaysia, Singapore, Indonesia, Thailand, Kampuchea, Laos, Vietnam, and the Philippines. Beekeeping is relatively new throughout most of this large region, except possibly in areas to the north that border on China or have been under Chinese influence, but the subject has been little explored. In the Introduction, I referred to the use of movable-comb top-bar hives in Vietnam, and perhaps this had its origin in China. The earliest dates I have been able to find for beekeeping anywhere in southeast Asia are not much more than a hundred years ago, and a few are known to be quite recent (Table III). Two islands where traditional beekeeping with *A. cerana* seems to have flourished earlier than on neighbouring lands are Samui Island in Thailand, where it is likely that Chinese traders introduced it (Wongsiri 1988), and Bali in Indonesia (Figs. 13 and 12). Statements are often made that beekeeping in a certain country existed 'many centuries ago', 'from earliest times' or 'in the mists of antiquity', but one needs supporting evidence before believing them.

Table III includes the earliest dates as I have been able to ascertain, and I am indebted to participants at the meeting in Malaysia for some of them.

In some countries, beekeeping seems not to have started until movable-frame hives were used. Where *A. mellifera* beekeeping has subsequently been introduced into suitable areas, as in China and Japan for instance, there has been less incentive to proceed with *A. cerana* beekeeping in those areas. There are, nevertheless, large areas where *A. cerana* is the only choice for modern beekeeping.

CONCLUSION

I believe that we should apply our present knowledge of the history of *A. cerana* beekeeping when seeking answers to the following questions:
-   Where is it most beneficial to promote *A. cerana* beekeeping?
-   Where should the use of movable-frame hives be taught and extended?
-   Should the use of movable-comb top-bar hives be promoted and, if so, where? These hives have not proved as popular for *A. cerana* as they have in some parts of the world for *A. mellifera*, but the reasons are not yet clearly assessed.
-   Where are the benefits of using *A. mellifera* likely to be so great that they should be weighed up against the dangers associated with importing this bee? These include the introduction of diseases and parasites, competition with and possible extinction of beekeeping with *A. cerana* - and of *A. cerana* itself - and associated ecological changes.
-   Finally, there are many areas where both *A. cerana* and *A. dorsata* are native, and the major honey production is still by collection from wild nests of *A. dorsata*. In which of these areas is the best aim for research and extension the extended use of *A. cerana* in hives? In which areas would it be better to concentrate on upgrading honey harvesting from *A. dorsata* - either unmanaged in the wild or managed, for instance in the way developed in India (Mahindre 1983; Crane 1990).

The present meeting, on beekeeping in Asia with *A. cerana*, follows one on beekeeping in Asia with *A. mellifera*, arranged by FAO in 1984. I think that a possible third international meeting should be considered, to be held before too many years have passed, on upgrading honey harvesting from *A. dorsata*, and on exploring possible types of beekeeping management with *A. dorsata*. This would largely complete a feasibility study on the exploitation of Asia's honeybee resources.

FIGURE 12. Two hives made from parts of the coconut palm and closed at the ends with half shells, under the eaves of a house in Bali, Indonesia, 1972 (photo: R. Verhagen).

FIGURE 13. Harvesting honey from a box hive of *Apis cerana* on Ko Samui, Thailand, 1986.

APPENDIX: DIAGNOSTIC FEATURES OF HIVES FOR *APIS CERANA*

The present paper is concerned specifically with the history of beekeeping in Asia with *A. cerana*. We are only at the start of exploring this subject, and there is a great need for archaeological evidence to support it, of the type that has been accumulated for beekeeping with *A. mellifera* (Crane 1983). Such evidence should be sought especially in the areas where beekeeping started relatively early, i.e. beyond the territory of *A. dorsata*. Searches in other areas may also bring some surprises. Diagnostic features of hives for *A. cerana* are listed below, adapted from Crane and Graham (1985), and it would be useful if these could be brought to the notice of archaeologists who may be working within *A. cerana* territory, to help them to recognize finds that might be remnants of hives. Asia is, at present, a virgin field for beekeeping archaeology.

A purpose-built hive for *A. cerana* is likely to be characterized by:

a) Its material(s) and construction: rigid, bee-proof, weatherproof, giving some thermal insulation, of almost any material except metal.

b) Capacity could be 10-50 litres, or even outside these limits; the larger hives would be expected in the north and at high altitudes, where bees are larger.

c) Entrance hole(s) for bees, commonly 1-2 cm across (or a slit about 1 cm wide). Entrances may be provided in the hive or in its closure, or by irregularities in construction, especially at the junction of two surfaces, e.g. between a hive and its closure or stand. Hives (and also certain other containers) may have small holes for ventilation or for cord used to secure two parts together.

d) Means of access by the beekeeper when removing honey combs. This can be provided, for instance: by using an open-bottomed hive standing on a base (lifting it up to take the combs); by cutting off the flat top of the hive (to which honeycombs were attached); or by incorporating a large, removable closure at one or both ends of a horizontal hive, or on one side of an upright hive. Alternatively, some primitive hives are made of disposable material such as mud (with or without animal dung). They are broken into to reach the honey combs, and immediately repaired by applying more mud.

e) Support for the combs: bees build their combs down from the top of their hive, so a hive must have a solid top. A horizontal hive may show combing (in pottery) or parallel grooves (in hewn wood) on the inner roof or upper part of the inner walls. The purpose of such treatment is to provide good attachment for the bees' combs, and/or to persuade the bees to build their combs in a certain direction. A hive used open at the top must have top-bars or similar provision to support the combs.

f) Pottery hives could retain vestiges of beeswax on the inner walls, where combs were attached to them, and confirmation of beeswax, e.g. by chromatography, has proved a valuable diagnostic aid (Graham 1975).

REFERENCES

A1 Ahmad, R. 1984. Country status report on beekeeping [in Pakistan]. *In* Proceedings of the Expert Consultation on Beekeeping with *Apis mellifera* in tropical and sub-tropical Asia. pp. 203-210.

A2 Akratanakul, P. 1984. Beekeeping industry with *Apis mellifera* in Thailand. *In* Proceedings of the Expert Consultation on Beekeeping with *Apis mellifera* in tropical and sub-tropical Asia. pp. 222-234.

A3 Alam, M.Z. 1983. Apiculture in Bangladesh. *In* Proceedings of the Second International Conference on Apiculture in Tropical Climates, 1980. pp. 82-86.

B1 Baron, F.J. 1988. School search. Gleanings in Bee Culture, 116(3): 118.

B2 Bee World. 1924. Bee-keeping in the Dutch Indies. Bee World, 6(1): 7.

Bilash, G.D. 1987. Personal communication.

C1 Cadapan, E.P. 1984. Personal communication.

C2 Chang, Shu-Young. 1988. Personal communication.

C3 Choi, Seung Yoon. 1984. Brief report on the status of Korean beekeeping. *In* Proceedings of the Expert Consultation on Beekeeping with *Apis mellifera* in tropical and sub-tropical Asia. pp. 170-189.

C4 Crane, E. 1983. The Archaeology of Beekeeping. Duckworth, London.

C5 Crane, E. 1988. Africanized bees, and mites parasitic on bees, in relation to world beekeeping. *In* Africanized Honey Bees and Bee Mites. G.R. Needham *et al.* (eds). Ellis Horwood, Chichester, UK.

Crane, E. 1990. Bees and Beekeeping: Science, Practice and World Resources. Heinemann Newnes, Oxford.

Crane, E. and A.J. Graham. 1985. Bee hives of the Ancient World. Bee World, 66: 25-41, 148-170.

Dollin, A. and L. Dollin. (1986). Tracing aboriginal apiculture of Australian native bees in the far north-west. Australasian Beekeeper, 88(6): 118-122.

D1 Drescher, W. and E. Crane. 1982. Technical Cooperation Activities: Beekeeping. A directory and guide. GTZ, Eschborn, GFR.

D2 Drieberg, C. 1920. Beekeeping in Ceylon. Bee World, 2(1/4): 38.

F1 Fang Yue-zhen. 1984. The present status and development plan of keeping European bees (Apis mellifera) in tropical and sub-tropical regions of China. In Proceedings of the Expert Consultation on Beekeeping with Apis mellifera in tropical and sub-tropical Asia. pp. 142-147.

F2 Fang Yue-zhen. 1988. Personal communication.

Galton, D. 1971. Survey of a Thousand Years of Beekeeping in Russia. Bee Research Association, London.

G1 Gassparian, S. 1977. Studies on Apis indica cerana in eastern part of Iran. In Proceedings of the 26th International Beekeeping Congress. pp. 293-296.

Gong, Yi-fei. 1983. The natural beekeeping conditions and honey bee races in China. Journal of Fujian Agricultural College, 12(3): 241-249.

Graham, A.J. 1975. Beehives from Ancient Greece. Bee World, 56(2): 64-75.

H1 Hanson, G.C. 1923. Apiculture in north Manchuria. Beekeepers Item (Bee World), 5(10): 166-167, 1924).

Harrer, H. 1954. Personal communication.

H2 Hiratsuka, Y. 1919. Bees and beekeeping in Japan. Bee World, 1(5): 100.

H3 Hiratsuka, Y. 1920/21. Bees and beekeeping in Formosa. Bee World, 2(5/11): 103.

J1 Jørgensen, A.S. 1983. Personal communication.

J2 Joshi, M.A., V.V. Divan and M.C. Suryanarayana. 1983. Bees and honey in Ancient India. In Proceedings of the Second International Conference on Apiculture in Tropical Climates, 1980. pp. 143-149.

Kloft, W. and E. Kloft. 1971. Bienenfunde in Nuristan und im südkaspischen Tiefland-weld. Allgemeine deutsche Imkerzeitung, 5(2): 26-30.

Lanerolle, G.A. 1984. Beekeeping in Sri Lanka. In Proceedings of the Expert Consultation on Beekeeping with Apis mellifera in tropical and sub-tropical Asia. pp. 217-220.

Langstroth, L.L. 1853. Langstroth on the Hive and the Honey-bee, a Bee Keeper's Manual.

Hopkins, Bridgeman & Co., Northampton, MA, USA.

L1 Lee, Sang-Kun. 1981. Beekeeping in Korea. In Proceedings of the 28th International Beekeeping Congress. pp. 193-196.

L2 Lim Choo Kiat. 1954. Beekeeping in Singapore. Gleanings in Bee Culture, 82(11): 649-650, 657.

M1 Ma De-Feng. 1984. Personal communication.

Ma De-Feng, Huang Wen-Cheng. 1981. Apiculture in the new China. Bee World, 62(4): 163-166.

Mahindre, D.B. 1983. Handling rock bee colonies. Indian Bee Journal, 45(2/3): 72-73.

M2 Massé, M. 1947. Arena. Bee World, 28(11): 80.

Mathpal, Y. 1984. Newly discovered rock paintings in central India showing honey collection. Bee World, 65(3): 121-126.

M3 Maung Maung Nyein. (1984). Study on traditional method of keeping Indian honey bees in Burma and keeping with modern method. Rangoon, Burma Research Association.

Melkania, N.P., U. Pandey and T. Sharma. 1983. Apiculture in the Himalayas: existing status, problems and strategies for development. Indian Bee Journal, 45(2/3): 67-68.

Moorcroft, W. and Mrs. G. Trebeck. 1940. Travels in the Himalayan provinces in Hindustan, 1819-1825. North Indian Bee Journal, (April):11-14, Extracts, under title 'Beekeeping in Kashmir'.

Mulder, V. 1988. Personal communication.

M4 Muttoo, R.N. 1944. Beekeeping in India: its past, present and future. Indian Bee Journal, 6(3/4): 54-77.

N1 Neve, E.F. 1931. Queries. Bee World, 12(8): 108.

Nogge, G. 1974. Die geographische Verbreitungsgrenze zwischen westlicher und östlicher Honigbiene. Allgemeine deutsche Imkerzeitung, 8(2): 163-165.

Ochi, T. 1985. [Japanese honeybees in Ehime prefecture.] Honeybee Science, 6(1): 31-38. In Japanese.

Ohkura. (1859). Remarks on Useful Products.

P1 Patra, K. and O. Suwanda. 1988. Bee-keeping with Apis cerana in Indonesia. Scout Movement Apiary Center & Deputy of Natural Resources Development, Jakarta.

P2 Phoon, A.C.G. 1983. Beekeeping in Malaysia. Pertanika 6 (review supplement): 3-17.

Pourasghar, D. 1986. Personal communication via A.B. Komeili.

P3 Punchihewa, W. 1988. Personal communication.

Ruttner, F. 1988. Biogeography and Taxonomy of Honeybees. Springer-Verlag, Berlin.

Sangyō-Yōhō. 1934. 1(1): 36; 1(2): 73.

Schneider, P. and A.S. Djalal. 1970. Vorkommen und Haltung der östlichen Honigbiene (*Apis cerana* Fabr.) in Afghanistan. Apidologie, 1(3): 329-341.

Seligmann, C.G. and B.Z. Seligmann. 1911. The Veddas. University Press, Cambridge.

Shah, F.A. 1975. Some facts about beekeeping in Kashmir. Bee World, 56(3): 103-108.

S1 Shah, F.A. 1984. The origin of beekeeping in Kashmir. Bee World, 65(1): 12-18.

S2 Singh, Y. 1983. Beekeeping in Uttar Pradesh - a review. *In* Proceedings of the Second International Conference on Apiculture in Tropical Climates, 1980. pp. 211-226.

S3 Soekiman Atmosoedaryo. 1976. Beekeeping as an activity in forest community development in Java. *In* Proceedings of the First International Conference on Apiculture in Tropical Climates, 1976. pp. 167-170.

S4 Straits Times. 1939. Bee World, 20(5): 59.

S5 Sukartiko, B. 1981. Country report on beekeeping in Indonesia. *In* Proceedings of the 28th International Beekeeping Congress. pp. 198-202.

T1 Takata, T. 1937. Old-style beekeeping in Korea. Bee World, 18(12): 132.

Thakar, C.V. 1976. Practical aspects of bee management in India with *Apis cerana indica*. *In* Proceedings of the First International Conference on Apiculture in Tropical Climates, 1976. pp. 51-59.

T2 Toumanoff, C. 1933. Documentation sur l'apiculture annamite. Bulletin économique de l'Indochine, 169-174.

T3 Toumanoff, C. and J. Nanta. 1933. Enquête sur l'apiculture au Tonkin. Bulletin économique de l'Indochine, 1015-1048.

Verhagen, R. 1971. Observations apicoles au Pakistan occidental. Abeilles et Fleurs (207): 5-7.

V1 Verma, L.R. 1988. Personal communication.

W1 Watanabe, K. 1981. [Beekeeping and bee-researches in Japan before the 19th century.] Honeybee Science, 2(2): 75-86. In Japanese.

W2 Watanabe, K. 1984. Personal communication.

W3 Wongsiri, S. 1988. Personal communication.

W4 Woyke, J. 1984. Beekeeping in Afghanistan. *In* Proceedings of the Expert Consultation on Beekeeping with *Apis mellifera* in tropical and sub-tropical Asia. pp. 124-130.

Note, May 1992

Since this paper was presented in 1988, a number of questions raised in it have been answered, and new information has been published, for instance on management of *Apis dorsata* colonies.

CHAPTER 2

BEES AND THE NATURAL ECOSYSTEM

S. APPANAH and P.G. KEVAN

INTRODUCTION

While we pay homage to the honeybees in this book, and in all probity too, we need to recognize that the true honeybees represent only four, or maybe five, species of one genus *Apis*, out of a huge diversity of bees known worldwide. It is also disquieting to say our interest in bees is still essentially that of a dacoit and his victims.

C.D. Michener's (1974) last sentence in his magnificent work on social behaviour of bees is, "It seems reasonable to believe, however, that bees, ..., are important in the maintenance of natural vegetation in most parts of the world." This, while alluding to the extremely important role that bees are playing in the pollination of probably a large portion of the world's angiosperms, also unmasks a truth: that we know practically nothing of the bees' role in the natural ecosystems - in the rain forests, swamps, prairies, meadows, deserts, and the polar regions. Even in the most depauperate vegetation zones at the poles, we have yet to assemble the full list of all the plants pollinated by bees, and by contrast the situation pales in the species-rich tropics.

Of late, man's accelerated pace of destruction of the various habitats, especially of the species-rich tropical forests, is becoming an issue of great concern internationally. In the present context, hardly anything is known about the destruction of the bees' habitats, and the consequences of such losses on the plants (Roubik, pers. comm.). While the effects of agricultural pesticides are troubling beekeepers (Hocking 1950; Johansen 1966), almost nothing is known on the effects of the widespread application of insecticides on the natural pool of bees (see Kevan 1986). That everything is not calm in the 'bee world' was dramatically exposed with the accidental release of Africanised honeybees in Brazil; this aggressive and defensive bee seems to displace the local bees, and the effects of such an introduction on the natural vegetation there is still only a subject of speculation (Roubik 1978, 1989).

With the above backdrop, it seems appropriate to examine the whole assemblage of bees within their natural ecosystems, not only to release the bees from the myopic view of man, not just to assert the true extent of their role in the ecosystem, but also to look for alternatives in the continuous search for solutions to many agricultural problems.

LET THERE BE BEES

The bees, which belong to the superfamily Apoidea, were a group of wasps that had abandoned their habits of provisioning their nests with insects and spiders, and instead fed their larvae with pollen and nectar collected from flowers or with glandular secretions ultimately derived from flowers. They are a large and diversified group, with some 21,000 species, and are usually categorized into nine families (see Table I: Michener [1965] provides a detailed systematics). A brief description of them is as follows:

1. Colletidae

    This is the most primitive family of bees. They nest in the soil, and in holes of logs and pithy stems. They are found worldwide but are better represented in the southern hemisphere. None are parasocial or eusocial (these terms are explained below).

2. Oxaeidae

    This is a small group of large bees from the American tropical and subtropical regions. They nest in deep burrows in the soil. None are parasocial or eusocial.

3. Halictidae

    This is an enormous group of small to middle-sized bees found worldwide. They are commonly called "sweat bees", and they nest in burrows of soil or in rotting wood. Their social behaviour ranges from communal, quasisocial, semisocial, to primitively eusocial.

4. Andrenidae

    This is a large group of bees found in all continents except Australia. Their nests are burrows in the soil, and a few of the species nest in colonies. The bees are mainly solitary, or communal but a few are parasocial.

5. Melittidae

    This small but diverse family occurs in all continents except Australia and South America. The bees nest in burrows in soil or wood. No parasocial or eusocial species are known.

TABLE I. Families, subfamilies, principal tribes, and the distribution of bees (superfamily Apoidea) (Based on Michener 1974).

Family	Subfamily	Distribution
1. Colletidae		World-wide
2. Oxaeidae		New World
3. Halictidae	Dufoureinae	Holarctic; African & Oriental regions; Chile
	Nomiinae	Old World tropics; South temperate regions; Holarctic
	t. Augochlorini	South & Central America; some in Canada
	t. Halictini	World-wide, but less abundant in neotropics because of
4. Andrenidae	Adreninae	Chiefly Holarctic; some in Africa & S. America
	Panurginae	Africa, Eurasia, New World
5. Melittidae	Ctenoplectrinae	Palaeotropics
	Macropidinae	Holarctic
	Melittinae	Holarctic, Africa
	Dasypodinae	Holarctic, Africa
6. Fidelidae		S. Africa & Chile
7. Megachilidae	Lithurginae	World-wide (tropical & warm regions)
	Megachilinae	
	t. Megachilini	All continents
	t. Anthidiini	All continents
8. Anthophoridae	Nomadinae	World-wide
	Anthophorinae	
	t. Exomalopsini	Neotropics
	t. Ancylini	Mediterranean & eastward into Asia
	t. Tetrapediini	Neotropics
	t. Melitomini	Western Hemisphere
	t. Canephorulini	S. America
	t. Eucerinodini	S. America
	t. Eucerini	All continents (except Australia)
	t. Anthophorini	World-wide
	t. Centridini	Americas (tropical & warm parts)
9. Apidae	Bombinae	
	t. Euglossini	Neotropics
	t. Bombini	Holarctic
	Apinae	
	t. Meliponini	Tropics world-wide
	t. Apini	Eurasia & Africa (introduced to all parts of the world)

6. Fideliidae

This family is found only in South Africa and Chile. The few genera studied nest in burrows in soil. No communal or eusocial species occur.

7. Megachilidae

This is a very large family found worldwide. Most nest in wood. No eusocial species occur. Many are solitary, and some are communal. The familiar leaf-cutting bees belong here.

8. Anthophoridae

This is also a very large and widely distributed family. They nest in soil or wood. So far as is known, most of these bees are solitary, but a few are communal.

9. Apidae

This is only a moderate family of worldwide distribution. It is unique in having all the high eusocial bees. Solitary as well as parasocial species are also present The genus *Apis* belongs here.

BEE SOCIETIES

The bee societies have a range of organizations, from unorganized two or three bees in a burrow to large, highly organized colonies of the honeybees. Their impact on the ecosystems probably varies just as extensively. Hence, an appreciation of their societies helps elucidate their role in the ecosystems. Below is a concise and over-simplified description of the bee societies. Readers should refer to Michener (1969) for details.

1. Solitary bees

Each female makes a nest or several of them independent of other nests. The female leaves after provisioning the cells with pollen and nectar, and ovipositing in them. Hence, usually there is no contact between generations.

2. Nest aggregations

In many solitary forms, especially the soil burrowing bees, the nests are grouped, from a few nests, small clusters, or enormous numbers.

3. Parasocial colonies

This is a collective term for communal, quasisocial and semisocial groups. The adults of these groups consist of a single generation only.

a. Communal colonies

A communal colony is made up of a group of females from the same generation using a single nest, each making, provisioning, and ovipositing in her own cells.

b. Quasisocial colonies

A small communal colony made up of a group of females of about the same age and generation that cooperatively construct and provision cells.

c. Semisocial colonies

These are like the quasisocial colonies, but are distinguished by showing division of labour among the females: both egg layers and worker-like females exist, although they are derived from the same generation.

4. Subsocial colonies

These colonies are family groups with one adult female and a number of immature offspring that are cared for by the mother. She leaves or dies when the young reach maturity.

5. Eusocial colonies

In all the previous colonies, the interactions among adults, if they occur, are within the same generation. However, the eusocial bees live in colonies which are family groups consisting of adult individuals of two generations, mothers and daughters. Usually only one queen exists in these colonies, and the bulk of the workers are daughters. Division of labour is often well characterized in recognizable castes.

a. Primitively eusocial colonies

In these colonies, castes of different females are generally indistinguishable externally. Swarming is not exhibited, and the gynes (the equivalent of queens) can live alone and establish colonies as lone individuals. Often the only food stored is in the brood cells.

b. Highly eusocial colonies

These are the well-known colonies where some of the most complex social interactions are exhibited. The female castes differ strongly between each other behaviourally, physiologically, and also in size. The gynes (queens) are unable to survive alone, and new colonies are established through swarming, with the aid of workers from the parent colony. Colonies can sustain themselves for long periods with food stored in non-brood cells. Communication concerning food sources and nest sites is mostly well developed, this feature perhaps has reached its acme in the true honeybees, *Apis*.

BEES IN THE ECOSYSTEM

Perhaps an ecosystematic study of all the bees inhabiting the diverse niches in a rain forest will illustrate the variety and complexity of interactions between the bees and the environment. Unfortunately, I know of no such single study. Nevertheless, based on personal experience and published material

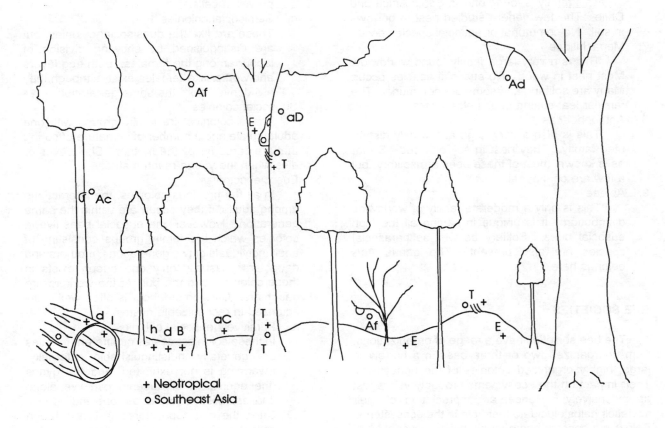

FIGURE 1. A tropical rain forest, showing potential nesting sites of bees.

Ac	*Apis cerana*	aC	*Augochlora*	h	*Halictus*
Ad	*Apis dorsata*	aD	Allodapine	l	*Lasioglossum*
Af	*Apis florea*	E	Euglossini	T	*Trigona*
B	*Bombus*	d	*Dialictus*	X	*Xylocopa*

of Malaysian and Neotropical forests, it is possible to compose a reasonable picture, as shown in Figure 1.

First, a comparison between the two forests indicates not all bees are common between them. The eusocial honeybees, *Apis* (Apidae), are not native to the neotropics (but have been introduced by man). Many solitary genera such as *Halictus*, *Dialictus* and *Augochlora* (Halictidae), *Euglossa*, *Eulaema*, *Euplusia*, *Lestrimelitta*, *Melipona* (Apidae), *Exomalopsis* (Anthophoridae) are not found in the Malayan forests. Although the genus *Trigona* (Apidae) is common to both forests, it is, however, much more diversified in the neotropics. For example, 183 species of stingless bees are known from the neotropics but only 42 have been recognized in Asia

(Kerr and Vilma Maul 1964).

The above disparity in the diversity of bees between the neotropics and palaeotropics is brought out when the family Apidae is compared (Table II). Although I have not been able to obtain the exact number of species occurring in the two regions, a preponderance of bee species in the neotropics is suggested.

The distribution of the bees within the rain forest habitat seems to be of interest too. Some restrictions to nest locations are discernible. For example, the giant honeybee, *Apis dorsata*, builds its large and exposed hive on the sturdy, more or less horizontal branches of tall emergent trees, such as the smooth-barked *Koompasia malaccensis* (Leguminosae).

TABLE II. A comparison of the genera in the family Apidae between the neotropics and Malesia.

| Family Apidae | Occurrence | |
Subfamily & Tribe/Genus	Neotropics	Malesia
Subfamily Euglossinae		
Euglossa	+	
Euplusia	+	
Eulaema	+	
Exaraete	+	
Subfamily Apinae		
Bombus	rare	rare
Subfamily Apinae		
Tribe Meliponini		
Lestrimelitta	+	
Melipona	+	
Trigona	+	+
Tribe Apini		
Apis	introduced	+

TABLE III. Colony size (number of adult workers and queens) in various social bees. For sources, see Michener (1974).

Species	Population size
Augochloropsis	2-4
Augochlorella	2-5
Lasioglossum versatum	5-60
L. marginatum	54-486
Bombus	50-2,000
Trigona	100-180,000
Melipona	160-900
Apis	4,000-60,000+

Apis florea builds its small exposed nests on small branches, usually in dense vegetation. In contrast, *Apis cerana* builds its nest in the hollow of a tree trunk.

Most Meliponini nest in cavities, usually in hollow tree trunks and branches. Some species characteristically nest at the foot of a tree in hollow roots or a hollow among the roots. Others nest in the soil, occupying nests of ants and termites.

Although most of the solitary bees like *Dialictus* and *Halictus* (Halictidae) nest in the ground, the Euglossine bees (Apidae) nest in natural cavities in the soil, tree trunk, nests of termites or as resin nests in stems. The Carpenter bees (Anthophoridae) which nest in holes drilled into wood of dead trees are usually found in the fringes of the main forest. Within the primary forest in Malaysia, they are nevertheless sighted nesting along river banks and large gaps. An unusual nesting site is that of the rare Brazilian *Bombus* (Apidae); it nests in the litter on the forest floor.

COLONY SIZE AND POPULATION DENSITY

There is a tremendous variation in the sizes of the colonies, but each species usually attains its characteristic strength (Table III). It can be seen that some colonies such as *Augochloropsis* have only a few adult females, but others like the *Trigona* can attain perhaps 180,000 individuals.

No detailed studies exist on the total population densities of bees in complex habitats such as the rain forests. Hubbell and Johnson (1972) found a density of approximately 1.4 nests/ha in a study on five species of *Trigona* in a neotropical forest. In a similar survey for all *Trigona* nests in the Malayan climax forests, only 0.6 nests/ha, of five species, were found (Appanah, unpublished). The paucity in *Trigona* in the Malayan forests is probably a reflection of the abundance of *Apis*, as evidenced by the latter's large populations converging on a tree in heavy flower (e.g. Kevan and Lack 1985).

WHAT DO BEES FORAGE?

a. Nest construction materials.

Although most bees construct cells by excavating in or building from the substrate material, a few such as the Megachilidae and some members of Apidae collect material from the outside to construct their nests. The Megachilidae bring back pieces of leaves, chewed leaf material, resin, mud, pebbles, or hairs removed from plants. These are used for cell walls and linings. The Meliponini (Apidae) have nests made up of wax mixed with resin gathered from plants. The resins are secretions from the surfaces of plants, and from cuts and damages to the bark. The bees may bite the soft tissue and collect the sap or latex. They have even been observed to collect oil and grease from machinery, and fresh paint, as well as DDT dust from walls (see Roberts *et al.* 1982).

b. Pheromones

The males of the neotropical Orchid bees (Euglossini) gather precursors of sex pheromones from orchid flowers.

c. Pollen and nectar

Bees forage for pollen avidly. The bees, even while solitary, are believed to have evolved hairs which retain pollen grains, and during normal grooming the pollen is brushed and collected into baskets under their abdomens or their legs (Jander 1976). However, the Colletidae and some Meliponini have the unique habit of carrying pollen in the crop, mixed with nectar.

Pollen contains 7-30% protein, all the necessary amino acids, vitamins and cholesterol (Herbert *et al.* 1980). Even an appetizer, an unsaturated C 18 alkane has been found in pollen (Johansson and Johansson 1977).

Nectar from floral nectaries is a sucrose solution with glucose and fructose, many amino acids, lipids, phenolics and alkaloids. The sugars provide the energy for metabolic activity, and the pollen-honey mixture is fed to larvae or to produce 'bee milk' for the young larvae and queens.

POLLINATION BY BEES

K. Faegri and L. van der Pijl, in their classic work on pollination ecology (1966), state that bees, on the whole, are better adapted for blossom visits than any other comparable group. This, in fact, is a modest statement of the performance of the best known pollinators of seed plants, both natural and planted, throughout the world.

There is a wealth of literature on the role of honeybees as pollinators, particularly on crop plants (e.g. Free 1974; McGregor 1976). So, for the sake of brevity, I shall adumbrate the main features only.

Bees, particularly the eusocial forms, are versatile and active foragers of flowers. They surpass other insects in remembering plant forms (Frisch 1950), and are able to communicate to their colony location (direction, distance) and sources of flowers. They are adept, too, at manipulating flowers and their mouthparts are well adapted for imbibing nectar. Their body parts are also specialized for collecting pollen. Bees are mostly vegetarian, and they provision cells with pollen and nectar for their larvae as well as for themselves during lean periods. All these factors dispose them to be highly successful pollinators of plants.

A great diversity of apoidean pollination systems can be recognized. Some complex bee-flower interrelationships have been discovered: the pseudo-copulation by male bees of female bee-mimicking orchids; gathering of essential oils by male bees from orchid flowers for lek, or lure, behaviour in mating.

Apart from the true honeybees, less is known of the pollinatory role of the other bees, and this state of affairs is even more pronounced in the tropics. It was only in recent times that the pollinatory role of Trigonid bees was recognized even though they are omnipresent in the tropics (e.g. Bawa 1977; Appanah 1981).

BEE FLOWERS

A whole syndrome of characters have been recognized among melittophilous flowers. Faegri and van der Pijl (1966) present a detailed outline of the characters of bee flowers. They are strongly zygomorphic with great depth effect; mechanically strong with landing surfaces, and are frequently intricate and semi-closed. Odours are fresh but not exceptionally strong. Nectar, produced in moderate quantities, is hidden though not very deeply. Sexual organs are concealed, with a few stamens but many ovules per ovary.

In terms of floral rewards too, specific patterns could be discerned. For example, the nectars of bee flowers are poorer in amino acids since they rely more on pollen for a protein source (Baker and Baker 1982). Bee flower nectars often possess proteins and lipids which bees can digest. For some reason, flowers with alkaloids are usually visited by bees.

Typical bee blossoms come from Labiatae, Scrophulariaceae, Papilionaceae, Orchidaceae, etc. As more on the pollination of plants becomes available, a compendium of bee flowers for each region has been compiled (see e.g. Crane et al. 1984). Many such regional/community directories exist, and more are beginning to appear for tropical areas (Kiew, this volume), along with information on their flowering schedules (Mardan and Kiew 1985).

A BEGINNING IN ECOSYSTEMS STUDIES

As knowledge on the bee fauna and flora within a community, such as in the species-rich tropics, increases, our understanding of the plant/bee pollinator interactions will throw light on resource competition, floral and bee pollinator population densities, and the degree of mutualism between the plant and bee.

In a comprehensive study on the pollination systems of a rain forest tree community in Costa Rica, Bawa et al. (1985) found medium-sized to large bees constituted the major pollinators. Together with small bees, they were the pollinators for 41.5% of the 143 tree species examined. The small bees were mostly Halictidae, Megachilidae, and Meliponini; the large bees were mostly Anthophoridae. They could further correlate floral types with the bees: all species in the Papilionaceae are pollinated by medium-sized to large bees. The medium-sized bees such as *Euglossa* and *Eulaema* foraged alone or in small numbers, while the large bees like *Centris* foraged in greater forces. They also found a very high proportion (44.2%) of canopy tree species are pollinated by the medium-sized to large bees.

No studies as the one above have been done, say in the Malayan tropics, for a comparison. Nevertheless, from other studies (Appanah 1987) and impressions, fundamental differences between the two forests, in terms of bee pollinators and flowering patterns, seem apparent. Unlike in the neotropics where flowering is regular and an annual event, a good proportion of the canopy trees in the Malayan climax forests are confined to the general flowering,

an event that may come at supra-annual intervals of 2-10 years (Appanah 1985).

The neotropical bee fauna foraging on canopy trees is well represented by a huge diversity of solitary bees. This niche seems to be chiefly replaced by the giant honeybee, *A. dorsata* in the Malayan forests. A single *A. dorsata* colony can contain as many as 50,000 workers. This bee, and to a lesser extent *A. cerana* and a few *Trigona* species, form the chief bee pollinators in the above canopy strata of the Malayan forest. Solitary bees are poorly represented. However, *Xylocopa*, a genus of solitary bee, which normally forages in the fringes of the forest on ever-flowering pioneer plants migrates into the forest during a general flowering, to forage on a series of Papilionaceous canopy trees.

The only eusocial bees of the neotropics that can match *A. dorsata* in colony size are some *Trigona* species. But these too are much smaller in body size, and probably do not match *A. dorsata* in flower foraging and flight capacities. *A. dorsata* seems to enjoy a further advantage as well; it is not limited in nesting sites in being able to build their open nests on emergent trees. Hence, they are capable of explosive build-up in populations during a heavy but long-intervalled flowering. *Trigona* species are nest-site limited (Hubbell and Johnson 1977) and are unlikely to respond in colony multiplication in response to an exceptional increase in flower abundance. These differences in the bee fauna, in terms of species, social behaviour, and nesting sites between the two hemispheres may provide part of the explanation for the evolution of such divergent flowering patterns in the two regions.

REFERENCES

Appanah, S. 1981. Pollination of androdioecious *Xerospermum intermedium* Radlk. (Sapindaceae) in a rain forest. Biological Journal of the Linnean Society, 18: 11-34.

Appanah, S. 1985. General flowering in the climax rain forests of South-east Asia.I Journal of Tropical Ecology, 1: 225-240.

Appanah, S. 1987. Plant-pollinator interactions in Malaysian rain forests. *In*: International Workshop on Reproductive Ecology of Tropical Forest Plants. K.S. Bawa (ed). Bangi, Malaysia.

Baker, H.G. and I. Baker. 1975. Studies on nectar-constitution and pollinator-plant coevolution. *In*: Animal and Plant Coevolution. L.E. Gilbert and P.H. Raven (eds.). University of Texas Press, Austin, Texas, pp. 100-140.

Baker, H.G. and I. Baker. 1983. Floral nectar sugar constituents in relation to pollinator type. *In*:

Handbook of Experimental Pollination Biology. C.E. Jones and R.J. Little (eds.). Scientific and Academic Editions, Division of Van Nostrand Reinhold Company Inc, New York, pp. 117-140

Bawa, K.S., S.H. Bullock, D.R. Perry, R.E. Coville, and M.H. Grayum. 1985. Reproductive biology of tropical lowland rain forest trees. II. Pollination systems. American Journal of Botany, 72: 346-356.

Crane, E., P. Walker and R. Day. 1984. Directory of Important World Honey Sources. London, U.K.: International Bee Research Association, pp. 384.

Faegri, K. and L. van der Pijl. 1966. The Principles of Pollination Ecology. Pergamon Press, London, p. 248.

Faegri, K. and L. van der Pijl. 1979. The Principles of Pollination Ecology. Third revised edition. Pergamon Press, Oxford, New York, Toronto, Sydney, Paris, Frankfurt, 244 pp.

Free, J.B. 1970. Insect Pollination of Crops. Academic Press, London and New York, 544 pp.

Frisch, K.v. 1950. Bees. Cornell University Press.

Herbert, E.W., J.A. Svoboda, M.J. Thompson and H. Shimanuki. 1980. Sterol utilization in honeybees fed on synthetic diet: effects on brood rearing. Journal of Insect Physiology, 26: 287-289.

Hocking, B. 1950. The honeybee and agricultural chemicals. Bee World, 31: 49-53. AA158/52.

Hubbell, S.P. and L.K. Johnson. 1977. Competition and nest spacing in a tropical stingless bee community. Ecology, 58: 949-963.

Jander, R. 1976. Grooming and pollen manipulation in bees (Apoidea): the nature and evolution of movements involving the foreleg. Physiological Entomology, 1: 179-194.

Johansen, C.A. 1966. Digest on bee poisoning, its effects and prevention, with an annotated list of 92 insecticides. Bee World, 47: 9-25. BRA Reprint No. 28. AA544/66.

Johansson, T.S.K. and M.P. Johansson. 1977. Feeding honeybees pollen and pollen substitutes. Bee World, 58(3): 105-118.

Kerr, W.R. and V. Maul. 1964. Geographic distribution of stingless bees and its implications. Journal of the New York Entomological Society, 72: 2-18.

Kevan, P.G. and A.J. Lack. 1985. Pollination in a cryptically dioecious plant, Decaspermum parviflorum (Lam.) A.J. Scott (Myrtaceae) by pollen-collecting bees in Sulawesi, Indonesia. Biological Journal of the Linnean Society, 25: 319-330.

Mardan, M. and R. Kiew. 1985. Flowering periods of plants visited by honeybees in two areas of Malaysia. Proceedings 3rd International Conference on Apiculture in Tropical Climates, Nairobi, pp. 209-216.

Michener, C.D. 1944. Comparative external morphology, phylogeny, and classification of the bees (Hymenoptera). Bulletin of the American Museum of Natural History, 82: 151-326.

Michener, C.D. 1969. Comparative social behavior of bees. Annual Review of Entomology, 1414: 299-342.

Michener, C.D. 1974. The Social Behavior of the Bees: A Comparative Study. Belknap Press, Harvard University, Cambridge, 404 pp.

Roubik, D.W. 1989. Ecology and Natural History of Tropical Bees. Cambridge Tropical Biology Series. Cambridge University Press, New York, Port Chester, Melbourne, Sydney, vii + 514 pp.

Vogel, S. 1990. The Role of Scent Glands in Pollination. On the Structure and Function of Osmophores. A.A. Balkema, Rotterdam, xvi + 220 pp.

SECTION II: BASIC BIOLOGY

CHAPTER 3

BIOLOGY OF THE EASTERN HONEYBEE *APIS CERANA* (FABRICIUS 1773)

NIKOLAUS KOENIGER

The true honeybees (the genus *Apis*) are a biologically well defined group within the family Apidae which comprises, besides *Apis*, the Euglossini (orchid bees), Bombini (bumble bees) and Meliponini (stingless bees). It is important to realize that all groups of Apinae share many traits, which they have inherited from their common ancestor. Nesting in a cavity seems to be a good example of an 'ancestral' feature which most Apidae have retained. According to Winston and Michener (1979) relation between the Meliponini and *Apis* is not as close as once thought. Many of their common characteristics, like the forming of perennial colonies and division of labour, have apparently arisen independently.

The main characteristics which separate *Apis* from all other bees are listed as follows:

1. The comb is constructed out of pure bee's wax. No other material is added as in bumble bees or Meliponini.
2. The construction of a vertical comb with horizontal hexagonal cells, which open to both sides and the repeated use of these comb cells for brood rearing and storage of pollen and honey.
3. The use of 9-oxo-2-decenoic acid as a main component of the queen's pheromone and as a major component of the queen's sexual attractant during mating.
4. The use of isopentyl acetate as the main alarm pheromone.
5. The dance communication which serves to direct colony members to newly found food sources.
6. Colony multiplication by swarming, which is initiated by the sudden departure of the old queen together with a large number of workers.

This list represents only a small number of the many common features in *Apis*. All traits, taken together, leave no doubt that all honeybees are closely related and have had a long common evolutionary path after separating from the other Apinae.

Traditionally, four species (Fig. 1) are recognized within the genus *Apis* (Lindauer 1952). These are the dwarf honeybee (*Apis florea* Fabr.), the giant honeybee or rockbee (*Apis dorsata* Fabr.), the

Eastern hive bee or Indian hive bee (*Apis cerana* Fabr.), and the Western hive bee (*Apis mellifera* L.). Each species is highly variable with a broad range of polymorphism which was, and is, subject to many attempts of reclassification. Intensive and careful biometrical and biogeographical analysis of *A. mellifera* (Ruttner 1988) shows that parameters of body size, hairs and colours vary widely. Many extremely different races of *A. mellifera* have been crossed and fertile hybrids were obtained. So, it is prudent to base decisions on recognition of species on characters of the reproductive and genital organs. In the case of the four species of *Apis*, the drones have clear species-specific structured endophalli (Fig. 2). As judged by genital characters, the large free-nesting bee of the Himalayan region, originally described by Sakagami *et al.* (1980), should be regarded as a subspecies named *A. dorsata laboriosa*.

The 'principal' difference among the honeybee species is the mode of nesting. It has an important impact on the colony as well as on the life of the single bee. Thus, the genus *Apis* can be divided into two subunits: the open-nesting honeybees, *A. florea* and *A. dorsata*, and the cavity-nesting species, *A. cerana* and *A. mellifera*. The open-nesting species normally build only a single comb per colony, but both species show several distinct differences in their nest construction. *A. florea* builds its comb around a small branch or other kinds of supports in such a way that the comb has an open convex surface on the top (Fig. 3). *A. dorsata* constructs its larger comb under a rock or large branch (Fig. 4), so the upper portion of the comb is never exposed.

The hive bees, *A. mellifera* and *A. cerana*, do not show any major differences in nest construction. Both species nest in cavities where they build several parallel combs. The combs are built under the ceiling of the cavity and attached to the cavity's walls. The arrangements and distribution on the combs is similar in all races of each species.

In the upper portion of the comb honey is stored. In the central and lower part the comb, cells are used for brood-rearing. Pollen storage cells are found between the brood-rearing area and the honey cells. Queen cells are constructed at the lower edge of the combs.

FIGURE 1. Four species of *Apis* (from left to right: *Apis florea*, *Apis dorsata*, *Apis cerana*, and *Apis mellifera*). Three specimens are from Sri Lanka. The European *A. mellifera* belongs to *A. mellifera carnica*.

NATURAL DISTRIBUTION

The natural distribution of the true honeybees is restricted to the old world (Asia, Europe, and Africa). *A. mellifera* was imported by immigrants from Europe to Australia and the America's.

The natural distribution of *A. mellifera* is restricted to Africa and Europe. In many parts of Asia all of the other three species, *A. florea*, *A. dorsata*, and *A. cerana*, share their habitats. Naturally, both species of hive bees are allopatric - meaning their territories are geographically isolated from each other. To the West, *A. cerana* is found as far as central Afghanistan. The eastern limit of the range of *A. mellifera* is Mashad in Iran (Ruttner *et al*. 1985). They are isolated from each other by more than 500 km of desert in which probably no bee colonies exist. In the north, *A. cerana* is found up to 46° latitude (Ussuria). The eastern territories of *A. cerana* include the Japanese islands (with the exception of Hokaido), Philippines, Celebes, and Timor. Wallace's line represents the eastern border in the South. No natural overlapping or direct contact between *A. cerana* and *A. mellifera* is known. Reports or speculations of the existence of bees transitional between *A. cerana* and *A. mellifera* (Deodikar and Thakar 1966; A.M. Shah 1980) are not supported by studies on their natural distributions.

DIFFERENCES BETWEEN *APIS MELLIFERA* AND *APIS CERANA*

Many morphological and biological characteristics show similarity between both species. A good example of this is the body size which can be precisely measured by the length of the forewing. The range of *A. mellifera* is 9.52 mm to 7.64 mm and for *A. cerana* 8.89 mm to 7.47 mm (Ruttner 1988). The smaller races of *A. mellifera*, like *A. mellifera yemenitica*, are smaller compared to the larger races of *A. cerana*. It is important to realize that both honeybee species are polymorphic and therefore differences found between one local population of *A. cerana* and another local population of *A. mellifera* may reflect regional adaptations to climatic or environmental conditions rather than species-specific differences. This polymorphism has led to many misinterpretations. Historically, many of the earlier descriptions of *A. cerana* were based on subtropical or tropical populations described by investigators who were familiar with populations of European *A. mellifera*. In consequence, many differences listed are not species-specific but are mainly differences between southern and northern honeybees. On the other hand, scientists who were familiar with *A. cerana* classified African populations of *A. mellifera* from Cameroon and Senegal as subspecies of *A. cerana* (Buttel-Reepen 1906; Maa 1953).

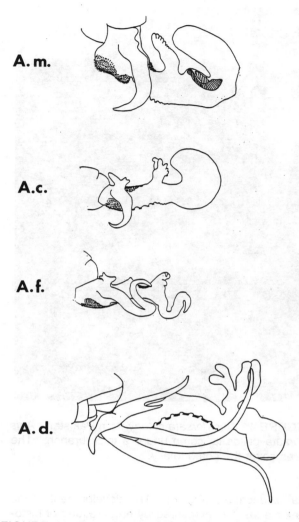

FIGURE 2. The male copulatory organ is a rather complex endophallus in *Apis*. The differences among the species are significant (A.m. - *Apis mellifera*, A.c. - *Apis cerana*, A.f. - *Apis florea*, A.d. - *Apis dorsata*).

Nevertheless, there are useful diagnostic differences between *A. cerana* and *A. mellifera* (below):
1. The tomentum on the 6th sternite is only found in workers of *A. cerana*.
2. The radial vein in the hindwing of *A. cerana* has an extension which is missing in *A. mellifera*.
3. The endophallus of drones of *A. mellifera* carries chitinous plates which are not found in the endophallus of *A. cerana*.
4. The cover of the capped drone brood cells has a pore only in *A. cerana*.
5. The position of the fanning bee is opposite in each species. In *A. mellifera* the fanning bee's head is directed towards the hive entrance; in *A.*

cerana the end of the abdomen points to the entrance.
6. *A. cerana* has a specific 'hissing' behaviour which is absent in *A. mellifera*. Colonies of *A. cerana* react to knocking on the hive or comb by producing a hissing sound (for details, see 'colony defense').

APIS CERANA AND *APIS MELLIFERA* AS 'GOOD' SPECIES

Because of the overlapping variation of many morphological and behavioural features, the question of whether or not *A. cerana* and *A. mellifera* are separate species, in the sense of strict reproductive isolation, has required research into their reproduction.

Initially it was demonstrated that the drones of *A. cerana* were visiting the same drone congregation areas as those of *A. mellifera* (Ruttner 1973). Indeed, drones of *A. cerana* did follow queens of *A. mellifera*. Drones of both *A. mellifera* and *A. cerana* react to 9-oxo-decenoic acid (Ruttner and Kaissling 1968) which is the sexual attractant emitted by queens of all *Apis* species (Shearer *et al.* 1976). Whether or not an interspecific copulation takes place regularly in drone congregations is not yet known. However, with instrumental insemination, interspecific sperm transfer is possible. Heterospecific sperm implanted into the queens' spermathecae survived for some time. Further, the sperm were seen to move out of the spermatheca to the egg, but the fertilized egg then died (Ruttner and Maul 1983). In conclusion, these experiments suggest that a genetic incompatibility between *A. cerana* and *A. mellifera* exists and therefore, in spite of all other similarities, *A. cerana* and *A. mellifera* must be recognized as well defined species.

DIVISION OF LABOUR

Although division of labour has been extensively studied in *A. mellifera* (Rösch 1927; Lindauer 1952; Seeley 1985), we have little information on this very important aspect of social life in *A. cerana*. In Oberursel some observations (Perk 1973) were carried out on a colony of *A. cerana* originating from Peshawar (North-West Frontier Province, Pakistan). A group of young bees (2-4 hours after emergence) was marked by small numbered tags on the thorax. One of these bees was observed during the following period of 15 days. During the first days the bee spent 40% to 60% of the observation time motionless

FIGURE 3. *Apis florea* colony from Iran. *A. florea* builds its comb around branches. The comb is covered by a layer of bees.

FIGURE 4. *Apis dorsata* colony from Pakistan. *Apis dorsata* builds its comb under a thick branch. The bees cover the comb totally.

in empty comb cells. Its other activities were patrolling and cleaning behaviour. On the third day the bee started to feed larvae. That was its main activity until day seven and eight when the bee joined others in comb building. Its first orientation flights were observed on the seventh day. After 15 days the bee began to forage for nectar and pollen outside. This bee did not act as a guard. Throughout the observation period of 140 hours, the bee spent most time patrolling (48%) and 'resting' motionless on the comb or inside a cell (38%). Some shorter activities such as food exchange, preparation of pollen, and fanning were also observed. Significantly different from the typical activities of *A. mellifera* was the large amount of grooming activity which occupied 2.75 h (2% of the observation time). For half of this time, the bee was groomed by other bees. A special behaviour was noted in which the bee would 'ask' to be groomed.

These observations were supplemented by measurements of the hypopharyngeal glands (Fig. 5). The diameters of the acini showed an increase during the first few days, but after the 15th day there

was a decrease (Fig. 6). The development of the wax glands was measured by preparations of histological sections by D. Mautz. The maximal development was on days 12 and 13. After day 22 the preparations showed degenerated gland cells. Altogether the development of the gland systems corresponded well with the behavioural changes.

These preliminary observations indicate a similarity between division of labour in *A. mellifera* and *A. cerana*. However, a more detailed study in the natural habitat of *A. cerana* may very well result in important quantitative differences.

DANCE COMMUNICATION

The dance communication enables all species of *Apis* to monitor, through a small group of scout bees, the nectar and pollen sources in the surroundings. The information gathered by the scouts is 'evaluated' centrally in the colony and the major force of foragers are directed to the optimal resources available at any

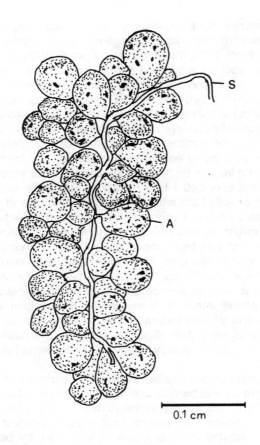

0.1 cm

FIGURE 5. Fully developed hypopharyngeal gland of an *Apis cerana* nurse bee (age 12 days).

given time. This 'information centre strategy' seems to be essential to understand the evolutionary success of honeybees (Seeley 1985).

A successful scout bee of *A. cerana* returns to the hive and, on the vertical comb, performs a dance which is similar to the dance of *A. mellifera* (Lindauer 1956). Food sources near the colony are indicated by round dances, typically performed by foragers running in circles and changing their direction from time to time. No information on the location of the food source is transmitted by the round dance. However, because the bees which follow the dance are in close contact with the dancer, they perceive the odour of the food source. This is, as demonstrated for *A. mellifera* (Frisch 1967), an important clue for finding the indicated food. Food sources at greater distances - in Sri Lanka beyond 10 meters - are communicated by means of the waggle dance which contains information on the location of the food source. The direction to the food source is indicated by the direction of the waggle run. The direction to the sun serves as reference in the flight orientation. The vertical direction on the comb represents the direction to the sun and serves as a reference during the dance. This transposition of horizontal direction (flight angle) into the vertical face of the comb (dance angle) is common to *A. cerana*, *A. mellifera*, and *A. dorsata*.

The distance of the food source correlates with the tempo of the dance. With increasing distances the dance tempo becomes slower. In this regard, a comparison of *A. cerana* from Sri Lanka and *A. melli-*

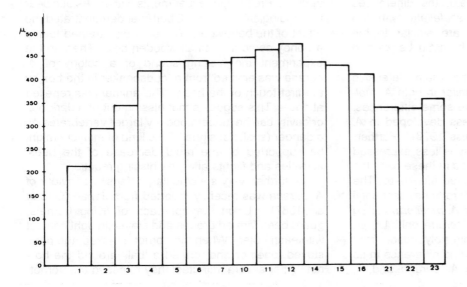

FIGURE 6. Development of hypopharyngeal glands. abscissa: age of the bees in days; ordinate: diameter of the acini in μm (meter x 10^{-6}).

fera of Europe (*A. mellifera carnica*) was undertaken by Lindauer (1956). He found that the dance tempo of *A. cerana* was much faster than that of *A. mellifera* for the same distance. A more recent study by Punchihewa *et al.* (1985) confirmed this. A faster dance facilitates a better and more exact communication of shorter distance. The average foraging distance of *A. cerana* during those experiments in Sri Lanka was less than 200 meters from the hive. Preliminary observations, made in Germany, of foraging distances of *A. cerana* from North Pakistan and China indicated larger foraging distances. Punchihewa was not able to train Sri Lankan *A. cerana* to feeding dishes beyond 500 meters and in the German experiments, foragers of *A. cerana* were easily trained up to distances of 1500 meters (Mautz pers. communication). It is suggested that these differences within *A. cerana* represent adaptation to specific environmental foraging requirements. So, the faster waggle dance and the shorter flight range of Sri Lankan *A. cerana* is an adaptation to a specific habitat rather than a species-specific character. It is known that southern races of *A. mellifera* (*A. mellifera lamarckii* and *A. mellifera scutellata*) have a faster dance tempo than northern races such as *A. mellifera carnica* (Frisch 1967).

COLONY DEFENSE

Differences in colony defense by hive bees vary from north to south. Southern, or more tropical, bees are more defensive than the northern races which are generally more 'gentle', e.g. the differences between African *A. mellifera scutellata* with the European *A. mellifera carnica* are similar to the differences between *A. cerana* from Sri Lanka and northern Pakistan.

The sting apparatus is the main defensive weapon. Its anatomy is very similar in both *A. mellifera* and *A. cerana* but there are some differences. The barbs of the lancets are less developed in *A. cerana* than in *A. mellifera* (Weiss 1978). Further, the mechanism of sting autotomy is less expressed in *A. cerana* (Sakagami 1960b), so in these bees the sting more often remains connected after use. The quantity of the main alarm pheromone, isopentyl acetate, is less in *A. cerana*. For *A. mellifera*, 2.3 µg per sting were found but for *A. cerana* only 1.5 µg (Koeniger *et al.* 1979). The main polypeptide from the venom is melittin and there is no difference in its amino acid sequence between *A. cerana* and *A. mellifera* (Kreil 1973).

The defense behaviour of *A. cerana* has some elaborate elements which are apparently missing in *A. mellifera*. A distinct reaction of *A. cerana* to opti-

cal stimuli, like flying insects, is described by several authors (Butler 1954; Sakagami 1960a; Schneider and Kloft 1971; Koeniger and Fuchs 1975). The bees react by a fast and sudden lateral body shaking. This behaviour can be observed readily when groups of guard bees react to hornets or wasps hovering at the nest entrance. Further, body shaking is frequently observed on swarms of *A. cerana*. The bees on the surface of the cluster react with simultaneous shaking behaviour and prevent the landing of flying insects on the cluster. Experiments showed that the speed (0.5 to 5 m/sec) corresponds well to flight speed of the intruding insects. The size of the optical stimulus is important for eliciting this reaction, with larger stimuli causing greater response. Further, *A. cerana* has been shown to react continuously to an optical stimulus for more than 90 minutes (Koeniger and Fuchs 1975). This behaviour seems to be a well adapted defense against flying insects. Preventing intruders from landing at the hive entrance or on the swarm cluster is more 'economic' and less risky than stinging, which, in the case of defense against wasps, always includes some risk of death.

Another defense behaviour of *A. cerana* can be elicited by mechanical stimuli. On a slight knock to the hive, the colony answers with a conspicuous hissing sound. This communicative sound production is transmitted from one bee to the other by body contact or by air movement produced by the wings. The speed of the transmission is fast (25 cm/sec) (Fuchs and Koeniger 1974). The colony or a swarm cluster reacts as a unit and the sound is highly audible. Preliminary experiments with an Asiatic bear in a zoological park near Oberursel demonstrated the effect of the behaviour. The bear was trained to find a honey comb in a small wooden box. Then, in the experiment the hissing sound of a colony of *A. cerana* was emitted from a loudspeaker in the box by the first touch of the bear. The animal was repelled at once. This suggests that hissing out of a dark box or cavity can be 'understood' by larger vertebrates as a danger (snake's) signal! This kind of mimicry might be supported by the rapid decrease of the bees' activities and flights after the hissing reaction.

A further, very spectacular, defense behaviour of *A. cerana* was recently reported from Japan (Ono *et al.* 1987). Upon the approach of flying hornets, guard bees formed groups and stayed in tight contact with each other. When the hornet attacked, the bees stayed together and formed a 'ball' around the hornet. After several minutes, they released the hornet,

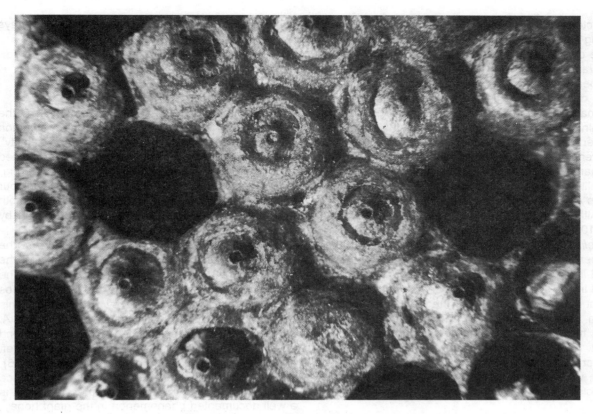

FIGURE 7. The drone cells of *Apis cerana* are covered by a dome-shaped cap which has a central pore.

MATING BEHAVIOUR

Drone development

The drone cells, which are larger in diameter (7 mm in Japan) than worker cells (4.8 mm in Japan) (Okada and Sakai 1960), are found mostly at the lower portion of the comb. The queen starts laying eggs into drone cells at the beginning of the flowering season. Towards the end of the drones' larval development, workers seal the cell with a wax cover. The larva spins its cocoon before metamorphosis starts. After some days, the bees remove the wax from the cell capping and a dome-shaped cover with its central pore is exposed (Fig. 7). Apparently the pore, which is found only in *A. cerana*, is the result of a locally applied secretion by the drone larva (Haenel and Ruttner 1985). Its function is not known. The total development of the drones of *A. cerana* takes 21 to 24 days in India (Singh 1962) which is longer than worker development at about 18 to 20 days (Singh 1962). The cappings of the drone cells are opened by the emerging drones and fall to the hive floor where they usually remain. The time of drone flight varies among locations. In Pakistan (North-West Frontier Province) drones flew between 1100 and 1500 hours and in Sri Lanka (North-Central Province) the drone flight was restricted to 1615 to 1715 hours (Koeniger and Wijayagunasekera 1976).

The number of sperm produced by drones of *A. cerana* is significantly smaller than that in *A. mellifera*. The vesiculae of *A. cerana* contained 1.5 million sperm but those of *A. mellifera* about 11 million sperm (Ruttner *et al.* 1973).

Queen development

Queen cells in *A. cerana* are constructed at the edge of the comb. They have the typical form and vertical orientation as in all *Apis* species. The development of the queen takes 15 to 16 days in India (Singh 1962). The number of queen cells per colony varies according to its strength. In Pakistan and Sri Lanka we found some colonies, after the first swarm had left, which had more than 20 sealed queen cells, while others in the same location had only two to five.

Mating time in India (Poona) is between 1400 and 1500 hours and the mean duration of the 'successful' flight was 27 minutes (Woyke 1975). The success of the mating was easily determined by the mating sign which protruded from the queen's sting chamber. It consists, in *A. cerana*, of a mucus plug and an orange sticky layer. Woyke (1975) dissected young queens returning from their first mating flight. The average volume of semen found in the oviduct of the queen was 1.94 mL. Because *A. cerana* drones produce about 0.2 mL of semen, it can be concluded that there were about 10 copulations during the mating flight. On average, the spermatheca of naturally mated queens of *A. cerana* contained 1.3 million spermatozoa, that is only one-quarter the number found in *A. mellifera carnica*. Different results were reported from experiments in Germany with *A. cerana* from Pakistan. There, about 3.5 million sperm were counted in spermatheca of a queen *A. cerana* (Ruttner and Maul 1983).

Although drones of *A. cerana* seem to produce only 10% of the amount of sperm found in drones of *A. mellifera*, there is only a small difference in the number of matings per mating flight: 10 in *A. cerana* and 8 in *A. mellifera carnica*. The amount of semen found in the spermatheca of *A. cerana* is about 25% of that in *A. mellifera*. Thus, the mechanism of the sperm transfer from the oviducts into the spermatheca must be twice as efficient in *A. cerana*. Of about 10 million sperm which are received in the oviduct of *A. cerana*, about 13% reach the spermatheca, whereas in *A. mellifera*, 80 million are in the oviduct and only 7-8% are found in the spermatheca.

SWARMING

In many areas of subtropical and tropical Asia, the flowering season depends on monsoon rains which usually occur twice a year. In these areas, *A. cerana* has two swarming seasons. In Sri Lanka (North-Central Province), for example, the first swarming takes place in March and April. This is after the rains which usually come in the middle of December. The second swarming season is in July and August after the summer rains. Normally, swarming starts at the end of or somewhat after the peak of the flowering season. The colonies have then collected enough honey to be 'invested' in colony multiplication by swarming. In Japan and temperate China, *A. cerana* has only one swarming season per year.

The number of swarms per colony seems to be higher in tropical and subtropical races. In Sri Lanka and Pakistan (Latif *et al.* 1960) three to eight swarms are reported, whereas Tokuda (1971) found only one to three swarms in Japanese *A. cerana*.

Swarms of *A. cerana* vary greatly in size. The prime swarms consist of up to 10,000 bees while some after-swarms are quite small: several times we counted less than 2,000 bees in North-West Frontier Province, Pakistan! A high percentage of swarms which were captured and put into hives absconded, sometimes even after having stayed for several days and initiated comb-building.

ABSCONDING AND DISPERSAL (MIGRATION)

Absconding is the deserting of the nest and the combs. In many tropical bees it is a common reaction to a decreasing environmental 'quality'. Scarcity of nectar and pollen sources (often caused by drought) diminishes or terminates brood-rearing. Under these conditions, honeybee colonies of all four species react to any kind of disturbance (wax moth infestation, honey harvesting by man, predation by hornets, etc.) by absconding.

In tropical *A. cerana*, absconding occurs at the end of the swarming season. By then, most of the bees have left the nest with previous swarms. The combs of the nest are no longer covered by bees and are immediately attacked by wax moths. This results in absconding. However, colonies of *A. cerana* which did not swarm previously also abscond easily. Often viable eggs and young larvae are left behind by *A. cerana* of southern India (Woyke 1976).

Migration, in the sense of a regular long distance movement from one location to another, far away, is a well documented phenomenon in the giant honeybee, *A. dorsata*. The colonies leave from and return to habitats seasonally as migratory swarms (Koeniger and Koeniger 1980).

In the other species, in particular in the tropical races, the colonies abscond and leave locations and areas whenever conditions become 'intolerable'. However, the direction of the moving swarms and the orientation does not seem to be consistent. The colonies of *A. cerana* seem to disperse rather than migrate. This seems to be the case in Sri Lanka (Anuradhapura) and in Pakistan (Peshawar). Also, a report of Woyke (personal communication) on *A. cerana* from India (Poona) indicated that there was no directionality detectable in moving swarms of *A. cerana* there. Field studies in areas with distinct sequences in flowering pattern, such as steep valleys, are recommended to decide whether a regular migration might exist in *A. cerana* under special environmental circumstances.

COEXISTENCE AND INTERACTION WITH THE OTHER ASIAN HONEYBEE SPECIES

Competition among closely related species can be disastrous so the question of how all three species, *A. cerana*, *A. dorsata*, and *A. florea* manage to live closely together has sparked some research.

Competition for nesting sites does not occur bec-

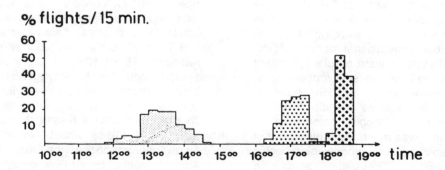

FIGURE 8. Time of drone flight in Sri Lanka (▨ *Apis florea*; ▦ *Apis cerana*; ▨ *Apis dorsata*).

ause *A. cerana* is the only species which needs cavities for the construction of its nest. Also, interaction among the honeybees during mating seems to be avoided. In Sri Lanka, a time-sharing mechanism prevents an interspecific overlap of mating (Fig. 8). Thus it is assured that the queen's pheromone, 9-oxo-2-decenoic acid, will always be directed at the drones of the same species.

Some experiments on food competition were made in Sri Lanka (Koeniger and Vorwohl 1979). Bees of four species, a meliponid bee *Trigona iridipennis*, *A. florea*, *A. dorsata*, and *A. cerana* were trained to feed at a common feeding dish simultaneously. *A. cerana* was more competitive than *A. dorsata* but less so than *A. florea*. Furthermore, the intraspecific fights among foragers of different colonies of *A. cerana* were significantly more frequent and of higher intensity than those of the other bees. A comparative analysis of pollen from honey samples of each species allowed conclusions on natural foraging habits to be drawn. The smaller bees (*Trigona* and *A. florea*) seemed to forage on many plant species within their small flight range. They showed a higher tendency to defend the feeding dish. *A. dorsata* did not show much defensiveness at the feeding dish. Honey of *A. dorsata* contained pollen of only a few plant species. This implies that it seems to concentrate its foraging activities on the more profitable flowers within its larger flight range. Honey of *A. cerana* contained a similar diversity of pollen grains as did that of *A. florea*. Thus, competition between the species for floral resources is reduced by different foraging strategies. Moreover, the annual migratory cycle of *A. dorsata* contributes to further reduce the competition once these bees have left the area entirely during dearth.

Though these studies are only in the initial stages, one gets the impression that the relationship among the Asian honeybee species is well balanced and that competition is avoided (mating) or at least reduced (food).

'MANMADE COEXISTENCE' BETWEEN *APIS CERANA* AND *APIS MELLIFERA*

With the successful establishment of *A. mellifera* in an Asian region, the indigenous *A. cerana* disappears. Good examples of this phenomenon are from Japan, some parts of India (Punjab), and some areas of Pakistan. The start of this competition between both species is 'manmade' because of import of the bees to areas outside their natural range. In addition, in the course of the establishment of *A. mellifera*, beekeepers, with their chemicals and other ways of protecting their honey producers, play an active and essential role. Therefore, *A. mellifera* is not the biologically 'dominant' species in Asia and it will remain there only in total dependence on humans. Even after beekeepers have destroyed many of its competitors, predators, and other natural 'problems', it will not survive without constant care.

The main problems of coexistence result from the similarity and general biological 'overlap' of both species. The best documented case is interspecific competition during mating. The species which has smaller numbers of drones at the congregation area fails in mating. Imported *A. mellifera* did not produce mated queens (Akratanakul 1976; Ahmad 1984) in Asia and imported *A. cerana* did not successfully mate in Germany. These problems can be solved by isolation of the imported species from indigenous bee colonies.

A further problem results from interspecific robbing behaviour. Although 'strong' colonies of hive bees normally defend themselves well against conspecific robbers, they have some inappropriate reactions in the case of heterospecific robbers. We observed that defending guard bees of *A. cerana* actually fed robbing foragers of *A. mellifera*. The latter then, because of the foraging success, recruited large numbers of additional robbers. At the end, the hives of *A. cerana* were regularly invaded and destroyed. In Pakistan we saw robbers of *A. cerana* entering colonies of *A. mellifera*, however losses of colonies of the latter as a result of robbing by *A. cerana* were rare. Robbing colonies of *A. mellifera* by *A. dorsata* was much more disastrous.

Great problems occur from interspecific exchanges of parasites. The natural adaptation 'protects' only the original host species. For the new species, the heterospecific parasite can cause severe damage. Examples of *A. cerana* suffering from parasites of *A. mellifera* are Thai Sac Brood Virus (Verma 1985) and *Acarapis woodi* (Ahmad 1984). The reverse cases are *A. mellifera* and the damage caused by the parasitic mites *Varroa jacobsoni* of *A. cerana* and *Tropilaelaps clareae* of *A. dorsata*.

REFERENCES

Ahmad, R. 1984. Country status report on beekeeping in Pakistan. Proc. Expert Consult. Bangkok, 203-210, FAO Rome.

Akratanakul, P. 1976. Honeybees in Thailand. American Beekeeping Journal, 116: 121-126.

Butler, C.G. 1954. The World of the Honeybee. Collins, London.

Buttel-Reepen, H. 1906. Apistica. Beiträge zur Systematik, Biologie sowie zur geschichtlichen und geographischen Verbreitung der Honigbiene, ihrer Varietäten und der übrigen Apisarten. Veroeff Zool. Mus. Berlin, 3: 118-120.

Deodikar, G.B. and C.V. Thakar. 1966. Cytogenetics of Indian honeybee and bearing on taxonomic and breeding problems. Indian Journal of Genetics, 36A: 386-393.

Frisch, K. von 1967. The Dance Language and Orientation of Bees. Harvard University Press, Cambridge, MA.

Fuchs, S. and N. Koeniger. 1974. Schallerzeugung im Dienst der Verteidigung des Bienenvolkes (*Apis cerana*). Apidologie, 5: 271-287.

Haenel, H. and F. Ruttner. 1985. The origin of the pore in the drone cell capping of *Apis cerana*. Apidologie, 16: 157-164.

Koeniger, N. and S. Fuchs. 1975. Zur Kolonieverteidigung östlicher Honigbienen. Zeitschrift für Tierpsychologie, 37: 99-106.

Koeniger, N. and G. Koeniger. 1980. Observation and experiments on migration and dance communication of *Apis dorsata* in Sri Lanka. Journal of Apicultural Research, 19: 21-34.

Koeniger, N. and G. Vorwohl. 1979. Competition for food among four sympatric species of Apini in Sri Lanka (*Apis dorsata*, *Apis cerana*, *Apis florea* and *Trigona iridipennis*). Journal of Apicultural Research, 18: 95-109.

Koeniger, N. and H.N.P. Wijayagunasekera. 1976. Time of drone flight in three Asiatic honeybee species (*Apis dorsata*, *Apis cerana*, *Apis florea*). Journal of Apicultural Research, 15: 21-34.

Koeniger, N., J. Weiss, and U. Maschwitz. 1979. Alarm pheromones of the sting in the genus *Apis*. Journal of Insect Physiology, 25: 467-476.

Kreil, G. 1973. Structure of melittin isolated from two species of honeybees. FEBS Letters, 33: 241-244.

Latif, A., A. Qayum, and M. Mansoor-ul-Haq. 1960. Multiple and two-queen systems in *Apis indica*. Bee World, 41: 201-209.

Lindauer, M. 1952. Ein Beitrag zur Frage der Arbeitsteilung im Bienenstaat. Zeitschrift für vergliechende Physiologie, 37: 263-324.

Lindauer, M. 1956. Ueber die Verstaendigung bei indischen Bienen. Zeitschrift für vergliechende Physiologie, 38: 521-557.

Maa, T.C. 1953. An inquiry into the systematics of the Tribus Apidini or honeybees. Treubia, 21: 525-640.

Okada, I. and T. Sakai. 1960. A comparative study on natural comb of Japanese and European honeybee with special difference in cell number. Bulletin of the Faculty of Agriculture, Tamagawa University, 1: 1-11.

Ono, M., I. Okada, and M. Sasaki. 1987. Heat production by balling in the Japanese honeybee, *Apis cerana japonica* as a defensive behavior against the hornet *Vespa simillima xanthoptera*. Experientia, 43: 1031-1032.

Perk, J. 1973. Arbeitsteilung bei *Apis cerana*. Examensarbeit, Inst. BK, Oberursel, Germany.

Punchihewa, R.W.K., N. Koeniger, P.G. Kevan and R.M. Gadawski. 1985. Observation on the dance communication and natural foraging ranges of *Apis cerana*, *Apis dorsata* and *Apis florea* in Sri Lanka. Journal of Apicultural Research, 24: 168-175.

Rösch, G.A. 1927. Ueber die Bautaetigkeit im Bienenvolk und das Alter der Baubienen. Weiterer Beitrag zur Frage nach der Arbeitsteilung im Bienestaat. Zeitschrift für vergliechende Physiologie, 6: 265-298.

Ruttner, F. 1973. Drohnen von *Apis cerana* auf einem Drohnensammelplatz. Apidologie, 4: 41-44.

Ruttner, F. 1988. Biogeography and Taxonomy of Honeybees. Springer Verlag, Berlin, Heidelberg, New York.

Ruttner, F. and K.E. Kaissling. 1968. Über die inter-spezifische Wirkung des Sexuallockstoffes von *Apis mellifera* und *Apis cerana*. Zeitschrift für vergliechende Physiologie, 59: 362-370.

Ruttner, F. and V. Maul. 1983. Experimental analysis of reproductive interspecific isolation of *Apis mellifera* and *Apis cerana*. Apidologie, 14: 309-327.

Ruttner, F., D. Pourashgar, and D. Kauhausen. 1985. Die Honigbienen des Iran. 2. *Apis mellifera meda* Skor, die persische Biene. Apidologie, 16: 241-264.

Ruttner, F., J. Woyke and N. Koeniger. 1973. Reproduction in *Apis cerana*. 2. Reproduction organs and natural insemination. Journal of Apicultural Research, 12: 21-34.

Sakagami, S.H.F. 1960a. Preliminary report of behavior and other ecological characters between European and Japanese honeybees. Acta Hymenopterologica, 1: 171-198.

Sakagami, S.H.F. 1960b. Two opposing adaptations in the post-stinging response of the honeybees. Studies on the Japanese honeybees VIII. Evolution, 14: 29-40.

Sakagami, S.H.F., T. Matsumura, and K. Ito. 1980. *Apis laboriosa* in Himalaya. The little known worlds largest honeybee. Insecta Matsumurana NS, 19: 47-77.

Schneider, P. and W. Kloft. 1971. Beobachtungen zum Gruppenverteidigungsverhalten der östlichen Honigbiene *Apis cerana*. Zeitschrift für Tierpsychologie, 29: 337-342.

Seeley, T.D. 1985. Honeybee Ecology. Princeton University Press, New Jersey.

Shah, A.M. 1980. Beekeeping in Kashmir. *In* Proceedings of the Second International Conference on Apiculture in Tropical Climates, New Delhi, 1980. pp. 197-204.

Shearer, D.A., R. Boch, R.A. Morse and F.M. Laigo. 1976. Occurrence of 9-oxodec-trans-2-enoic acid in queens of *Apis dorsata*, *Apis cerana* and *Apis mellifera*. Journal of Insect Physiology, 16: 1437-1441.

Singh, S. 1962. Beekeeping in India. ICAR, New Delhi.

Tokuda, Y. 1971. On the biological characteristics of the indigenous Japanese bees. Proceedings of the International Beekeeping Congress, 23: 348-349.

Verma, L.R. 1985. Sac brood in *Apis cerana*. Newsletter for Beekeepers in Tropical and Sub-tropical Countries, 6: 4. IBRA Cardiff, GB.

Weiss, J. 1978. Vergleichende Morphologie des Stachelapparates bei den vier Apis-Arten. Apidologie, 9: 19-32.

Winston, M.L. and C. Michener. 1979. Dual origin of highly social behavior among bees. Proceedings of the National Academy of Science USA, 74: 1135-1137.

Woyke, J. 1975. Natural and instrumental insemination of *Apis cerana indica* in India. Journal of Apicultural Research, 14: 153-159.

Woyke, J. 1976. Brood rearing efficiency and absconding in Indian honeybees. Journal of Apicultural Research, 15: 133-143.

CHAPTER 4

APIS CERANA: BIOMETRIC, GENETIC AND BEHAVIOURAL ASPECTS

L.R. VERMA

DEDICATION

This chapter is respectfully dedicated to Professor Dr. F. Ruttner, former Director Institute of Honeybee Science, G.W. Goethe University, Frankfurt am Main, F.R.G., who inspired and introduced me to the fascinating field of honeybee biometry.

INTRODUCTION

In many Asian countries, beekeeping with the native hive bee, *Apis cerana* F., has been practised for at least 2,000 years. The species has been exploited extensively by honey hunters and beekeepers. Log and pot hives are still in use as relics of ancient honey collection techniques. Sir Louis Dane (1908) was the first hobbyist beekeeper who kept *A. cerana* in modern hives especially designed to suit its smaller size. He did this in the Kullu valley of Himachal Pradesh, India. Since then, this species, like the European honeybee (*Apis mellifera* L.), has been domesticated for commercial honey production and pollination services. As a result, today there is a thriving beekeeping industry with *A. cerana* in Asia and great strides are being made in modernizing it (Verma 1990, 1991).

A. cerana is very closely related to *A. mellifera*. It is similar to *A. mellifera* in its nesting and dancing behaviour, sequence of melittin amino acids, and in building of parallel combs (Ruttner 1988). *A. cerana* is gentle in temperament, industrious and easy to handle. However, this species has not become popular with the beekeepers because of its frequent swarming, absconding and robbing habits, production of a large number of laying worker bees, and helplessness against the attacks of some predators (Verma 1984).

For a long time, *A. cerana* was considered a sub-species of *A. mellifera*. However, on the basis of several genetic, morphological, and behavioural characteristics, it has been established that they are two completely isolated species. Hybridization of *A. cerana* with *A. mellifera* through instrumental insemination technique has resulted in the formation of hybrid zygotes but they died at an early stage of development (Ruttner and Maul 1983). Both domesticated species of honeybees can also be distinguished from each other by a number of morphological characters. For example, *A. cerana* has an extra radial vein on the hindwing, additional tomentum on the 6th sternite, and its endophallus has 3 additional pairs of cornuae with no chitin plates as compared to *A. mellifera*. These two species of honeybees also show marked quantitative differences in forewings and cubital index (Ruttner 1986). Similarly, certain behavioural and related patterns such as perforated cappings of drone cells nest, inverse position of worker bees while fanning, lack of propolis in the hive, higher degree of resistance to *Nosema apis* and co-existence with the *Varroa* mite without any damage to the host makes *A. cerana* distinct from *A. mellifera* (Ruttner 1986). Recently, we also found that *A. cerana* is less prone to the attack of wasps as compared to *A. mellifera* possibly because of the stronger direct flight muscles in the former species. On the other hand, *A. mellifera* is resistant to Thai sacbrood virus disease of *A. cerana* (Dulta and Verma 1987; Verma 1987).

A. cerana has many characteristics of economic and biological value which must be explored in order to obtain better honey crops and pollination services. It is with this background that different aspects of *A. cerana*'s biology have been reviewed in this chapter with the hope that they will stimulate further research in this scientifically neglected species of honeybee.

GEOGRAPHIC DISTRIBUTION OF *APIS CERANA*

Of the four species of the genus *Apis* found in Asia, *A. cerana* F., *A. dorsata* F. and *A. florea* F. are sympatric through much of their ranges. *A. mellifera*, the European bee, is exotic to Asia.and naturally its range is allopatric. Sakagami *et al.* (1980) reported *A. laboriosa* from the Himalayas as another new distinct honeybee species even larger than *A. dorsata*. Our biometric investigations on honeybee samples collected from the Himalayas reveal that all such samples were similar to *A. dorsata* in morphological characters. The conclusions of the Japanese researchers need further confirmation.

The geographic distribution of *Apis* species in the Oriental region was extensively reviewed by Maa (1953). According to him, the primary distribution centre was in the Malayan sub-region, where the number of species was greater than elsewhere and the various degrees of specializations co-existed. He further suggested that sub-genus *Sigmatapis* included honeybees from Oriental, Palaearctic and Manchurian sub-regions. In all, he described more than 10 species. Michener (1974) reported wide distribution of *A. cerana* in southeast Asia, extending from Sri Lanka and India to Japan and southeast to the Moluccas. Kellogg (1938) discussed the distribution of *A. cerana* in China. He considered the bees in China to be a variety of *A. indica* and different from the Japanese variety. *A. indica pernoi* was the largest race of Oriental honeybees found in Fukan Province of southeast China. According to Sakagami (1959), the native *A. cerana* in Japan was being replaced by the European honeybee, *A. mellifera*, but the former species was still found in the mountainous regions in the wild and also in hives. However, Sakai and Matsuka (1982) reported wide occurrence of *A. cerana* throughout Japan except in the northern-most island of Hokkaido. Reports of the distribution of *A. cerana* in various parts of Afghanistan, Philippines, and Sri Lanka have been given by Schneider and Djalal (1970), Morse and Laigo (1969), and Fernando (1979) respectively.

Distribution of honeybees in different parts of India has been studied by various investigators from time to time. Hussain (1939a, 1939b) claimed that honeybees originated in India as did Muttoo (1944, 1956). He described three species of honeybees from India, i.e. rock bee (*A. dorsata*), indigenous bee (*A. indica*), and pigmy bee (*A. florea*). Rahman and Singh (1940) reported *A. cerana indica* from all over India. These authors distinguished smaller and yellowish plain strains and larger and darker hill strains of this species. Rahman (1944) reported for the first time the presence of *A. cerana indica* at a height of 3030 to 3333 metres in a wild state. Muttoo (1944, 1956) described the following species of honeybees in India: *A. indica*, *A. dorsata*, and *A. florea*. A hill variety of *A. indica* was named *A. indica gandhiana*. Sharma (1945) described the distribution of *A. indica* in the plains of Northern India and reported the absence of this species from the Rajputana desert. Lal (1945) and Khan (1947) described three different species of honeybees in India and two strains of *A. florea* (one smaller and another bigger strain) were reported from Bhopal. Deodikar (1959), while studying the ecotypes of *A. cerana indica*, found a gradual variation in some traits such as body size, tongue length, and number of hamuli. Sometimes the extent of these variations approached the values found in *A. mellifera*. He also showed differences in the genitalia of *A. indica* from the northern and southern regions of India. Narayana *et al.* (1960) suggested the existence of three races

of *A. cerana indica* in India which were distinguished as Himalayan, the Gangetic plains, and the South Indian plains races. Singh (1962) reported *A. cerana indica*, *A. dorsata*, and *A. florea* at elevations of 2424, 1515-2424, and 606-757 metres respectively.

Ruttner (1985, 1986, 1987b) has recently reviewed the geographic distribution of *A. cerana*. According to him, this species is found in a very wide area comprising mostly southern and eastern Asia. Its range extends from Afghanistan in the west to the Philippines in the east, and in the north from Ussuria to Java and Timor in the south. Thus, *A. cerana* is found not only in tropical and sub-tropical regions of Asia, but also in cooler climates such as Siberia, north China, and the higher altitudes of the central Asian Mountains (Koeniger 1976).

RACES AND ECOTYPES OF *APIS CERANA*

Before discussing the different geographic races and ecotypes of *A. cerana*, it is important to make a distinction between these two concepts based on the earlier studies on *A. mellifera*. As a result of the continuous process of natural selection, different geographic races of a particular species of honeybee have evolved. Such geographic or natural races are different from the races of other domestic animals because the latter resulted from planned breeding by man. In the case of honeybees, such geographic races have evolved under the influence of natural abiotic and biotic factors existing in the environment. The geographic races of *A. mellifera* existing in tropical Africa, north Africa, and the near east and west Mediterranean regions have been identified through computer-based biometric analyses (Ruttner 1985, 1986). These results reveal that even each geographic race of honeybee species has further locally adapted populations called ecotypes which differ from each other in several biological and economic characteristics. The biological and economic differences existing between different geographic races and ecotypes of honeybees provide an excellent opportunity for their genetic improvement by selection and breeding. These differences have been extensively exploited in *A. mellifera* with remarkable success.

For example, by crossbreeding *A. mellifera* races, it is possible to increase honey production by 200 per cent (Fresnaye and Lavie 1976) and to develop low and high preference lines for better pollination of agricultural crops (Nye and Mackensen 1970). However, very little is known about natural variation in *A. cerana*, except for the rather subjective distinctions between hill and plain varieties (Kapil 1956; Narayanan *et al.* 1960, 1961a, 1961b; Kshir-

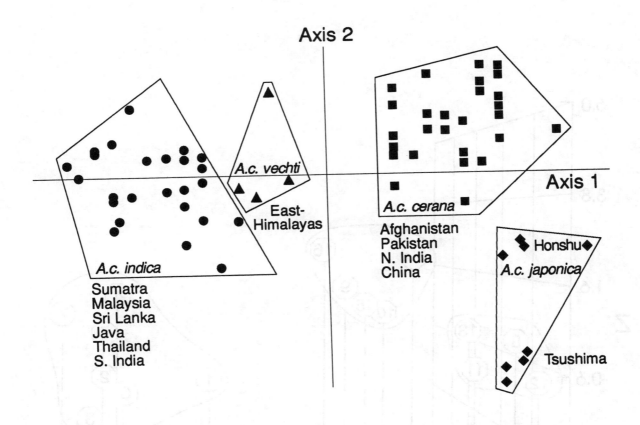

FIGURE 1. Principal component analysis (34 characters) with 68 *Apis cerana* samples of 20 worker bees each (after Ruttner 1986).

sagar 1976). These earlier biometric investigations were based on a few morphological characters and geographical samples and also lacked proper statistical analysis of data. However, in the recent past, attempts have been made to identify different races of *A. cerana* by using computer-assisted standard statistical methods. These results are reviewed as follows:

Ruttner (1985, 1986, 1987a,b) has distinguished four different races of *A. cerana*; namely *A. c. cerana*, *A. c. himalaya*, *A. c. indica*, and *A. c. japonica* (Fig. 1). His study was based on 34 morphological characters studied in 68 samples of *A. cerana* collected from different parts of Asia. Statistical methods included principal component analysis, discriminant analysis, and cluster analysis. Our research group has also carried out biometric studies on workers of *A. cerana* found in northeast, northwest and southern India, representing different physiographic conditions (Fig. 2). From each locality, 60 field bees (workers) were collected in summer from 4 to 5 wild colonies located in forests. In all, 55

morphological characters related to tongue, antenna, forewing, hindwing, hind leg, tergites, and sternites were studied. These characters were selected on the basis of previous work of Alpatov (1929) and Ruttner *et al.* (1978). Statistical analyses were carried out by using computer-based univariate and multivariate discriminant analyses in collaboration with Professor Howell V. Daly at the University of California, U.S.A. The results of these analyses as well as those of Ruttner (1985, 1986, 1987a,b) are given below:

1) *Apis cerana cerana*

This subspecies/race is distributed over northern China, northwest India, northern Pakistan, and Afghanistan. In northwest India, we (Mattu and Verma 1983, 1984a, 1984b; Verma and Mattu 1982; Verma *et al.* 1984) made detailed biometric studies on worker bees of *A. cerana* from 12 localities of Himachal Pradesh (Himachal region) and 8 localities of Jammu and Kashmir (Kashmir region) representing different altitudes (Fig. 2).

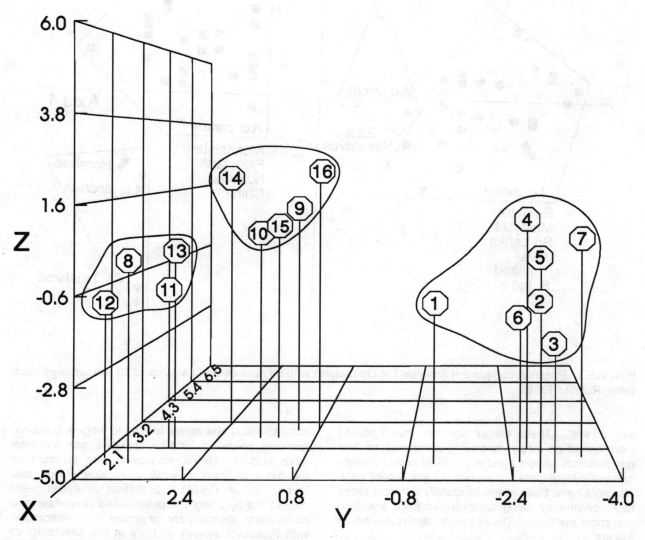

FIGURE 2. Three dimensional view of the biometric relationships of bees from 16 localities of north-east India. Axes X, Y, Z are the first 3 canonical discriminant functions that account for 59.79, 13.85 and 6.96 per cent, respectively, of the total variations. Centres of circles mark positions of centroids. Number within circles are codes for localities. Localities 1 to 7 = Naga and Mizo Hills. Localities 8, 11 to 13 = Brahmputra Valley. Localities 8, 10, 14 to 16 = Main Axis of Himalayas (Assam, Arunachal Pradesh and Sikkim).

Univariate analysis of data computed for 55 morphological characters of *A. c. cerana* showed significant differences in 28 characters in Himachal region and 18 characters in Kashmir region. In the bees of Himachal, 40 characters showed a significant positive correlation with altitude whereas, in Kashmir, 22 characters were positively correlated with altitude.

Worker bees from mountainous zones were significantly bigger in size and darker in colour than those of sub-mountainous zones. Bees of Kashmir region were significantly larger in 39 morphometric characters as compared to Himachal region. This subspecies is also larger in body size as compared to bees of northeast and south India. These findings are contrary to the observations of Ruttner (1985) who reported smaller size of bees from the Himalayas.

We (Verma *et al.*, unpublished results) also made discriminant analyses of *A. c. cerana* found in Kashmir and Himachal regions by computing their centroids based on the mean values. In this analysis, 97.04 per cent of the bees were correctly classified according to geographic regions. These results also supported our earlier univariate analysis results (Mattu and Verma 1983, 1984a, 1984b) that bees from Kashmir and Himachal regions of northwest India can be clustered biometrically into two separate sub-groups. Thus, *A. c. cerana* in northwest India may further comprise two separate ecotypes or geographic populations.

2) *Apis cerana himalaya*

Ruttner (1985) reported that bees from the eastern Himalayas form a separate cluster from the bees of the western Himalayas. These bees are possibly a separate race which he named *A. c. himalaya* (Ruttner, personal communication). Our (Verma *et al.*, unpublished results) biometrical results on *A. cerana* from northeast India (comprising of Nagaland, Manipur, Mizoram, Assam, Meghalaya, Arunachal Pradesh, and Sikkim) support these observations of Ruttner (1985) because out of 55 morphological characters, more than 45 were larger in *A. c. cerana* as compared to *A. c. himalaya*.

The F values for a univariate analysis for each of 55 characters for 16 localities of northeast India (Fig. 2) were all highly significant (significance probability < 0.0001). The discriminant analysis indicated that 16 localities were largely distinct. The reclassification of the individual bees by the discriminant co-efficients gave 80 to 100 per cent correct classification with an overall average of 91.6 per cent. The biometric relationships of the bees from 16 localities of northeast India are shown in a 3-dimensional graph (Fig. 3). This graph shows that from northeast India, the following three geographic ecotypes of *A. c. himalaya* were recognized: (1) Naga and Mizo Hills, (2) Brahamputra Valley, and (3) Main axis of Himalayas.

3) *Apis cerana indica*

The worker bees of *A. cerana* from south India, Sumatra, Malaysia, Sri Lanka, Java, and Thailand have been separately grouped through principal component analysis and named *A. c. indica* (Ruttner 1985). Our (Verma, unpublished results) univariate and discriminant analysis results from 14 localities of south India comprising of Kerala, Tamil Nadu and Karnataka revealed that these 14 localities were largely distinct biometrically (Fig. 3). Worker bees of this group were the smallest in size. This is evi-

denced by the fact that out of 55 morphological characters, 44 and 37 were significantly larger in *A. c. cerana* and *A. c. himalaya* respectively as compared to *A. c. indica*.

Based on the discriminant functions, biometrical relationships of the bees from 19 localities are shown in the 3-dimensional graph (Fig. 3). The first three axes of the graph represent the first three discriminant functions evaluated at the centroids of these groups. These functions account for 74.8 per cent of the total variations. The per cent of the variance explained by each of the three functions, i.e. x, y, x, are 49.3, 19.86, and 5.63 per cent respectively. This graph shows only approximate relationships because the remaining 25.2 per cent of the variations is not represented in the graph.

The discriminant analysis indicated two separate biometric sub-groups/ecotypes in south India. The first group is distributed in the Kerala region along the southwest boundary of India, whereas the second lies in the Karnataka and Tamil Nadu regions.

We also made biometric studies on *A. cerana* samples collected from 5 localities of the Andaman Islands (Fig. 3) with the idea that bees in these islands might be an isolated distinct race as these islands in the Indian Ocean are cut off from the rest of the world by long sea distances. However, by tracing the history of beekeeping in these islands, it was found that *A. cerana* is not a native of these islands but had been introduced from Bengal and possibly from other parts of India only two decades ago. Multivariate discriminant analysis for 5 geographic localities of these islands also revealed that these bees are biometrically similar to the bees from south India.

4) *Apis cerana japonica*

This sub-species is well adapted to the temperate climate of Japan except Hokkaido island in the north. However, *A. c. japonica* is gradually being replaced by *A. mellifera* (Okada 1986). Ruttner (1985) reported that this sub-species can further be divided into two separate ecotypes or sub-groups, i.e. Honshu (Tokyo region) and Tshushima bees. These two ecotypes differ from each other in tongue length, forewing length, hair length and colour patterns. This sub-species also has a higher cubital index and more slender abdomen as compared to other races of *A. cerana*.

From the above results, the following conclusions can be drawn:
a) Morphometrical comparison of three races of *A. cerana* found in India revealed significant differences in size (northwest India > northeast India > south India).

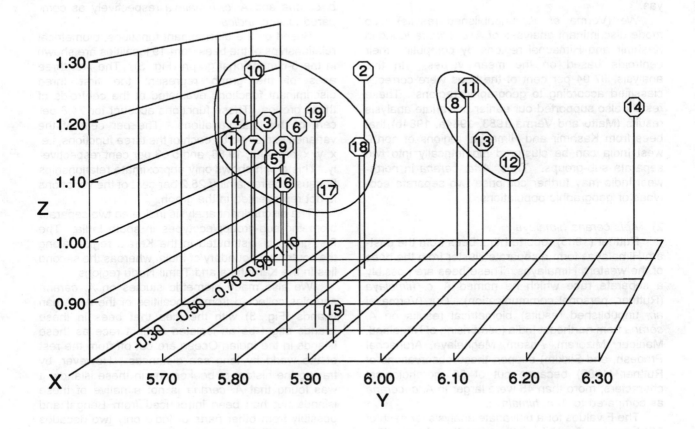

FIGURE 3. Three dimensional view of the biometric relationship of bees from 19 localities of South India and Andaman Islands. Axes X, Y, Z are the first 3 discriminant functions that account for 49.33, 19.86 and 5.63 per cent, respectively, of total variations. Centres of circles mark positions of centroids. Localities (1 to 14) are from South India and (15 to 19) are from Andaman Islands. Localities 1, 3 to 7, 9 and 10 = Kerala. Localities 15 to 19 = Andaman Islands. Localities 2, 8, 11 to 14 = Karnataka and Tamil Nadu.

b) Although at present we only know four races of A. cerana in the Asian region, there may be additions made to this list if detailed investigations are made in other regions of Asia. The above-mentioned works of Ruttner (1985, 1986, 1987) on biometry of A. cerana provide an excellent base for such studies.

c) Each race of A. cerana can further be divided into different ecotypes or geographic populations. These ecotypes are biologically meaningful because they occupy the adjacent geographic areas. So far, we have identified seven such sub-group/ecotypes in different races of A. cerana in India but there may be a much greater

number of ecotypes representing the different geographical regions.

d) Present results also suggest that any taxonomic decisions or construction of evolutionary relationships among the races of A. cerana should be based on total distribution of the species in the geographic region wherever it is found.

SELECTION AND BREEDING OF APIS CERANA

Present biometric results suggest that there exists a great variety of different geographic races and ecotypes of A. cerana in the entire Asian continent. Such great phenotypical variability provides an excellent opportunity for genetic improvement of native A. cerana by selection and breeding. The most productive approach is through the selection and rearing of proven valuable geographic races and ecotypes, development of new varieties, and reproduction of selected stock. An efficient method to improve an ecotype or strain is by analytical breeding, i.e. with assessment of queens according to the value of their progeny. This allows selection of the best stock and elimination of unwanted stock in a short time. A still better method is the mass production of hybrid honeybee colonies. Such hybrids are produced by crossing queens and drones of geographically and ecologically distant races or ecotypes. This method must, and can, become one of the most important means to increase the efficiency of beekeeping industry in all the major beekeeping regions of Asia. Based on two different geographic ecotypes existing in the northwest Himalayas, i.e. Kashmiri and Himachali ecotypes, such selection and breeding work on A. cerana has been started by our research group (Verma 1986a, 1986b) and results are summarized as follows:

A selection programme was started by making surveys of colonies of A. cerana at different places in Himachal Pradesh at different altitudes (30-36°N latitude, 74-81°E longitude) and climatic conditions. In Himachal Pradesh, the State Horticulture Department is maintaining bee colonies at 43 different beekeeping stations with more than 200 colonies at each apiary. Out of these apiaries, the best colonies were selected on the basis of such biological and economic characters as honey yield, pollen stores, area under brood, fecundity, foraging efficiency, temperament, hygiene, strength of colony, etc.

There were significant differences between colonies of A. cerana with regard to honey yield, pollen store, egg production, larvae, sealed brood, total brood, fecundity, and foraging efficiency. For example, honey yield per colony ranged from 1.205 to 8.480 kg; pollen stores from 56.80 to 588.71 sq cm; total brood area from 606.16 to 1862.66 sq cm; fecundity from 115.46 to 354.79 eggs per day, and foraging efficiency 2.13 to 12.60 pollen loads per minute in different colonies of A. cerana.

Significant positive correlations (P<0.01) were observed among different biological and economic characters. For example, honey yield was positively correlated with prolificness, pollen stores with foraging efficiency and fecundity, total brood area with pollen stores, fecundity and honey yield.

Pollen store area, total brood area, fecundity and sealed brood area were maximum in May-June and during September-October, the two major honey flow seasons in northern India.

In the breeding experiments, inbred lines of A. cerana of the Himachal region were developed by Brother X Sister system of mating in an isolated mating yard and its effect was studied in terms of change in morphological characters of worker bees and fecundity of queen bees. Data collected from worker bees revealed significantly lower values (P<0.01, P<0.05) for length of apical portion of radial cell, veins RL and IL, femur, tibia, third and fourth tergite, tongue, hindwing and sixth sternite, breadth of fore and hindwing and distance between wax mirrors in F1 inbred generations than the parent stock. Besides the above characters, length of forewing, radial cell, 2nd abscissa, vein ML, vannal lobe and breadth of metatarsus and sixth sternite also showed significant decrease in F_2 inbred generations as compared to the parent stock.

Inbreeding also affected the fecundity of F_1 and F_2 queens as compared to the parent stock. For example, egg laying rate was 343, 256, and 163 eggs per day for parent, F_1 and F_2 inbred queens respectively. These results also suggest that the inbreeding depression was more pronounced in F_2 (Parent>F_2, P<0.01) than the F_1 inbred (Parent>F_1, F_1>F_2, P<0.05) queens.

Cross-breeding experiments were conducted by crossing Himachali and Kashmiri ecotypes of A. cerana in an isolated mating yard. The results were studied in terms of change in morphological characters of workers and fecundity of queens. Cross-breeding experiments between Himachali queens and Kashmiri drones showed significantly higher values (P<0.01, P<0.05) for breadth of forewing, length of vein VL, 2nd abscissa, hindwing, jugal lobe and third sternite and distance between the wax mirrors of hybrid than parent worker bees of Himachal region. On the contrary, the length and breadth of the wax mirror were significantly smaller in such hybrid worker bees than in the Himachali parent stock. Thus, these studies revealed that certain morphological characters of hybrid worker bees were intermediate between those of the parent stock.

Hybrid queens obtained by crossing Kashmiri queens with Himachali drones showed an increase of 102.55 per cent (397 eggs/day) in fecundity compared to the Kashmiri parent stock (196 eggs/day). However, in hybrid queens obtained by mating Himachali queens with Kashmiri drones, the fecundity decreased by 13.53 per cent (to 147 eggs/day) by comparison with the Himachali parent stock (170 eggs/day). Because of the incidence of sacbrood virus disease in A. cerana colonies during the course of investigation (April, 1984), these breeding experiments could not be carried further and, at this stage, we had to deviate our research programme to investigations on sacbrood virus disease (see below).

The above work on selection and breeding of *A. cerana* can be extended further by using analytical and hybrid breeding techniques. Such research work may help in improving the economic, biological, and morphometric characters of this species to increase the honey production and better pollination of agricultural crops in Asia. This is a potentially valuable area for future research.

BREEDING FOR RESISTANCE TO THAI SACBROOD VIRUS DISEASE

Thai sacbrood virus disease of *A. cerana* has been reported from Thailand, Burma, and Nepal. In India, it was noticed for the first time in 1978 in Meghalaya (Kshirsagar *et al.* 1981; Kshirsagar 1983). The incidence and severity of this disease is increasing at an alarming rate and more than 95 per cent of colonies infected in various parts of the country were killed by this disease (Rana *et al.* 1986, 1987). There was a great economic loss to Indian beekeeping not only in terms of honey and beeswax production but also through adversely affected pollination services. The problem was particularly severe in the temperate regions of the country where the disease is more widespread than in the tropical and subtropical regions.

We confirmed the presence of Thai sacbrood virus in *A. cerana* in northern India by conducting electron microscopic and serological (immunodiffusion test) studies. For immunodiffusion tests, specific antiserum against Thai sacbrood was obtained from Rothamsted Experimental Station, England. The results of these investigations have been presented by Rana *et al.* (1986, 1987).

Different preventative control measures, recommended to control the spread of sacbrood disease in *A. mellifera*, were unsuccessful in *A. cerana* (Rana *et al.* 1986) However, about 5 per cent of colonies in affected areas were resistant to, or escaped from, the disease. In such colonies, resistance to Thai sacbrood virus disease was studied in detail. Out of 52 colonies, 3 developed severe symptoms of the disease and they were destroyed. The remaining 22 colonies were reared for five generations to test for resistance: each generation was fed the purified virus suspension in sugar syrup.

Our results showed that the symptoms of the disease appeared in previously symptom-free colonies within 4 to 10 days of feeding the purified virus suspensions in sugar syrup. Such symptoms appeared earlier in parent colonies than in colonies from subsequent generations. For example, disease symptoms appeared in 4, 5, 4, 7, 10 and 8 days in parent, F_1, F_2, F_3, F_4, and F_5 generations respectively.

Also, the percentage of affected brood was more in parent than in daughter colonies and, hence, a continuous decrease in infection was observed in subsequent generations. The amount of infection was 50, 20, 10, 5, 5, and 4 per cent in parent, F_1, F_2, F_3, F_4, and F_5 generation colonies respectively.

During our studies, we noted that recovery from infection occurred within 30 days from the appearance of disease in the colonies. Parent colonies took longer to recover from the attack of this disease than did daughter colonies (25, 23, 20, 16 and 15 days for F_1, F_2, F_3, F_4, and F_5 generations respectively). In parent colonies, abnormal behaviour such as no coverage of brood by nurse bees, greater tendency to abscond, increased aggressiveness, reduced fecundity, and reduced hygienic behaviour (disposal of the dead brood) was observed. However, in subsequent generations (F_1 to F_5), there was a gradual improvement and colonies showed a return to normal behaviour.

We also repeated the above experiments of feeding purified virus suspension to healthy *A. mellifera* colonies but no symptoms of the disease appeared in them.

Our results indicate that there is some mechanism of resistance to Thai sacbrood virus disease in *A. cerana*. In nature, the epizootic lasts for about four years after which surviving colonies start multiplying and populations recover. For example, in Himachal Pradesh (India), the disease was observed from 1982 to 1986/87. The surviving colonies are now multiplying and 25 per cent of the previous population has been restored during the last two years or so.

SCOPE OF BEEKEEPING WITH *APIS CERANA* VERSUS *APIS MELLIFERA* IN ASIA

Large scale importation and multiplication of exotic *A. mellifera* for higher honey production in Asia has become a controversial subject among bee scientists. This species may not adapt well to the tropical and sub-tropical parts of Asia with different climatic conditions, flora, mating competition with *A. cerana* and hazards of predators and diseases (Koeniger 1976) It is recognized that native bees are the best adapted to any specific climate and environment. However, so far, *A. mellifera* is doing well in the plains and sub-mountainous regions of northern India except above 1500 m ASL. Thus, both species seem to be complementary to each other for beekeeping in the plains and hilly regions of northern India.

Information on interspecific behaviour can be of great practical value to both beekeepers and bee scientists. Behaviour of honeybees may vary according to species and sub-species and also depends upon environmental factors. Our research group in Himachal Pradesh University has made detailed investigations on comparative biological and economic characteristics of *A. mellifera* and *A. cerana* under Indian conditions for the last 15 years. These results are reviewed as follows:

Foraging behaviour on apple bloom

Our previous biometric works on *A. cerana* and *A. mellifera* suggest that many of the morphological characters related to foraging and pollination efficiency are significantly different in the two species (Mattu and Verma 1983; Mattu and Verma 1984a,b). The foraging behaviours of the two species may also be different on some other agricultural crops. Therefore, our research group (Verma and Dulta 1986) has made detailed investigations on the foraging behaviour of *A. cerana* and *A. mellifera* in relation to the pollination of apple bloom under different agroclimatic conditions.

Worker bees of *A. cerana* started foraging significantly earlier (P<0.01) and ceased later (P<0.01) than did *A. mellifera*. Average duration of foraging activity in *A. cerana* (13.10 hours) was significantly more than in *A. mellifera* (12.28 hours). The duration of foraging trips was significantly longer (P<0.01) for *A. mellifera* than for *A. cerana*. In *A. cerana*, no pollen + nectar collectors were found, whereas, in *A. mellifera*, the percentage of such forager bees varied from 6 to 11 per cent. In both species, nectar collectors outnumbered pollen collectors (Verma and Dulta 1986).

Hourly fluctuations in the number of bees leaving the hive showed the peak activity of *A. cerana* was between 0900 and 1130 hours (mean 132 bees/5 minutes) at temperatures from 15.5 to 21.0°C and that of *A. mellifera* was between 1100 and 1300 hours (mean 118 bees/5 minutes) when the temperature ranged from 21-25°C during the months of March-April in Shimla hills. The interspecific difference is remarkable from the pollination point of view because by keeping both species of honeybees in the same orchard, the duration of peak period of foraging activity can be prolonged to ensure better pollination.

However, there were no significant differences between *A. cerana* and *A. mellifera* with regard to the number of stigmas touched per minute, time spent per flower, their visits to apple trees in the same or different rows in the orchard, number of flowers visited per apple tree, number of apple trees visited per foraging trip, and in the ratio of top- and side-working bees on apple bloom throughout the day.

Results on foraging behaviour of *A. cerana* and *A. mellifera* at three different altitudes - 1350, 1875 and 2400 metres ASL - showed that initiation of foraging activity was delayed and its cessation was earlier with the increasing altitude. Duration of each foraging trip in both species increased with the increase in altitude of the orchard.

Altitude had no significant effect (P>0.01) on other parameters like bees' preference for pollen or nectar or both during a visit, peak hours of foraging activity, pollen load, number of stigmas touched per visit, and time spent per flower.

Comparative foraging behaviour of *A. mellifera* and *A. cerana* shows marked differences. This may be because the foraging efficiency and flight range in honeybees depend upon the number and diameter of the flight muscle fibres and their fuel content. Our investigations (Dulta and Verma 1987) revealed that the number of fibres in dorsolongitudinal, dorsolateral, dorsoventral, pleurosternal, and intersegmental muscles of *A. mellifera* were significantly greater than in *A. cerana* (P<0.01). Similarly, diameter of flight muscles of *A. mellifera* was significantly greater (P<0.01) than in *A. cerana*. Fuel content in terms of glycogen, total lipids, and associated enzyme systems were greater in *A. mellifera* than in *A. cerana* (Dulta and Verma 1988). Our morphometric results show that *A. mellifera* is bigger than *A. cerana* and the flight range of *A. mellifera* is double that of *A. cerana*. Thus, characteristics of flight muscles and their fuel content correspond to body size and also appear to be related to flight range and foraging efficiency.

In India, the Himachal Pradesh State Horticulture Department and a few private beekeepers rent *A. cerana* and *A. mellifera* colonies to the fruit-growers at the time of apple bloom for pollination. Generally, at the onset of winter season (November-December), colonies of both *A. cerana* and *A. mellifera* are taken from the temperate hilly region to the sub-tropical plain area. There, brood-rearing usually starts in the first or second week of February. By mid-March, colony strength reaches its maximum and this is the time when flowering in apple orchards starts. Colonies are transported in trucks directly to the apple-growing belt of the state and distributed to the fruit-growers at the cost of Rs.25/- per colony for one flowering season (13 Rs = 1 U.S. Dollar). However, private beekeepers charge a higher rental fee than do state-owned apiaries. At present, colonies are distributed to about 1000 fruit-growers and each gets about two to five colonies irrespective of the size of the orchard. Although the number of colonies distributed for pollination is perhaps too small, and given the large area of land under fruit cultivation in Himachal Pradesh, apple-growers are now aware of the important role honeybees play in apple pollination. As a result of this practice by the State Horticulture

Department, many fruit-growers now maintain their own colonies of bees for the purpose of pollination and honey production.

Our findings on foraging behaviour of *A. mellifera* and *A. cerana* suggest that both species of honey-bees are complementary for pollination of horticultural and agricultural crops. Instead of providing two colonies of the same species per hectare of crop in bloom, one strong colony each of *A. mellifera* and *A. cerana* could be kept to ensure efficient pollination. During low temperatures, *A. cerana* should be preferred to *A. mellifera*. Additional research on comparative foraging behaviour of *A. cerana* and *A. mellifera* on other agricultural and horticultural crops in tropical and sub-tropical parts of Asia should be carried out to augment our data.

Aggressive behaviour and robbing

A. cerana colonies are robbed by *A. mellifera*, causing the former to abscond. Robbing of diseased and weak colonies of *A. cerana* by strong colonies of *A. mellifera* leads to the spread of tracheal mites (*Acarapis woodi*) to the latter. Hanging ball experiments show that *A. mellifera* is more aggressive than *A. cerana* (Verma *et al.*, unpublished results). Given the overall dominance of *A. mellifera* over *A. cerana*, to keep both species in the same habitat, special management techniques should be developed. Otherwise large-scale introduction of *A. mellifera* may lead to the extinction of *A. cerana* in India.

Swarming and absconding

Frequent swarming and absconding are serious problems in beekeeping with *A. cerana* but it is a much lesser problem with European races of *A. mellifera*. Frequent swarming and absconding may be beneficial for the survival and propagation of *A. cerana* but it sometimes poses a serious problem to beekeeping, especially when it occurs during the honey flow. To some extent, swarming can be prevented by improving the environment of the colony through provision of shade, ventilation, proper arrangement of brood, removal of uncapped queen cells or capped drone brood, artificial division of the colony, introduction of a new queen, etc. (Singh 1962).

Absconding by bees usually happens because of starvation, robbing, attack of diseases and enemies, excessive handling or exposure, poor ventilation, etc. The absconding rate of *A. cerana* may vary from 30 to 100 per cent/season. About two to three weeks before absconding, the fecundity, brood-rearing and pollen collection decline sharply, reaching zero level on the day of absconding. It has been found that *A. cerana* of Kashmir is less prone to abscond than that of Himachal (Verma 1986c).

Temperature regulation

All species of the genus *Apis* are actively or passively involved in regulating the temperature of their nest. They maintain the brood nest temperature remarkably constant at 34-35°C. Verma (1970) investigated the possible differences between *A. mellifera* and *A. cerana* in their ability to regulate the hive temperature against outside air temperature changes. This information should help in assessing the adaptability of the two species to different climates.

In summer, when the outside air temperature was maximum (39°C ± 0.35), both species significantly lowered their hive temperatures (P<0.01). When the outside air exceeded 40°C, *A. cerana* colonies absconded frequently but no such absconding tendency was observed in *A. mellifera*. At temperatures above 40°C, fanning was more regular and frequent in *A. mellifera* than in *A. cerana*. Further, evaporation rates in hives of *A. mellifera* were significantly higher than in those of *A. cerana* (P<0.01).

In winter, the mean cluster temperature of *A. cerana* and *A. mellifera* fluctuated between 36.7°C and 37.1°C and 33.0°C and 33.9°C respectively against air temperatures of 3.6°C to 17.3°C. The cluster temperature of the *A. cerana* colony was significantly higher (P<0.01) than that of *A. mellifera* possibly because of differences in compactness of cluster and colony strength.

Studies on high temperatures did suggest that *A. mellifera* survived high lethal temperatures (50°C) longer than did *A. cerana*. This is remarkable considering that the *A. mellifera* originated in a much cooler climate. The survival time at 5°C was not different between the species (Verma and Edwards 1972).

At present, we use Italian honeybees (*A. mellifera ligustica*) in northern India. The above data on temperature regulation and tolerance suggest that *A. m. ligustica* is better suited to the hot climate whereas *A. cerana* is well adapted to the cold one. This fact should be kept in mind while introducing exotic bees to the other new parts of Asia also.

Hoarding behaviour and longevity

Over a period of 14 days, *A. mellifera* hoarded (100.40 mgm/bee/day) significantly greater amounts of sugar syrup than *A. cerana* (78.87 mgm/bee/day) (P<0.01). However, there was no significant difference within the 6 colonies of *A. mellifera* or of *A. cerana* in their hoarding behaviour. Longevity of caged worker bees of *A. cerana* (range 23.82 to 36.31) was significantly less than for *A. mellifera* (range 26.30 to 30.90) as determined by probit analyses (Verma 1986c).

These results support the general view that *A. mellifera* produces three times as much honey as does *A. cerana*. However, there is a considerable scope to improve the honey production of *A. cerana* through selection, breeding and better management techniques.

Mating behaviour and fertility

One of the major difficulties in any breeding programme is the mating habit of the queens and drones. This difficulty in *A. mellifera* has been overcome by the use of instrumental insemination. However, this technique with *A. cerana* has unexpectedly turned out to be difficult because of obtaining enough semen ejaculate from drones. Individual *A. cerana* drones ejaculate about 0.35 μl of semen containing about 1.20 million spermatozoa and these values are 5 to 6 times lower than that of *A. mellifera* drones. Therefore, the breeding programme for *A. cerana* is generally carried out by allowing natural mating in isolated mating yards to avoid mixing of the drones of different genetic origins.

The number of premating flights in *A. cerana* and *A. mellifera* are the same. However, the duration of such flights was significantly more (P<0.01) in the former than the latter. Queens at the time of mating and oviposition were significantly older (P<0.01) in European honeybees than in *A. cerana*. The peak period of mating flights of the queen bee and drones coincided in both species. The queen bees of both species secrete a pheromone of the same chemical composition during the mating flight which attracts the drones of both species. These results suggest that drones of one species may try to mate, but unsuccessfully, with the queen bee of the other species. Queens of *A. mellifera* possess double the number of ovarioles, their spermathecae can store three times the number of spermatozoa and the daily egg-laying rate is also triple that of queens of *A. cerana*.

REFERENCES

Alpatov, W.W. 1929. Biometrical studies on variation and races of the honeybee (*Apis mellifera* L.). Quarterly Review Biology, 4: 1-58.

Deodikar, G.B. 1959. Geographical distribution based on morphological characters (structure of genitalia and crossability among different bee species). Indian Bee Journal, 23: 60-61.

Dulta, P.C. and L.R. Verma. 1987. Comparative biometric studies on flight muscles of honeybees in the genus *Apis*. Journal of Apicultural Research, 26: 205-209.

Dulta, P.C. and L.R. Verma. 1989. Biochemical studies on flight muscles of genus *Apis*. Comparative Biochemistry and Physiology, 28: 136-141.

Fernando, E.F.W. 1979. Some biometrical features of *Apis cerana* F. from Sri Lanka. Indian Bee Journal, 41: 5-8.

Fresnaye, J. and P. Lavie. 1976. Selective and crossbreeding of bees in France. Proceedings of the International Symposium on Bee Genetics, Selection and Reproduction. Moscow, U.S.S.R. pp. 212-218.

Hussain, S.W. 1939a. Present position of beekeeping in India. Indian Bee Journal, 1: 53-55.

Hussain, S.W. 1939b. Hindustan, the home of the honeybee. Indian Bee Journal, 1: 56.

Kapil, R.P. 1956. Variations in the biometrical characters of the Indian honeybee (*Apis indica* F.). Indian Journal of Entomology, 18: 440-457.

Kellogg, C.R. 1938. Some characteristics of Oriental honeybees (*Apis indica* F.) in China. Journal of Economic Entomology, 34: 717-720.

Khan, M.S.A. 1947. Bhopal is a home of honeybees. Indian Bee Journal, 9: 144.

Koeniger, N. 1976. The Asiatic honeybee *Apis cerana*. Proceedings of the International Apicultural Congress in Tropical Climate. London, England. pp. 47-49.

Kshirsagar, K.K. 1976. Studies on Indian Apidae with special reference to Indian hive bee, *Apis cerana indica* F. Ph.D. thesis, University of Pune, India.

Kshirsagar, K.K. 1983. Spread of Sacbrood disease in Uttar Pradesh. Indian Bee Journal, 45: 41-42.

Kshirsagar, K.K., M.C. Mittal and R.M. Chauhan. 1981. Occurrence of Sacbrood disease in *Apis cerana indica*. Indian Bee Journal, 43: 44.

Lal, K.B. 1945. The distribution of *Apis indica* F. in the plains of India. Indian Bee Journal, 7: 133-134, 144.

Maa, T. 1953. An inquiry into the systematics of the tribus Apidinii or honey bees (Hym.). Treubia, 21: 525-640.

Mattu, V.K. and L.R. Verma. 1983. Comparative morphometrical studies on the Indian honeybee of the north-west Himalayas. 1. Tongue and antenna. Journal of Apicultural Research, 22: 79-85.

Mattu, V.K. and L.R. Verma. 1984a. Comparative morphometric studies on the Indian honeybee of the north-west Himalayas. 2. Wings. Journal of Apicultural Research, 23: 3-10.

Mattu, V.K. and L.R. Verma. 1984b. Comparative morphometric studies on the Indian honeybee of the north-west Himalayas. 3. Hindleg, Tergites and Sternites. Journal of Apicultural Research,

23: 117-122.

Michener, C.D. 1974. The Social Behaviour of the Bees. Harvard University Press, Cambridge, Massachusetts.

Morse, R.A. and F.M. Laigo. 1969. The potentials and problems of beekeeping in Philippines. Bee World, 50: 9-14.

Muttoo, R.N. 1944. Beekeeping in India, its past, present and future. Indian Bee Journal, 6: 54-57.

Muttoo, R.N. 1956. Facts about beekeeping in India. Bee World, 37: 125-133.

Narayanan, E.S., P.L. Sharma and K.G. Phadke. 1960. Studies on biometry of Indian bees. 1. Tongue length and number of hooks on the hind wings of Apis indica F. Indian Bee Journal, 22: 58-63.

Narayanan, E.S., P.L. Sharma and K.G. Phadke. 1961a. Studies on biometry of Indian bees. III. Tongue length and number of hooks on the hind wings of Apis indica F. collected from Madras state. Indian Bee Journal, 23: 3-9.

Narayanan, E.S., P.L. Sharma and K.G. Phadke. 1961b. Studies on biometry of Indian bees. IV. Tongue length and number of hooks on the hind wings of Apis indica F. collected from Uttar Pradesh. Indian Bee Journal, 23: 69-74.

Nye, W.P. and O. Mackensen. 1970. Selective breeding of honeybees on alfalfa pollen collection with tests in high and low alfalfa pollen collection region. Journal of Apicultural Research, 9: 61-64.

Okada, I. 1985. Biological characteristics of the Japanese honeybee, Apis cerana japonica. Proceedings of the XXXth International Apicultural Congress. Nagoya, Japan. pp. 119-121.

Rahman, K.A. 1944. Distribution of Apis indica F. Indian Bee Journal, 6: 155.

Rahman, K.A. and S. Singh. 1940. The editor's clip on Indian honeybee, Apis indica F. Indian Bee Journal, 2: 93.

Rana, B.S., I.D. Garg, S.M. Paul Khurana, L.R. Verma and H.O. Agrawal. 1986. Thai Sacbrood virus of honeybees (Apis cerana indica F.) in north-west Himalayas. Indian Journal of Virology, 2: 127-131.

Rana, B.S. I.D. Garg, S.M.Paul Khurana, L.R. Verma and H.O. Agrawal. 1987. Incidence of Thai Sacbrood virus disease in Apis cerana indica F. in south-east Asia. In Chemistry and Biology of Social Insects. J. Eder and H. Rembold (eds.), Peperny Verlag, Munchen. pp. 640-641.

Ruttner, F. 1985. Characterization and variability of Apis cerana F. Proceedings of the XXXth International Apicultural Congress. Nagoya, Japan. pp. 130-133.

Ruttner, F. 1986. Geographic variability and classification. In Bee Genetics and Breeding. T.E. Rinderer (ed.), Academic Press, New York. pp. 23-56.

Ruttner, F. 1987a. Taxonomy of Honeybee. In Chemistry and Biology of Social Insects. J. Eder and H. Rembold (eds.), Peperny Verlag, Munchen. pp. 59-62.

Ruttner, F. 1987b. Biogeography and Taxonomy of Honeybee. Berlin: Springer Verlag. pp. 120-161.

Ruttner, F. 1988. (personal communication).

Ruttner, F. and V. Maul. 1983. Experimental analysis of reproductive interspecies isolation of Apis mellifera and Apis cerana. Apidologie, 14: 309-324.

Ruttner, F., L. Tassencourt and J. Louveaux. 1978. Biometrical-statistical analysis of the geographic variability of Apis mellifera L. 1. Material and Methods. Apidologie, 9: 363-381.

Sakagami, S.F. 1959. Some interspecific relations between Japanese and European honeybees. Journal of Animal Ecology, 28: 51-68.

Sakagami, S.F., T. Matsumura and K. Ito. 1980. Apis laboriosa in Himalayas, the little known world's largest honeybee (Hymenoptera, Apidae). Insecta Matsumurana, 19: 47-77.

Sakai, T. and M. Matsuka. 1982. Beekeeping and honey resources in Japan. Bee World, 63: 63-71.

Schneider, P. and A.S. Djalal. 1970. Vorkommen and haltung der ostlichen Honigbiene (Apis cerana Fab.) in Afghanistan. Apidologie, 1: 329-341.

Sharma, P.L. 1945. Distribution of Apis indica F. in the plains of northern India. Indian Bee Journal, 7: 53-54.

Singh, S. 1962. Beekeeping in India. Indian Council of Agricultural Research, New Delhi.

Verma, L.R. 1970. A comparative study of temperature regulation in Apis mellifera L. and Apis cerana indica F. American Bee Journal, 110: 390-391.

Verma, L.R. 1984. Beekeeping in northern India. Major constraints and potentials. Proc. F.A.O. (United Nations) Expert consult. on beekeeping with Apis mellifera in tropical and sub-tropical Asia. Bangkok, Thailand. pp. 148-155.

Verma, L.R. 1986a. Studies on genetic improvement of Indian honeybee Apis cerana indica F. by selection and breeding. Proc. Group monitoring workshop on DST funded projects in Env. Biol., Entomol. Reprod. Biol. and Socio. Biol. Ministry of Science and Technology, GoI, New Delhi. pp. 11-14.

Verma, L.R. 1986b. Biological and economic

characters of *Apis cerana indica* F. Honeybee Science, 7: 151-157.

Verma, L.R. 1986c. Comparative comb structure, temperature regulation and foraging behaviour of *Apis cerana indica* F. and *Apis mellifera* L. *In* Chemistry and Biology of Social Insects. J. Eder and H. Rembold (eds.), Peperny Verlag, Munchen. p. 540.

Verma, L.R. 1987. Current status of parasitic mites in relation to beekeeping with *A. cerana* F. and *A. mellifera* L. in India. Proc. F.A.O. Workshop on Parasitic Bee Mites and their Control. Pulawy, Poland. pp. 195-200.

Verma, L.R. 1990. Beekeeping in Integrated Mountain Development. New Delhi: Oxford and IBH Publishing Co. Pvt. Ltd. 367 pp.

Verma, L.R. 1992. Honeybees in Mountain Agriculture. New Delhi: Oxford and IBH Publishing Co. Pvt. Ltd. 274 pp.

Verma, L.R. and P.C. Dulta. 1986. Foraging behaviour of *Apis cerana indica* F. and *Apis mellifera* L. in pollinating apple flowers. Journal of Apicultural Research, 25: 197-201.

Verma, L.R. and D.K. Edwards. 1972. Metabolic acclimatization to temperature and temperature tolerance in *Apis mellifera* L. and *Apis cerana indica* F. Journal of Apicultural Research, 20: 105-108.

Verma, L.R. and V.K. Mattu. 1982. Ecotype studies on *Apis cerana indica* F. *In* the Biology of Social Insects. M.D. Breed, C.D. Michener, and H.E. Evans (eds), West View Press, Boulder, Colorado. p. 413.

Verma, L.R. V.K. Mattu and M.P. Singh. 1984. Races of Indian honeybee in Himalayas. Proceedings of the XVIIth International Congress of Entomology, Hamburg, F.R.G. p. 508

TEMPERATURE AS A CAUSATIVE FACTOR OF THE SEASONAL COLOUR DIMORPHISM IN *APIS CERANA JAPONICA*

M. MATSUKA, T. TSURUTA and M. SASAKI

INTRODUCTION

Variation in body colour of *Apis cerana* has been described as characteristics of local strains or varieties (Tokuda 1924; Muttoo 1956).

Japanese honeybees (*A. cerana japonica*) are dimorphic in body colour (Okada 1986); the yellow type appears in colonies from July to October, whereas the black type emerges from October to May. In the present study, we examined the body colour of several colonies during a year and laboratory-tested the effect of temperature as a causative factor affecting body colour (*cf* Tsuruta *et al.* 1989).

MATERIALS AND METHODS

A. cerana japonica colonies were obtained from several different regions in 1985 and 1986 and kept in the apiary of the Institute of Honeybee Science, Tamagawa University.

To determine the seasonal change of the dimorphs in the colonies, two hundred bees were collected at intervals from each colony and the colour grade of following body parts was examined:

Scutellum (Sc): yellow or black

Third abdominal tergite (T3): grade 1 (2 black spots present) to grade 6 (totally black)

Fourth abdominal tergite (T4): yellow or black (if any black part)

Abdominal sternites (St): yellow (if milky-white or yellow without black mark) or black (if any black part)

As a preliminary test to examine the effect of temperature on body colour, parts of combs containing pupae were taken out and put in an incubator in which compartments were set to 25 to 38°C. The colour of the body parts was examined after emergence of bees. The colour pattern did not change after emergence.

Pupae were collected, divided into separate developmental stages according to the grade of eye pigmentation and subjected to 30 or 34°C in filter paper dishes to determine the temperature sensitive stage(s).

The temperature in various parts of a colony was automatically recorded from 15 to 18 November 1985

by using microthermistors (Takara Ind. Co., TZL-64) in which sensory pin-points were inserted into cells or left free. During this period, the ambient temperature was low enough to easily detect temperature differences, if any, within a colony.

RESULTS AND DISCUSSION

Colour change in colonies

Body colour was partially genetically determined. Dark strains, which came from Ehime, Shikoku Island, showed a predominance of dark bees with colour grades for T3 of more than 4, except during August to October. Strains from Kumamoto, Kyushu Island, were lighter in colour. The colour grade of winter-type bees in this strain was 3 on T3. These genetic variations correspond to colour varieties as reported in the cited references.

Colour grades changed seasonally to produce summer and winter bees as reported by Okada (1986). Figure 1 represents the results obtained with a Ehime strain. Yellow bees (T3 grade less than 2) appeared from July until October. Dark ones (T3 grade more than 5) decreased strikingly during this period but reappeared in October.

Temperature treatment in an incubator

Since the seasonal colour change may reflect the temperature at which bees developed, the effect of temperature during the pupal stage was examined. Sealed brood was removed from colonies and put in a temperature-programmed incubator. Emerged bees were examined for their colour types. The T3 colour in the Kumamoto strain at 38, 34, 30, and 25°C was 1.1, 1.7, 2.6, and 5.8, respectively. The lower the temperature, the more dark-coloured bees emerged. The colour of abdominal sternites in this strain was more sensitive to temperature. No dark spot appeared at 38°C, only 6.7% bees were dark at 34°C, and a 100% black abdomen appeared at 30°C or lower. Mortality was high at temperatures lower than 28°C.

In the next experiment, pupae at known developmental stages were treated with high and low temperatures. The high experimental temperature was 34°C; the low was 30°C. Results are shown in Figure

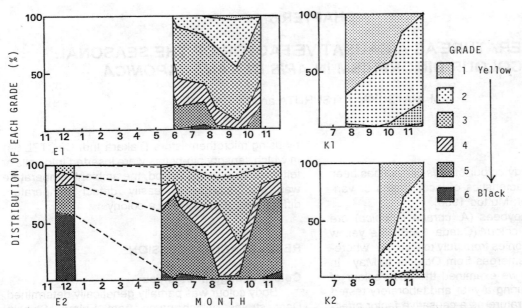

FIGURE 1. Seasonal colour change in the third abdominal tergite of *Apis cerana japonica*.

EFFECT OF TEMPERATURE CHANGE DURING PUPAL PERIOD ON THE PIGMENTATION

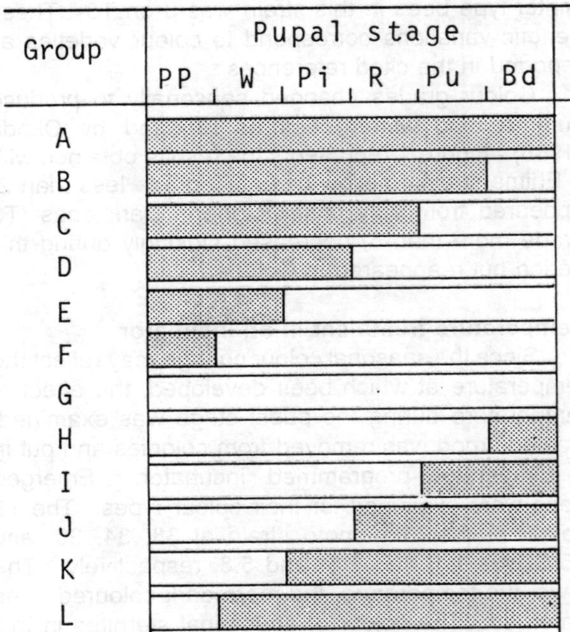

Group	Pupal stage						N	Mortal-ity (%)	T3 Grade	Pigmentation (%)		
	PP	W	Pi	R	Pu	Bd				Sc	T4	St
A							10	70	3.7	67	100	100
B							8	25	3.5	67	83	83
C							5	0	3.6	60	80	80
D							6	67	3.0	0	100	100
E							7	0	3.3	29	100	57
F							8	13	3.0	0	43	43
G							13	0	3.0	0	0	8
H							5	40	3.0	0	67	0
I							7	0	3.0	0	71	71
J							7	43	3.0	0	100	100
K							6	33	2.8	25	100	100
L							7	14	3.3	67	100	100

30°C   34°C

FIGURE 2. Effect of temperature changes during pupal period on the pigmentation of *Apis cerana japonica*.

2. The T3 colour grade of the high-temperature treated individuals was 3.0 and 0-8% of bees were dark at other parts (Sc, T4, and St). However, the same pigmentations were 3.7 and 67-100%, respectively, in bees kept at the low temperature through their pupal stages. From transference experiments

(shown in the figure), we found that the earlier or longer the treatment with high temperature, the lighter bees appeared, and vice versa. The results indicated that the temperature-sensitive period is the early pupal stage with white or pink eyes.

Temperature fluctuation in a colony

Brood area temperature in a honeybee colony is known to be constant (Free 1977). If this is always true, however, the colour change described above is difficult to explain based on temperature change alone, and the phenomenon has to be explained by other factor(s). Thus, we checked temperatures at various parts of an *A. cerana* hive with microthermistors in the autumn. Ambient temperature in the experimental period showed diurnal fluctuation between 5-18°C (10.0 ± 3.1, average). Temperature at the central brood area was very stable at 34°C (33.9 ± 0.3°C). However, the peripheral brood area temperature was lower than the centre with some diurnal fluctuation (31.3 ± 1.7°C). The honey storage area was also kept much warmer than the air but was affected by the diurnal change (25.9 ± 3.4°C).

The temperature difference (about 2.5 degrees) between the central and peripheral brood area could affect colour morph of adult bees. Although other factors such as photoperiod could determine colour dimorphism in *A. cerana*, we conclude temperature is a major factor in the mechanism. Also, the variation in pupal period in *A. cerana* (10-12 days, Kapil 1959) may reflect the temperature differences in the brood area. Verma (1970) also reported temperature differences in a colony.

REFERENCES

Free, J.B. 1977. The social organization of Honeybees. E. Arnold, London. pp. 68.

Kapil, R.P. 1959. Variation in the developmental period of the Indian bee. Indian Bee Journal, 21: 3-6 and 26.

Muttoo, R.N. 1956. Facts about beekeeping in India. Bee World, 37(7): 125-133.

Okada, I. 1986. Biological characteristics of the Japanese honeybee, *Apis cerana japonica*. Proceedings of the 30th International Apicultural Congress Apimondia. pp. 119-122.

Tokuda, Y. 1924. Studies on the honeybee, with special reference to the Japanese honeybee. Trans. Sapporo National Hist. Society, 9: 1-27 (Reprint: Bull. Imper. Zootech. Exp. Sta. No. 15, 1935).

Tsuruta, T., M. Matsuka and M. Sasaki. 1989. Temperature as a causative factor in the seasonal colour dimorphism of *Apis cerana japonica*

workers. Apidologie, 20: 149-155.

Verma, L.R. 1970. A comparative study of temperature regulation in *Apis mellifera* L. and *Apis indica* F. American Bee Journal, 110(10): 390-391.

CHAPTER 6

SOME BIOLOGICAL ASPECTS OF THE NORTH-ADAPTED EASTERN HONEYBEE, *APIS CERANA JAPONICA*

M. SASAKI, M. ONO and T. YOSHIDA

INTRODUCTION

The Eastern honeybee, *Apis cerana*, is a polytypic species which is distributed from tropical to northern temperate Asian areas. There are a vast variety of biotypes and a high plasticity of adaptation that is comparable with the Western honeybee, *Apis mellifera*, distribution from tropical Africa to northern Europe. The origin, route, and time of advance of the Eastern honeybee into Japan is not clear but morphometric and statistical data enabled Ruttner (1988) to classify Japanese *A. cerana* (Fig. 1) as an independent subspecies, *A. cerana japonica* (abbreviated ACJ).

Probably, the spread of ACJ into the Japanese northern climate is related to the large body size, which is similar to the West-Himalayan biotype. In addition to retaining characteristics of their ancestral biotype, Japanese *A. cerana* may have evolved some new survival tactics that adapt it to the northern climate. The biology of ACJ has already been outlined by Tokuda (1924), Sakagami (1960), and Okada (1985). This article reviews our recent studies of north-adapted Japanese *A. cerana*.

REARING METHODS

Keeping in modified Langstroth hives

ACJ is usually kept in various types of traditional hives (Fig. 2). It also inhabits natural nests (Fig. 3) such as dark, confined spaces in hollow trees or under graves throughout Japan except Hokkaido island. Although rearing ACJ in movable frame hives has been very limited, Okada (1985) succeeded in raising several successive generations at Tokyo in a standard Langstroth hive with two important modifications: (1) comb foundation of smaller cell size (576.5 cells/100 cm^2), and (2) two-story hive with empty bottom box. Recently, further modifications have been made to the thickness of the frame resulting in a shallower cell depth, to the width of the spacers resulting in a narrower bee space, and to the shape of the bottom corner of the foundation (Yoshida *et al.* 1990). Queen rearing with plastic queen cell cups has become possible as a result of a systematic survey of the most acceptable cup size and colony

conditions (Fig. 4). Usage of mating nuclei and artificial swarming techniques have also been established. Only one absconding was recorded in 1987 for our ten 4- to 8-frame Langstroth hives and several nuclei or observation hives.

Rearing in glass observation hives

There is no problem in raising small or middle-sized colonies consisting of 2,000 to 12,000 bees in glass observation hives throughout the year (Fig. 5). Modified UC Davis-type observation hives (Gary 1976) were placed in rooms at 24° to 28°C with an 8 to 16-hour photoperiod and bees were allowed to forage through the transparent pathway to the outside. No special care was needed except for occasional removal of comb debris and occasional supply of honey and pollen substitutes. A shortage of stored honey and/or bee-bread might cause absconding or associated cannibalism of brood. A varied behavioural repertoire was observed including: oviposition by either queen or laying workers, retinue behaviour, trophallaxis, various types of dancing, shimmering, fanning, grooming for *Varroa* mite, feeding and hoarding, and seasonal construction of queen and drone cells (Fig. 6).

REPRODUCTIVE BIOLOGY

Reproductive capacity of queen

The number of ovarioles in the ACJ queen is only half (134.6±36.5, n=5) that of *A. mellifera* (276.6±22.5, n=5) (Fig. 7). This is the reason for the lower egg productivity and consequently seems to be reflected in the smaller colony size. However, the number of ovarioles in ACJ workers is greater (11.9±3.7, n=150) than in *A. mellifera* (7.8±2.5, n=150). This suggests that caste differentiation in ACJ is less developed than in *A. mellifera*. The ability of the laying ACJ queen to take flight, however, might be a secondary adaptation to enable easy absconding in response to attack by enemies or to environmental change in the ancestral subtropical forest habitat. It should also be pointed out that ACJ has a great potential egg production by queens and in beeswax secretion by workers. They may exceed *A. mellifera* on a single ovariole and single bee basis.

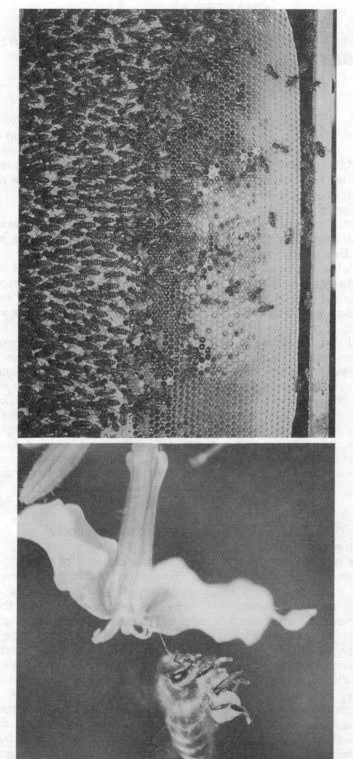

FIGURE 1. Japanese honeybee, *Apis cerana japonica*, foraging for pollen and nectar (left). A typical arrangement of stored honey, bee bread and brood areas of *Apis cerana japonica* (right). Note the orientation of workers in negative geotactic manner.

FIGURE 2. Two types of traditional hives for *Apis cerana japonica*. A. Log hive. B. Wooden box covered with straw.

This is clearly observed when new comb foundation is introduced under favourable conditions; more than 2,000 eggs are found in completed comb after three days.

Queen behaviour in hive

The behaviour of a mated ACJ queen was monitored for 24 hours on 18 October 1983. The queen's behaviour was composed of two sequential phases: (1) translocation with oviposition, and (2) resting with trophallaxis from workers. This behaviour was repeated throughout the day under a 12-hour photoperiod and no daily rhythm was detected. Time spent in translocation was 59% of the total and the average number of ovipositions was 33/hour. The queen received milk from an average of 4.1 workers/resting phase and the duration of trophallaxis/worker was about 1 minute. There was no correlation between the number of ovipositions/

translocation phase and the duration of the preceding or following resting phase.

Mating flight and its artificial photoperiodic control

In Tokyo, the ACJ breeding season ranges from mid-April to mid-June. During the season, drones take flight from 13:00 to 16:30 with the peak from 14:30 to 15:30. This is about 1 to 1.5 hours later than that of sympatric *A. mellifera*. The number of flights/drone/day was 1.73 ± 0.23 (52 marked drones of 8-9 days old). Flight and interflight time varied with individuals and weather conditions. The flight time of drones and new queens is determined by both their own circadian clocks, which are entrained by environmental photoperiod, and cues from other colony members. It is interesting that the mating flight time can be artificially shifted by giving an appropriate photoperiod regime inside the hive (Yoshida and Sa-

FIGURE 3. Feral colonies of *Apis cerana japonica*. A. Nest constructed under house floor. B. An "open air nest" constructed under tree branch.

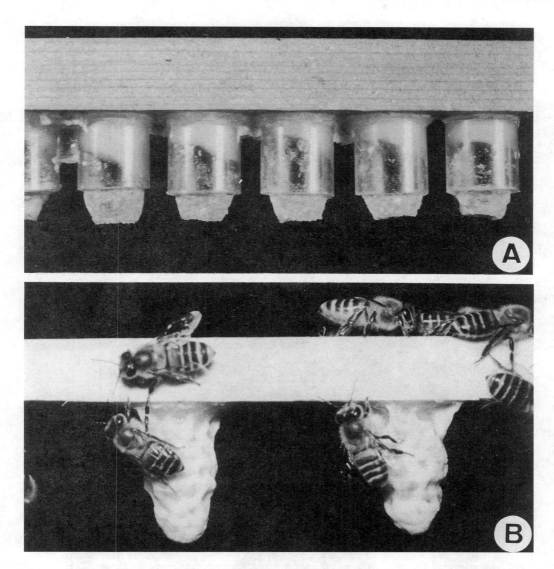

FIGURE 4. Queen rearing of *Apis cerana japonica* with plastic queen cell cups. A. Accepted artificial queen cell cups with royal jelly. B. Sealed artificial queen cell.

saki 1987; Sasaki 1990). For example, drones or virgin queens flew at around 10:00 (when they never fly normally) after exposure to artificial illumination from 01:00 to 13:00 (Fig. 8). In this case, the photoperiod within the hive should be well protected from that outside.

This technology may be applicable to (1) keep pure line in co-existence with other strains of bees in the same apiary, and (2) make planned crossings without artificial insemination.

In our experiments, despite the inhibition of foraging after "lights-out" in the hive, no notable adverse effect was seen on colony activities, such as in the amount of stored honey or brood production, for more than 6 months of treatment. Ultraviolet light is essential for effective entrainment of the biological clocks of all three castes, so that glass rather than acryl should be used when mating nuclei and drone-source hives are constructed.

Drone mandibular gland pheromone

The mandibular gland (MdGld) of ACJ drones is very small and difficult to see even under a microscope but it secretes a substance(s) which may attract other drones and/or virgin queens. The attractivity of drone MdGld secretion to other drones was first pointed out by Gerig (1971, 1972) and was further studied by Lensky *et al.* (1985). To check Lensky's behavioural observation and test the possible responsiveness of queens to the MdGld secre-

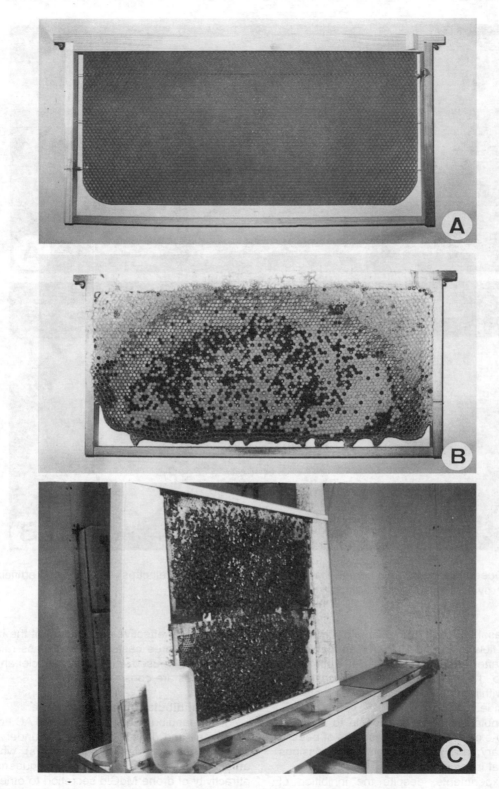

FIGURE 5. Rearing *Apis cerana japonica* in glass observation hive with movable frames. A. Comb foundation for *Apis cerana japonica*. B. Completed comb with honey, pollen and brood. C. Glass observation hive for research.

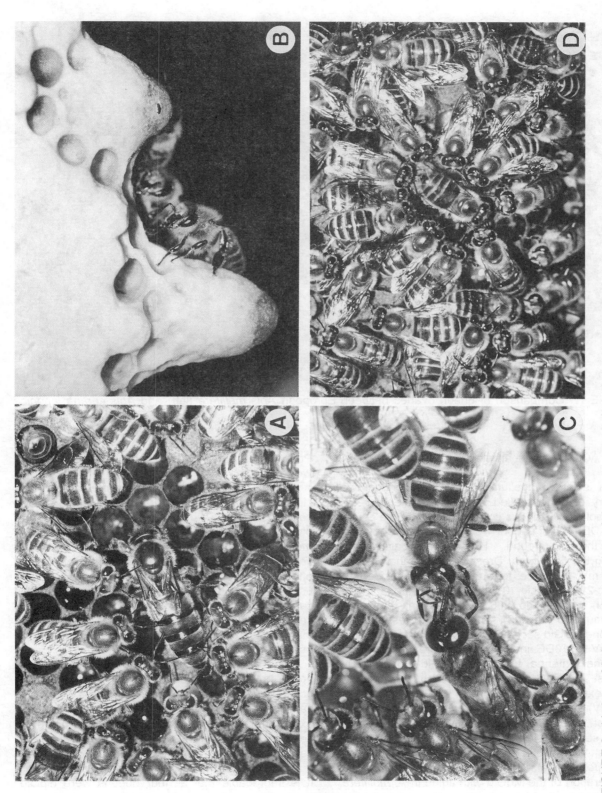

FIGURE 6. Variety of behavioural repertoires of *Apis cerana japonica*. A. Laying queen and her attendants. B. Two queen cells (note that the wax layer at the top of the cells is removed). C. Drone receiving food from a worker. D. Foraging dance.

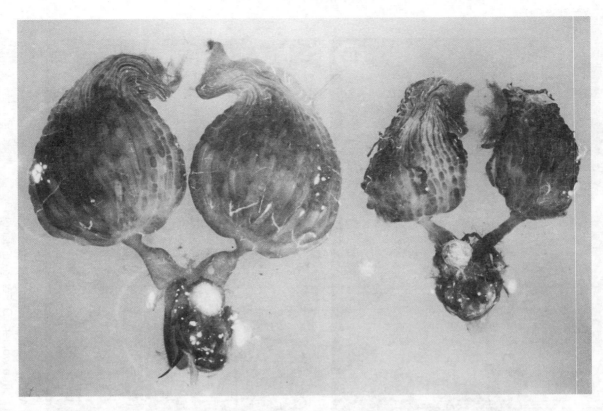

FIGURE 7. Comparison of queen ovaries between European *Apis mellifera* (left) and *Apis cerana japonica* (right).

tion in ACJ, we made an electroantennogram (EAG) study.

An isolated flagellum was used to bridge two capillary electrodes filled with *Apis* saline and Ag-AgCl$_2$-solution. Various concentrations (drone equivalent: DE) of test vapour were injected for about 0.1 s into the background. H$_2$O-saturated air stream flushing the flagellum. Drone ACJ antenna showed a 1.3 mV response for 10 μg of synthesized 9-oxodec-2-enoic acid, 0.3 mV for 100 μg of nerol (control), and 0.03 to 0.06 mV for a blank (mechanical stimulus of air puff). The average response to the drone MdGld secretion was 0.09 mV for 1DE and 0.37 mV for 10DE, indicating a clear responsiveness of drone antenna to drone MdGld odour. By contrast, the EAG amplitude of ACJ queen antenna to the extract was much smaller: 0.23 mV (blank = 0.11 mV) even for 10DE. This evidence of a positive receptor level response suggests that the drone MdGld secretion attracts both other drones and virgin queens. Interspecific cross-activity between ACJ and *A. mellifera* has also been found (unpublished). The degeneration of the MdGld with aging in *A. mellifera* (Lensky *et al.* 1985) might indicate that the secretion is involved in chemical communication in the hive.

Possible multiple control of drone production by workers

Differentiation of drone and worker cells is less clear in ACJ than *A. mellifera*. A typical ACJ drone cell is 15% to 16% larger than a worker cell in diameter and the figures are 22% smaller than for *A. mellifera* (Okada and Sakai 1960) and 62% for *A. florea*. The cell size is sometimes continuous and is often hard to classify. Drone cells are constructed usually in April at the bottom of combs or in spaces caused by heavy gnawing of combs. The queen seems to lay unfertilized eggs in these cells. This is the first control of drone production and is the same as that used by *A. mellifera*.

The second possible control is elimination of drone brood from "worker cells". This seems to occur out of the reproductive season. When we sampled young larvae from worker cells of four experimental colonies in autumn and determined the sex after rearing on modified *A. mellifera* royal jelly, several males were obtained from these colonies. At that time, no adult drone was allowed in the colonies. It is improbable that all four queens were diploid-drone layers because there had been 10 healthy colonies from three different localities in the apiary.

It seems well known that the first instar larvae of diploid drones are removed by *A. mellifera* (Woyke 1963), but the elimination of the drone larvae by ACJ occurred at later stages even after the cells were sealed. If the laying of normal haploid eggs and the following elimination of such drones is true, it might be attributed to a residual behaviour of year-round drone production in ancestral southern *A. cerana*.

A third possibility, direct drone production by workers in normal queen-right colonies, should also be mentioned. Laying workers in queen-right colonies have been reported by Sakagami (1960) and the behaviour seems to be related to the above-mentioned incomplete caste differentiation of ACJ. Our impression, however, is that this behaviour is not common and may be restricted to the reproductive season when inhibition of worker ovary development by the queen appears to weaken.

Emergency queen cells

Emergency queen cells (Fig. 9) are rarely seen in ACJ (Tokuda 1924; Sakagami 1960). But we have observed several colonies were continued by the queens emerged from emergency queen cells. This can be used as a rescue technique as in *A. mellifera* beekeeping.

The reason why emergency queen cells are rarely seen may be related to the evidence that the emergency queen cells are often destroyed and cleaned off in a short while. In warm areas allowed year-round reproduction, the abrupt colony mode change to drone production, by which workers may be able to inherit their genes directly, may have an adaptive value. Indeed, the onset of worker laying in ACJ is very quick and there seems to be no latent time for the possible rescue mechanism (Sakagami and Akahira 1958). This might also be an effective strategy in applying the stored resources of the colony to full production of drones. Has this nature been inherited without modification even in the northern-distributed ACJ? By contrast, *A. cerana* in Pakistan has a good plasticity in using the emergency-cell rescue system in response to climatic (may be fixed in populations of different altitudes) and environmental conditions (Ahmad, personal communication).

Pore in drone cell cap

A feature peculiar to ACJ is the removal of the wax seal from both queen and drone cells usually within a few days after pupation (Fig. 10). In drone cells, a tiny pore appears at the centre of the cocoon after the wax seal removal. From evidence that the silk is molten at the wall of the pore and inner central portion of the cocoon, cocoonase activity from spinning drone larva seems likely (Hänel and Ruttner 1985). However, it should be noted that the pore is made before impregnation and melting of the silk. Spinning behaviour without production of silk at the central portion, which becomes the pore, has been observed. Also, serial sampling during the later stages of cocoon formation yields a pale-yellow cocoon with pore but no trace of silk melting.

Although a promeric pore function was assumed by Tokuda (1924), its real biological significance has not been specified. However, behavioural evidence indicates that the pore is used for recognition or communication by workers because insertion of worker antenna through the pore has often been observed.

Seasonal colour change

The body colour of ACJ workers changes with the season in addition to the strain-specific local colour variation. A yellowish type appears from July to October and a black type emerges from October to the following May (Fig. 11). In the past, the three colour morphs were classified as three different subspecies: *Apis indica japonica*, *A. i. nigrocincta*, and *A. i. pernoi* (Yano 1950; Shiraki 1973).

Matsuka *et al.* (1989) demonstrated that body colours of various grades can be induced in an incubator by subjecting the pupae to constant temperatures between 25° to 38°C. The lower the temperature, the more dark-coloured bees emerged. For example, the abdominal sternites had no dark spot at 38°C, but were black in 6.7% of bees at 34°C, and all black at 30°C or lower (see Chapter 5).

Swarming on orchid flowers

Reproductive swarms and all castes of individual bees of ACJ are strongly attracted to the flowers of a particular oriental orchid (*Cymbidium pumilum*). The evidence of drone attraction is of particular interest because they are known to never work nor visit flowers (Sasaki *et al.* 1991). Both workers and drones visit orchid flowers individually and insert their head and thorax deep into flowers between the column and lip. During the effort to escape from the flower, pollinia stick to the bee's scutellum. When they visit the next flower, the pollinia are trapped into a hole of stigma and pollination takes place. In the case of swarm attraction, on the other hand, a few workers first visit the flowers and gnaw the petals without any visible excitement. Then the bee swarm clusters onto the flowers (Fig. 12). The active principle(s) that is attractive to ACJ has not been isolated and no such response is seen in *A. mellifera*. The attractant might be used as an effective lure for trapping swarms of ACJ and other subspecies of *A. cerana*.

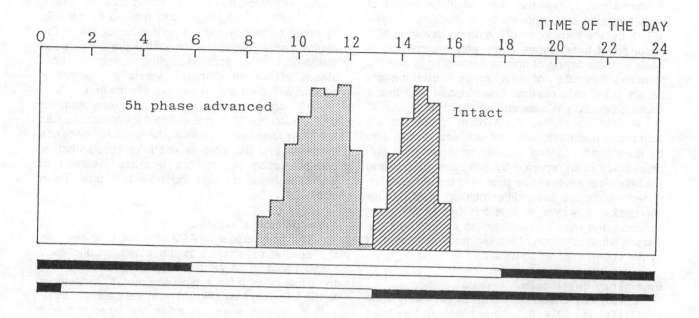

FIGURE 8. Photoperiodically controlled mating flight time (there is no overlap of the two activity peaks).

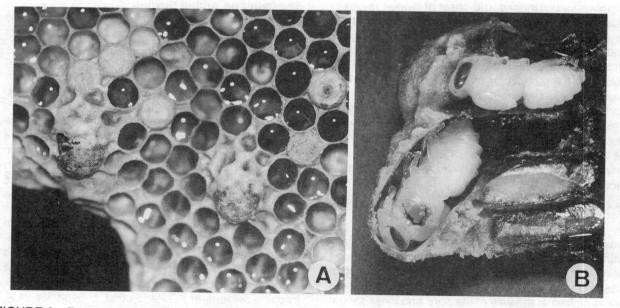

FIGURE 9. Emergency queen cells of *Apis cerana japonica*. A. Two emergency queen cells constructed on comb. B. Cutaway view of emergency queen cell (note the wound on the thorax made by the queen mandible).

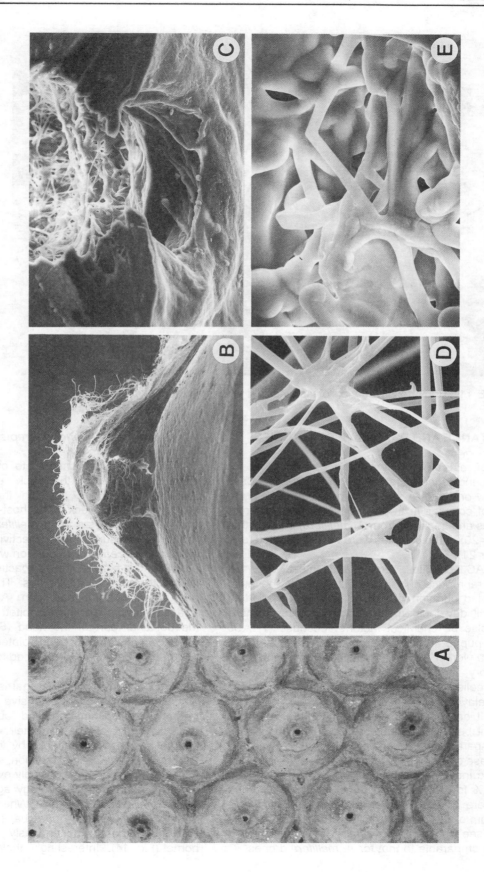

FIGURE 10. Pore in drone cell cap. A. Tiny pore at the center of each drone cell cap. B. Cutaway view of drone cell cap. C. Close-up of inner surface of the pore. D. Layer of silk fibers spun in earlier phase of seal formation. E. Molten silk inside pore.

FIGURE 11. Body color variation of *Apis cerana japonica* workers.

RESISTANCE AND DEFENSIVE STRATEGIES

Mode of resistance to *Varroa jacobsoni*

The incidence of parasitic *Varroa* mite on ACJ is very low or zero. A survey of nest debris from the floors of colonies in traditional hives (from different localities and separate from *A. mellifera*) showed that 50% (n=20) of the colonies were weakly infested (see Chapter 21).

In ACJ colonies, female adult mites (Fig. 13) usually reproduce only in drone cells mainly because the sealed duration of worker cells is too short to allow full development of *Varroa* offspring. There might also be chemical factor(s) because (1) ACJ worker pupae attracted less mites than males or *A. mellifera* worker pupae in a choice-experiment in the laboratory, and (2) 37% of *Varroa* that invaded worker cells could not lay eggs, or oviposition tended to be delayed if any occurred.

ACJ drone pupae seem not to be chemically resistant because we have observed an abnormally heavily-parasitized queenless colony which was in a late phase of drone production by worker laying. The parasitic incidence for adults was 5.3% for workers and 10% for drones while 38.4% of the 700 drone cells were invaded by *Varroa*. It was likely that a maximum of 5 to 7 female mites/drone could be produced (see Chapter 21 for details). This reproduction rate is comparable to that for *A. mellifera* drones.

Infestation by *Pseudoacarapis indoapis* and *Acarapis externus*

Two species of small mite other than *Varroa* were detected from the neck region. *Acarapis externus* was found only on the intersegmental membrane of the neck. The host-parasite relationship seems to be as in *A. mellifera* (Eckert 1961). When we measured the radioactivity of the blood of mites parasitized for 24 hours on worker bees injected with ^{14}C-dextrane, the radioactivity was detected from both larval and adult mites. Thus, the mite must be a potent vector of pathogen. Another species of *Pseudoacarapis indoapis* inhabited the tentorial pit of the posterior part of the head (Sakai and Sasaki 1989). As has already been pointed out by Lindquist 1968), they seem not to be blood feeders.

Balling defensive strategy against hornets

ACJ has a variety of defensive measures. Some of them, like "shimmering" and "abdomen shaking", seem to be retained from their ancestral biotype adaptations to heavy attacks by various predators. Others, like the balling reaction, described below, might be new, and have possibly evolved as a specific group-counterattack strategy against the hornet, *Vespa simillima xanthoptera*. When a hornet attacks an ACJ colony, many guard bees (*ca* 180 to 300) rush out almost simultaneously and engulf the hornet (Fig. 14). Interestingly, they produce heat for

FIGURE 12. Reproductive swarm of *Apis cerana japonica* clustered on oriental orchid flowers (*Cymbidium pumilum*). A. Swarming colony on oriental orchid. B. Attracted workers (before formation of the swarm, many workers are attracted to the flowers). C. Worker gnawing flower tip. D. Orchid set in front of an empty hive (this method is used to trap feral swarming colonies by some local beekeepers).

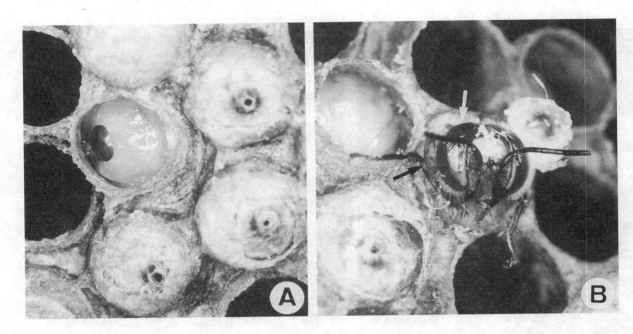

FIGURE 13. Female *Varroa* mite parasitizing drone. A. Gravid female entering drone cell just before sealing. B. Mother mite (white arrow) and offspring female adult (black arrow) parasitizing emerging drone.

as long as 20 minutes, causing the temperature inside the ball to rise to more than 46°C (Fig. 15). This high temperature is lethal to the hornet but not to the bees; the upper lethal temperature for ACJ is 48° to 50°C. We observed 36 ballings and all the victim hornets were killed. The balling bees were passive and no sting was found in the hornet corpses. Evidence of defense by heat production in poikilothermic animals has not been found previously. Although a similar balling reaction has also been observed in *A. mellifera*, the workers readily use their stings during balling. As a result of the *A. mellifera* sting anatomy two or three stings usually remain in the intersegmental membrane of the dead hornet. The average maximum temperature inside the *A. mellifera* ball is 42.8°C, which is significantly lower than inside the ACJ ball (Ono *et al.* 1987).

COLD HARDINESS

Colony size and nesting site

We have no statistical records of ACJ colony sizes but the number of workers ranges from several thousand to twenty-five thousand. The larger number is estimated from evidence that standard Langstroth frame (21x42 cm) colonies can be kept without any problem. Usually, our colonies contained 4 to 8 frames with about 3,000 bees per frame.

As already pointed out by Seeley (1985) for the

European (versus African) honeybee, the *A. mellifera* large colony size and large amount of stored honey must be a prerequisite for long winters. Essentially, in Tokyo, there is no nectar flow from November until mid-March. Colony reproduction is restricted to the period from April to the beginning of June and production of reproductive castes begins in March in strong colonies. Thus, there is about five months for a swarmed colony to expand and store honey before overwintering.

Feral nests of ACJ in bright, open locations are rare. This is in contrast to *A. mellifera* which sometimes make feral nests in open spaces under branches of trees, etc. (Sasaki and Okada 1988; Sasaki *et al.* 1990).

In tropical and subtropical areas where the three Asian honeybee species originated, three different strategies seem to have evolved against heavy predation. *A. florea*'s choice of nesting site is not specific and it has a strong nest-relocating tendency. *A. dorsata* is aggressive and strongly nest protective. It nests under branches of tall trees or under overhanging rocks and tends to aggregate, probably to increase the nest guarding efficiency. *A. cerana* chooses dark confined spaces. Confined spaces like hollow trees should be advantageous for insulation and protection. However, they restrict abundance. Bees can concentrate their guarding attention at the nest entrance. This habit might explain the northward distribution of ACJ. Although ACJ chooses dark

FIGURE 14. Behavioural sequence of defensive balling in *Apis cerana japonica*. A. Hornet hunting in front of hive entrance. B. Ball of approximately 250 worker honeybees with ball internal temperature monitored by micro-thermistor (copyright Birkhäuser Verlag). C. Hornet dead 30 minutes later. D. Ball on palm of hand; no stinging (copyright Birkhäuser Verlag).

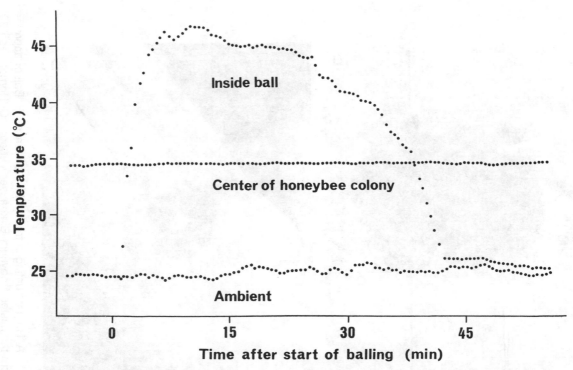

FIGURE 15. Typical record of temperature change monitored inside ball of *Apis cerana japonica* (copyright Birkhäuser Verlag).

FIGURE 16. Wall-like rampart structure of comb frequently seen in nests built in wide spaces.

places, it does not seem to mind bright illumination in observation hives. Darkness may just be merckmal coincidental with the requirements for confined, protected nest sites.

Winter clustering

ACJ over-winters by forming winter clusters just like north-adapted *A. mellifera*. We do not know if tropical or subtropical *A. cerana* responds in a similar manner to low ambient temperatures. There has been no analytical study on the dynamics of the ACJ cluster. Sakagami and Kouta (1958) mentioned that ACJ tends to cluster in the space made by comb gnawing to conserve heat. As far as we can see, however, the winter cluster is composed of bees distributed in several inter-comb bee spaces, and distinct comb gnawing begins after clustering.

Nest architecture and perennial use of same nesting site

The parallel comb architecture and its usage by ACJ is essentially the same as that of *A. mellifera* except for the smaller cell size and narrower bee space. An interesting feature is the occasional use of a trans-comb rampart in feral nests in wide spaces (Fig. 16). It apparently functions as a windbreak and insulation structure and often has shallow cells that are not used for storing food or rearing brood. Usually the structure is built *ad libitum* after the nest has been expanded to full size and partially joins the basal (upper) parts. It is not built in autumn in response to falling temperatures.

The original purpose of this rampart might be to increase nest strength. Often in ACJ nests, part of a comb or a few whole combs fall down. This may be related to the low plasticity of ACJ beeswax (Takamatsu unpublished) or to the lack of propolis usage. It may also be partially due to comb weakness resulting from the tendency of small amounts of silk linings due to lack of repetitive brood rearing. ACJ does not like old comb and tends to tear it down and build new comb. Local beekeepers report that feral ACJ colonies inhabit the same nest site for several years. Distinct comb gnawing and comb rebuilding may have evolved to maximize use of the limited nesting space.

Heavy gnawing begins from the end of February or beginning of March in Tokyo and appears to be related to early drone-comb production. This is good timing because it is followed by a big nectar flow.

DIFFICULTY OF CO-EXISTENCE BETWEEN *APIS CERANA* AND *APIS MELLIFERA*

We saw several cases where both ACJ and *A.*

mellifera colonies were placed side by side for more than three years (Sakai and Ono 1990). But it is difficult to keep ACJ colonies with *A. mellifera* colonies in an apiary. Sometimes severe group robbing by *A. mellifera* occurs in the summer when nectar is scarce. ACJ shows almost no defensive response to the robbers presumably because group robbing has only occurred since *A. mellifera* was introduced to Japan about 100 years ago. ACJ allow *A. mellifera* into the hive or nest and trophallaxis or parental care is seen between the two species. Conversely, group robbing by ACJ from *A. mellifera* is not common. Individual bees sometimes steal honey but a long stay in an *A. mellifera* colony by ACJ or the occupation of the colony is seldom observed.

Estimating from our preliminary dialect curve according to training up to 1.3 km and distance indications of dances for natural resources, the usual foraging range of ACJ covers 1.5 to 2.5 km from their hives. This figure is far beyond that reported for tropical *A. cerana* in Sri Lanka (Punchihewa *et al.* 1985), although it is still narrower than that of temperate *A. mellifera* (Visscher and Seeley 1982; our unpublished data). The tendency to utilize selected batches (species) of nectar or pollen resources investigated as a diversity index of pollen spectra of pollen loads (unpublished data) was just comparable to that of *A. mellifera* in the same biotope. Considering these two criteria and others, the two species have very similar ecological niches, meaning that ACJ must come in conflict with introduced *A. mellifera*.

There is no visible conflict between foragers of the two species. However, according to experimental observation by Sakagami (1959) and our unpublished data, if two sugar dishes, to which foragers of each species have been trained to visit, are brought close together, both dishes are always occupied by *A. mellifera*. This suggests a long-lasting dominance of *A. mellifera* over ACJ in natural conditions.

Another important factor is susceptibility to damage caused by the greater wax moth, *Galleria mellonella*, which usually inhabits *A. mellifera* colonies and readily moves into ACJ colonies. The smaller wax moth, *Achroia innotata*, which is widely distributed in Asian countries and is distinguished from *A. grisella* (Inoue 1988), has been found inhabiting feral ACJ colonies. However, *A. innotata* is less vigorous in fecundity than *A. grisella* and lives mainly in comb debris so it is not so harmful. Rather, it appears to be symbiotic with ACJ (Okada 1988), and also its population is held under natural control by *Apanteles galleriae* (Shimamori 1987; Watanabe 1987) (Fig. 17).

Removal of old, remnant combs by ACJ might have adaptive significance to protect the comb body

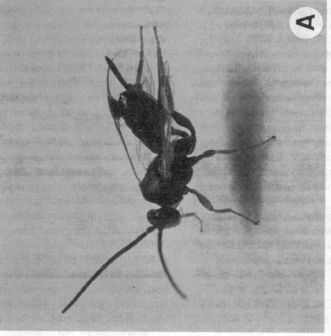

FIGURE 17. *Apanteles galleriae*, parasitic wasp of *Achroia innotata*. A. Adult female. B. Cocoon of the parasite (left) and host remnant (right).

from intrusion by the wax moth larvae. However, *G. mellonella* larvae do intrude deep into comb under use and often many ACJ pupae are killed. Queenless colonies are especially susceptible although it is not known why.

CONCLUDING REMARKS

Although we are far from fully understanding the whole biology of ACJ, the fragmental evidence shows ACJ to be an interesting species with some primitive features but also with a highly sophisticated and flexible mode of life. North-adapted ACJ has increased in colony size but has retained the survival skills of small colonies. We have even observed a colony consisting of only a few hundred workers with a normal queen, eggs, sealed brood and stored beebread and honey.

A. mellifera colonies rapidly increase their population in favorable conditions but they are also readily weakened in hot summers when the resources are limited and in overwintering, while ACJ tends to keep colony strength more or less constant in such a summer dearth period and in winter.

The queen has a great potential egg production but sometimes stops laying eggs for up to one month even in warm months. She can fly while able to lay. ACJ sometimes absconds, leaving behind much invested wax, stored food and even brood. Instead, workers show a high wax secretion rate and it is said the rate exceeds that of *A. mellifera*. ACJ can both produce drones without building specific drone cells and can control drone production by eliminating the developing larvae or pupae. Sometimes, larvae are translocated from one cell to another. Cannibalism often occurs when protein resources are short.

Little is known about the biology of ACJ outside, i.e. foraging range, nectar and pollen plant spectra, DCA and mating behaviour, conflict with *A. mellifera*, swarming distance, fate of absconding colonies. Further extensive studies are needed for both scientific and applied purposes.

ACKNOWLEDGEMENTS

We are most grateful to Profs. I. Okada and T. Sakai for their encouragement and helpful discussions throughout the study. We are indebted to T. Kurihara, H. Toshikiyo, T. Ochiai, S. Yamazaki, M. Hamano, T. Tsuruta, and M. Funatsu for their share in the study. Thanks are due to T. Ochi, M. Fukuda, and S. Fujiwara for their kind supply of material colonies and cooperation. Special thanks are also due to Dr. Robert Hancock for reviewing this manuscript.

REFERENCES

Eckert, J.E. 1961. Acarapis mites of the honeybee, *Apis mellifera* Linnaeus. Journal of Insect Pathology, 3: 409-425.

Gary, N.E. 1976. How to construct and maintain an observation bee hive. Division of Agricultural Science, University of California, Leaflet 2853.

Gerig, L. 1971. Wie Drohnen auf Königinnentrappen reagiren. Schweiz Bienenztg, 12: 3-7.

Hänel, H. and F. Ruttner. 1985. The origin of the pore in the drone cell capping of *Apis cerana* Fabr. Apidologie, 16: 157-164.

Inoue, H. 1988. On two species of *Achroia* Hübner (Pyralidae, Galleriinae) from Japan. Jaan Heterocerists' Journal, 149: 377-378.

Lensky, Y., P. Cassier, M. Notkin, C. Delorme-Joulie and M. Levinsohn. 1985. Pheromonal activity and fine structure of the mandibular glands of honeybee drones (*Apis mellifera* L.) (Insecta, Hymenoptera, Apidae). Journal of Insect Physiology, 31: 265-76.

Lindquist, E.E. 1968. An unusual new species of *Tarsonemus* (Acarina: Tarsonemidae) associated with the Indian honey bee. Canadian Entomologist, 100: 1002-1006.

Matsuka, M., T. Tsuruta and M. Sasaki. 1989. Temperature as a causative factor of the seasonal colour dimorphism of *Apis cerana japonica*. Apidologie, 20: 149-155.

Okada, I. 1985. The Japanese honeybee in nature. The Heredity, 39: 58-68.

Okada, I. 1988. Three species of wax moths in Japan. Honeybee Science, 9: 145-149. [In Japanese, with English summary]

Okada, I. and T. Sakai. 1960. A comparative study on natural comb of the Japanese and European honeybee, with special deference to cell number. Bull. Fac. Agr., Tamagawa University, 1: 1-11.

Ono, M., I. Okada and M. Sasaki. 1987. Heat production by balling in the Japanese honeybee, *Apis cerana japonica* as a defensive behaviour against the hornet, *Vespa simillima xanthoptera* (Hymenoptera: Vespidae). Experientia, 43: 1031-1032.

Punchihewa, R.W.K., N. Koeniger, P.G. Kevan and R.M. Gadawski. 1985. Observation on the dance communication and natural foraging ranges of *Apis cerana*, *Apis dorsata* and *Apis florea* in Sri Lanka. Journal of Apicultural Research, 24: 168-175.

Ruttner, F. 1988. Biogeography and Taxonomy of Honeybees. Springer-Verlag, Berlin Heidelberg. pp. 284.

Sakagami, S.F. 1959. Some interspecific relations between Japanese and European honeybees.

Journal of Animal Ecology, 28: 51-58.

Sakagami, S.F. 1960. Preliminary report on the specific difference of behaviour and other ecological characters between European and Japanese honeybees. Acta Hymenopterologica, 1: 171-198.

Sakagami, S.F. and Y. Akahira. 1958. Comparison of ovarian size and number of ovarioles between the workers of Japanese and European honeybees. Kontyu, 28: 103-109.

Sakagami, S.F. and S. Kouta. 1958. An attempt to rear the Japanese bee in a framed hive. Journal of the Faculty of Science, Hokkaido Univ. VI, Zool., 14: 1-8.

Sakai, T. and M. Ono. 1990. Comparative studies on the bionomics of *Apis mellifera* L. and *A. cerana japonica* Radoszkowski. I. Differences in the seasonal foraging activity. Bull. Fac. Agr., Tamagawa Univ., 30: 73-86.

Sakai, T. and M. Sasaki. 1989. *Tarsonemus indoapis* (Acarina: Tarsonemidae) from Japanese honeybee, *Apis cerana japonica*. Honeybee Science, 10: 37-38. [In Japanese, with English summary]

Sasaki, M. 1990. Photoperiodic regulation of honeybee mating-flight time: Exploitation of innately phase-fixed circadian oscillation. Advances in Invertebrate Reproduction, 5: 503-508.

Sasaki, M. and I. Okada. 1988. Feral nest of *Apis cerana japonica* constructed in an open space. Honeybee Science, 9: 77-78. [In Japanese, with English summary]

Sasaki, M., J. Nakamura, M. Tani and T. Sakai. 1990. Nest temperature and winter survival of a feral colony of the honeybee, *Apis mellifera* L., nesting in an exposed site in Japan. Bull. Fac. Agr., Tamagawa Univ., 30: 9-19.

Sasaki, M., M. Ono, S. Asada and T. Yoshida. 1991. Oriental orchid (*Cymbidium pumilum*) attracts drones of the Japanese honeybee (*Apis cerana japonica*) as pollinators. Experientia, 47: 1229-1231.

Seeley, T.D. 1985. Honeybee Ecology. A study of adaptation in social life. Princeton University Press, New Jersey. pp. 201.

Shimamori, K. 1987. On the biology of *Apanteles galleriae*, a parasite of the two species of wax moths. Honeybee Science, 8: 107-112.

Shiraki, T. 1973. Classification of insects. Hokuryukan, Tokyo, Japan. p. 625.

Tokuda, Y. 1924. Studies on the honey bee, with special reference to the Japanese honey bee. Trans. of Sapporo Natural History Society, 9: 1-27.

Visscher, P.K. and T.D. Seeley. 1982. Foraging strategy of honeybee colonies in a temperate deciduous forest. Ecology, 63: 1790-1801.

Watanabe, C. 1987. Occurrence of *Apanteles galleriae* (Hymenoptera, Baraconidae), parasite of wax moth, in Japan. Kontyu, 55: 165.

Woyke, J. 1963. What happens to diploid drone larvae in a honeybee colony. Journal of Apicultural Research, 2: 73-75.

Yano, M. 1950. Iconographia insectorum japonicorum (eds. T. Ishi *et al.*) Hokuryukan, Tokyo, Japan. p. 1494.

Yoshida, T., M. Ono and I. Okada. 1989. Keeping of the Japanese honeybee, *Apis cerana japonica* Radoszkowski using a modified Langstroth style movable-frame hive. Bull. Fac. Agr., Tamagawa Univ., 29: 41-55. [In Japanese, with English summary]

SECTION III: GENETICS, BREEDING AND MATING

CHAPTER 7

HONEYBEE GENETICS

THOMAS E. RINDERER

INTRODUCTION

Honeybee genetics is in its youth. The generation of honeybee geneticists that began their careers about 40 years ago is the first group of scientists to devote themselves exclusively to this field of study. The inspiration to study honeybees most probably came 40 years ago, as it often does today, because of the rich natural history of honeybees, and because of the excitement caused by the announcement that techniques had been developed to instrumentally inseminate queen honeybees (Watson 1927; Nolan 1929, 1932; Laidlaw 1944; Mackensen 1947; Mackensen and Roberts 1948).

Instrumental insemination provided the remarkable ability to control the male parentage of a bee colony. It was the perfect complement to the long-standing methods of Doolittle (1889) which permitted the control of the source of a colony's queen. In combination, these two techniques made the study of honeybee genetics possible. For the first time, the mating of honeybees could be absolutely controlled.

Other techniques previous to the development of instrumental insemination have also made the study of honeybee genetics easier. The discovery of bee space and the resulting development of the movable frame hive by Langstroth (1853) permitted the routine examination of colonies. The management of movable-frame hives for queen and drone production (reviewed by Harbo 1986) is a straightforward extension of Langstroth's contributions.

All this technology development had to occur prior to the genetical study of bees. Since the technology was developed using *Apis mellifera*, most of the genetical studies of honeybees have been done with this species (Rinderer 1986). Nonetheless, some work has been done with *Apis cerana*. A review of that work will provide a starting point for a discussion of some possible new directions for work on the genetics of *A. cerana*.

GENETICS OF *APIS CERANA*

Mating biology

A. cerana is closely related to *A. mellifera* and displays similar behaviour in many respects. Nest architecture, swarming biology, and other characteristics are all sufficiently similar that one might hope that at least infertile hybrids could be formed between the two species. Unfortunately, sufficient genetic differences exist between the species that adult hybrids cannot occur. Instrumental insemination procedures do function in crosses between the species. Spermatozoa migrate to the spermatheca, are stored there, and are used to fertilize eggs. Eggs are fertilized and, during the first 24 hours, undisturbed cleavage proceeds. However, at the blastoderm stage, embryological development stops and the zygote disintegrates (Ruttner and Maul 1983). Most likely, the successful early embryonic process is driven by enzymes contributed to the egg by the queen. As these enzymes or other factors are exhausted or as other metabolic products are required for further development, the embryonic sequence is arrested. The hybrid genome does not seem able to promote the successful metabolic operations of zygote development.

Drones of *A. mellifera* may interfere with the natural mating of queens of *A. cerana* in some cases. In Germany, imported queens of *A. cerana* could not successfully mate when drones of *A. mellifera* were abundant (Ruttner *et al.* 1972, 1973). However, numbers of colonies and their relative locations, as well as numbers of drones, probably influence such results. Currently, beekeeping with *A. mellifera* is thriving in several parts of Asia and with locally produced and mated queens. However, at least in Thailand, the initial importation was about 100 colonies of *A. mellifera* and now several thousand colonies are in the general area (Wongsiri, per. comm.). While potentially successful, the importation of *A. mellifera* has three clear dangers. First, the seriously negative experiences in South America with the Africanized *A. mellifera* from *A. m. scutellata* shows that not all stocks of *A. mellifera* are desirable for importation. Quite simply, many sources of germplasm are best left at home. Second, if breeding populations of *A. mellifera* become established and the mating of *A. cerana* is prevented because of competition by drones, or *A. cerana* is in some other way harmed, then potentially interesting and scientifically and economically useful variation in genomic material of *A. cerana* may be lost. Such loss is very serious and steps should be taken to prevent it. Third, the accidental introduction of pests and diseases is an ever present danger. Unnoticed or unimportant symbionts of the honeybees in one area may be devastating to the honeybees of another area.

Tools for genetical studies

The fundamentals for doing genetical studies with *A. cerana* are available. For example, instrumental insemination technology has been successfully employed with *A. cerana* to produce inbred lines of bees (Woyke 1973, 1975, 1979). However, there were some important adaptations that were required for successful inseminations. Only those queens inseminated with the semen of more than 15 drones laid normal numbers of fertilized eggs. In part, this requirement for more drones comes because drones of *A. cerana* only produce about 0.2 μl of semen, one-tenth of what is common for drones of *A. mellifera*. However, the efficiency of the movement of spermatozoa from the median oviduct to the spermatheca is greater for *A. cerana* than it is for *A. mellifera* (Woyke 1975). Also, the spermathecae of queens of *A. cerana* have far fewer spermatozoa after natural mating than do the spermathecae of queens of *A. mellifera* (Woyke 1975). Thus, although a greater number of drones is required for the successful instrumental insemination of queens of *A. cerana*, the number is less than might be predicted from some of the data.

After observing the process of instrumental insemination of queens of *A. cerana* in Thailand, I can offer several suggestions to those new to the techniques. If possible, the techniques should be first perfected with *A. mellifera*. Small queens of *A. mellifera* can prove difficult to inseminate. In the initial development of instrumental insemination, Watson discarded a stock of queens as unsuitable because of their small size (Rothenbuhler, per. comm.). The technique is best learned with larger queens. If queens of *A. mellifera* are not available, then at least larger *A. cerana* can be used. The entire process of insemination involves the collection of semen and then its insertion into the median oviduct of the queen. In order to facilitate learning, it is useful to learn each part of the process separately. Collecting semen is an art in itself and is best learned as a separate task. The successful insertion of semen into the median oviduct of a queen can also be learned separately. Cow's milk or similar material can be used instead of semen and insemination successes can be inferred if little or no fluid leaks from the queen as it is injected. A complete description of the insemination process is available in English along with excellent photographs and drawings (Harbo 1986).

The management techniques of queen rearing and drone production are apparently rather straightforward adaptations of these techniques as they are employed with *A. mellifera* (Wongsiri, per. comm.). Good descriptions of these management techniques have been provided by Harbo (1986). However, attention should be paid to specific requirements of bees in different climates and ecosystems.

Generally speaking, the use of instrumental insemination is best reserved for specific genetic studies. Its use in bee stock improvement programs has limited practical value. The costs of a breeding program based on instrumental insemination are usually prohibitive. Breeding programs are still able to have the use of reasonable control of mating. The use of island mating stations or the mainland use of drone flooding techniques combined with reductions in the populations of unmanaged drones in mating areas are often better alternatives for controlling mating in breeding programs.

Cytogenetics

The first important study of the genetics of *A. cerana* was the description of its karyotype (Deodikar *et al.* 1959). The chromosome number of N = 16 has since been confirmed by other investigators (Sharma *et al.* 1961; Hoshiba *et al.* 1981). The chromosome number of N = 16 is the same for all species of the genus (Fahrenhorst 1977). Also, one large metacentric chromosome is common to all species of the genus. These commonalities indicate that radiating evolution within the genus has been the result of events different from simple polyploid formation (Moritz 1986). Cytogenetic work with honeybees has proved difficult. In all cases, chromosomes are quite small and no tissues containing polytene chromosomes have been discovered. It may be that a search of various tissues will yield sources of polytene material as has occurred with several other nondipteran insects.

Sex determination

Sex determination in *A. cerana* was studied by Woyke (1973, 1975, 1979). He had substantial prior experience with studying the sex determination of *A. mellifera* (Woyke 1986) and consequently he tested the hypothesis that sex determination was genetically controlled in both species in similar ways. By producing inbred lines of bees, he created the possibility that the brood of the inbred queens would have a percentage of inviable eggs or larvae. This indeed was the case and he hypothesized that there are multiple alleles (X^a, X^b, X^c, etc.) at the sex locus (X). Males develop from unfertilized eggs (all of which are hemizygotes at the X locus) or from fertilized eggs which are homozygous at the X locus. For example, a queen inseminated by one drone (X^aX^b x X^c) produces haploid drones X^a and X^b from unfertilized eggs and diploid females X^aX^c from fertilized eggs. If one of these daughters (X^aX^c) is inseminated by her brother, X^a, then this daughter will produce two types of fertilized eggs: normal heterozygotes (X^aX^c) from which females will develop and homozygotes (X^aX^a) from which diploid males will develop. Similar progeny ratios were observed by Hoshiba et al. (1981) who confirmed the hypothesis of Woyke for sex determination of A. cerana.

The issue of diploid drones is an interesting one. In A. mellifera, these newly hatched larval drones are eaten by worker bees (Woyke 1963). It is thought that they may produce sufficient quantities of a substance called "cannibalism substance" which marks them and stimulates workers to eat them (Woyke 1967; Dietz 1975). With A. cerana, diploid drone larvae are not eaten by the workers just after hatching but are sometimes reared to the age of four days. Presumably, drones of A. cerana also produce cannibalism substance but the quantities or timing of production are different. Hopefully, further work will clarify these issues.

DNA studies

A few studies have examined DNA of A. cerana, the principal molecule of heredity. Jordan and Brosemer (1974) examined the DNA from three species of Apis (mellifera, cerana, and florea). First, the buoyant densities were determined for double stranded DNA in cesium chloride gradients. The DNA peak of A. florea was regular and narrow. However, the DNA peaks of A. mellifera and A. cerana were broad and rather asymmetrical. Both showed a low guanine-cytosine content but this was especially so for A. cerana. Generally, these results indicate that the Apis species have an unusually heterogeneous base pair composition compared to other animals.

Jordan and Brosemer (1974) also studied the reassociation kinetics of the DNA of A. mellifera and A. cerana. These experiments showed that these honeybees have very little repetitious DNA - only about 3-5% of the genome. An amazingly high 89% of these honeybee genomes is composed of unique DNA sequences. This result is especially curious when contrasted with the results of Sperlin et al. (1975). They found that only about 60% of the DNA of A. mellifera forms heterochromatin with DNA of A. cerana. This divergence is truly remarkable in a sister-species system where the two species are so similar and where so little of the DNA is repetitious. Further investigations in these areas are bound to reveal interesting facts.

Biogeography

The range of A. cerana is quite large with a distribution that is allopatric to that of A. mellifera. This range encompasses a broad diversity of ecological conditions. In some portions of this range, the biotype or subspecies variations of A. cerana has received scientific attention and has been described, especially for morphological characteristics (Ruttner 1987). However, there is clearly more to do to fully document the morphological variation of A. cerana throughout its range. Even more importantly, the behavioural variation which is bound to exist in a species so widely distributed has been studied very little in controlled comparative experiments. This is not surprising since such behavioural investigations are far more difficult and expensive than morphometric studies. Indeed, only in Europe, a small portion of the range of A. mellifera, has sufficient work been accomplished to fully describe the variation of the local A. mellifera. Naturally occurring behavioural variation in all the honeybees in the remainder of the world has received very little scientific attention. This undescribed variation will be a chief source of scientifically and economically important questions for future generations of geneticists.

EXAMPLES FROM APIS MELLIFERA

Beyond the work already cited, little is known of the genetics of A. cerana. However, several examples of possible areas of genetical work with the Eastern hive bee come from work already done with its Western sister species.

Classical genetical studies

Several visible mutations have been described and studied in A. mellifera. Most of them are mutations which interfere with normal pigment development which leads to the typical black or brown eye colour of honeybees. Other mutants involve the cuticular colour, the presence or absence of body hair, or the morphology of the eyes, wings, and sting. Most of these mutants are recessive gene forms, but their transmission and interactions can be studied using instrumental insemination as a basic tool. The vast majority of mutants of A. mellifera have been discovered in drone honeybees (Tucker 1986). The sex determination system which causes naturally occurring drones to be haploid is very fortunate for those interested in finding mutants. The haploid drones display recessive as dominant ones. Certainly such mutants are to be found in A. cerana. When they are, the classical studies of mode of inheritance, dominance, allelism, linkage, viability, and penetrance all can be conducted.

Behavioural genetics

Behavioural genetic studies in *A. cerana* await clear behavioural descriptions. As differences between stocks or colonies are brought to light, it will become difficult for honeybee biologists to avoid wanting to explore the genetic source of these differences. There is already a strong beginning in behavioural genetics with *A. mellifera*. The classic work of Rothenbuhler (1964) is widely cited in the larger field of behavioural genetics. This work investigated the variation between stocks in their tendency to clean their nests of dead brood, a trait called hygienic behaviour. Using a special genetical approach called the inbred line - single drone insemination technique in a backcross experiment, Rothenbuhler created colonies having worker bees all having the same genotype. With these techniques, genetic segregation could be studied at the colony behaviour level. In this way, Rothenbuhler showed that hygienic behaviour "depends upon homozygosity for two recessive genes". Many other examples of behavioural genetic studies in honeybees exist (Rinderer and Collins 1986). Most students of honeybees are attracted to them because of their rich and diverse behaviour. Because of this interest, many other examples of behavioural genetic studies will be forthcoming. Not all such work requires the special insemination procedures used by Rothenbuhler (Rinderer and Collins 1986), so many studies can already be undertaken. However, it is possible that one day someone will learn how to apply the single drone insemination technique to *A. cerana*.

Biochemical genetics

The most striking thing about the biochemical genetics of honeybees and other Hymenoptera is the lack of variation which is found when their allozymes are analyzed. This is equally true for studies with *A. cerana*. Tanabe *et al.* (1970) found that esterases of *A. mellifera* and *A. cerana* were different but did not find differences between groups of *A. cerana* from three different locations. This result suggests that allozyme studies will probably not prove especially useful throughout the genus *Apis*. Since other characteristics do vary, including DNA characteristics, it will probably be more productive to focus efforts in other areas.

Quantitative genetics and honeybee breeding

Quantitative traits usually involve many genes, each contributing a small effect. In some cases, there are modifier genes at other loci which have indirect, or pleiotropic, effects on the genes directly affecting the character. There is no difference in basic chromosomal mechanics for these two types of genes, although in some cases the genes involved in controlling a continuous character may be rather closely associated on a chromosome (Falconer 1981). Such groups of many genes affecting a single character are called polygenes.

Many of the characters of honeybees that have economic importance are quantitative. To aid in more clearly defining the underlying genetic complexity, the visible expression of characters, the phenotype, must be clearly described. Some traits, such as morphological ones, are easily measured. Physiological traits, such as hormone or pheromone levels and disease resistance, may require more complex assessment. Behavioural traits, such as pollen collection and honey production, may require the development of a measurement system that divides the complex behaviour into smaller, more easily studied parts.

One of the basic objectives of quantitative genetics is predicting the outcome of a selection or breeding program based on observations of existing populations. Measurements are made on groups of relatives which are used to predict how future offspring will express a character. The process uses estimates of population parameters such as means, variances, and covariances.

The statistical tools of quantitative genetics are well worth having before embarking upon programs to select improved stock. The genetic potential for change in populations of *A. mellifera* is amazing. Even after long-term culturally-based artificial selection in Europe, the bees of Europe respond to selection for economic traits very quickly and very well (Kulincevic 1986). *A. cerana* has been under less artificial selection in Asia, in part because of its tendency to abscond. However, there are suitable examples of colonies of *A. cerana* that do not abscond, even in conditions that trigger the absconding response in other colonies. The potential for stock improvement programs using selective breeding of *A. cerana* is tremendous. The possibilities of using native bees, selected for improved economic performance, should not be overlooked in a rush to import mite-susceptible *A. mellifera*.

CONCLUSION

The potential of *A. cerana* as an animal to use in genetical studies is largely untapped. However, the tools exist to study the genetics of *A. cerana* in much the same way that the genetics of *A. mellifera* has been studied. In addition, the potential for the improvement of *A. cerana* as an economically valuable animal is large and mostly unexploited. Selection programs should yield considerable success with this species in reasonably short periods of time.

ACKNOWLEDGEMENT

This review was prepared in cooperation with the Louisiana Agricultural Experiment Station.

REFERENCES

Deodikar, G.B., C.V. Thakar and N.S. Pushpa. 1959. Cytogenetic studies in Indian honeybees. I. Somatic chromosome complement in *Apis indica* and its bearing on evolution and phylogeny. Proceedings of the Indian Academy of Science, 49: 196-207.

Dietz, A. 1975. The influence of the "cannibalism substance" of diploid drone honey bee larvae on the survival of newly hatched worker bee larvae. Proceedings of the XXVth International Apiculture Congress (Apimondia), 25: 297-269.

Doolittle, G.M. 1889. Scientific Queen-Rearing. Thomas G. Newman, Chicago, Ill.

Fahrenhorst, H. 1977. Nachweis Ubereinstimmender Chromosomen-Zahlen (N=16) bei allen 4 *Apis*-Arten. Apidologie, 8: 89-100.

Falconer, D.S. 1981. Introduction to Quantitative Genetics. 2nd edition. Ronald Press, New York.

Harbo, J.R. 1986. Propagation and instrumental insemination. *In* Bee Genetics and Breeding. (T.E. Rinderer, ed.), Academic Press, Orlando, Florida. pp. 361-389.

Hoshiba, H., I. Okada , and A. Kusanagi. 1981. The diploid drone of *Apis cerana japonica* and its chromosomes. Journal of Apicultural Research, 20: 143-147.

Jordan, R.A. and R.W. Brosemer. 1974. Characterization of DNA from three bee species. Journal of Insect Physiology, 20: 2513-2530.

Kulincevic, J.M. 1986. Breeding accomplishments with honey bees. *In* Bee Genetics and Breeding. (T.E. Rinderer, ed.), Academic Press, Orlando, Florida. pp. 391-413.

Laidlaw, H.H. Jr. 1944. Artificial insemination of the queen bee (*Apis mellifera* L.): morphological basis and results. Journal of Morphology, 74: 429-465.

Langstroth, L.L. 1853. Langstroth on the Hive and the Honey-Bee, a Beekeeper's Manual. Saxton, New York.

Mackensen, O. 1947. Effects of carbon dioxide on initial oviposition of artificially inseminated and virgin queen bees. Journal of Economic Entomology, 40: 344-349.

Mackensen, O. and W.C. Roberts. 1948. A Manual for the Artificial Insemination of Queen Bees. U.S.D.A. Bureau of Entomology and Plant Quarantine ET-250.

Moritz, R.F.A. 1986. Genetics of bees other than *Apis mellifera*. *In* Bee Genetics and Breeding. (T.E. Rinderer, ed). Academic Press, Orlando, Florida. pp. 121-154.

Nolan, W.J. 1929. Success in the artificial insemination of queen bees at the Bee Culture Laboratory. Journal of Economic Entomology, 22: 544-551.

Nolan, W.J. 1932. Breeding the Honey Bee under Controlled Conditions. U.S.D.A. Technical Bulletin No. 326.

Rinderer, T.E. (ed.) 1986. Bee Genetics and Breeding. Academic Press, Orlando, Florida.

Rinderer, T.E. and A.M. Collins. 1986. Behavioural genetics. *In* Bee Genetics and Breeding. (T.E. Rinderer, ed.), Academic Press, Orlando, Florida. pp. 155-176.

Ruttner, F. 1987. Biogeography and Taxonomy of Honeybees. Springer-Verlag, Berlin.

Ruttner, F. and V. Maul. 1983. Experimental analysis of the reproductive interspecific isolation of *Apis mellifera* L. and *Apis cerana* Fabr. Apidologie, 14: 309-327.

Ruttner, F., J. Woyke and N. Koeniger. 1972. Reproduction in *Apis cerana*. 1. Mating behaviour. Journal of Apicultural Research, 11: 141-146.

Ruttner, F., J. Woyke and N. Koeniger. 1973. Reproduction in *Apis cerana*. 2. Reproductive organs and natural insemination. Journal of Apicultural Research, 12: 21-34.

Rothenbuhler, W.C. 1964. Behavior genetics of nest cleaning in honey bees. IV. Responses of F_1 and backcross generations to disease-killed brood. American Zoologist, 4: 111-123.

Sharma, G.P., B.L. Gupta and C.G. Kumbkarni. 1961. Cytology of spermatogenesis in the honey bee *Apis indica* F. Journal of the Royal Microscopic Society, 79: 337-351.

Sperlin, A., R. Campbell and R.W. Brosemer. 1975. The hybridization of DNA from two species of honeybee. Journal of Insect Physiology, 21: 373-376.

Tanabe, Y., Y. Tamaki and S. Nakano. 1970. Variations of esterase isozymes in seven species of bees and wasps. Japanese Journal of Genetics, 45: 425-428.

Tucker, K.W. 1986. Visible mutants. *In* Bee Genetics and Breeding (T.E. Rinderer, ed.), Academic Press, Orlando, Florida. pp. 57-90.

Watson, L.R. 1927. Controlled mating of the honeybee. American Bee Journal, 67: 300-302.

Woyke, J. 1963. What happens to diploid drone larvae in a honeybee colony. Journal of Apicultural Research, 2: 73-76.

Woyke, J. 1967. Diploid drone substance - canni-

balism substance. Proceedings of the XXIst
International Apiculture Congress (Apimondia),
21: 471-472.

Woyke, J. 1973. Instrumental insemination of *Apis
cerana indica* queens. Journal of Apicultural
Research, 12: 151-158.

Woyke, J. 1975. Natural and instrumental insemination of *Apis cerana indica* in India. Journal of
Apicultural Research, 14: 153-159.

Woyke, J. 1979. Sex determination in *Apis cerana
indica*. Journal of Apicultural Research, 18: 122-
127.

Woyke, J. 1986. Sex determination. *In* Bee Genetics and Breeding (T.E. Rinderer, ed.), Academic
Press, Orlando, Florida. pp. 91-119.

CHAPTER 8

BIOTECHNOLOGICAL POTENTIAL OF *APIS CERANA*

H. ALLEN SYLVESTER

INTRODUCTION

Recent advances in genetics and related disciplines have made it possible to move from traditional methods of controlling genetic change in organisms, such as controlled breeding programs and selection, to the ability to directly manipulate the DNA, the genetic code itself. One major focus is on the area of biotechnology known as recombinant-DNA technology, locating or assembling specific genes and placing them in the chromosomes of an organism. Also, genes that appear to have the same function can be obtained from different organisms, and the sequence of the nucleotides, the building blocks of DNA, may be compared in the finest detail to analyze what differences are present. This technology is best developed in the fruit (or vinegar) fly, *Drosophila melanogaster*, in which known genes have been placed in chromosomes and are stably inherited.

Methods of inserting genes into chromosomes are presently the major block to the application of the technology developed with *Drosophila* to other insects. Many efforts to apply *Drosophila* gene transfer technology to other insects have failed to demonstrate stable gene transfer on a repeatable basis. Most efforts have been completely unsuccessful. Therefore the original hopes of simple technology transfer have been dashed. Efforts are now being concentrated on developing the technology of manipulating genes. This involves techniques such as locating specific genes, assembling new or modified genes from existing or synthesized parts, and alternative methods of gene transfer.

While our ability to apply these new methods is mainly limited to *Drosophila*, some plants and some lower organisms, there is very active research in progress to learn how to apply similar methods of genetic manipulation to other organisms. One of those organisms is the honeybee. The present research is limited to *Apis mellifera*, but preliminary research is under way to expand this research effort to *Apis cerana*.

PRESENT RESEARCH WITH HONEYBEES

Biotechnology-related research with honeybees is presently being conducted by the USDA, Agricultural Research Service, Honey-Bee Breeding, Genetics, and Physiological Laboratory at Baton Rouge, Louisiana. The goals of this cooperative research are to develop the technology to locate, manipulate and transfer genes in honeybees. The specific genes may very well not be originally from honeybees. In fact, they might be at least partially synthetic genes created in a laboratory.

Research is also being conducted to identify desirable genes or parts of genes to transfer. The first gene to transfer will be one which can be identified easily so that verification of a successful transfer is simplified. Once a reliable transfer method has been developed, other genes that will result in an improved stock of honeybees can be transferred.

One class of genes that is being evaluated as the most promising for improving honeybees are the genes coding for proteins known as cecropins. These genes are from insects and produce proteins that have very strong bactericidal and fungicidal effects, even at low concentrations. Thus, by transferring a single gene into honeybees, resistance to American foul brood (AFB), European foul brood (EFB) and chalkbrood might all be obtained simultaneously. Preliminary research at Baton Rouge has already shown that one cecropin is bactericidal to AFB with an LD50 of about 1 to 5 micromolar. The effects of this cecropin on EFB and chalkbrood are now being investigated. It is possible that honeybees already contain cecropins but that in some cases they are induced or "turned on" too late (after a larva is infected) to provide acceptable levels of disease resistance. Therefore, we are examining honeybee DNA to determine whether there is a sequence similar to that of this particular cecropin. If a cecropin-like gene is found in bees, it might be possible to modify the expression of this gene in honeybee larvae so that the cecropin protein is present to respond to the challenge of various diseases. It should be equally possible to conduct this transformation with *A. cerana* as with *A. mellifera*, if DNA laboratory facilities are available at a location where *A. cerana* is available.

Another area of biotechnology-related research which is beginning is that of mite resistance. *A. cerana* is the natural host of the parasitic mite *Varroa jacobsoni*. In some way it is resistant to the effects of this mite to the extent that it can keep levels of infestation of this mite very low with no assistance from beekeepers. Research by Dr. Siriwat Wongsiri and cooperators, Chulalongkorn University, Bangkok, Thailand, into the nature of this resistance is presently under way. Dr. Christine Peng, University of California, Davis, California and cooperators in China are also conducting research on the nature of the mite resistance in *A. cerana*.

As an alternative to chemical and management methods of mite control, it would be desirable to have the same resistance in *A. mellifera* as is present in *A. cerana*. Since these two species do not hybridize, the use of recombinant-DNA methods is the only feasible way to transfer this resistance. However, in order to make this transfer, the mechanism of resistance must be identified, its genetic basis determined, the specific controlling gene(s) located, the desired gene removed, and this gene transferred. These will all be time-consuming steps, so it is important that research begin and be pursued so that the feasibility of this approach can be determined.

Even if DNA transfer is not feasible or takes a very long time, the results of research into the mechanism of mite resistance in *A. cerana* will yield useful information. Knowledge of behavioural or physiological responses contributing to mite resistance in *A. cerana* may very well lead to identification of similar characteristics in *A. mellifera* and permit more efficient selection to increase their effect.

RECOMBINANT-DNA PROCEDURES

Specific procedures must be determined for each organism and, often, even for each laboratory, due to variations in enzymes, proteins, etc., which must be removed, chemicals used, and equipment used. Therefore, no specific procedures for bees can reasonably be presented yet. Specific protocols will also tend to change rapidly as research yields improved procedures. However, procedures which have been found to be effective in other organisms are available in laboratory manuals, including Maniatis *et al.* (1982) and Berger and Kimmel (1987). Berger and Kimmel's manual also includes the section "Requirements for a Molecular Biology Laboratory", which discusses equipment and procedures.

The general procedure is basically as follows:

DNA extraction - A suitable tissue or life stage is determined (whole larvae or testes of drone pupae are both used for bees). The tissue or organism is ground in an appropriate buffer solution. Various chemicals are added to disrupt the cells and remove the other components of the cells (e.g. membranes,

fats, proteins, enzymes that destroy DNA and RNA). This often occurs in a two-phase system (water and hydrocarbon), or through centrifugation. The purified DNA can then be used in several ways.

DNA fractionation - Enzymes (restriction enzymes) are available which cut the DNA at specific places (restriction sites, which are short specific sequences of component nucleotides). The pieces of DNA (restriction fragments) can then be separated by their size in a procedure called electrophoresis.

DNA hybridization - The fractionated DNA can then be transferred to a treated membrane and fixed in place. Under proper conditions, known DNA (a probe) can be applied to the membrane. If any areas of the fractionated DNA are sufficiently similar to the probe, the DNA molecules will align and pair (hybridize). If the probe has been treated with a suitable marker before hybridization, the location of any similar fractionated DNA, if present, can be detected. By varying the conditions of hybridization, the degree of similarity can be estimated.

DNA cloning - Once the location on a membrane or in a gel of a particular piece of DNA (usually a gene) has been determined, it can be separated from the rest of the DNA pieces. To increase the available amount of a particular gene, the gene can be inserted into the DNA of one of various micro-organisms, and it will then be reproduced (cloned) as the micro-organism reproduces. The total DNA can then be extracted and the desired gene removed using restriction enzymes. The desired gene can be increased to any quantity by controlling the reproduction of the micro-organism.

DNA library - If no similar gene is available or if changes have been too great for hybridization to occur, "all" of the DNA pieces produced by a restriction enzyme acting on the DNA from that organism can be cloned. This produces a great number of different clones (groups of micro-organisms containing the same piece of cloned DNA) which together are called a "DNA library". Then the clones are examined for some characteristic (screened).

Gene construction - Successful expression of a gene in a foreign organism depends on two factors. First, the gene of interest must be inserted. Second, the accompanying DNA regions that control production of the gene's product must be present and work in the new organism. These controlling elements are often quite specific in their activity. Many studies have demonstrated that the best expression is derived from a combination of the gene of interest with controlling elements from the organism to be transformed. The technology is already available to construct such a gene, if the structural gene and control elements can be identified. The procedure is basically the same as for cloning a gene, except that two or more pieces of DNA must be inserted.

Vectors - After the desired gene has been obtained, it must be introduced into the DNA of the organisms to be transformed. Various methods have been used or proposed, with varying rates of success in different organisms. One method in use with *Drosophila* uses a particular piece of DNA (P-element) with the capability to actively insert itself into *Drosophila* DNA rather than depending on some type of passive incorporation. A piece of DNA which can actively insert itself into host DNA is called a vector. If available, use of a vector is much more efficient than passive incorporation. In *Drosophila* a modified P-element, with the desired gene inserted in the P-element, can introduce the gene into a chromosome. Insertion of the gene into a vector is basically the same process as cloning a gene.

Transformation - Transformation is the stable integration of the gene of interest into the host's chromosomes, with subsequent production of the gene product. In *Drosophila* this is accomplished by injecting a solution containing the vector, with the desired gene incorporated, into an egg of suitable age. This requires a micromanipulator, a high quality dissecting microscope, a very fine pointed syringe containing the DNA vector in solution, and appropriate treatment of the egg. In a few percent of the injected eggs, the vector will successfully integrate into a chromosome. However, if it integrates within a required gene, it will probably inactivate that gene and kill or be detrimental to those eggs. Therefore, only some of the eggs where the vector has successfully integrated will be viable. Unfortunately, no experiments to date have been able to repeatably demonstrate successful use of the *Drosophila* P-element for transformation in any insect outside a small group of species in the Diptera. Even within the Diptera, the success rate quickly falls to zero in more distantly related species. Therefore, P-elements are unlikely to be usable in bees. Hopefully, another vector will be located. Viruses appear to be the most likely alternative, particularly the DNA viruses. Unfortunately, no DNA viruses have been reported from bees.

Propagation - The treated individuals must then be propagated to select transformants and to obtain the beneficial results of the insertion of the foreign gene. Compared to *Drosophila*, raising the treated

individuals will probably be much more difficult in a social insect such as bees, since the workers may be able to identify treated individuals and may reject them. However, a successfully transformed queen bee will be able to produce many more offspring over a much longer period of time than is possible in *Drosophila*.

Selection of transformants - Individuals that were successfully transformed must be separated from those that were not transformed. Occasionally this can be done by examining or testing (screening) those individuals which were produced from the treated eggs. Usually, however, treated individuals contain both transformed and untransformed germ cells. Therefore, they must reproduce to produce offspring with the gene of interest distributed homogenously throughout their body. Screening the offspring allows selection of offspring of parents that were transformed.

CONCLUSION

Because the technology is still not developed, particularly the availability of vectors, recombinant-DNA cannot yet be applied to bees. However, it probably will not be very long until the technology is available. It is therefore important to begin to consider potential uses. More uses are apparent for *A. mellifera* because problems, such as mites and diseases, and possible solutions, such as transfer of mite resistance from *A. cerana* and transformation for the cecropin gene, have already been identified. Also, *A. mellifera* is much more important economically and so more resources are available to conduct research.

In *A. cerana*, transformation for the cecropin gene is an obvious choice. However, an important problem for some *A. cerana* beekeepers is a virus disease, the so-called "Thai sacbrood". A disease caused by a virus probably would not be affected by the cecropin protein. Identification of a gene in *A. mellifera* which conferred resistance to this sacbrood would then provide a gene which would be important to *A. cerana* beekeepers and would only be available through recombinant-DNA technology. Location of such a gene (if it even exists or is a single gene) would undoubtedly be a major undertaking with no guarantee of success, which means it may not even be attempted. Many of the characteristics of *A. cerana*, such as absconding, swarming and honey production, which need improvement to achieve the relative economic level found in *A. mellifera*, are behavioural characteristics which will not lend themselves to solutions at the DNA level. Attention therefore needs to be directed to characteristics of *A. cerana* which are probably under simpler genetic control and thus are more amenable to modification at the DNA level.

A. cerana has significant potential to be improved by recombinant-DNA technology and to contribute to the improvement of *A. mellifera*. However, its potential can only be fulfilled if those who are working with *A. cerana* are made aware of the uses and limits of recombinant-DNA technology and expend the effort to determine where DNA-level improvements could be made.

ACKNOWLEDGEMENTS

This review was prepared in cooperation with the Louisiana Agricultural Experiment Station.

REFERENCES

Berger, S.L. and A.R. Kimmel (eds). 1987. Guide to molecular cloning techniques. Vol. 152 in Methods of Enzymology, eds.-in-chief J.N. Abelson and M.I. Simon, Academic Press, San Diego, Ca. 812 pp.

Maniatis, T., E.F. Fritsch and J. Sambrook. 1982. Molecular cloning (A Laboratory Manual). Cold Spring Harbor Laboratory, Cold Spring Harbor, New York. 545 pp.

CHAPTER 9

QUEEN PRODUCTION

SIRIWAT WONGSIRI

INTRODUCTION

In China, *Apis cerana* Fabr. has been "domesticated" for 3,000 years. However, for most of this time the hives were wooden boxes, buckets, and rustic bamboo hives (Fang 1984). Improving the queen production of *A. cerana* was not possible until this century when the modern queen rearing methods used for *Apis mellifera* were introduced into China (Wongsiri *et al.* 1986). In the late 1950's, the method of transferring *A. cerana* colonies and then maintaining them in modern hives was first popularized intensively. Because of this development, comparative studies on breeding of *A. cerana* and *A. mellifera* were in process for several years. However, by the mid-sixties, it became evident that *A. mellifera* was not especially suitable for the southern part of China (Liu 1984). From this period on, beekeepers decided to concentrate on the selection of *A. cerana* for honey production (Wongsiri *et al.* 1986).

The honey production of *A. cerana* in Asia was limited by outdated management methods for a long time. The number of small colonies and the low yields did not increase until new methods of beekeeping and queen rearing were adopted. Before 1960, in Chonghue county, Guangdong (Canton) province, there were a total of 2,000 colonies of *A. cerana* with an annual yield of approximately 10,000 kg honey or an average of less than 5 kg of honey from each colony. After the adoption of modern beekeeping and queen rearing methods, the colony numbers and honey yields increased year by year. By 1963, honeybee populations had increased to about 6,000 colonies with an annual yield of 300,000 kg honey, or an average of almost 50 kg of honey per colony (Liu 1984). These figures clearly demonstrate the economic value of *A. cerana*.

Information on *A. cerana* queen rearing in general beekeeping manuals is limited. I hope that this compilation of information from specialized books and research articles written in Chinese and Thai on queen rearing will stimulate more beekeepers in Asia to try this fascinating side-line of their craft (Doolittle 1915; Laidlaw and Eckert 1962; Laidlaw 1979; Lai 1982; Wongsiri 1984; Pothichot and Wongsiri 1987; Wongsiri *et al.* 1988).

THE QUEEN

A normal colony of Asian honeybees, *A. cerana*, is composed of one queen, several thousand workers, and a few hundred drones. The laying queen is longer than the worker (Fig. 1). Her body colour is black to dark brown and similar to *A. mellifera carnica*. It is not true that *A. cerana* queens are necessarily smaller than *A. mellifera* queens. The worker bees of these species greatly overlap in size (Ruttner 1986) and this is also true of queens. The northern biotypes (*A. cerana cerana* and *A. cerana japonica*) are generally larger than southern biotypes (*A. cerana indica* and *A. cerana indica (javana)*. In any event, the wings of the *A. cerana* queen cover only a portion of her abdomen, which is considerably longer than the rest of her body. Although her wings seem to be smaller than those of the workers, they are actually longer and broader. Her thorax is bigger than that of a worker. Actually, the thorax size of most *A. cerana* laying queens makes it impossible for them to pass through a queen excluder for *A. mellifera*. The drones (Fig. 2) are broader than either the queen or the workers, but are not as long as a laying queen. The queen is typically found within the brood area unless the colony has been disturbed, a behaviour also common in *A. mellifera* (Laidlaw and Eckert 1962; Ruttner *et al.* 1973).

The queen is the mother of all members of the colony, drones, workers and daughter queens. Because of this and the mating system of bees, the queen is the repository of all of the inherited characteristics of the colony. Eggs she lays contain her genes and, if females, are fertilized by the sperm held in her spermatheca since the time of mating. Thus the queen is responsible for the colour of the bees (*A. cerana indica* is darker than *A. cerana cerana*), their industry (*A. cerana cerana* is a better egg laying queen than *A. cerana indica*), degree of gentleness, resistance to disease, swarming and absconding tendencies, longevity, comb-building propensities, and all other colony attributes dependent upon genetics (Rinderer 1986). By merely changing the queen in a colony, one can change many of the colony's characteristics within a few weeks (Laidlaw 1979). Such results were observed when *A. cerana*

FIGURE 1. A queen of *Apis cerana*.

FIGURE 2. A drone of *Apis cerana*.

queens were introduced into the colonies of *A. cerana indica* in Thailand (Wongsiri *et al.* 1986).

A normally mated queen is capable of laying two kinds of eggs, fertilized eggs from which female bees arise, and unfertilized eggs which, through the phenomenon of parthenogenesis, produce males. Dzierzon (1845) published a brief note stating that worker bees and queens develop from fertilized eggs which are females, while drones (males) develop from unfertilized ones (Woyke 1986). Eggs destined to produce females are laid in worker or queen cells; those which are to develop into drones are laid in drone cells. Unfertilized eggs usually produce only drones, but all female larvae can develop into queens or workers, depending on the food and care given them during their early larval stages (Laidlaw and Eckert 1962). Sex determination in *A. cerana* was investigated by Woyke (1979) in India. Hoshiba (1984) and Woyke (1986) indicated that the mechanism of sex determination was similar to that of *A. mellifera*. *A. cerana* and *A. mellifera* have a common number of chromosomes (n=16); drones are haploid, workers and queens are diploid. Hoshiba *et al.* (1981) confirmed the production of haploid drone larvae and unusual diploid drone larvae in *A. cerana*. They found 16 chromosomes in the haploid and 32 in the unusual diploid drones of *A. cerana*.

The virgin queen

In unmanaged colonies, queens are reared in three circumstances: queenlessness, swarming, and supersedure (Laidlaw and Eckert 1962). All methods that stimulate colonies of *A. cerana* to build queen cells take advantage of the basic behaviour by which colonies produce emergency cells in the absence of a queen. The cells are capped in 5 days (15 days from egg to adult queen in *A. cerana*) and then transferred to queenless colonies or mating nuclei, where the virgin queens emerge, fly and mate (Dietz *et al.* 1975; Sanford *et al.* 1975; Dietz 1983; Wongsiri *et al.* 1988).

Mating of the queens

Observation of the mating flight of 72 *A. cerana cerana* queens showed that the majority of them making flights were 6-8 days old, although flight ages ranged from 3 to 16 days (Gong *et al.* 1987). The results were close to those reported for *A. mellifera* by Gary (1975). He found queens of *A. mellifera* usually made mating flights 8-9 days after emergence. Queens of *A. cerana* started orientation flights at a younger age than queens of *A. mellifera* (Sharma 3.6 days, Adlakha 2.9 days). Adlakha (1971) reported mating on only one flight while Sharma (1960) and Ruttner *et al.* (1972) reported matings on two flights. Gong *et al.* (1987) found

most queens of *A. cerana cerana* went on 1 to 3 mating flights and most mating occurred on the first flight. They found that the mean duration of non-mating flights of *A. cerana cerana* was 7.5 minutes while mating flights averaged 22.3 minutes. The mating sign is a thread of male genitalia brought back by a successfully mated queen, which protrudes from her vagina when the mating flight is finished. This mating sign was often seen by Gong *et al.* (1987). The drones eventually die after mating, however this often takes more than an hour.

Similar to *A. mellifera*, mating flights took place only between 1:00 and 5:00 P.M., with the greatest frequency between 2:00 and 4:00 P.M. (Gary 1975). Gong *et al.* (1987) reported that queens of *A. cerana cerana* made their flights at about 2:00 P.M. in March, at about 3:00 P.M. in April and from 3:00 to 5:00 P.M. in May and June. The suitable temperature for queen flight was between 25 and 30°C. It was shown that queen flight was often limited by the temperature and weather.

Oviposition

Most *A. cerana cerana* queens begin to lay eggs within 2 to 3 days after mating. However, the range of the age of first oviposition was from 2 to 18 days. Before laying an egg, the queen of *A. cerana* walks over the comb and places her head in the cell in a fashion like that of *A. mellifera* (Gary 1975). Then she withdraws her head, curves her body, and quickly pushes her abdomen into the cell. In a few seconds she turns to the right or to the left and withdraws the abdomen out of the cell. The egg-laying process takes approximately 8 to 10 seconds. A normal queen of *A. cerana cerana*, under favourable colony and environmental conditions, lays an average of 557 (346-1,067) eggs each day (Table I).

METHODS FOR REARING QUEENS

In about 1870, G.M. Doolittle became interested in rearing queens of *A. mellifera*. During the next 18 years he gradually developed an improved system after testing a variety of methods (Laidlaw and Eckert 1962). The development of this method provides the foundation for all queen breeding programs.

A first category of queen rearing programs involves the small-scale production of queens by individual beekeepers. They are characterized by having small base populations, and usually do not involve control stocks which permit precise evaluation of success (Kulincevic 1986).

The next category of queen rearing programmes are those usually undertaken by commercial bee-

TABLE I. The production of eggs from *Apis cerana cerana* naturally produced queens and *A. cerana cerana* grafted queens (from Wongsiri *et al.* 1988).

Number of colonies	Average eggs per day (April - June)						Source of queens
	1-12/4	12-24/4	24/4-6/5	6-18/5	18-30/5	30/5-11/6	
3	629	717	800	733	808	941	Natural
4	363	463	551	733	900	346	Natural
16	421	533	800	941	1067	663	Grafted
17	413	429	668	600	1023	608	Grafted

keeping companies and bee research institutes. The more successful commercial queen rearing programs often have taken advantage of information gained by the small pioneering projects. Commercial queen rearing programs are characterized by having large numbers of colonies in base populations, selected generations, and a lack of costly control stocks (Kulincevic 1986). Since 1957, the modern beekeeping systems and queen rearing methods of *A. mellifera* were introduced for use with *A. cerana* in China. The Chinese have developed techniques to transfer *A. cerana* into modern hives, to increase colony reproduction, select for high honey yield, control bee diseases, rear queens and divide colonies commercially, under their conditions. Fang (1984) reported that there are now 1,000,000 colonies of *A. cerana* in China.

Environmental factors necessary for the production of queens

In the production of good queen cells of *A. cerana*, it is important to approximate the conditions which exist in nature when a strong colony produces cells under the swarming impulse. At such times, the colony is usually at its peak of strength numerically, thus insuring an abundance of honey and pollen, nurse bees, wax builders, ventilators and field bees. The combs in the hive are well filled with honey, pollen and brood. The incoming nectar and pollen create conditions favourable for the production of both wax and brood food. The crowded condition of the brood nest and the restriction in the available space to rear brood result in an overabundance of nurse bees and the production of royal jelly in excess of the colony's needs. Wax builders are stimulated to wax production by the evaporation and storage of nectar and by the increased heat of the hive. Drone production is in full swing and mature drones are present in numbers. This combination of factors generally results in the preparation of numerous queen cell cups in which the queen will lay, the construction of queen cells, and finally, swarming, unless unfavourable weather intervenes (Laidlaw 1979). The method for rearing queens of *A. mellifera* was applied to queen rearing of *A. cerana* at the Chulalongkorn University Bee Biology Research Station, Samut Songkhram province, Thailand. Up to 90% of the transplanted larvae were accepted during the swarming season and less than 30% were accepted during the rainy season and when there was a lack of food (Wongsiri *et al.* 1988).

Blooming season conditions are not always present when queens are reared in a supersedure process or under the emergency of queenlessness. In either of these cases, the colony may be weak or other environmental conditions may not be favourable. The production of queens of *A. cerana* is clearly favoured by good external environmental conditions. Only a small number of cells could be produced in the rainy season and the virgin queens mostly were small and weak. In emergencies, as when a queen is removed from a colony, the bees may rear only a few emergency queen cells (Fig. 3) but the number may depend on environmental conditions.

Queen production from natural sources

It is possible to secure and select a few good queen cells from a colony which is preparing to replace an old or failing queen (supersedure). If all supersedure cells are removed, the colony will make others, and the old queen does not disturb them. Occasionally, we see an old and a young queen living together in the same colony.

Queen cells from colonies preparing to swarm under "natural" conditions are also usable (Fig. 4). This method has been used by beekeepers of *A. cerana* in Thailand. Similarly, Laidlaw (1979) recommended manipulating colonies of *A. mellifera* to stimulate the building of cells in preparation for swarming. The value of this idea is supported by the recent findings that queens from swarm cells have on

FIGURE 3. An emergency queen cell.

FIGURE 4. Swarm queen cells.

TABLE II. Queen cells from natural sources.

Queen cells	Emergency	Supersedure	Swarming
Number	1-20	1-5	5-30
Position	Surface and bottom of the comb and the corners	Surface of the comb and the corners	Bottom of the comb
Age	Approximately similar (10-12 days)	Approximately similar (14-15 days)	Widely variable
Contents of worker cells	Old eggs and young brood present	Eggs and young brood present	Eggs absent

average more ovarioles than queens from emergency cells (Pothichot and Wongsiri 1987).

Queen cells with reddish-brown tips, caused by bees removing most of the wax over the membranous cocoon, are "ripe" and the queens are due to emerge (10-11 days after cell building began). All the ripe queen cells must be removed but the longest and most perfect queen cell may be left for the colony. This is because the first virgin queen that emerges will inhibit queen cell production, and destroy any remaining queen cells. After their removal, the ripe cells are then separated, and small or poorly formed cells are discarded. The cells are placed between layers of padded cloth to protect the queens in the cells and carried to the nucleus or prepared mating hive.

Queen cells may be reared under emergency conditions, as when a queen is removed from a colony. The bees will rear a few emergency cells in 1 to 2 days in young brood comb. If the emergency occurs when natural conditions are unfavourable, the resulting queen larvae may be poorly fed. If one wishes to rear queens this way at a time other than during the swarming season, it is necessary to stimulate and feed the colony. A colony of bees can be strengthened by the addition of the required number of young bees and emerging brood from other colonies. The production of brood food can be increased by feeding a heavy sugar syrup and pollen substitute which is a dry soybean powder, in an external feeder (Fig. 5). The feeding of a pollen supplement (Fig. 6) along with sugar syrup also stimulates brood rearing and increases production of brood food when unsealed brood is present. The characteristics listed in Table II distinguish emergency supersedure and swarm cells.

"Artificial" queen cell production (queen rearing)

All methods that stimulate the colony to build queen cells from wax cell cups take advantage of the basic behaviour by which the colony produces emergency cells in the absence of a queen. Queen rearing of A. cerana uses a frame with 1 or 2 bars of cell cups which have 10-30 cells mounted at intervals (Fig. 7).

We developed a process for producing cell cups for A. cerana based on the process for A. mellifera as discussed by Laidlaw (1979). This uses wooden dipping sticks made from pieces of dowelling (6 mm in diameter), rounded and smoothed at one end. The stick is dipped and redipped into the just molten wax until a cell is formed. The cell is removed and fastened to the grafting bar. In addition, we place a frame (Fig. 7) holding the wax cups into a colony for a few hours or overnight before grafting larvae so that the bees can clean and prepare the cups (Wongsiri et al. 1988).

We prime the cells with royal jelly before placing larvae in them. A. cerana prefer "wet" grafts. A damp cloth or paper towelling kept over the frames from which the larvae are being taken, as well as the cell cups that will receive them, minimizes drying of the larvae. Bees will have been brushed off the grafting comb before use. Adequate illumination is needed in front of the operator, who uses a transfer tool (Fig. 8); this may be purchased, or fashioned from a matchstick, toothpick, twisted feather, bamboo stick or grass stem. The chosen tool is inserted underneath a larva (less than 1 day old) to lift it from the worker cell. The larva is placed in one of the cell cups primed with royal jelly which are located on the frame bars and returned to the queenless hive as quickly as possible. In the absence of a honey flow, sugar syrup must be fed at least 3 days prior to grafting and throughout the cell building period.

The queenless colony or cell builder hive (Fig. 9) is a single-story colony with a minimum of 3 or 4 combs of honey and pollen and an abundance of nurse bees (Fig. 10). If necessary, we add frames of emerging worker brood without eggs a few days in advance. These conditions simulate the conditions

FIGURE 5. A dry soya bean powder in external feeder.

FIGURE 6. Pollen supplement on top of frames in a mating hive which can be fed by the same method to stimulate brood rearing in cell builder hive.

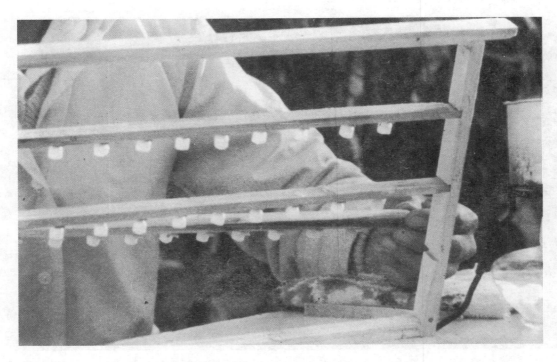

FIGURE 7. A queen rearing frame with 3 bars which has 30 cells.

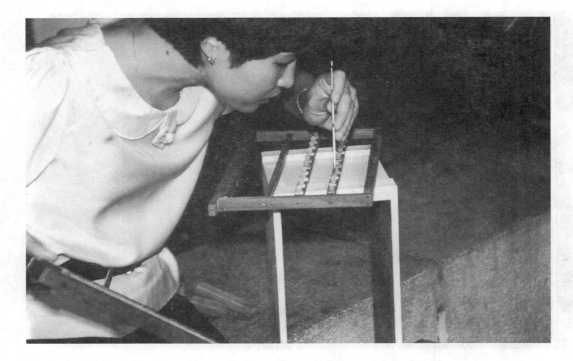

FIGURE 8. Grafting.

FIGURE 9. A queenless colony hive or cell builder hive with a single story.

FIGURE 10. A frame with an abundance of nurse bees from a cell builder hive.

TABLE III. Approximate queen production time table.

Day	First cycle	Second cycle	Third cycle	Example date
1	graft			March 16
3*	remove royal jelly (if needed)	graft		March 19
6		remove royal jelly (if needed)	graft	March 22
10	cells to nuclei		remove royal jelly (if needed)	March 26
13		cells to nuclei		March 29
16			cells to nuclei	April 1
18	mating flights			April 3
21**	eggs	mating flights		April 6
24	larvae	eggs	mating flights	April 9
27		larvae	eggs	April 12
30***	capped brood		larvae	April 15
33		capped brood		April 18
36			capped brood	April 21
43****	emerging workers			April 28
46		emerging workers		May 1
49			emerging workers	May 4

*	The larvae must be discarded from cells where royal jelly is harvested, so such cells do not produce queens.
**	Usually the first cycle can be checked on or after this day to see if the queen mated successfully. If good weather allowed mating flights at the proper time, *A. cerana* take mating flights from 3-10 days after emerging.
***	Usually the first cycle can be checked on or after this date (if eggs were present on 21) to see if cells are capped as workers (queen mated successfully) or drones (mating was unsuccessful).
****	Emerging workers (not drones) confirm successful mating.

in a colony preparing to swarm.

In queen rearing, the time table for procedures must be followed strictly once it is begun. Regardless of conditions, certain management activities must be done so the colonies used should be gentle as well as populous (Table III).

In "double grafting" a worker larva is grafted (transferred) into a queen cell, and the next day it is replaced with a young larva (less than 24 hours old) (Table III). The queens of *A. cerana* produced by this technique are slightly heavier than those from single grafts. This process, theoretically at least, provides the second larvae with abundant food because of food fed to the first larvae (Table III) and generally insures that considerably more food is put into the queen cells than the larvae can eat (Laidlaw (1979). During preliminary observations of *A. cerana* under optimum conditions, the number of cells accepted in single grafting is less than that accepted with double grafting. More than 90% of the double-grafted larvae were accepted and reared by the workers as the queens (Fig. 11) (Wongsiri *et al.* 1988).

When cells are double grafted, care should be exercised in the second transfer. The first larva must be discarded carefully. Unless the larvae are removed without materially changing the consistency of the royal jelly, the bees may remove all of the jelly and start over again, thus eliminating any beneficial effect the double graft might have.

One to three days before the queen cells are "ripe", a queenless nucleus is made up (Fig. 12) or the queen is removed from an existing colony. One queen cell from the cell builder hive is then placed in each such colony, to await emergence and mating.

CONTROLLED MATING

The first successful instrumental insemination of queens of *A. cerana indica* was by Woyke (1973) in Germany and the egg-laying activity of these queens was investigated in Poland.

Artificial insemination is important in selective breeding because it is the only way that a breeder can control which drones mate with a queen. Bee breeders and beekeepers are well aware of the importance of artificial insemination and controlled mating. However, one can also improve stock in a breeding program that uses only natural mating. Artificial insemination should not be seen as a replacement for natural mating but as an additional tool that gives a breeder absolute control of mating (Harbo 1976).

To increase the productivity of *A. cerana*, controlled mating must be assured, but a successful method of artificial insemination of this species can be worked out only when the details of its reproduction, and especially of its mating behaviour are better known. The reproductive biology of *A. mellifera* has been studied by many authors, but such studies on *A. cerana* have only just started (Ruttner 1985). Sharma (1960) and Adlakha (1971) investigated the mating behaviour of *A. cerana indica* in India. Ruttner *et al.* (1972, 1973) studied reproduction of this species in the Federal Republic of Germany. Lai You-shen and Liu Zhi-song in the Division of Apiculture, Guangdong province, China carried out investigations of artificial insemination of *A. cerana cerana* in China but never published in English (Wongsiri 1984).

For *A. cerana indica*, the amount of semen in the oviducts of one queen returning from a mating flight was measured by Ruttner *et al.* (1973) in Germany.

They also counted the number of spermatozoa in the spermathecae of two queens mated naturally in Germany and of one naturally mated in Pakistan. Woyke (1975) studied natural and instrumental insemination of *A. cerana indica* in India. Queens of *A. cerana indica* inseminated instrumentally in India with 6 mm^3 of semen had 1.441 million spermatozoa in the spermatheca (Woyke 1973). Queens inseminated by Woyke (1973) with 4 mm^3 in Germany had more (1.95 million) but inseminations in China with 6 mm^3 had still more (2-3 million).

Queens of *A. cerana indica* inseminated with 4 mm^3 of semen (Woyke 1973), or queens of *A. cerana cerana* inseminated with 4-6 mm^3 in China as described here, produced exclusively worker brood during the first year. An artificially inseminated queen of *A. cerana cerana* under favourable colony and environmental conditions, lays an average of 761 (highest 1,067) eggs each day (Wongsiri *et al.* 1989).

As a source for semen, it is best to choose drones that have aged 7-15 days after emergence. Drones younger than 7 days are often not yet sexually mature, and those older than 15 days are more likely to cause disease in the queens or leave a residue of semen in the oviducts (Woyke and Jasinski 1973). Both conditions will kill a queen before she begins to lay eggs.

The mating biology of *A. cerana indica* in India and Thailand and *A. cerana cerana* in China differs in some respects from that of *A. mellifera*. However, although queens of *A. cerana indica* are smaller in India and Thailand, they can be satisfactorily instrumentally inseminated (Figs. 13, 14, 15 and 16). However, the procedure with *A. cerana* and especially *A. cerana indica* is much more time consuming than it is with *A. mellifera*.

CONCLUSION

Critical factors in successful queen production with *A. mellifera* are summarized by Johansson and Johansson (1973). These can be applied to *A. cerana* as follows:

1. Schedules for queen rearing must arrange for the mating of queens to coincide with the availability of mature drones.
2. Optimal conditions prevail during the swarming season, or in the early part of a honey flow.
3. Bees must be fed if there is no honey flow.
4. Colonies must have ample stores of honey and pollen.
5. Colonies should have an abundance of young bees.
6. Simple methods should be used while the operator learns more demanding techniques such as grafting.

FIGURE 11. Double grafted queen cells.

FIGURE 12. Separating a new queen colony.

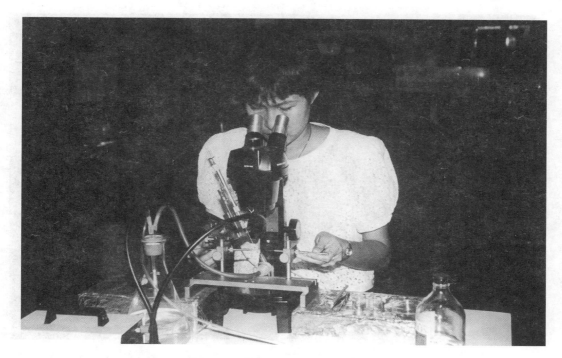

FIGURE 13. Instrumental insemination apparatus of *Apis cerana*.

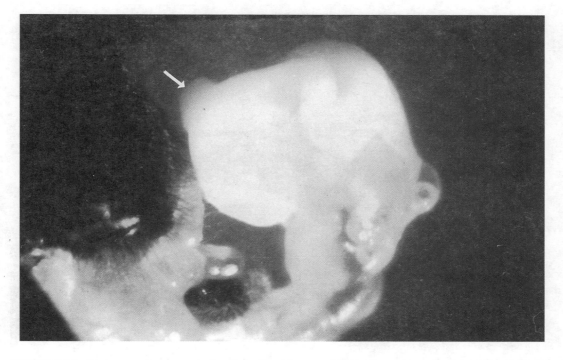

FIGURE 14. Release of semen to the exterior (drone endophallus with semen (→) and mucus).

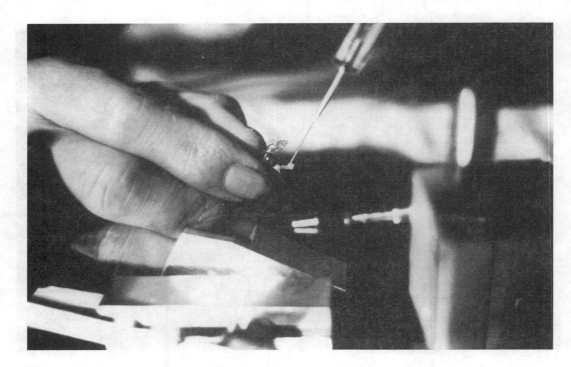

FIGURE 15. Obtaining semen by taking semen into the syringe.

FIGURE 16. Injecting semen.

Queen production with *A. cerana* provides a challenge to bee breeders for the propagation of bee stock in a selection program in the future. Easier rearing of many queens will predictably improve stock more rapidly (Rinderer 1986). In the future, *A. cerana* will probably become the favoured species for commercial beekeeping in tropical and subtropical Asia, especially if the problems of queen production and absconding can be solved.

ACKNOWLEDGEMENTS

The preparation of this review and the newly reported research were done in cooperation with Dr. Lai You-sheng, Division of Apiculture, Guangdong Entomological Institute, People's Republic of China. Drs. T.E. Rinderer and H.A. Sylvester made several useful suggestions for improvements on earlier manuscript drafts.

REFERENCES

Adlakha, R.L. 1971. Preliminary studies on the mating behaviour of *Apis mellifera* and *Apis indica* queens and their age of starting oviposition. XXIII International Beekeeping Congress, pp. 420-425.

Dietz, A. 1983. An accelerated honey bee queen rearing method. Journal of the Georgia Entomological Society, 18: 145-151.

Dietz, A., M.T. Sanford and Y. Lensky. 1975. Mating success of virgin queen honey bees of different ages (*Apis mellifera ligustica*). Journal of the Georgia Entomological Society, 10: 296-300.

Dzierzon, J. 1845. Gutachten uber die von Herrn Direktor Stohrin eraten und zweiten Kapitel des General-Gutachtens aufgestellten Fragen. Bienenzeitung, 1, pp. 109-113, 119-121.

Doolittle, G.M. 1915. Scientific queen rearing. American Bee Journal. Hamilton, Ill., pp. 21-46.

Fang, Y.Z. 1984. The present status and development plan of keeping European bees (*Apis mellifera*) in tropical and sub-tropical regions of China. Proceedings of the Expert Consultation on Beekeeping with *Apis mellifera* in Tropical and Sub-tropical Asia. Rome. FAO. pp 142-147.

Gary, N.E. 1975. Activities and behaviour of honey bees. *In*: The Hive and The Honey Bee. Dadant and Sons, Inc. Hamilton, Ill., pp. 185-264.

Gong, Y., Q. Zhang and R. Su. 1987. Observation and discussion on Chinese bee mating biology. Proceedings of the XXXIst International Apicultural Congress, Warsaw, Poland, pp. 184-186.

Harbo, J.R. 1976. The effect of insemination on the egg-laying behaviour of honey bees. Annals of the Entomological Society of America, 69: 1036-1038.

Hoshiba, H. 1984. The C-banding analysis of the diploid male and female honeybee (*Apis mellifera*). Proceedings of Japan Academy, 60 (Ser.8): 238-240.

Hoshiba, H., J. Okada and A. Kusanagi. 1981. The diploid drone of *Apis cerana japonica* and its chromosomes. Journal of Apicultural Research, 20: 145-147.

Johansson, T.S.K. and M.P. Johansson. 1973. Methods for rearing queens. Bee World, 54(4): 149-175.

Kulincevic, J.M. 1986. Breeding accomplishments with honey bees. *In*: Bee Genetics and Breeding. T.E. Rinderer (ed.). Academic Press, N.Y., pp. 391-413.

Lai, Y. 1982. Chinese Beekeeping Handbook. Division of Apiculture, Guangzhu, China (in Chinese).

Laidlaw, H.H. Jr and J.E. Eckert. 1962. Queen Rearing. Dadant & Sons, Hamilton, Ill.

Laidlaw, H.R. Jr. 1979. Contemporary Queen Rearing. Dadant & Sons, Hamilton, Ill.

Liu, Z. 1984. Apiculture in Guangdong Province. Division of Apiculture, Guangzhu, China (unpublished observation).

Pothichot, S. and S. Wongsiri. 1987. Research on Chinese bee, *Apis cerana cerana*, queen rearing. Report to Chulalongkorn University (unpublished observation).

Rinderer, T.E. 1986. Selection. *In*: Bee Genetics and Breeding. T.E. Rinderer (ed.). Academic Press, N.Y., pp. 305-319.

Ruttner, F. 1985. Characteristics and geographic variability of *Apis cerana* Fabr. Proceedings of the XXXth International Apicultural Congress, Nagoya, Japan. pp. 49-50.

Ruttner, F. 1986. Geographical variability and classification. *In*: Bee Genetics and Breeding. T.E. Rinderer (ed.). Academic Press, N.Y., pp. 23-52.

Ruttner, F., J. Woyke and N. Koeniger. 1972. Reproduction in *Apis cerana*. 1. Mating behaviour. Journal of Apicultural Research, 11(3): 141-146.

Ruttner, F., J. Woyke and N. Koeniger. 1973. Reproduction in *Apis cerana*. 2. Reproductive organs and natural insemination. Journal of Apicultural Research, 12(1): 21-34.

Sanford, M.T., A. Dietz and Y. Lensky. 1975. Experimental introduction and acceptance of aged virgin honey bee queens (*Apis mellifera ligustica*). Journal of the Georgia Entomological

Society, 10: 291-296.

Sharma, P.L. 1960. Observation on the swarming and mating habits of the Indian honeybee. Bee World, 41(5): 121-125.

Wongsiri, S. 1984. Beekeeping in China. Science, Science Society of Thailand, 39(8): 418-420 (in Thai).

Wongsiri, S., Y. Lai and Z. Liu. 1986. Beekeeping in the Guangdong province of China and some observations on the Chinese honey bee *Apis cerana cerana* and the European honey bee *Apis mellifera ligustica*. American Bee Journal, 126: 748-752.

Wongsiri, S., S. Pothichot and F. Chao. 1988. Queen rearing with *Apis cerana* in Thailand. Proceedings of the Fourth International Conference on Apiculture in Tropical Climates, Cairo, Egypt. pp. 466-470.

Wongsiri, S., C. Lekprayoon, S. Pothichot and Y.S. Lai. 1989. Efficiency of crossing the Chinese strain *Apis cerana cerana* with the Thai strain *Apis cerana indica* (Apidae: Hymenoptera) by artificial insemination. Honeybee Science, 10(3): 112-119.

Woyke, J. 1973. Instrumental insemination of *Apis cerana indica* queens. Journal of Apicultural Research, 12(3): 151-158.

Woyke, J. 1975. Natural and instrumental insemination of *Apis cerana indica* in India. Journal of Apicultural Research, 14(3/4): 153-159.

Woyke, J. 1979. Sex determination in *Apis cerana indica*. Journal of Apicultural Research, 18: 122-127.

Woyke, J. 1986. Sex determination. *In*: Bee Genetics and Breeding. T.E. Rinderer (ed.). Academic Press, N.Y., pp. 91-115.

Woyke, J. and Z. Jasinski. 1973. Influence of external conditions on the number of spermatozoa entering the spermatheca of instrumentally inseminated honeybee queens. Journal of Apicultural Research, 12: 145-149.

CHAPTER 10

ARTIFICIAL CONTROL OF THE MATING FLIGHT TIME OF HONEYBEES BY PHOTOPERIODIC TREATMENT WITHIN THE HIVE

T. YOSHIDA and M. SASAKI

INTRODUCTION

The difficulty in breeding honeybees is often attributed to the facts that mating sites are far from colonies and that honeybees never mate on the ground. This has long prevented programmed natural mating for effective selection of desirable bee genetic lines. Recent advances in instrumental insemination have made it possible to hybridize desired strains or varieties without using spatially-isolated places (Ruttner 1976). However, the artificially-inseminated queens require a longer preovipositional period and tend to be less vigorous than naturally-mated queens (Harbo and Szabo 1983). We tried to control the timing of natural mating by photoperiodic treatment for both chronobiological and possible commercial applicability reasons.

MATERIALS AND METHODS

Apis cerana japonica was used for flight-time studies of queens. *Apis mellifera* was used for flight-time studies of drones and to check the possible side-effect of the photoperiodic treatment on worker foraging activity. A glass observation hive (for drones) and 5 nucleus hives with glass lids (for queens) were placed in a darkroom at 25°C. The hive entrances were connected to the outside by a light-tight passage. Light-dark (LD) regimes in the darkroom and, consequently, within the hives, were controlled by a 24-h time switch. Light sources were 15W white fluorescent tubes and/or tubes emitting additional UV (Matsushita Electric, FL10, BA-37). Light intensity on the comb surface ranged from 5 to 50 lux. Drone flight time was evaluated by counting the outgoing and returning drones for 10 min every 30 min. The queens' movements to the outside were read from continuous video records by a video monitor system of the transparent passage. Queens were monitored even during the scotophase by using a red safety light.

An *A. mellifera* colony was reared in a modified Langstroth hive placed outside. The hive had a light-tight entrance attachment and no light leaked in from the outside. The inside of the hive was lit by fiber optics. Outgoing and returning drones were counted by eye and worker activity was automatically monitored by an infrared beam also fitted in the attachment. Environmental conditions such as air temperature, cumulative radiation, wind speed, and precipitation were also recorded automatically.

RESULTS AND DISCUSSION

Control of drone flight time

First we checked the normal flight time of drones in the experimental *A. mellifera* colony under an LD 12:12 regime with light-on at 0600 and light-off at 1800 (Fig. 1). On 26 September 1986, the period during which drones flew was from 1300 to 1600 with the peak activity at around 1500. This agrees with the time of drone flight of intact colonies in the natural mating season in May. When the LD regime inside the colony was advanced by 3 h, drones began to fly at 1030. When the advancing LD phase shift was 5 h (photophase 0100 to 1300), the time of drone flights ranged from 0830 to 1230, indicating that the phase of the drones' circadian rhythm had been advanced by approximately 4.5 h (Fig. 1). There was no overlap between the artificially shifted phase and the natural one.

As shown in Figure 2, the transient time was about 3 days for each of the first 3 h and the additional 2 h of phase advance. However, phase delay took longer. The phase is still transient at 6 days after returning to the original LD scheme. This is inconsistent with the usual behaviour of circadian rhythmicity.

Control of queen flight time

Queen flight time was evaluated by monitoring the movement of queens of *A. cerana* in the transparent passage to the outside. It was also controllable, as is evident from Figure 3 when the internal photophase was from 0100 to 1300. The earliest queen passage to the outside was seen at 0852 and the latest one was seen at 1248, which is about 4 h earlier than the normal queen flight time.

Possible side effects on worker activity

Reduction of foraging activity in total darkness within the hive during the day time was checked by

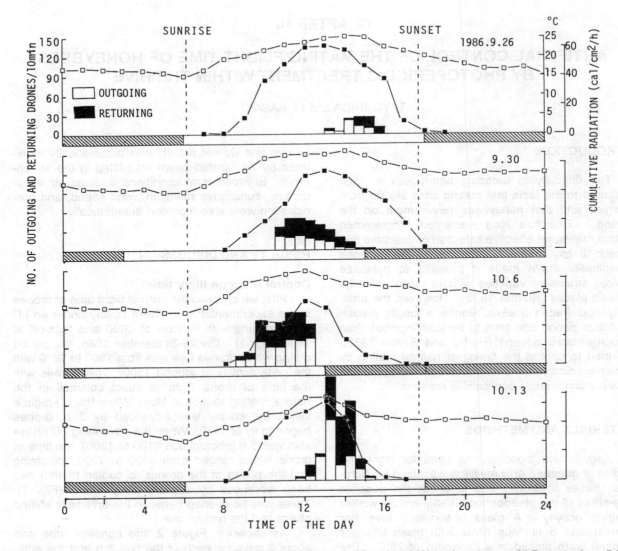

FIGURE 1. Advancement of the drone flight time of *Apis mellifera* by shifting the phase of LD cycle 3 or 5 h.

two different systems. In the *A. mellifera* colony placed outside (see Methods), there was little or no inhibition of worker activity and normal foraging continued until dusk. However, significant reduction of foraging activity was monitored in *A. cerana* nucleus colonies. This point should be reinvestigated, especially in relation to the possible "Social Zeitgeber" from foragers. On the other hand, newly-mated queens began to lay eggs normally while in the shifted LD regime.

Applied aspects

The time of drone and queen flights was well synchronized even under a 5 h phase-advanced regime (Figs. 1 and 2). As has been mentioned (Sasaki 1990), this implies that chronological repro-

ductive isolation could be artificially induced. This might be applicable to: maintenance of at least two pure lines of different varieties in sympatric condition; and programmed crossing with natural mating. As far as we could tell from the nucleus hives, which were placed side-by-side but marked with different colour patterns, virgin queens could discriminate their own hives even when the hives were closely aligned. This makes it possible to construct joined nuclei for collective photoperiodic treatment. A drone-supplying colony with synchronized LD regime may be required, especially for the cross between different strains. Any possible adverse effect on foraging, if it occurs, can be ignored because the treatment is not for honey production.

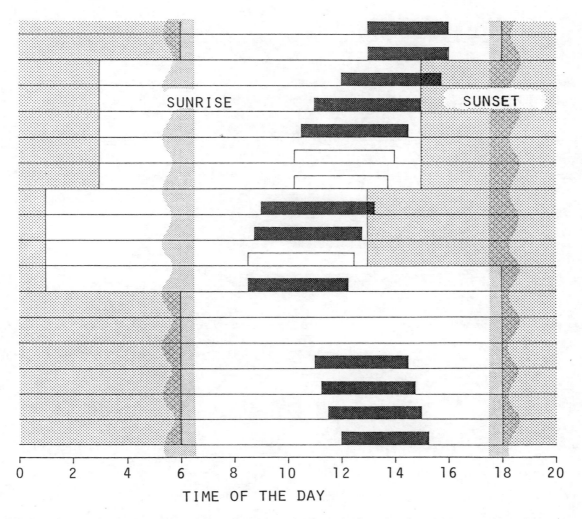

FIGURE 2. Schematic representation of the transient state of phase shifting. Timings shown with black bars were estimated from partial records. There was no flight in the first two days of returning phase because of rain.

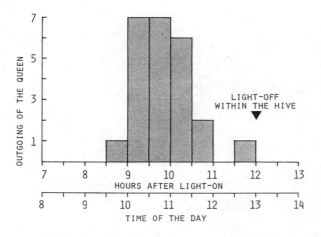

FIGURE 3. Queen flight time under 5 h phase-advanced state.

REFERENCES

Harbo, J.R. and T.I. Szabo. 1983. A comparison of instrumentally inseminated and naturally mated queens. Journal of Apicultural Research, 23: 31-36.

Ruttner, F. (Ed.) 1976. The instrumental insemination of the queen bee, its origin and development. Printing house of Apimondia, Bucharest.

Sasaki, M. 1990. Photoperiodic regulation of honeybee mating-flight time: Exploitation of innately phase-fixed circadian oscillation. Advances in Invertebrate Reproduction, 5: 503-508.

SUNSET

TIME OF THE DAY

FIGURE 2. Schematic representation of the transient state of phase shifting. Timing is shown with black bars when exhibited from plot of records. There was no flight in the first two days' phase-shifting phase because of ...

REFERENCES

Hardie, J.R., and T.H. Stace. 1983. A comparison of instantaneously insemnated and naturally mated aphens. Journal of Applied Insect Research 23:91.

Lumb, F.Sd. 1975. The instrumental insemination of the queen bee. Its origin and development. Printing house of Apimondia, Bucharest.

Saaez, M. 1990. Photoperiodic regulation of honey bee mating flight time. Exploitation of innately fixed circadian oscillation. Advances in Invertebrate reproduction, 5:605-608.

FIGURE 3. Queen flight line under 3 h flower, advanced state

SECTION IV: BEE BOTANY, FORAGING,

AND POLLINATION

CHAPTER 11

BEE BOTANY: POLLINATION, FORAGING AND FLORAL CALENDARS

P.G. KEVAN

Flowers are the mainstay of bees' lives. From flowers they obtain pollen, the protein-rich food used mostly to feed the brood, and nectar, the carbohydrate fuel for flight, foraging, hive activity and for developing brood. Ultimately, beeswax is made from nectar, physiologically processed within the bee and secreted by the wax glands. The bees are automated micro-manipulators by which man can harvest floral resources which would be otherwise unobtainable. These micro-manipulators also work to bring about pollination, which is absolutely required by many economically important plants if a crop is to be produced. Other crop plants benefit from cross-pollination, and some do not require it.

Although many kinds of insects visit flowers of crop plants, weeds and the natural vegetation (Kevan and Baker 1983), honeybees are the most important pollinators in agriculture. Other bees and other insects may be useful for specific crops and are invaluable in their roles in the pollination of the native flora. The process of pollination involves the movement of pollen, each grain of which is a microscopic male plant in haploid (i.e. half the number of chromosomes of the parent plant) form. This pollen must move from the anthers, in which it is produced, to the stigma of the female parts of a flower. If this takes place within the same flower or same plant, it is self-pollination. If flowers of different plants of the same species are involved, it is cross-pollination. Many plants can self-pollinate automatically and do so regularly to produce a crop, others can do so but favour cross-pollination by the structure of the flowers or an off-set in the timing of the release of pollen and receptivity of the stigma. Other plants require cross-pollination and have incompatibility mechanisms which prevent self-pollen from developing on the stigma (Figure 1). There are also plants which set fruit without pollination. This is called apomixis as the shuffling of genes (mixis), which is brought about by sexual reproduction, does not take place. There are many examples of these reproductive strategies in crop plants. A few crop plants produce fruit without seeds. This is called parthenocarpy and pollination is not required.

Once the pollen has arrived on a receptive stigma of the right kind, pollination is complete and it germinates. The cell nuclei leave the grain and migrate down the pollen tube as it grows through the female parts of the flower and into the ovary. There, the process of double fertilization takes place, involving two nuclei from the pollen (sperm nuclei) and two from the ovule, and embryo, seed and fruit development proceed.

Pollinators do not render this service to plants for no return. It is thought that pollination in primitive flowering plants was accomplished by pollen-feeding beetles but for advanced pollinators, nectar is the main reward they obtain.

Nectar contains a variety of carbohydrates, mostly sucrose, glucose and fructose. The ratio of these sugars influences the quality of honey and its tendency to crystallize. Some minor sugars found in nectar, such as lactose, galactose and raffinose are poisonous to honeybees. Nectar also contains other minor constituents, such as amino acids, lipids, ascorbic acid, minerals and sometimes phenolics and poisonous alkaloids. The latter two are more common in the nectars of tropical lowland plants than in temperate zone plants. Sometimes minerals, such as potassium, may make nectar undesirable to honeybees.

Pollen contains proteins, peptides, amino acids, lipids, starch, carbohydrates, minerals and vitamins and may have oils externally to act as a scent attractant and to help the grains adhere to the pollinators.

In foraging for nectar or pollen bees have developed strategies which increase the efficiency of cross-pollination. Bees do not forage enthusiastically on very dilute nectars (less than 10% sugar): the energy cost of foraging is not met by energy gain in the nectar. Thus, bees may wait until nectar evaporates to become sugary enough to be worth harvesting. Honeybees taste threshold for sugar solution is at about 10%. Highly concentrated nectar (60% or more) is viscous and cannot be sucked up as quickly by foraging bees, thus the constraints of speed and time enter the picture. Honeybees communicate between each other to indicate good nectar sources but other bees work more individualistically. Once at a nectar source, a patch of flowers, bees proceed from one flower to another so as to maximize energy gain and minimize energy expenditure. They do this by changing the direction of flight, moving rapidly in a nectar rich patch. This way they stay longer in the patch and visit more flowers. They also forage by climbing up tight vertical arrays

Selfing and Crossing

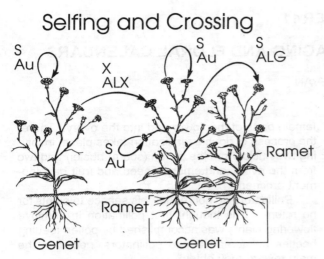

FIGURE 1. Pollen movement in self- (S) and cross-pollination (X) showing autogamy (Au), allogamy (AL) and geitonogamy (G).

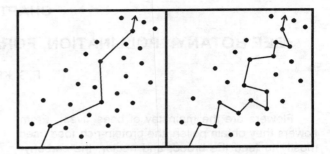

FIGURE 2. Path of pollinator foraging at a patch of poorly or non-rewarding flowers (left) and a patch of richly rewarding flowers (right). Note the overall "forwarding" motion, but shorter hops and sharper angles between flowers in the richly rewarding patch.

of flowers, and flying down to the next array. If flowers are more spaced on such arrays, as in trees, then they should fly up between plants and fly down the longer zig-zag route on a particular plant. Figures 2 to 4 summarize these patterns of movement.

Bees not only learn the location of plants and nectar sources, they also learn how to manipulate flowers efficiently. Complex flowers take longer for the bees to learn, but the rewards are greater as fewer bees forage on them. Bees develop floral constancy by which they forage from only one species of plant. In this way they can forage efficiently by reacting rapidly to the image of the flower (search image) and then manipulating it rapidly in an assembly-line familiarity manner. Through this constancy, pollen is efficiently moved within the population of a species of plant.

Bees prefer to forage close to the hive as in this way they expend less energy to bring back more. Nevertheless, European honeybees forage over long distances (several kilometres if need be) but cannot produce as much honey. They spend more time in travel and burn energy fast while flying. The Asiatic hive bee, A. cerana, does not forage over such long distances, staying within a kilometre or so of the hive, at least in Sri Lanka (Punchihewa et al. 1985).

It is important for beekeepers to understand something of the biology of the plants from which the bees acquire their food. Some flowers, such as poppies and some pulses, produce only pollen. Other produce nectar and pollen. Not all flowers produce the same amounts of nectar, nor nectar of the same quality for honey. Some flowers produce nectar deeply hidden within and which honeybees

cannot obtain. It is not enough to have flowers for beekeeping, the flowers must be of the right kind. Thus, studies in bee botany need to include: first, the identification of the flora for beekeeping and then an evaluation of the species in terms of their nectar and pollen production as those relate to bee foraging.

Another important aspect of bee botany is the flowering time of important bee plants. This is particularly valuable information for planning management schedules. Good pollen and nectar availability will stimulate active foraging, brood rearing and rapid colony growth in the bees. The beekeeper should be ready for adding supers to hives, making splits, rearing queens, etc. before colonies start to build up. In this way the best conditions can be used to full advantage. At times of heavy nectar flows, the honey crop can be predicted to be high. Supering must be planned and extracting equipment readied. At times when there is a dearth of flowers, nectar or pollen, beekeepers must also be ready. They may wish to leave honey in the hive, feed sugar water or pollen substitute, or any of these in combination. The length of the dearth is an important factor as that determines how much food the bees in a colony of a certain size must have.

A floral calendar, which catalogues the flowers, their value to bees, their abundance and time and duration of bloom, contains essential information for sound management in beekeeping. Floral calendars need to be produced for the ecological regions in which beekeeping is practised. Sometimes, especially in mountainous or hilly country, the ecological regions can be quite small and diverse in terms of their floras.

Floral calendars for several regions can be used to plan for migratory beekeeping. When dearth commences in one ecological region, the bees can be moved to another where bee flowers are abun-

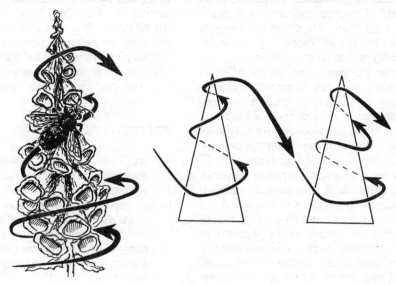

pollinator movements from bottom to top - both on a large inflorescence and on plants

FIGURE 3. Pollinator movement on vertical arrangement of flowers in and between inflorescences. Note, pollen is taken from younger flowers in male phase of one plant to older flowers in female phase of the next.

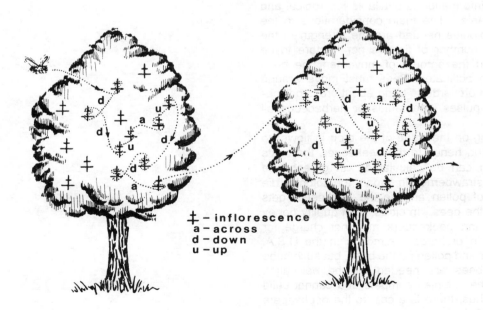

‡ – inflorescence
a – across
d – down
u – up

FIGURE 4. Generalized foraging path of large bees on flowering trees with inflorescences: based on several species of large bees in two genera *Bombus* and *Xylocopa* on eight species of tree in seven genera from temperate Canada and Scandinavia and the tropics of Indonesia, Malaysia, and the Maldive Islands. Upward movements on inflorescences, whether upright or pendant, are the general rule with shallow to steep downward and lateral movements between well separated inflorescences (*d* and *a*). If inflorescences are close together the bees trend upwards or laterally (*u* and *a*).

dant. In this way, extra honey crops can be harvested.

For keeping bees for pollination purposes, floral calendars are useful. For crop pollination it is desirable to have strong colonies. Thus, the beekeepers should build up the colonies at places of good nectar and pollen availability some weeks before they are needed on the crops. Some crops do not offer all the resources needed by bees to continue colony growth, or at least rapid colony growth. Thus, colonies used for pollination may become weakened, especially in greenhouses and beekeepers may wish to remove the bees to better forage after the pollination season for the crop in question is over.

Keeping bees for pollination purposes requires not only a knowledge of floral calendars in general, but also a knowledge of the flowers in the vicinity of the crop to be pollinated. Sometimes other plants compete with the crop for pollinators as happens in pear orchards and cranberry bogs in Canada and the U.S.A. Pears produce weak nectar, cranberries produce little pollen and nectar: both are unattractive to bees. Thus, bees will forage elsewhere if there is a choice.

The number of colonies needed to pollinate a given crop varies with the crop. Recommendations for temperate zone crops are given in various manuals, but little information is available for tropical and sub-tropical Asia. The main considerations in the number of colonies needed are the strength of the colonies, the number of flowers per hectare to be pollinated and the amount of movement the bees must have to pollinate. Bees must move around much more in orchards to bring about cross-pollination than on pulses, vegetables or herbaceous oil plants.

Depending on the value of the crop in flower to honeybees, and hence to the beekeeper, the costs for pollination can be calculated. In greenhouse pollination of strawberries in Japan, the colonies die out for lack of pollen and so the beekeeper gets nothing from the bees. In citrus, high quality honey is produced and beekeepers may not charge for putting bees in orchards. Almonds in the U.S.A. provide nectar and pollen for the bees, but such huge numbers of bees are needed for the pollination service that the colonies compete and cannot build up rapidly. Thus, there is a cost to the beekeepers whose bees of elsewhere would be more productive. In as much as there is usually a charge for bees for pollination on crops, the growers paying for the service want to be sure that the bees will do the job. Obviously, a beekeeper with bees available for pollination must be able to assure the growers that he understands the requirements in which the pollination services are needed.

The fundamental importance to beekeeping of understanding bee botany, foraging behaviour of bees and pollination is clear. However, beekeepers cannot be expected to undertake detailed studies themselves. This research necessary to build up the body of knowledge upon which the beekeeping industry can rely must be done by trained researchers at universities, colleges and government laboratories working together with beekeepers.

REFERENCES

Kevan, P.G. and H.G. Baker. 1983. Insects as flower visitors and pollinators. Annual Review of Entomology, 28: 407-453.

Punchihewa, R.W.K., N. Koeniger, P.G. Kevan and R.M. Gadawski. 1985. Observation on the dance communication and natural foraging ranges of *Apis cerana*, *Apis dorsata* and *Apis florea* in Sri Lanka. Journal of Apicultural Research, 24: 168-175.

CHAPTER 12

BEE BOTANY IN TROPICAL ASIA, WITH SPECIAL REFERENCE TO PENINSULAR MALAYSIA

R. KIEW

Of all the bees in Malaysia, *Apis cerana indica* is the only species that can readily be kept in hives, and thus it holds the greatest potential for beekeeping. However, the history of modern beekeeping in Malaysia is still young and so many problems need to be faced to make beekeeping more productive and profitable.

Although this chapter deals with aspects of bee botany, in particular the problems of obtaining adequate forage, it is necessary to stress that in Malaysia the colonies used are basically wild colonies, and within the same area the annual honey harvest can vary between colonies from nothing to about 5 kg (Mardan and Kiew 1985). It is clear then, that of equal importance in the improvement of the honey yield is the selection and breeding of high-yielding colonies.

One of the major factors that impedes honey production in Malaysia is the lack of abundant food supplies throughout the year. This may come as a surprise to those from temperate countries who are impressed by the profusion of plants in the tropics. However, because plants flower throughout the year, they tend to present relatively fewer flowers at any one time. In addition, because *A. cerana* has evolved in warmer regions, it has not needed to evolve hoarding behaviour which results in a large honey surplus to tide it over a season of inactivity. This means that colonies can survive at a baseline level for most of the year.

However, in contrast to plants of open areas, many of the forest trees in Malaysia are distinctly seasonal in their flowering. It is the native fruit trees, such as rambutan *Nephelium lappaceum* (Sapindaceae) and durian *Durio zibethinus* (Bombacaceae), that allow honey surpluses to be built up during their short and intense flowering seasons. Perhaps surprisingly too, there are dearth periods of flowering in equatorial Malaysia, not only during the rainy season (November-December), but also at other times of year, for example in June after the main flowering season. It is necessary then to devise ways to provide sufficient forage during these dearth periods or else the colonies of *A. cerana* tend to abscond.

FLOWERING SEASONS IN MALAYSIA

The main flowering season (including the refoliation of rubber) begins in February with a sequence of species in flower until May. The major nectar sources during this period, which are grown on a plantation scale, are first the refoliation of rubber *Hevea brasiliensis* (Euphorbiaceae) in February, followed by the flowering of rambutan and durian (February and March). The nectar source in rubber is the extrafloral nectaries on the young leaves. In Malaysia this nectar source is only just beginning to be exploited, compared with India where rubber honey accounts for between a third to a half of all honey produced (Suryanarayana 1983).

It is interesting to note that rambutan (and also pulasan *Nephelium mutabile*, which flowers less regularly than rambutan from one year to another) are members of the Sapindaceae to which litchi *Litchi chinensis*, longan *Dimocarpus longan* and soapnut *Sapindus* spp. all belong. All these species are major honey plants: litchi in Bangladesh (Dewan 1983), Burma (Zmarlicki 1984), China (Lui 1985), northern India (Seethalakshmi 1983) and northern Thailand (Akratanakul 1984); longan in China, Sri Lanka (Baptist and Punchihewa 1983) and northern Thailand; and soapnut in coastal areas of India. One of the highest honey yields for *A. cerana*, 15-20 kg per annum, is reported for litchi honey in China (Lui 1985).

Flowers of the Sapindaceae are not typical "bee flowers" as judged by their floral structure. Rambutan flowers are small, open, greenish-brown and produce a slight fruity scent. Rambutan is not pollinated by bees, but is apomictic; the stamens in the hermaphrodite flower do not open to release pollen (male trees are not grown as they do not produce fruit). Neither is the durian flower pollinated by bees. It is a well-known night-flowering bat pollinated flower. Bees, *Apis dorsata* as well as *A. cerana*, collect nectar the subsequent morning.

The nectar flow of this main flowering season of rambutan and durian can be tapped by transporting hives to the plantations for the duration of their flowering season. This strategy is also used in India for the refoliation of rubber for its 2-2.5 month season (Suryanarayana 1983).

This major flowering season is followed by a dearth period in June. A second minor flowering season occurs between July and September. Flowering is usually less intense and more prolonged, except for rambutan, which in some years flowers more heavily during this second flowering period. Next comes the dearth period in November and December associated with the rainy season, when not only are bees less active, but there is some suggestion that flowering in non-seasonal species such as coconut *Cocos nucifera* (Palmae) is also depressed.

NON-SEASONAL FLOWERING BEE PLANTS

The challenge to the bee botanist is therefore to recommend species that can provide adequate forage throughout the year so that the colony is strong and can take full advantage of the major flowering seasons of the seasonal plants and secondly so it can maintain itself during the dearth periods.

Tropical regions have a wealth of flowering plants (8,000 species for Peninsular Malaysia alone) and it is not surprising that the list of plants visited by *A. cerana* in cultivated areas exceeds 90 species and is continually growing (Kiew and Muid 1991). In areas adjacent to forest, the number of species is even greater.

In Malaysia, most commercial beekeeping is carried out in areas with coconut, which is now often intercropped with cacao (*Theobroma cacao*, Sterculiaceae). Other areas with potential are starfruit-growing areas (*Averrhoa carambola*, Oxalidaceae) and areas with mixed farming. Coconut and starfruit flower throughout the year. Coconut supplies both pollen and nectar, but throughout its range, although it is a reliable honey plant, annual honey yields are low. Yields are up to 10 kg per colony, but 4-5 kg is more usual, in Malaysia (Mardan and Osman 1983), Sri Lanka (Baptist and Punchihewa 1983) and southern Thailand (Akratanakul 1984). Starfruit is primarily a nectar plant, so an additional source of pollen needs to be provided. In starfruit plantations, there is the additional management problem of insecticide spraying during the flowering periods.

Plants recommended for planting for additional bee forage include those which flower throughout the year and produce a good supply of nectar, pollen or both. These should be planted close to the hive and in sufficient abundance to attract the bees. *A. cerana* forages within 500 m (and usually within 300 m) of the hive, but it will forage further afield for preferred food sources. In addition, these plants should be hardy and demand little care. Many potential bee plants are weeds. Most Malaysian weeds are not so vigorous that they cannot be kept under control by regular cutting rather than by using herbicides. Woody plants are preferred as they are less liable to be eaten by goats.

Flower preference by *A. cerana* can have economic implications. For example, in using it as a pollinator in starfruit plantations, observations indicate that it preferentially forages on *Asystasia intrusa* (Acanthaceae), an herbaceous weed, rather than on starfruit.

POLLEN SOURCES

Pollen resources are not a problem in coconut plantations, where a single coconut inflorescence produces over a thousand male flowers. However, there is a dearth of pollen in starfruit orchards and rubber plantations, where *A. cerana* forages primarily for nectar. Naturally occurring weeds which satisfy the pollen requirement include *Mimosa pudica* (Leguminosae), which is found throughout the region, and local weeds such as grasses and composites, the species of which vary from country to country. However, with proper management, pollen need never be a limiting factor as maize *Zea mays* (Gramineae) can easily be grown close to the hive to provide pollen throughout the year.

NECTAR SOURCES

Major nectar producing plants in Malaysia which result in surplus honey are rather few: coconut, starfruit, cashew *Anacardium occidentale* (Anacardiaceae), rubber, rambutan and durian, and plants used in mixed farming. The pollen spectrum of Malaysian honey (MaiShihah and Kiew 1989) confirms this (see below). In tropical Asia, a wider range of plants are important besides litchi, longan and soapnut. These include tamarind *Tamarindus indica* (Leguminosae) and neem *Azadirachta indica* (Meliaceae). Eucalyptus species (Myrtaceae) are playing an increasingly important role in reafforested regions in Burma (Zmarlicki 1984), China (Lui 1985), Thailand (Akratanakul 1984) and Sri Lanka where Baptist and Punchihewa (1983) report yields of 14-17 kg per season.

Minor bee plants within the Asian region are varied and include banana *Musa* cvs (Musaceae), *Eugenia* and *Syzygium* species (Myrtaceae), guava *Psidium guajava* (Myrtaceae), drumstick *Moringa oleifera* (Moringaceae) and species of *Vitex* (Verbenaceae).

Some plants should be avoided during the season when honey is accumulated as they make the honey taste unpleasant. In Malaysia, examples of these plants include oil palm *Elaeis guineensis* (Palmae), a copious pollen producer, and elephant tapioca (ubi gajah) *Manihot esculenta* cv. 'Dulcis' (Euphorbiaceae), which is a copious nectar producer. However, elephant tapioca is recommended as a nectar plant for dearth periods but it should be pruned of its flowers before the main flowering season begins (Muhammad Muid, pers. comm.).

Whether the bee forages on a particular plant depends on a number of factors whose relative importance has yet to be assessed. These factors include:

(i) the quantity and sugar concentration of nectar,
(ii) the types of sugars in nectar,
(iii) the timing of release of nectar,
(iv) the intensity of flowering and proximity to the hive.

Investigation of these factors has only just begun in Malaysia and facts and figures are known for only a handful of species.

(i) Quantity and sugar concentration of nectar

Table I gives nectar concentrations and volume of some important plants for *A. cerana* in Malaysia. Members of the Sapindaceae, the rambutan and soapnut, stand out as having high nectar concentrations. However, the majority have sugar concentrations below 25% and with a mean of 16.4% (Table II). The contents of the honey crop of bees returning to the hive have a similar concentration of 17% (Mai-Shihah 1987). This contrasts with figures given for *A. mellifera*, which is generally reported to forage for nectar with 30-50% sugars.

Other studies in the tropics (Table II) indicate that even for *A. mellifera* in the tropical lowlands, e.g. in Jamaica, it forages for nectar with a lower concentration (19-27%). There are two possible explanations for these lower nectar concentrations in the tropics. One is the effect of environmental factors. Nectar secreted by a plant tends to be more dilute when soil moisture is high (Fahn 1946), which it might be expected to be in the humid tropics. This is to some extent borne out by the differing nectar concentrations reported for *Tecomaria capensis* (Bignoniaceae) in drier regions (Mexico and Palestine) 18.4% and 20% compared with 12.7% in Malaysia. However, this cannot be the whole story, as 20% is still well below 30-50% reported for *A. mellifera*. Another explanation may be bee physiology. With higher ambient temperatures, less energy is expended in flight (hence less need for concentrated nectars), while more dilute nectars may be advantageous for thermoregulation by evapotranspiration during flight (M. Mardan, pers. comm.).

Nectar concentration frequently varies inversely with its volume and indeed rambutan besides being concentrated is also present in minute amounts. Two plants stand out in Table I as producing copious quantities of nectar, namely durian and *Tecomaria*. Durian is pollinated by bats and *Tecomaria* by sunbirds. In general, both bird and bat-pollinated flowers produce more nectar than those pollinated by insects.

(ii) Types of sugar in nectar

The few figures available for types of sugars in nectar of Asian plants are shown in Table III. Baker and Baker (1983) have already noted that although feeding experiments show that *A. mellifera* prefers sucrose dominated nectars, in practice in the wild, they will also take nectars with a predominance of hexoses. Table III shows that for the species so far tested, sucrose-dominated nectars and hexose-dominated nectars are in roughly equal proportions. Again, it is notable that members of the Sapindaceae, rambutan and soapnut, have sucrose-dominated nectars. However, it is too early to assess the effect of bee preference for sugar type in nectar as determining preference in foraging.

(iii) Timing of nectar section

The general daily pattern of nectar secretion for species such as *Asystasia intrusa* (Acanthaceae), *Callistemon speciosa* (Myrtaceae), *Tecomaria capensis*, and *Vitex pinnata* (Verbenaceae) is a major peak in the early morning, falling towards midday, probably as a result of evaporation, then another small peak in late afternoon (Che Tek Kamariah 1985). Concentration varies inversely with volume so the small afternoon peak is more concentrated than the larger morning peak.

A few species, such as coconut, Manila palm *Veitchia merrillii*, rambutan and coffee *Coffea canephora* (Rubiaceae) have a single peak of nectar secretion in the early morning. For exposed flowers such as those of rambutan or coconut, if the nectar is not collected by bees in the early morning, the nectar rapidly becomes viscous and dries up and is no longer available to the bee.

A third pattern is shown by relatively few species, such as *Antigonon leptopus* (Polygonaceae) or the thrum flowers of starfruit, which have a major peak in the afternoon.

The timing of nectar secretion has profound implications for bee foraging behaviour. Nectar from rambutan and coconut flowers needs to be collected before 10 a.m. For the heterostylous starfruit, the

TABLE I. Sugar concentrations and volume of nectars collected by *Apis cerana*.

Nectar Sources	Sugar Concentrations (%)		Volume (μl)
Major Nectar Sources:			
Litchi chinensis	62		
Nephelium lappaceum			
hermaphrodite flower	48.3		0.46
Sapindus emarginatus			
male	30		1.6
female	30		5.09
Cocos nucifera	24	(Burma)	
male	13.4*		
female	10-19*		
Averrhoa carambola			
pin	16.5		0.69
thrum	10.7		1.37
Durio zibethinus	13.5		600.0
Anacardium occidentale			
male	11.9		1.98
hermaphrodite	10.8		3.9
Minor Nectar Sources:			
Eupatorium odoratum	45		
Vitex pinnata	28*		1.69
Musa cv.	27.4	(Palestine)	
	24	(Burma)	
Antigonon leptopus	17.2	(Mexico)	4.02
	21.6*		1.03
Asystasia intrusa	23		1.09
	21.4*		0.97
Tecomaria capensis	21	(Palestine)	
	18.4	(Mexico)	11.33
	12.7*		7.84
Callistemon speciosa	6.7*		1.46
Coffea canephora	6*		0.54
Veitchia merrillii			
male	5.3*		1.69
female	7.3*		18.5

*unpublished data (Che Tek Kamariah 1985).

TABLE II. A comparison between tropical countries for nectar concentrations collected by *Apis* species.

Country	Bee	Nectar concentration (%)		No. species sampled
Malaysia	*A. cerana*	16.4	6-48	12
Jamaica	*A. mellifera*	21	19-27	14
Costa Rica	Honeybee	-	24-35	2

nectar secretion patterns are bound up with effecting cross-pollination between pin flowers (with a morning nectar peak) and the thrum flowers (with an afternoon nectar peak) (Phoon 1985).

To maximize honey production, the provision of bee forage with a good morning and a good afternoon peak may be necessary. It is possible that the ceiling of honey production in coconut plantations is the result of the single morning peak of nectar secretion by coconut and that higher yields may be possible by planting bee forage with a strong afternoon peak.

CHARACTERIZATION OF HONEY USING POLLEN TYPES

In Malaysia, demand exceeds supply for local honey, which commands high prices (M$25 per kilo, M. Mardan, pers. comm.) compared with imported honey from Australia or China (about M$9 per kilo). The preference for local honey is partly due to belief in its medicinal properties. There is therefore the temptation to sell adulterated honey. Mardan and Osman (1983) described the practice of adulteration of local honey with palm sugar (jaggery) as rampant,

TABLE III. Types of sugars in nectar collected by *Apis cerana*.

	Sucrose	Glucose	Fructose
Sucrose dominated:			
*Antigonon leptopus**	44.6	33.4	22.0
*Averrhoa carambola**	66.9	12.8	18.2
*Nephelium lappaceum**	78.3	5.0	8.8
Sapindus emarginatus	85.5	7.25	7.25
*Veitchia merrillii**	99.8	0.2	ND
*Vitex pinnata**	98.8	1.2	ND
Hexose dominated:			
*Anacardium occidentale**			
male	20.8	43.3	35.9
female	12.5	47.8	38.0
*Asystasia intrusa**	12.6	51.7	35.7
*Callistemon speciosa**	0.7	54.0	45.3
*Tecomaria capensis**	3.0	45.5	51.5
Tecoma stans	2	50	47

* analyses by I. Baker.

TABLE IV. Pollen spectrum of some Malaysia honeys.

Beekeeping Area	Pollen Types		
	Predominant (+45%)	Secondary (16-44%)	Minor (3-15%)
Coconut	Coconut (65-100%)	-	Coffee Starfruit Sago palm Compositae *Cleome*
Starfruit	Starfruit (70-90%)	-	*Acacia* *Leucaena* Compositae Coconut
Mixed farming	-	Coconut Guava Starfruit	*Veitchia* *Acacia* *Sporobolus*

Mimosa pudica is excluded as being over-represented.

even to the extent of adding a dead bee to make the "honey" look more authentic. As yet, there are no reported cases of passing off foreign honey as the local product.

With the expansion of beekeeping in Malaysia, particularly among the lower income groups, it is important that they are protected from competition from the sale of adulterated honey which also brings beekeeping in general into disrepute. In addition, as beekeeping becomes more sophisticated, unifloral honeys can be specifically labelled.

While the detection of adulteration with palm sugar is best detected by analysis of the sugars in honey, the problem of adulteration with foreign honeys and the determination of whether particular honeys are unifloral are best approached by the analysis of pollen in honey.

As a first step we (Kiew and Muid 1991) prepared a pollen atlas of Malaysian bee plants as a means of accurately identifying pollen. Analysis of pollen in honey then reveals the pollen spectrum for each type of honey. So far, we have analyzed honey from coconut, starfruit, rubber, and mixed farming areas, with a view to identifying marker pollen by which to distinguish Malaysian honey from foreign honey (MaiShihah and Kiew 1989).

MaiShihah (1987) has shown that honey from coconut or starfruit growing areas is unifloral (Table IV) compared with honey from a mixed farming area, which has a wider range of pollen types. Results for the pollen spectrum were remarkably constant between samples from different areas for coconut honey and starfruit honey. It would, therefore, be

valid to label and market these two honeys as unifloral.

Seethalakshmi (1983) found similar results for different types of Indian honeys, of which the majority were unifloral. He pointed out the interesting case of rubber honey, in which pollen is not present because the nectar is collected from the leaves not flowers. Instead of rubber pollen, coconut and *Mimosa pudica*, the pollen sources usually associated with rubber plantations, were the predominant pollen types in rubber honey.

This predominance of pollen from pollen source plants in honey, to which Seethalakshmi drew attention, was also found in Malaysian honey. *M. pudica* pollen was generally over-represented in most samples.

However, the range of pollen types in honey is small. In ten samples, MaiShihah and Kiew (1989) recorded a total of 26 species with a mean of 8 species (range 3-14) in any one sample. Seethalakshmi recorded a total of 44 species in 12 types of honey, for honeys from all over the Indian subcontinent. Again the mean number of species per honey type was low, with a mean of 6 (range 3-9). This supports the observation that if there is a good nectar or pollen source close to the hive, the bees will exploit rather few species.

Distinguishing Malaysian honey from honey from Australia or China presents no problem as none of the common Malaysian types of pollen (Table V) are found in these two foreign honey types (MaiShihah and Kiew 1989).

However, Malaysian honey has a short shelf life

TABLE V. Frequency of the presence of pollen types in Malaysian honeys.

Species	Frequency (%)
Coconut	100
Mimosa pudica and *M. invisa*	75
Starfruit	75
Asystasia intrusa	62
Sporobolus spp.	50

as it tends to ferment. During the pollen analysis, no fungal spores, in particular yeast, were encountered. The honey we used was freshly bottled, which may indicate that contamination by yeast in Malaysia is a post-harvest problem.

CONCLUSION

It is one thing to compile a list of plants visited by bees and to study their flowering seasons, pollen and nectar yields. It is quite another to assess their relative importance to the economy of the bee colony. MaiShihah (1991) has addressed this aspect by monitoring, among other things, the daily activities of colonies by sampling pollen and nectar loads of incoming bees in relation to honey storage in the hive.

Finally, I should emphasize that of equal importance to an understanding of bee botany in increasing honey yield is the management of the apiary, particularly the problem of overstocking, as well as the importance of genetic improvement of bee strains.

REFERENCES

Akratanakul, P. 1984. Beekeeping industry with *Apis mellifera* in Thailand. *In* Proceedings of the Expert Consultation on Beekeeping with *Apis mellifera* in tropical and sub-tropical Asia, Thailand. pp. 222-232.

Baker, H.G. and I. Baker. 1983. A brief historical review of the chemistry of floral nectar. *In* B. Bentley and T. Elias (eds.), The Biology of Nectaries. Columbia University Press, New York.

Baptist, B.A. and R.K.W. Punchihewa. 1983. A preliminary analysis of the principal factors which will affect apiary honey production in Sri Lanka.

In Proceedings of the Second Conference on Apiculture in Tropical Climates, New Delhi, 1980. pp. 87-99.

Che Tek Kamariah, K. 1985. Nilai gula dan struktur nektari bagi beberapa tumbuhan utama lebah Malaysia. Honours Project Thesis, Department Biology, Universiti Pertanian Malaysia.

Dewan, A.L. 1983. The role of the Central Bee Research Institute, Pune, in the process of development of apiculture in Bangla Desh. *In* Proceedings of the Second International Conference on Apiculture in Tropical Climates, New Delhi, 1980. pp. 24-28.

Fahn, A. 1946. Studies in the ecology of nectar secretion. Palestinian Journal of Botany, 41: 207-224.

Kiew, R. and M. Muid. 1991. Beekeeping in Malaysia: Pollen Atlas. Malaysian Beekeeping Research and Development Team, Universiti Pertanian Malaysia.

Lui, X. 1985. Advancing Chinese apiculture. *In* Proceedings of the Third International Conference on Apiculture in Tropical Climates, Nairobi, 1984. pp. 93-95.

MaiShihah, A. 1987. Kajian permulaan perlakuan lebah madu (*Apis cerana*) dalam pemilihan tumbuhan debunga dan nectar. Honours Project Thesis, Department Biology, Universiti Pertanian Malaysia.

MaiShihah, A. 1991. Foraging activities of *Apis cerana* in a coconut plantation. M.Sc. Thesis, Universiti Pertanian Malaysia.

MaiShihah, A. and R. Kiew. 1989. The pollen spectrum as a means of characterizing Malaysian honeys. *In* Proceedings of the Fourth International Conference on Apiculture in Tropical Climates, Cairo, 1988. pp. 274-278.

Mardan, M. and R. Kiew. 1985. Flowering periods of plants visited by honeybees in two areas of Malaysia. *In* Proceedings of the Third International Conference on Apiculture in Tropical Climates, Nairobi, 1984. pp. 209-216.

Mardan, M. and M.S. Osman. 1983. Beekeeping in coconut small holdings in Pontian, Johor, West Malaysia. *In* Proceedings of the Second International Conference on Apiculture in Tropical Climates, New Delhi, 1980. pp. 179-186.

Phoon, A.C.G. 1985. Pollination and fruit production of carambola, *Averrhoa carambola*, in Malaysia. *In* Proceedings of the Third International Conference on Apiculture in Tropical Climates, Nairobi, 1984. pp. 129-133.

Seethalakshmi, T.S. 1983. Melittopalynological investigations of some Indian honeys. *In* Proceedings of the Second International Conference on Apiculture in Tropical Climates, New Delhi,

1980. pp. 609-621.

Suryanarayana, M.C. 1983. The rubber tree (*Hevea brasiliensis*) - an important nectar source in the tropics. *In* Proceedings of the Second International Conference on Apiculture in Tropical Climates, New Delhi, 1980. pp. 656-658.

Zmarlicki, C. 1984. Evaluation of honey plants in Burma - a case study. *In* Proceedings of the Expert Consultation on Beekeeping with *Apis mellifera* in tropical and sub-tropical Asia, Thailand. pp. 57-76.

CHAPTER 13

POLLINATION MANAGEMENT PRINCIPLES

SOESILAWATI HADISOESILO

INTRODUCTION

Pollination is an essential stage in the reproduction of flowering plants. It is the transfer of pollen from the male to the female part of a flower (Chapter 11) (McGregor 1976; Crane and Walker 1984).

Many insects visit flowers of plants and play a vital role in their pollination. However, honeybees are the most important pollinators in agriculture because they develop floral constancy by which they forage from only one species of plant. Through this constancy, pollen is efficiently transferred within the population of a plant species. Moreover, honeybees are easily handled and manipulated and they can be concentrated within a crop to the degree desired (McGregor 1976; Kevan 1984).

The roles of honeybees in pollinating many crops has long been recognized. Moving honeybee colonies into a field crop is expected to improve crop productivity, yet the results are not always encouraging. The crop production does not always demonstrate promising increases as one anticipates.

There are several factors that might cause the failure to increase crop productivity, one of them being pollinator management. Beekeepers and/or growers often do not have enough knowledge on the pollination management principles, especially for those in the tropical and sub-tropical zones.

Many research workers have conducted research in crop pollination and have given recommendations on pollination management. Unfortunately, most of them deal with temperate crops and *Apis mellifera* as a pollinator. Research in the pollination management in the tropics, especially with *Apis cerana* as a pollinator, is urgently needed to suggest ways of improving crop productivity.

This chapter briefly discusses the principles of pollination management which include:
1. The distance of colonies to a field crop.
2. The number of colonies needed.
3. The distribution of colonies.
4. Plant competitors.
5. Floral calendars.
6. The time of colony introduction.

Jay (1986) provides a review of much of this topic in respect to the management of *A. mellifera* in temperate regions. Many of the principles he elucidates apply to *A. cerana*.

THE DISTANCE OF COLONIES TO A FIELD CROP

Because honeybees show a tendency to forage at the nearest location on any given species, it is important that colonies should be placed near the target crop (Gary 1969; Kevan 1984). Moreover, Gary (1969) stated that it is not uncommon that 50% of the bees forage on a crop within 300 m from the hive, even though *A. mellifera* forage over long distances when a particular plant species is not ubiquitous in the area.

Malakhova and Ponomareva (1977) observed that as the distance from an apiary increased, bee visitations to the apple flowers decreased markedly, thus the fruit sets were lower. Kurennoi (1977) also stated that the saturation of sunflower with bees was influenced by the location of the apiary in the immediate vicinity of the crop to be pollinated.

The right distance of colonies to the field crop is important to ensure that bees fly to pollinate the target crop. This distance is probably different for *A. mellifera* and *A. cerana*. *A. cerana* does not forage over such long distances as does *A. mellifera*, with the average foraging distance of *A. cerana* being less than a kilometre from the hive (Punchihewa *et al.* 1985; Kevan 1984; Sulaksono *et al.* 1986).

THE NUMBER OF COLONIES NEEDED

The fundamental consideration to achieve the desired level of pollination is whether enough bees visit the target crop (Gary 1969). Whether or not there are enough bees to visit the flowers will be determined by the number of colonies brought into the field. Nevertheless, the strength of colonies, the number of flowers to be pollinated, the presence of plant competitors, and the attractiveness of the flowers are the main considerations in the number of colonies needed (McGregor 1976; Kevan 1984).

The number of colonies needed to pollinate varies widely with the crop. Various authors recommended 1-2 strong colonies per hectare for sunflower. On the other hand, 8-15 colonies per hectare are recommended for mango because the flowers are not very attractive to honeybees, and tend to open in large numbers at a time (McGregor 1976).

The species of bee might also influence the

number of colonies needed because their foraging behaviours are different.

THE DISTRIBUTION OF COLONIES

The number of colonies per hectare alone is not too meaningful. Distribution of colonies to give thorough coverage of all blooms is highly important (McGregor 1976). Moreover, Free (1970) mentioned that bees tended to confine foraging to a small area during most of their foraging trips until the pollen and nectar rewards became reduced, thus the distribution of colonies in the field becomes a very important factor that will influence crop productivity.

The distribution of colonies will also vary with the crop. In almond orchards, colonies should be distributed in the orchards in small groups, 150-200 m apart (McGregor 1976), but in rape fields, colonies should be placed all around a field rather than clustered in one spot (Oschmann 1977). Jay (1986) has indicated that European honeybees seem to forage so as to distribute themselves throughout blooming crops. Thus special placement patterns may not be useful, at least on some crops.

The distribution of colonies is probably different if *A. cerana* is used for pollination instead of *A. mellifera*, however data are lacking for making recommendations

PLANT COMPETITORS

The attractiveness of any given species is a function of variables such as flavour, colour, nectar volume, sugar concentration, and fragrance (Frisch 1967). Even when apparently adequate foraging areas are located near the hive, a significant proportion of the colony population flies over and beyond nearby species to other species. It seems this is because of differences in the above factors. When all other factors are equal, however, greater bee populations fly to species that yield the greatest resources (Gary 1969).

Knowledge of the flowers in the vicinity of the crop to be pollinated is required (Kevan 1984). Other plants compete with the crop to be pollinated primarily because of deficiencies in nectar and pollen rewards produced by the target crop (Gary 1969). Savchenyuk (1977) observed that buckwheat growing in the vicinity of red clover distracted the bees from pollination of the latter. Buckwheat is a strong nectar-producing plant and as long as buckwheat is in bloom, bees do not pollinate red clover intensively. The influence of dandelions in detracting from honeybee pollination of apples is also well known (Free 1970).

To achieve the desired level of pollination, the presence of more attractive plants than the target crop should be avoided, so that bees will not forage elsewhere.

FLORAL CALENDARS

Adequate pollination which results in good crop yields requires strong colonies to pollinate. Floral calendars are very useful for keeping bees for pollination. It is important for beekeepers to plan their management schedule. They should build up their colonies so that they will have strong colonies by the time they are needed for pollination.

It is also important for beekeepers to know where to take their colonies after pollination is complete. Some crops do not offer all of the resources needed by the bees to continue their growth, thus colonies used for pollination become weakened. Therefore, beekeepers may wish to take their colonies to better forage (Kevan 1984).

THE TIME OF COLONY INTRODUCTION

The right time for introducing colonies into the fields needs to be established. Different plants might have different times for introduction although, according to Traynor (1966), it has been established that colonies brought into the orchard at first bloom work most efficiently. Colonies brought too early into the field fail to pollinate effectively because they establish flight patterns to other crops, which are difficult to break. Cirnu (1960, cited by McGregor 1976) recommended that colonies should be moved to sunflower fields when 3-5% of the plants are already in bloom. For pears, the recommendation is at 25% bloom (Free 1970).

For pollinating greenhouses, the time to move in colonies may differ from the time for pollinating an open field. Kitagawa (1986) mentioned that the best time for introduction of a colony in a greenhouse for strawberries is apparently 4-5 days after the blooming of the first flower when the anthers open and pollen emerges. If the colony is introduced at this time, all the flowers, including the ones which bloomed first, can be completely pollinated. If the colony is introduced earlier, there is no pollination work until the fourth day, and if the colony is introduced after the number of flowers ready for pollination has already increased, some flowers whose petals have already fallen will remain unpollinated.

REFERENCES

Crane, E. and P. Walker. 1984. Pollination Directory for World Crops. International Bee Research Association, London. 187 pp.

Frisch, K. von. 1967. The Dance Language and Orientation of Bees. The Belknap Press of Harvard University Press, Cambridge, Massachusetts. xiv + 566 pp.

Free, J.B. 1970. Insect Pollination of Crops. Academic Press, London. 544 pp.

Gary, N.E. 1979. Factors that affect the distribution of foraging honey bees. Proceedings of IVth International Symposium on Pollination. pp. 353-358.

Jay, S.C. 1986. Spatial management of honeybees on crops. Annual Review of Entomology, 31: 49-65.

Kitagawa, S. 1986. Pollination of strawberries in the green house by honeybees. Proceedings of the XXXth International Apicultural Congress. pp. 378-380.

Kevan, P.G. 1984. Bee botany: pollination, foraging and floral calendars. Proceedings of the Expert Consultation on Beekeeping with *Apis mellifera* in Tropical and Sub-Tropical Asia. Food and Agricultural Organization of the United Nations, Rome. pp. 51-56.

Kurennoi, N.M. 1977. Intensive bee pollination and increase in yield of sunflower. *In*: Pollination of agricultural crops by bees, Volume III. Mel'nichenko, A.N. (ed). Amerind Publishing Co., Pvt., Ltd., New Delhi. pp. 212-222.

Malakhova, L.P. and E.G. Ponomareva. 1977. Effect of bees as pollinator on apple production. *In*: Pollination of agricultural crops by bees, Volume III. Mel'nichenko, A.N. (ed). Amerind Publishing Co., Pvt., Ltd., New Delhi. pp. 350-353.

McGregor, S.E. 1976. Insect Pollination of Cultivated Crop Plants. Agricultural Handbook No. 496. U.S. Department of Agriculture, Washington, D.C. viii + 411 pp.

Oschmann, H. 1977. Experience of the German Democratic in organizing bee pollination of agricultural crops. *In*: Pollination of agricultural crops by bees, Volume III. Mel'nichenko, A.N. (ed). Amerind Publishing Co., Pvt., Ltd., New Delhi. pp. 80-85.

Punchihewa, R.W.K., N. Koeniger, P.G. Kevan and R.M. Gadawski. 1985. Observation on the dance communication and natural foraging ranges of *Apis cerana*, *Apis dorsata* and *Apis florea* in Sri Lanka. Journal of Apicultural Research, 24: 168-175.

Savchenyuk, D.M. 1977. Improving the qualities and accessibility of red clover nectar. *In* Mel'-nichenko, A.N. (ed.): Pollination of agricultural crops by bees, Volume III. Amerind Publishing Co., Pvt., Ltd., New Delhi. pp. 236-245.

Sulaksono, S., T. Suryati, Nismah and R.C.H. Susilo-hadi. 1986. Biologi *Apis cerana* dengan tekanan pada kegiatan mencari makan. Prosiding Lokakarya Pembudidayaan Lebah Madu Untuk Peningkatan Kesejahteraan Masyarakat. Perum Perhutani, Jakarta. pp. 49-64.

Thorp, R.W. 1979. Honey bee foraging behavior in California almond orchards. Proceedings of IVth International Symposium on Pollination. pp. 385-392.

Traynor, J. 1966. Increasing the pollinating efficiency of honey bees. Bee World, 47(3): 101-110.

CHAPTER 14

INSECT POLLINATION OF ECONOMICALLY IMPORTANT PLANTS OF TROPICAL AND SUBTROPICAL ASIA

P.G. KEVAN

The requirements for pollination by insects of crop plants throughout the world are presented in two encyclopedic volumes which summarize the state of knowledge on a crop by crop basis. These books, one by J.B. Free (1970) and another one by S.E. McGregor (1976), are indispensable as reference material for development in beekeeping and the role of bees and other insects in pollination. What also emerges from these books is the lack of knowledge about tropical and subtropical crops. Research in crop pollination in the tropics is urgently needed to fill the gaps in our knowledge, to resolve confusing and conflicting results of some studies and to suggest ways of improving crop productivity by pollinator management.

In this chapter, I will briefly discuss the pollination requirements of as many of the economically important plants of tropical and subtropical Asia as possible, making special references to bees as pollinators. I have divided the crops into:
1. Fruits and nuts.
2. Vegetables and pulses.
3. Cereals.
4. Drug, beverage, condiment and spice plants.
5. Oil crops.
6. Forage crops.
7. Timber trees and natural vegetation.
8. Fibre plants and rubber.

FRUITS AND NUTS

Tropical and subtropical fruits are very diverse. The pollination requirements of many are, at best, poorly understood.

In *Citrus*, the situation is complex. It seems that the mandarin oranges are dependent on and greatly benefit from cross-pollination. Pummelo should be inter-planted with other cultivars for cross-pollination and fruit set to take place. Oranges do not depend on insects for pollination, but may benefit from it. Lime pollination has not been well studied, but cross-pollination may be beneficial. In lemons the data are conflicting, ranging from statements about pollination by insects being completely unnecessary to outcrossing being required, depending perhaps on the variety of lemon considered. Grapefruits do not require cross-pollination. *Citrus* trees are excellent sources of nectar and pollen.

Apples (*Pyrus malus*) require inter-plantings of varieties and insect-mediated cross-pollination. Pear (*P. communis*) is similar, but is not a good bee plant as the nectar is watery: bees do collect pollen. Plums and prunes (*Prunus* spp.) are mostly self-incompatible, require insect pollination and offer good nectar and pollen forage for bees (Zmarlicki 1984 for *Pr. insitia* in Burma). Apricots (*Pr. armenica*) are variable in their pollinator requirements depending on variety. Cherries (*Prunus* spp.) mostly cannot self-pollinate, but some are self-compatible. Thus, inter-plantings of varieties and bees for pollination are recommended. Peach and nectarine (*Prunus persica*) pollination is not well studied, despite the economic importance of this crop. Although at least some varieties appear to be self-fruitful, cross-pollination by bees is recommended for good crops. All are good nectar and pollen plants for bees.

Avocado (*Persea gratissima*) is grown widely throughout Asia. It is dependent on cross-pollination by insects. Carambola or star fruit (*Averrhoa carambola*) and bilimbi (*A. bilimbi*) are heterostylous (i.e. having different forms of the same flower on different plants) and so show similar dependence. *Ziziphus* spp. (*Z. jujuba*, jujube and *Z. mauritiana*, ber), *Nephelium* spp. (*N. litchi*, *N. chiensis*, *N. lappaceum*, *N. longan*, litchi or lychee, rambutan and longan) are excellent honey plants and seem to depend on insect cross-pollination as well. Mango (*Mangifera indica*) requires insects for pollination, but cross-pollination between cultivars is not needed. Papaya (*Carica papaya*) has a complete breeding system of male, hermaphrodite (3 types) and female flowers in which the best fruit results from cross-pollination. Bees are recommended as pollinators. They collect pollen from male and hermaphrodite flowers. Persimmon (*Diospyros kaki*) has not been adequately investigated; some cultivars produce fruit without pollination, others cannot. Other *Diospyros* spp. (sapote, date plum, etc.) have not been studied. McGregor (1975) lists *D. discolor*, the mabolo, as dependent on insects for pollination. Honeybees are the most important pollinators of phalsa (*Grewia asiatica*) in India. In the loquat (*Eriobotrya japonica*) the pollination requirements are not understood.

The durian (*Durio zibethinus*) is cross-pollinated by bats. The flower are also an abundant source of nectar which is used by bees. It has a slimy consistency and an off-smell. The soursops and custard apples (*Annona* spp.) have not been studied in Asia, but the cherimolla (*A. cherimola*) of South America seems to require, at least partially, cross-pollination.

The breadfruit, jackfruit (*Artocarpus* sp.), mombins (*Spondias* spp.), jambus, jambolans and related plants (*Syzygium* and *Eugenia* spp.), bignay (*Antidesma* spp.), otaheite-gooseberry and mirobalan (*Phyllanthus* spp.), lingaro (*Eleagnus philippensis*), wampi (*Clausena lansium*), sapote relatives, star apple, sapodilla (*Manilkara achras*), egg fruit (*Pouteria campechiana*) introduced from South America, all probably benefit from insect pollination (McGregor 1975). The green sapote (*Calocarpum viride*), Runeala plum (*Flacourtia cataphracta*), kei apple and kitembilla (*Doryalis* spp.) require insect pollination (McGregor 1975). Other Indian plum relatives (*Flacourtia* spp.), mangosteens (*Garcinia* spp.), mamey apple (*Mammea americana*), and guava (*Psidium* spp.) are known to benefit from cross-pollination by insects, but the extent of their dependence is not known (McGregor 1975).

Bananas (*Musa* spp.) in the wild are pollinated by vertebrates (Nur 1976) whereas cultivated ones set fruit parthenocarpically.

Among the viney fruit plants, the Chinese gooseberry or kiwi (*Actinidia chinensis* is dioecious and requires cross-pollination by pollen collecting bees. Wild grape species (*Vitis* spp.) are similar, but the domestic grape (*V. vinifera*) can set fruit by self- or wind-pollination. Bee pollination seems to increase fruit set in some varieties. Pollination in passion fruits (*Passiflora* spp.) is complicated by the structure of the flower. They require cross-pollination, but honeybees may not always accomplish this. Carpenter bees (*Xylocopa* spp.) seem to be best. The shrubby pomegranate (*Punica granatum*) has not been well studied. The flowers produce only pollen. Pineapple (*Ananas sativus*) requires cross-pollination for seed to be produced, but this is undesirable for table fruit. Honeybees mostly cannot reach the nectar hidden at the base of the reddish tubular flowers which are pollinated by hummingbirds in South and Central America. Prickly pear (*Opuntia*) flowers provide large amounts of pollen. Their pollination requirements are unknown.

From the foregoing, one can appreciate that there are many gaps in our knowledge of fruit pollination. Incomplete and conflicting reports need resolution. Numbers of fruits, such as dukus, jambus and others are unknown from the viewpoint of their pollination and their importance as bee plants.

Among the nut plants of Asia, coconut and nutmeg are discussed below. The cashew (*Anacardium occidentale*) is an important cash crop. India is the world leader in production. The pollination requirements are for cross-pollination, apparently by insects. Peanut (*Arachis hypogaea*) flowers are visited by insects, including bees which trip the flowers and collect pollen; there is no functional nectary. These visits seem to have a beneficial effect in increasing crops. The almond (*Prunus amygdalus*) is dependent on insects, primarily bees, for fruit set.

VEGETABLES AND PULSES

In many vegetable plants it is not the fruit which is eaten and so production does not depend on insect pollination in a direct sense. However, insect cross-pollination is important in obtaining the seeds of these plants and the flowers are often good forage for bees. Included in this list are carrots (*Daucus carota*), cabbage, broccoli, cauliflower and other cole crops (*Brassica oleracea* and *B. pekinensis*), chicory (*Cichorium intybus*), lettuce (*Lactuca sativa*), onions (*Allium cepa*), radish (*Raphanus sativus*), fennel or saunf (*Foeniculum vulgare*) and others. Sweet potato (*Ipomoea batates*) and manioc or cassava (*Manihot esculenta*) are good nectar plants and the flowers well visited by honeybees. Their role in pollination is not known. The plants are propagated by cuttings, but seeds are used in breeding programmes.

For vegetables in which the fruit is eaten, pollination must be considered. The eggplant (*Solanum melongena*) is poorly studied but requires pollination and bees can be used. Tomatoes (*Lycopersicon esculentum*) are not automatically self-pollinating but movement of the plant causes pollen to fall from the anthers onto the stigmas. Thus, wind, insects or artificial vibration will bring about fruit set. The peppers (*Capsicum* spp.) seem to be able to function in the same way as tomatoes but do better if cross-pollinated. The flowers of solanaceous crop plants (including potatoes, *S. tuberosum* from which seeds are grown to produce seed-potatoes for planting) are not attractive to bees but probably would benefit from their foraging by being more productive in fruit quantity and quality. The cucurbit vegetables, pumpkins and squash (*Cucurbita* spp.), cucumbers and gherkins (*Cucumis sativus*), balsam pear (*Momordica charantia*), musk melon (*Cucumis melo*), other melons (*Citrullus* spp.) and gourds, including bottle gourd (*Lagenaria siceraria*), ash gourd (*Benincasa hispida*) and sponge gourd or luffa (*Luffa aegyptica*) require pollinators for fruit set; bees are the principal pollinators. Okra (*Hibiscus esculentus*) is self-pollinating but is well visited by bees. The value of out-crossing has not been assessed.

Of the pulses, cowpeas (*Vigna sinensis*) are highly attractive to bees. Pollination is best effected by large bees rather than honeybees. Such bees, like *Xylocopa*, are probably the chief pollinators of the horse bean (*Canavalia ensiformis*), at least in Java (Sastrapradja *et al.* 1975) although this species and the sword bean (*C. gladiata*) are reported to be self-pollinating. The lentil (*Lens esculenta*), mung bean (*Phasiolus aureas*), and gram (*Cicer arietinum*) are thought to be self-pollinating. Horsegram (*Lablab niger*) requires pollination by insects. However, the pollination requirements of many leguminous crops are unknown (Free 1970). Soya beans (*Glycine max*) have been considered to be self-fertile. However, the benefits that bees bring in terms of increased seed set and oil yield suggest that more research is needed.

CEREALS

Most cereals are independent of insects for pollination. Wind pollination prevails in the grasses. Maize, although a pollen source for bees, is wind-pollinated. Many cereals do not reproduce by pollination, the grain develops automatically. Pearl millet (*Pennisetum typhoides*) may benefit from insect pollination, as bees are sometimes abundant, collecting pollen from the flowers (Leuck and Burton 1966).

DRUG, BEVERAGE, CONDIMENT AND SPICE PLANTS

There is no comprehensive account of the pollination needs of the wide variety of medicinal plants grown throughout Asia. Many are not economically prominent and are grown in small patches for specific uses. Poppy (*Papaver omniferum*) is grown for the illicit drug trade. It produces only pollen and is visited extensively by pollen-foraging bees. The number of seeds produced is greater when pollinators are abundant. Hemp (*Cannabis sativa*) is wind-pollinated, but the male flowers are visited by bees for pollen. Tobacco (*Nicotiana*) cross-pollination can be brought about by honeybees for hybrid seed production.

Coffee (*Coffea*) production can be considerably enhanced by augmented pollination by honeybees. Coffee flowers are a good source of nectar. Tea (*Camellia sinensis*) is not a good bee plant. The small flowers are usually pollinated by flies. Cocoa (*Theobroma cacao*) is also pollinated by small flies (*Forcipomyia*: Ceratopogonidae), but some pollen-

collecting bees (e.g. *Trigona* and *Lasioglossum*) may also pollinate the small flowers.

Condiment and spice plants are not well studied from the viewpoint of their pollination or value as bee plants. Cardamom (*Elettaria cardamomum*) crops are much improved by honeybee pollination. Pepper (*Piper nigrum*) remains an enigma and self-pollination by rain is suggested. Coriander (*Coriandrum sativum*) is grown extensively in India and seems to benefit from cross-pollination by bees and other insects in Europe. Sesame (*Sesamum indicum*) is grown for its oil-rich seeds and is reportedly self-pollinating. Bees collect nectar and pollen from the flowers, but their importance in crop production has not been studied much. In Egypt, the wide variety of flower visitors, mostly honeybees, substantially increased seed yield in open-pollinated plants compared with those in cages (Rashad *et al.* 1979). Vanilla (*Vanilla* spp.) is grown in Asia. Pollination is usually done by hand. The mustards (*Brassica* spp.) are variable in their pollination needs, but offer good bee forage and benefit from out-crossing.

The pollination in cloves (*Syzygium aromaticum*) requires out-crossing. Bees are probably important, but other insects are also involved and may be more important in some places. The cloves themselves are not produced by pollination as they are the immature flowers. Nutmeg and mace are produced from *Myristica fragrans*. This plant is dioecious and so requires cross-pollination. However, how this is achieved is unknown; small insects, bees and wind have been suggested. Allspice (*Pimenta dioica*) is also dioecious and is effectively pollinated by honeybees in Jamaica. Cinnamon (*Cinnamomum zeylandicum*) requires insect pollination.

OIL CROPS

The rapeseed, mustards and related *Brassica* spp. are grown extensively for oil seed production in Asia. *Brassica campestris* is dependent on insects for pollination; it is an excellent source of pollen and nectar for bees. *B. juncea* is also more fruitful if bees are present (Kamal and Akhtar 1976). Niger (*Guizotia abyssinica*) is a good bee plant and seed yields are greater when bees are placed in niger fields. Sunflower (*Helianthus annuus*) is being grown more and more in Asia. Even though new self-compatible varieties are available, they benefit from cross-pollination and oil yields are greater. Non-self-compatible varieties require insect pollination and bees are the primary agents. The flowers provide high quality nectar and pollen. Flax (*Linum usitatissum*) is grown for oil and fibre and benefits from out-crossing by bees. Safflower (*Carthamus tinc-*

torius) is a good source of nectar and pollen used by bees and yields more oil when cross-pollinated. The oil palm (Elaeis guineensis) is a very important oil-producing plant in tropical Asia. It is pollinated most effectively by beetles (weevils) (Syed 1979). Although bees sometimes collect the pollen, it is not a good bee plant. The coconut (Cocos nucifera) is grown for the fruit which provides food, drink, oil and fuel. Evidence is accumulating slowly that coconut production may be improved by augmented pollination by bees. Wind pollination is most important. The coconut offers good forage, nectar and pollen, to bees.

Castor bean (Ricinus communis) is not understood in terms of its pollination requirements. Clauss (1982) in Crane and Walker (1983) indicates that it is pollinated by bees in Botswana.

Tung (Aleurites fordii) and tong (A. montana) are grown for their nuts which, when pressed, yield oil which is used in varnishes, electrical insulators and protective coatings. A. fordii may be dependent on insects for pollination, but this is not clear (Free 1970; McGregor 1976).

FORAGE CROPS

Alfalfa (Medicago sativa) is grown in drier parts of tropical Asia. It requires insects for pollination, honeybees and leaf-cutter bees are the most effective. Kudzu (Pueraria thunbergiana) is pollinated by bees. Berseem (Trifolium alexandrium) has a wide variety of pollinators on which it is dependent for seed set. Honeybees are effective pollinators.

TIMBER TREES AND NATURAL VEGETATION

It is very difficult to obtain information on the pollination biology of important timber trees of tropical and subtropical Asia. Appanah and Chan (1981) have discussed the role of thrips in pollination of dipterocarps in Malaysia and Appanah (1981) discusses, in a general way, the roles of bees in pollination in Malaysian primary forests. There are a few publications on the pollination of plants of the tropical forests (Faegri and van der Pijl 1976) but, in general, this is a much neglected area of botany, forestry and applied ecology. The importance of the forest trees in honey production is well known but there is no account of the trees and their relative importance.

FIBRE PLANTS AND RUBBER

The most important fibre plant is cotton

(Gossypium spp.), however, it is not considered to depend on insects for cross-pollination. In fact, cross-pollination has been considered detrimental as the resultant seeds and progeny are not necessarily truly bred for the desired cultivar. Nevertheless, benefits do accrue from cross-fertilization, larger crops, more oil and hybrid vigour in progeny. Honeybees are used extensively on cotton fields where pure-line seed is not sought. The flowers produce abundant pollen and nectar. Kapok (Ceiba pentandra) is a copious nectar producer and excellent bee forage. In nature, bats are important pollinators but the trees also seem to be self-fertile. Kenaf (Hibiscus cannabinus) pollination is not fully understood but out-crossing by honeybees may be more important than now thought. Sunn (or sann) hemp (Crotalaria juncea) seems to require pollination by bees, at least for maximum fruit set. Carpenter bees (Xylocopa) may be more valuable than honeybees. Cannabis sativa is wind-pollinated but is used by bees for its pollen. Information on flax and coconut is given above.

Rubber is pollinated by insects, mostly midges. However, it is an important honey plant in the tropics as bees forage for nectar from the extra-floral nectaries on the petioles of the leaves.

With the continued large-scale cutting of tropical and subtropical forests in Asia, attention must be paid to reafforestation programmes. In some cases, as with Calliandra introduced into Java, beekeeping projects have gone hand-in-hand. Nevertheless, all too little is known of the reproductive biology of most valued timber trees of the forests. To obtain seeds for reafforestation, either by natural processes or man-induced, the trees must be pollinated. If the trees are highly specific in their requirements for pollinators and the pollinators are finely attuned to the tree for their own reproduction, then over-cutting could produce a vicious cycle of decline in both plant and pollinator. These issues are urgently in need of consideration, but this is beyond the scope of this consultation, except in that honeybees may become involved in ameliorating such situations.

From the foregoing, one can readily appreciate that many economically important plants of tropical and subtropical Asia are unknown from the viewpoint of their pollination requirements. Those listed are the most important and those which have received some attention, if only to indicate the lack of information about them. Certainly, of those economic plants for which documentation on breeding systems is available, the number requiring insect pollination is high. If to those are added the plants which certainly benefit from cross-pollination by insects and those which are suspected of being in this category, only the cereals, bananas, and seedless fruits remain. At the same time, one can see that most of the economic plants for which insect cross-pollination is at least beneficial are also good honeybee plants. Thus, beekeeping and agricultural productivity are as clearly interwoven in the tropics as they are in the temperate regions of the world.

REFERENCES

Appanah. S. 1981. Pollination in Malaysia primary forests. Malaysian Forester, 44: 37-42.

Appanah, S. and H.T. Chan. 1981. Thrips: pollinators of some dipterocarps. Malaysian Forester, 44: 234-252.

Crane, E. and P. Walker. 1983. The Impact of Pest Management on Bees and Pollination. Tropical Development and Research Institute, London. ix + 129 pp + Annex A, 79 pp + Annex B, 9 pp.

Faegri, K. and L. van der Pijl. 1976. The Principles of Pollination Ecology - 3rd Edition Revised. Pergamon Press, Oxford University. 244 pp.

Free, J.B. 1970. Insect Pollination of Crops. Academic Press, Ltd. London. xi + 544 pp.

Kamal, S. and M. Akhtar. 1976. Symposium on Pollination, pp. 231-234. Role of insects in pollination of raya (*Brassica juncea* H.F.&T.) flowers. Pakistan Journal of Agricultural Science, 13: 65-72.

Leuck, D.B. and G.W. Burton. 1966. Pollination of pearl millet by insects. Journal of Economic Entomology, 59: 1308-1309.

McGregor, S.E. 1975. Insect pollination of tropical crops. Proceedings III International Symposium on Pollination. pp. 47-55.

McGregor, S.E. 1976. Insect Pollination of Cultivated Crop Plants. U.S. Department of Agriculture, Agriculture Handbook, No. 496. Washington, D.C. viii + 411 pp.

Nur, N. 1976. Studies on pollination in Musaceae (bananas). Annals of Botany, 40: 167-177.

Rashad, S.E., M.A. Ewies and H.G. El-Rabie. 1979. Insect pollinators of sesame (*Sesame indicum* L.) with special reference to the role of honeybees. Proceedings of IV International Symposium on Pollination. pp. 231-34.

Sastrapradja, S., S.H. Aminah, I. Lubis and D. Sastrapradja. 1975. Studies on Javanese species of *Canavalia* I. Floral biology and cytology. Annales Bogoriensis, 6: 43-55.

Syed, R.A. 1979. Studies on oil palm pollination by insects. Bulletin of Entomological Research, 69: 213-224.

Zmarlicki, C. 1984. Evaluation of honey plants in Burma - a case study. *In* Proceedings of the Expert Consultation on Beekeeping with *Apis mellifera* in Tropical and Sub-Tropical Asia, F.A.O., Rome. pp. 57-76.

CHAPTER 15

CROP POLLINATION AND *APIS CERANA*

R.C. SIHAG and R.C. MISHRA

The range of *Apis cerana*, the Asiatic honeybee, extends from tropical Asia across China as far as Siberia. The vast natural distribution and diverse climatic zones provide this honeybee with associations with a diverse flora of wild plants and cultivated crops from tropical, sub-tropical and temperate regions and from the plains and hills of each region. A large body of literature is available on *Apis mellifera* and its relationship with temperate crops (Free 1970; McGregor 1976). However, the role of *A. cerana* in pollination has been studied fragmentarily and most of the reports available come from India. Nevertheless, these records show that *A. cerana* is associated with the flowers of all categories of entomophilously pollinated crops:

1. Fruit trees.
2. Vegetables and pulses.
3. Oilseed crops.
4. Condiment and spice crops.
5. Fibre crops.
6. Forage and fodder crops.
7. Crops producing dyes.

This chapter attempts to summarize the available information on *A. cerana* and its relationships in pollination and flower visiting with these crop types.

FRUIT TREES

The association of *A. cerana* with fruit trees is well established. The trees for which clear documentation has been made include almond *Prunus dulcis* (Miller) D.A. Webb (Muttoo 1950; Bhalla *et al.* 1983b), apple *Malus domestica* Borkh (Sharma 1961; Rai and Gupta 1983; Verma and Dutta 1986), lime *Citrus aurantifolia* (Christm.) Swingle (Anonymous 1981), cranberry *Vaccinium macrocarpon* Ait. (Sharma 1961), litchi *Litchi chinensis* Sonner (Pandey and Yadav 1970; Dhaliwal *et al.* 1977; Phadke and Naim 1974; Dhoble and Shinde 1982), plum *Prunus domestica* L. (Sharma 1961), peach *Prunus persica* (L) Batsch. (Bhalla *et al.* 1983b; Kumar *et al.* 1984), phalsa *Grewia asiatica* L. (Parmar 1976), strawberry *Fragaria vesca* L. (Singh 1979), Chinese jujube *Ziziphus jujuba* Mill. (Ackerman 1961), durian *Durio zibethinus* Murray (Crane and Walker 1983), carambola *Averrhoa carambola* L. (Nand 1971), coconut palm *Cocos nucifera* L. (Anonymous 1982), borassus

palm *Borassus flabellifer* L. (Seethalakshmi and Percy 1979), and pear *Pyrus communis* L. (Sharma 1961). Muttoo (1950) cited the lack of fruit set in cultivated almonds resulted from failure in pollination, and he pleaded for the use of honeybees for the production of fruits in India. Sharma (1961) reported that 50-78 per cent of the insect visitors to pear and cranberry were honeybees and on plum, apple, cherry, and peach the population of honeybees represented 33, 70, 45 and 63 per cent respectively. *A. cerana* represented the largest number and was essential for fruit set. He further reported that pollinating insects greatly increased fruit set in four varieties of apple (Red-, Golden-, Red-delicious and American mother), pear, plum and cranberry. Persimmon, peach and cherry gave a commercial set even in the absence of pollinating insects but the set was higher on flowers receiving insect visits. Singh and Mishra (1986) observed the populations of bees and flies at different elevations in Himachal Pradesh (India), and flies were found to outnumber *A. c. indica* at all locations on all fruit blossoms. Mishra *et al.* (1976) reported that visits by honeybees on apple during 1200 and 1500 h were more than all other pollinators and red-delicious had higher fruit set near the bee colonies but that fruit set decreased with distance from the colonies. Verma and Dutta (1986) also compared the foraging behaviour of *A. c. indica* and *A. mellifera* in pollinating the flowers of apple. Without giving the relative abundance of different visitors, Bhalla *et al.* (1983b) reported that plum, peach, and almond were visited by honeybees *A. c. indica* along with other insects. Rai and Gupta (1983) also reported the role of honeybees in apple and pear pollination. Strawberry flowers are also visited by honeybees *A. c. indica* (Singh 1979) and among the insect visitors, their number was highest in a study in strawberry by Singh (1979). Pandey and Yadav (1970) studied pollination in litchi. They reported that 98-99% of the visitors were Apoidea and *A. cerana* constituted 28% of the total visitors. Phadke and Naim (1974) and Dhaliwal *et al.* (1977) also reported that *A. cerana* constituted 15% of insect visitors to litchi blooms. Honeybees were the most important pollinating agents of phalsa and the plants of seedling origin were reported to be benefited by insect pollination (Parmar 1976). Fruit yield in lime was found to be increased from 15-17 times by the honeybees in Tamil Nadu, India (Anonymous 1981). Coconut was also found to double the fruit yield when honeybee colonies were moved near the trees. On durian (*Durio zibethinus* Murray) in Singapore, honeybees collected pollen and *A. c. indica* visited the plants for nectar (Crane and Walker 1983) but their role in pollination is probably minimal.

VEGETABLE CROPS

Several reports are available on the visits of honeybee *A. c. indica* to cauliflower *Brassica oleracea* L. var. *botrytis* (Raula 1972; Dhaliwal and Sharma 1973; Adlakha and Dhaliwal 1979; Chakrabarti and Sinha 1980; Kakkar 1980, 1981; Tewari and Singh 1983; Verma and Joshi 1983). Thirty-four species of insects, including honeybees, visited the cauliflower blooms at Solan, (Himachal Pradesh), India (Sharma *et al.* 1974) but *A. c. indica* was the most abundant (Kakkar 1980) and helped in seed production of this crop (Kakkar 1981). The honeybee was found to prefer cauliflower blooms in comparison to flowers of *Berberis* sp., a weed of the surrounding area (Dhaliwal and Sharma 1973). Adlakha and Dhaliwal (1979) reported that *A. c. indica* was the most abundant pollinator of cauliflower in Himachal Pradesh and that it was a better pollinator than *A. mellifera*. Raula (1972) reported that 18% of the visitors to cauliflower were *A. c. indica*. That species was also found to be a superior pollinator of cauliflower compared to other visiting insects in northern India (Verma and Joshi 1983). They noted that pod setting, number of seeds per pod, and seed weight were increased by bee pollination. Similar results were reported by Tewari and Singh (1983) and they also reported higher pod set near the hives of *A. c. indica*. Bhambhure (1957, 1958a) reported the importance of honeybees in fruit yield of cucurbits. In okra *Abelmoschus esculentus* (L.) Moench, bees were the important pollinators (Mishra *et al.* 1988) and *A. c. indica* was the chief pollinator (Chaudhary *et al.* 1973). Weight and length of capsules of okra and seed number were found to be significantly higher in open pollinated than in bagged flowers (Mishra *et al.* 1988). In onion, *Allium cepa* L., more than 70% of the total insect pollinators on Patnar-red variety were honeybees and uncaged (insect pollinated) plants produced 72-79% more seed than caged/bagged plants (Jadhav 1981). Jadhav and Ajri (1981) found 74% seed set with 3.83 g seed per umbel in open as compared to 8% and 0.18 g per umbel in bagged inflorescences. Singh and Dharamwal (1970) also obtained 72-79% higher seed set in bee pollinated crop than in bagged plants. Kumar *et al.* (1985) found that three onion species, *A. cepa*, *A.*

fistulosum and *A. cepa fistulosum*, were greatly benefited by insect pollination. *A. cerana* was one of the visitors to blooms of these cultivars. Rao and Lazar (1980) observed that *A. c. indica* constituted 6.83% of the total visitors to onion blooms and bee pollination increased the seed yield. In bee pollinated umbels, 93.5% fruit set took place and each fruit carried an average of 4.3 seeds. The respective figures for bagged umbels were 9.8% and 1.9 seeds.

No reports on *A. cerana* as pollinators of pulses have come to light. However, many pulses are known to set fruit independently of insect pollination (Free 1970).

OILSEED CROPS

A. cerana is known to be an important pollinator of many oilseed crops, especially rape seed and mustard *Brassica* spp. (Rahman 1940; Latif *et al.* 1960; Bisht *et al.* 1980; Bhalla *et al.* 1983a), niger *Guizotia abyssinica* (Bhambhure 1958b), sesame *Sesamum indicum* L. (Rao *et al.* 1981) and sunflower *Helianthus annuus* L. (Rangarajan *et al.* 1974; Thakar 1974; Deodikar *et al.* 1976; Panchabhavi and Devaiah 1977; Panchabhavi *et al.* 1976; Wakhle *et al.* 1978; Basavanna 1979; Bhattacharya *et al.* 1982; Swaminathan and Bhardwaj 1982). Relative abundance of *Apis* spp. visitors to mustard bloom are given by Naim and Phadke (1976). *A. cerana* had a high degree of fidelity but *A. dorsata* was absent. The flowers of rape *Brassica campestris* var. Pusa Kalyani were well visited by *A. c. indica* along with other honeybees. The flowers visited by *Apis* spp. had higher pod set, greater number of seeds per pod, and the weight of seeds was also higher in comparison to those where no pollinators visited (Bisht *et al.* 1980). *A. cerana* was also found to be an important pollinator of *B. campestris* L. (Mohammad 1935; Rahman 1940; Latif *et al.* 1960). In niger (*Guizotia abyssinica* (L.f.) Cass.), flowers caged with *A. cerana* produced 2.6 times more seed than in the open, and provision of honeybees in the field was found to increase crop yield. *A. c. indica* was the most frequent visitor to *Sesamum indicum* (Rao *et al.* 1981) and was particularly active in the morning, foraging for nectar and pollen. *A. c. indica* on sunflower showed its highest activity during the afternoon (Rangarajan *et al.* 1974; Deodikar *et al.* 1976; Panchabhavi and Devaiah 1977). Seed set in sunflower covered with nylon net was markedly lower than that of an open pollinated crop (Dhoble and Shinde 1982) as expected for self-incompatible varieties. Moving honeybee colonies to sunflower fields increased seed setting by 27% (Panchabhavi *et al.* 1976; Basavanna 1979), and much higher seed yields and weights from plots with *A. cerana* colonies than from plots without bees were reported (Thakar 1974; Deodikar *et al.* 1976). Wakhle *et al.* (1978) reported increases in oil contents after bee pollination in sunflower. Shrivastava and Shrivastava (1986) found *A. c. indica* and *Xylocopa* sp. as the most important pollinators of sunflower throughout the flowering span of the crop. In pollinated plants, there were 658 grains per head out of which 226 grains were full. In non-pollinated flowers, none of the grains was full. Bhattacharya *et al.* (1982) also reported that honeybees were the chief pollinators of sunflower, and excluding honeybees by bagging of floral heads resulted in a reduction in seed yield, seed weight, seed viability and oil contents.

CONDIMENT/SPICE CROPS

A. cerana is known to be an excellent pollinator of some condiment and spice crops. Narayanan *et al.* (1960) reported that honeybees (*A. cerana, A. florea* and *A. dorsata*) were the chief pollinators of fennel (*Foeniculum vulgare* L.) but the number of *A. cerana* visitors was much lower than that of *A. florea*. Shelar and Suryanarayana (1981) found that seed weight of umbels visited by honeybees was greater than those obtained from caged umbels of coriander. In cardamom (*Elettaria cardamomum* (L) Maton), the main pollinators appear to be honeybees, particularly *A. cerana* which collects pollen from the flowers in the morning and nectar later. The flowers pollinated by bees gave 66% fruit set, but it was only 11% in the control flowers (Pattanshetti and Prasad 1973). The plots supplied with bee hives gave 34-35% higher yield than control (Madhusoodnan and Dandin 1981). Chandran *et al.* (1980) also found that *A. c. indica* was the main pollinator of cardamom. Increase of 37.2 and 27.9 per cent in fruit set was observed in Malabar and Mangirabad varieties of cardamom respectively in plants having access to bee visits compared to plants which had no insect visits (Chandran *et al.* 1980). Siddappaji and Channabassavanna (1980) reported that honeybees constituted 98 per cent of visitors to cardamom flowers and even one bee visit was sufficient to pollinate the flower. The cardamom panicles exposed from a layer of leaf mulch to open pollination by bees improved fruit set by about 14 times (Pattansheetti and Prasad 1974).

FIBRE CROPS

A. c. indica is found to visit some fibre crops also, e.g. cotton *Gossypium herbaceum* L. (Sidhu

and Singh 1961, 1962; Tanda and Goyal 1979a,b), congo jute *Urena lobata* L. (Crane and Walker 1983), tussa jute *Corchorus olitorius* L., white jute *C. capsularis* L. (Kundu *et al.* 1959) and sunnhemp *Crotalaria juncea* L. (Jitendra Mohan 1973). On Asiatic cotton, 6% of the total visitors were from *A. c. indica* and their role in pollination of cotton flowers was established (Tanda and Goyal 1979a,b). Sidhu and Singh (1961, 1962) studied the insect pollinators of cotton and found that plants caged with *A. c. indica* and *A. florea* gave 17.19% more seed cotton than plants without insects (Sidhu and Singh 1962). On sunnhemp, *A. c. indica* played no role in pollination, perhaps due to the larger size of the flowers. The bees robbed the nectar by simply biting through the lateral part of the keel (Jitendra Mohan 1973). Honeybees have also been reported collecting nectar from the flowers of congo jute in Indonesia (Crane and Walker 1983) but no information on its pollination is available. However, Kundu *et al.* (1959) reported that in tussa jute and white jute, the rate of cross pollination was 12% and 2.3% respectively, and only small numbers of bees visited the flowers.

FORAGE/FODDER CROPS

A. cerana is known as a visitor to the flowers of some forage or fodder crops, e.g. alfalfa *Medicago sativa* L. (Shelar and Suryanarayana 1983), berseem *Trifolium alexandrium* L. (Narayanan *et al.* 1961), fenugreek *Trigonella foenum-graecum* L. (Crane and Walker 1983) and horse gram *Macrotyloma uniflorum* (Lam.) Verdc. var. *uniflorum*. Shelar and Suryanarayana (1983) recommended 12.25 colonies of *A. cerana* per hectare for the pollination of alfalfa (*M. sativa*). The berseem seed set per head is about 70% provided enough pollinating insects, which are essential for profitable seed production, are present. *A. cerana* has been reported to pollinate the flowers of berseem in India (Narayanan *et al.* 1961) but wind was found to affect adversely the activity of the bees (Dhaliwal and Atwal 1976). *A. cerana* has also been observed collecting nectar from the flowers of fenugreek in Maharastra, India (Crane and Walker 1983) but their role in pollination of this crop has not been reported. Plots of horse gram pollinated by *A. cerana* gave yields 6 times higher than plots caged to exclude insects (Anonymous 1981).

CROPS PRODUCING DYES

The only two dye-producing crops where *A. cerana* has been reported as pollinator are Java indigo *Indigofera arrecta* A. rich.) and Sumatrana indigo (*Indigofera tinctoria* L. var. *tinctoria*). The flowers set seed only if they are tripped by bees (Howard and Howard 1915). When they were tripped artificially (resulting in self-pollination only) less seed was set than when they were visited by bees.

FAVOURABLE POLLINATING CHARACTERISTICS OF *APIS CERANA*

In addition to its general pollinating ability, *A. cerana* possesses several positive characteristics which make it a superior pollinator, even compared to *A. mellifera*. Such characteristics include foraging behaviour, foraging rate, foraging range, flower constancy, and colony strength (Jhajj and Goyal 1979a,b). *A. cerana* foragers show the usual foraging behaviours on crops as is known for *A. mellifera*, i.e. the foragers include only pollen gathers, pollen as well as nectar gatherers, and only nectar gatherers. The different proportions of these categories of foragers vary during the course of the day and flowering span of the crop (unpublished).

A. cerana has a higher wing-beat frequency (305±16.2 per sec) than does *A. mellifera* (235.2±7.5) (Goyal and Atwal 1977) and its foraging rate is also higher on *B. juncea* (unpublished). These characteristics should make it a more efficient pollinator, at least in certain categories of crops where smaller numbers of pollen grains are required for pollination and flower size is small, e.g. cruciferous, umbelliferous, and many papilionaceous crops.

The small foraging range of *A. cerana* (about 1 km) in comparison to *A. mellifera* (3-4 km) (Goyal 1978; Punchihewa *et al.* 1985) may be an additional advantage to breeders and seed growers. This is because the foragers would tend to restrict themselves to smaller radii where pesticidal operations could be regulated more effectively by the growers and, if desired, the breeders could establish the isolation yards for genetic purity of a cultivar easily by keeping *A. cerana* as a pollinator for self-pollination. This would be especially beneficial in cruciferous crops where contamination of genotypes is common (Adlakha and Dhaliwal 1979).

A. cerana has been reported to have a high floral fidelity (Chaudhary 1978) and out of 5,600 pollen loads analyzed, only 56 contained pollen from more than one plant species. Dhaliwal and Atwal (1986) reported that only 66.5% of *A. mellifera* foraging on alfalfa carried pure pollen.

A. cerana colonies have smaller strength (not greater than 30,000) than those of *A. mellifera*, which can reach even 60-70,000 (Mishra and Sihag 1987). The larger size of *A. mellifera* colonies present problems for management for pollination and smaller nuclei or packages are often used. This problem is overcome if *A. cerana* is used as a pollinator of crops. The colonies with smaller strength and small honey stores can be transported with little difficulty. However, for large crop fields, higher numbers of colonies of *A. cerana* would be required. *A. cerana* is also better adapted to higher altitudes as compared to *A. mellifera*.

Thus, it is clear that *A. cerana* is a pollinator of a large number of cultivated crops. Like *A. mellifera*, *A. cerana* can also be easily managed. In spite of its being less of a producer than *A. mellifera*, several of the favourable pollination attributes of *A. cerana* put this bee ahead in terms of its usefulness as a pollinator of crops not only possibly in areas of its natural distribution but also in new ones where it is not indigenous.

ACKNOWLEDGEMENTS

The funds for the preparation of this article were utilized from the Project 'C (b)-Ento-2-I.C.A.R.' financed by the Indian Council of Agricultural Research New Delhi. The authors wish to thank Dr. S.K. Sharma for extending cooperation during the preparation of the manuscript.

REFERENCES

Ackerman, W.L. 1961. Flowering, pollination, self-sterility and seed development of Chinese jujubes. Proceedings of the American Society of Horticulture Science, 77: 265-269.

Adlakha, R.L. and H.S. Dhaliwal. 1979. Insect pollination of seed cauliflower (*Brassica oleracea* var. *botrytis*) with particular reference to the role of honeybees. Indian Bee Journal, 41(1/2): 13-16.

Anonymous. 1981. Work on bee pollination in India. Indian Bee Journal, 43(4): 140-145.

Anonymous. 1982. Does cocopalm benefit by bee pollination? Indian Bee Journal, 44(1): 24.

Basavanna, G.P.C. 1979. Role of insect pollinators in sunflower production. Current Research, 8(1): 1-3.

Bhalla, O.P., A.K. Verma and H.S. Dhaliwal. 1983a. Insect visitors of mustard bloom (*Brassica campestris* var. *sarson*), their number and foraging behaviour under mid-hill conditions. Journal of Entomological Research, 7(1): 15-17.

Bhalla, O.P., A.K. Verma and H.S. Dhaliwal. 1983b. Foraging activity of insect pollinators visiting stone fruits. Journal of Entomological Research,

7(2): 91-94.

Bhambhure, C.S. 1957. Importance of honeybees in the pollination of *Luffa aegyptica*. Indian Bee Journal, 19(11/12): 149,151.

Bhambhure, C.S. 1958a. Further studies on the importance of honeybees in pollination of cucurbitaceae. Indian Bee Journal, 20(10): 148-149.

Bhambhure, C.S. 1958b. Effect of honeybee activity on niger seed production. Indian Bee Journal, 20(12): 189-191.

Bhattacharya, P., R.C. Samui, M.R. Ghos, S.K. Dasgupta and A. Roy. 1982. Sunflower seed yield as influence by pollination and insect pests. Proceedings of 10th International Sunflower Conference, Sulfers Paradise, pp. 132-134.

Bisht, D.S., M. Naim and K.N. Mehrotra. 1980. Studies on the role of honeybees in rapeseed production. Proceedings of 2nd International Conference on Apiculture in Tropical Climates, New Delhi. pp. 491-496.

Chakrabarti, A.K. and S.N. Sinha. 1980. Bee pollination and its impact on cauliflower seed production. Proceedings of 2nd International Conference on Apiculture in Tropical Climates, New Delhi. pp. 649-655.

Chandran, K., P. Rajan, D. Joseph and M.C. Suryanarayana. 1980. Studies on the role of honeybees in the pollination of cardamom. Proceedings of 2nd International Conference on Apiculture in Tropical Climates, New Delhi. pp. 497-504.

Chaudhary, B., M.L.A. Choomsai and M.G.R. Menon. 1973. Insect pollination in some vegetable crops. Haryana Journal of Horticulture Scient, 2(1/2): 56-62.

Chaudhary, R.K. 1978. Floral fidelity in Indian honeybee (*Apis cerana indica* F.). Indian Bee Journal, 40(2): 33-35.

Crane, E. and P. Walker. 1983. The Impact of Pest Management on Bees and Pollination. Tropical Development and Research Institute, London. 232 pp.

Deodikar, G.B., V.S. Seethalakshmi and M.C. Suryanarayana. 1976. Floral biology of sunflower with special reference of honeybees. Journal of Palynology, 12(1/): 115-125.

Dhaliwal, H.S. and P.L. Sharma. 1973. The foraging range of the Indian honeybee on two crops. Journal of Apicultural Research, 12(2): 131-134.

Dhaliwal, H.S., S. Scrivastava and R.L. Adlakha. 1977. Insect pollination of lychee, *Litchi chinensis* Sonn in the Valley areas in the Himalayas. Proceedings of XXVIth International Apiculture Congress, Adelaide. p. 396.

Dhaliwal, J.S. and A.S. Atwal. 1976. Note on the effect of air temperature, relative humidity and wind velocity on bees visiting berseem at Ludhiana. Indian Journal of Agricultural Sciences, 46(1): 50-51.

Dhaliwal, J.S. and A.S. Atwal. 1986. Factors influencing tripping efficiency of bees on alfalfa (*Medicago sativa* L.). In: Pollination Biology: An Analysis. Kapil, R.P. (ed). Inter-Indian Publication, New Delhi. pp. 79-90.

Dhoble, S.Y. and Y.M. Shinde. 1982. Role of insect pollinators for effective seed setting in sunflower. Journal of Maharashtra Agricultural Universities, 7(1): 103.

Free, J.B. 1970. Insect Pollination of Crops. Academic Press, London. 544 pp.

Goyal, N.P. 1978. Performance of *Apis mellifera* and *A. indica* as observed in Punjab plains. Indian Bee Journal, 40(1): 3-5.

Goyal, N.P. and A.S. Atwal. 1977. Wing beat frequency of *Apis indica* and *Apis mellifera*. Journal of Apicultural Research, 16(1): 47-48.

Howard, A. and G.L.C. Howard. 1915. First report on the improvement of indigo in Bihar. Bulletin of Agriculture Institute, Para. 51.

Jadhav, L.D. 1981. Role of insects in the pollination of onion (*Allium cepa*) in the Maharashtra State, India. Indian Bee Journal, 43(3): 61-63.

Jadhav, L.D. and D.S. Ajri. 1981. Insect pollinators of onion (*Allium cepa*) in Ahmednagar district of Maharashtra, India. Indian Bee Journal, 43(4): 109.

Jhajj, H.S. and Goyal, N.P. 1979a. Comparative behaviour of pollen foragers of *Apis cerana indica* and *Apis mellifera*. Journal of Apicultural Research, 18(4): 279-284.

Jhajj, H.S. and N.P. Goyal. 1979b. Comparative studies on the flower constancy of *Apis cerana indica* F. and *Apis mellifera* L. Proceedings of 4th International Symposium on Pollination, Maryland. pp. 333-339.

Jitendra Mohan, K.V. 1973. Some observations on the bee pollination in Sunnhemp (*Crotalaria juncea*) and their importance in breeding work. Jute Bulletin, 35: 214-216.

Kakkar, K.L. 1980. Prospects of bees as pollinating agents of cauliflower. Proceedings of 2nd International Conference on Apiculture in Tropical Climates, New Delhi. pp. 545-556.

Kakkar, K.L. 1981. Foraging behaviour of insect pollinators of cauliflower bloom. Indian Journal of Ecology, 8(1): 126-130.

Kumar, J., R.C. Mishra, J.K. Gupta and G.S. Dogra. 1984. Pollination requirements of some peach cultivars. Indian Bee Journal, 47: 3-6.

Kumar, J., R.C. Mishra and J.K. Gupta. 1985. The effect of mode of pollination on *Allium* species with observations on insects as pollinators.

Journal of Apicultural Research, 24(1): 62-66.

Kundu, B.C., K.C. Basak and P.B. Sarcar. 1959. Jute in India. Leonard Hill, London.

Latif, A., A. Qayum and M. Abbas. 1960. The role of *Apis indica* in the pollination of oilseed toria and sarson (*Brassica campestris* var. *toria* and *dichotoma*). Bee World, 41: 283-286.

Madhusoodanan, K.J. and S.B. Dandin. 1981. Floral biology of cardamom (*Elettaria cardamomum* L.) in relation to the foraging behaviour of honeybees (*Apis* spp.) Indian Bee Journal, 43(4): 104-108.

Mishra, R.C., G.S. Dogra and P.R. Gupta. 1976. Some observations on insect pollinators of apple. Indian Bee Journal, 38(1-4): 20-22.

Mishra, R.C., J. Kumar and J.K. Gupta. 1988. Effect of modes of pollination on yield and oil potential of *Brassica campestris* var. *sarson* with observations on insect pollinators. Journal of Apicultural Research, 27(3): 186-189.

Mishra, R.C. and R.C. Sihag. 1987. Apicultural Research in India. All Indian Co-ordinated Project on Honeybee Research and Training, Haryana Agricultural University Press, Hissar. 120 pp.

Mohammad, A. 1935. Pollination studies in toria (*Brassica napus* var. *dichotoma* Prain). Indian Journal of Agriculture Sciences, 5: 125-154.

Muttoo, R.N. 1950. Honeybees and fruit crops. Indian Journal of Horticulture, 7(3/4): 17-20.

Nand, D. 1971. Pollination, fruit set and fruit development in carambola (*Averrhoa carambola* L.). Indian Journal of Horticulture, 28(4): 278-284.

Narayanan, E.S. and P.L. Sharma 1960. Studies on requirements of various crops for insect pollinators. I. Insect pollinators of saunf (*Foeniculum vulgare*) with particular reference to the honeybees at Pusa, Bihar. Indian Bee Journal, 22(1): 7-11.

Narayanan, E.S., P.L. Sharma and K.G. Phadke. 1961. Studies on requirements of various crops for insect pollinators. Insect pollinators of berseem-Egyptian clover (*Trifolium alexandrinum* L.) with particular reference to honeybees and their role in seed setting. Indian Bee Journal, 23(4/6): 23-30.

Panchabhavi, K.S. and M.A. Devaiah. 1977. A note on the activities of insect pollinators on sunflower during winter and summer seasons at Bangalore. Current Science, 6: 88-89.

Panchabhavi, K.S., M.A. Devaiah and G.P.C. Basavanna. 1976. The effect of keeping *Apis cerana indica* F. colonies on the seed set of sunflower, *Helianthus annuus* Linn. Mysore Journal of Science, 10(4): 631-636.

Pandey, R.S. and R.P.S. Yadav. 1970. Pollination

of litchi (*Litchi chinensis*) by insects with special reference of honeybees. Journal of Apicultural Research, 9(2): 103-105.

Parmar, C. 1976. Pollination and seed set in phalsa (*Grewia asiatica* L.). Agriculture and Agro-Industries Journal, 9(6): 12-14.

Pattanshetti, H.V. and A.B.N. Prasad. 1973. Bees help pollination of cardamom flowers. Current Research, 2(8): 56-57.

Pattanshetti, H.V. and A.B.N. Prasad. 1974. Exposing the cardamom panicles from a layer of leaf mulch to open pollination by bees thereby improving the fruit set. Current Research, 3(8): 90.

Phadke, K.G. and M. Naim. 1974. Observations on the honeybee visitation to the litchi (*Nephelium litchi*) blossom at Pusa (Bihar, India). Indian Bee Journal, 36(1-4): 9-12.

Punchihewa, R.W.K., N. Koeniger, P.G. Kevan and R.M. Gadawski. 1985. Observation on the dance communication and natural foraging ranges of *Apis cerana*, *Apis dorsata* and *Apis florea* in Sri Lanka. Journal of Apicultural Research, 24: 168-175.

Rahman, K.A. 1940. Insect pollinators of toria (*Brassica napus* Linn. var. *dichotoma* Prain) and sarson (*Brassica campestris* Linn. var. *sarson* Prain) at Lyallpur. Indian Journal of Agriculture Sciences, 10: 422-447.

Rai, K.M. and B.P. Gupta. 1983. Role of honeybees and other insects as pollinators in apple and pear. Indian Bee Journal, 45(2/3): 56-57.

Rangarajan, A.V., N.R. Mahadevan and S. Iyemperumal. 1974. Note on the time of visit of pollinating honeybees to sunflower. Indian Journal of Agriculture Sciences, 44(1): 66-67.

Rao, G.M. and M. Lazar. 1980. Studies on bee behaviour and pollination in onion (*Allium cepa* L.). Proceedings of 2nd International Conference on Apiculture in Tropical Climates, New Delhi. pp. 580-589.

Raula, T.S. 1972. Pollination studies in cauliflower (*Brassica oleracea* var. *botrytis* L.). Journal of Research, Ludhiana, 9(4): 580-585.

Seethalakshmi, T.S. and A.P. Percy. 1979. *Borassus flabellifer* (palmyrah palm) a good pollen source. Indian Bee Journal, 41(1/2): 20-21.

Sharma, P.L. 1961. The honeybee population among insects visiting temperate zone fruit flowers and their role in setting fruit. Bee World, 42(1): 6-8.

Sharma, P.L., H.S. Dhaliwal and K.L. Kakkar. 1974. Insect visitors and pollinators of cauliflower (*Brassica oleracea* var. *botrytis*) seed crop bloom. Himachal Journal of Agriculture Research, 2(2): 74-78.

Shelar, D.G. and M.C. Suryanarayana. 1981. Preliminary studies on pollination of coriander (*Coriandrum sativum* L.). Indian Bee Journal, 43(4): 110-111.

Shelar, D.G. and M.C. Suryanarayana. 1983. Effect of pollination by honeybee (*Apis cerana indica* Fabricius) on the yield of lucerne. Indian Journal of Agriculture Sciences, 53(3): 190-191.

Shrivastava, O.S. and G.P. Shrivastava. 1986. Nocturnal pollination in sunflower *Helianthus annuus* L. *In*: Pollination Biology: An Analysis. Kapil, R.P. (ed). Inter-India Publication, New Delhi. pp. 59-65.

Siddappaji, C. and G.P. Channabasavanna. 1980. Role of honeybees in the pollination of cardamom (*Elettaria cardamomum* (L) Meton). Proceedings 2nd International Conference on Apiculture in Tropical Climates, New Delhi. pp. 640-648.

Sidhu, A.S. and S. Singh. 1961. Studies on agents of cross pollination in cotton. Indian Cotton Growers Review, 15(6): 341-353.

Sidhu, A.S. and S. Singh. 1962. Role of honeybees in cotton production. Indian Cotton Growers Review, 16(1): 18-23.

Singh, J.P. and S.S. Dharamwal. 1970. The role of honeybees in seed setting on onion at Pantnagar, Dist. Nainital, U.P., India. Indian Bee Journal, 32(1/2): 23-27.

Singh, Y. 1979. Pollination activity on strawberry at Jeolikot, Dist. Nainital, India. Indian Bee Journal, 41(1/2): 17.

Swaminathan, R. and S.C. Bhardwaj. 1982. Bee pollinators of sunflower and their foraging behaviour. Indian Bee Journal, 44(2): 32-34.

Tanda, A.S. and N.P. Goyal. 1979a. Some observations on the behaviour of *Apis mellifera* Linn. and *Apis cerana indica* Fab. workers in the field of desi cotton (*Gossypium arboreum* Linn.). American Bee Journal, 119(2): 106.

Tanda, A.S. and N.P. Goyal. 1979b. Insect pollination in asiatic cotton (*Gossypium arboreum*). Journal of Apicultural Research, 18(1): 64-72.

Tewari, G.N. and K. Singh. 1983. Studies on insect pollinators in relation to seed production in cauliflower (*Brassica oleracea* var. *botrytis* L.). Indian Bee Journal, 45(1/2): 54-55.

Thakar, C.V. 1974. Experiments on pollination of sunflower. Indian Bee Journal, 36(1-4): 36-38.

Thakur, A.K., O.P. Sharma, R. Garg and G.S. Dogra. 1982. Comparative studies on foraging behaviour of *Apis mellifera* and *Apis indica* on mustard. Indian Bee Journal, 44(4): 91-92.

Verma, L.R. and P.C. Dutta. 1986. Foraging behaviour of *Apis cerana indica* and *Apis mellifera* in pollinating apple flowers. Journal of Apicultural Research, 25(4): 197-201.

Verma, S.K. 1983. Studies on the foraging behaviour of *Apis cerana indica* Fab. in Jeolikot (Nainital, India). Indian Bee Journal, 45(1): 5-7.

Verma, S.K. and N.K. Joshi. 1983. Studies on the role of honeybees in the pollination of cauliflower (*Brassica oleracea* var. *botrytis*). Indian Bee Journal, 45(2/3): 52-53.

Wakhle, D.M., K.S. Nair and R.P. Phadke. 1978. Effect of bee pollination on the oil and protein content in the seeds of sunflower (*Helianthus annuus* L.). Indian Bee Journal, 40(1): 1-2.

CHAPTER 16

POLLINATION ECOLOGY OF APPLE ORCHARDS BY HYMENOPTEROUS INSECTS IN MATIANA-NARKANDA TEMPERATE ZONE

L.R. VERMA

INTRODUCTION

Himachal Pradesh is the principal temperate fruit-growing state in India with more than 1.27×10^5 hectares of land under fruit cultivation. Apple is the most important of the temperate fruits cultivated, and every year more and more land is coming under cultivation for this important commercial crop. With such a drastic increase in the area under apple cultivation continuing each year, some management problems inevitably have arisen. A major problem has been pollination. In general, apples are self-incompatible and require cross-pollination by bees. This applies to the most delicious and valuable varieties of apple, like Royal and Red Delicious, grown in the state. Maximum yield is only possible through efficient and sufficient pollination.

The most efficient way of assuring adequate pollination is by the introduction of honeybees into the orchards at the time of blossoming; a practice well adapted for apples in North America, Western Europe, Eastern Europe and so on.

It is with this background that the present research project was started in April, 1983, as part of the Himalayan Eco-Development Project at Himachal Pradesh University, Shimla.

OBJECTIVES

1. Diversity, abundance and distribution of insect pollinators in apple orchards.
2. Comparative foraging behaviour of the hive bees, *Apis cerana indica* F. and *Apis mellifera* L., on apple bloom.
3. Effect of insect pollinators on set, drop and quality of apple fruit.
4. Comparative biometric and biochemical studies on the flight muscles of genus *Apis*.
5. Eco-physiology of *Plectranthus* spp.: A major source of honey in Northern India.
6. Laboratory and field studies on the effect of biocides on insect pollinators.

DISTRIBUTION, ABUNDANCE, AND DIVERSITY OF INSECT POLLINATORS IN APPLE ORCHARDS OF SHIMLA-NARKANDA TEMPERATE ZONE

In the present investigation, we have collected and identified 44 species of insect pollinators belonging to the orders Hymenoptera (14 species), Diptera (11 species), Lepidoptera (9 species), Coleoptera (7 species) and Hemiptera (1 species) visiting apple blossoms. Among them, the frequent pollinators were: *A. cerana indica*, *A. mellifera*, *Eristalis tenax*, *Eristalis* sp., *Eristalis angustimarginalis* and *Halictus dasygaster*. Efficiency ratings and pollination indices data reveal that besides honeybees, other insect pollinators also play an important role in the pollination of apple bloom. Techniques should be developed for their mass rearing, and survey of their natural nesting sites should also be carried out.

COMPARATIVE FORAGING BEHAVIOUR OF *APIS CERANA INDICA* F. AND *APIS MELLIFERA* L. ON APPLE BLOOM

During the period of apple bloom (March-April), the environmental temperatures are generally low, and thus other naturally-occurring insect pollinators are not found in sufficient number for the adequate pollination of apple bloom. It is, therefore, essential to keep honeybee colonies in the orchards for adequate pollination. It is with this idea that the comparative foraging behaviour of *A. cerana indica* and *A. mellifera* on apple blossoms was studied in apple orchards of Matiana-Narkanda Zone which is a major apple growing belt of Himachal Pradesh.

Worker bees of *A. cerana* started their foraging activity significantly earlier in the morning (mean time 0603 hours) than *A. mellifera* (mean time 0627 hours) (P<0.01). In the evening, *A. mellifera* ceased its foraging activity significantly earlier (mean time 1855 hours) than *A. cerana* (mean time 1913 hours) (P<0.01). The duration of foraging trips of *A. mellifera* (17.92 minutes ± 0.36) was significantly longer than that of *A. cerana* (11.85 minutes ± 0.36) (P<0.01). In both species, nectar collectors outnumbered pollen collectors. Mean ratio of pollen and nectar collectors for *A. cerana* was 1:2.08 and for *A.*

mellifera it was 1:2.78. In *A. cerana*, no pollen plus nectar collectors were found, whereas in *A. mellifera* the percentage of such worker bees varied from 6 to 11 during different hours. Peak foraging activity of *A. cerana* was between 0900 and 1130 hours when the temperature ranged from 15.5 to 21.0°C, and that of *A. mellifera* was between 1100 and 1320 hours when the orchard temperature ranged from 21 to 25°C. This is remarkable from the pollination point of view because by keeping both species of honeybees in the same orchard, the duration of peak periods of foraging activity can be prolonged to ensure better pollination. Worker bees of *A. mellifera* carried significantly heavier pollen loads than *A. cerana* throughout the day (P<0.01). *A. cerana* contacted on an average 3.09±0.39 stigmas per visit and spent 5.90±0.22 seconds on each flower, whereas these values for *A. mellifera* were 3.33±0.32 stigmas per visit and 6.63±0.23 seconds on each flower respectively. These differences between the two species were non-significant.

The length and breadth of direct and indirect flight muscles of *A. mellifera* were significantly (P<0.01) greater than *A. cerana indica*. The number and diameter of flight muscle fibres in these two species of honeybees also followed a similar pattern. The fuel content (glycogen and lipids) and associated enzyme systems (glycogen phosphorylase, succinic dehydrogenase and α-glycerophosphate dehydrogenase) were also significantly higher in *A. mellifera* than *A. cerana*. These results on biometry and biochemical composition of flight muscles correspond to the body size of bees and are also related to their flight ranges. The flight range of *A. mellifera* is double that of *A. cerana indica*.

EFFECT OF INSECT POLLINATORS ON FRUIT SET, FRUIT DROP AND FRUIT QUALITY OF APPLE

Honeybees play a significant role in the pollination of apple bloom. Different important biological and economic aspects of pollination, such as fruit set, fruit drop and fruit quality of the apple crop depend upon their visits to apple blossoms.

Effect of insect pollinators on fruit set

In self-compatible varieties like Golden Delicious, the percentages of fruit set in control (no insect visitors), open (all naturally occurring insect visitors), and honeybee pollinated flowers were 24.57, 30.73 and 34.53 per cent respectively, without any significant difference (P>0.01). Similarly, in another self-compatible variety, Red Gold, the percentages of fruit set in control, open and honeybee pollinated flowers

were 15.76, 18.34 and 22.45 per cent respectively with no significant difference (P>0.01). In self-incompatible varieties like Royal Delicious and Red Delicious, there was no fruit set at all in the absence of any insect pollinator, but the fruit set was significantly higher (P<0.01) in honeybee pollinated flowers of Royal Delicious (23.33 per cent) and Red Delicious (19.69 per cent) than in open pollinated flowers of Royal Delicious (13.21 per cent) and Red Delicious (11.42 per cent).

Effect of insect pollinators on fruit drop

Fruit drop in self-compatible varieties of apples was significantly higher (P<0.01) in fruits from flowers in the control than the fruits from open and honeybee pollinated flowers. For example, in Golden Delicious and Red Gold, the greatest fruit drop (38.45 and 38.07 per cent respectively) occurred in the control and the least (25.22 and 25.02 per cent respectively) occurred in honeybee pollinated flowers. In open pollinated flowers of Golden Delicious and Red Gold, the fruit drop was 27.62 and 28.38 per cent respectively with no significant difference (P>0.01) from open or honeybee pollinated flowers. In a self-incompatible variety like Royal Delicious, the fruit drop in open pollinated and honeybee pollinated flowers was 28.69 and 25.50 per cent respectively without any significant difference (P>0.01). The same trend was observed in another self-incompatible variety, Red Delicious, where the fruit drop in open and honeybee pollinated flowers was 28.86 and 25.73 per cent respectively, with no significant difference (P>0.01).

Improvement in the quality of fruit due to insect pollinators

Improvement in the quality of apple fruits resulting from honeybee pollination was observed in terms of increase in weight (gm), length (cm), breath (cm), volume (ml) and number of seeds per fruit.

In Golden Delicious, there was an increase in the weight, length, breadth, volume and number of seed per fruit by 22, 9, 7, 17 and 17 per cent respectively in the fruits which developed from flowers exclusively pollinated by honeybees as compared to the open pollinated flowers. Likewise, in Red Gold the weight, length, breadth, volume and number of seeds per fruit were increased by 18, 9, 9, 9, and 32 per cent respectively by placing two additional colonies of honeybees in the orchard at the time of 10-15 per cent bloom. Weight, length, breadth, volume and number of seeds per fruit in self-compatible varieties like Golden Delicious and Red Gold were greatest (P<0.01) in the fruits from honeybee pollinated flowers and lowest in the fruits under control experimental conditions.

In Royal Delicious, the increase in weight, length, breadth, volume and number of seeds per fruit was 33, 15, 10, 51 and 49 per cent respectively in fruits which developed from flowers exclusively pollinated by honeybees as compared to the open pollinated flowers. Similarly, in Red Delicious, the increase in weight, length, breadth, volume and number of seeds per fruit which developed from flowers exclusively pollinated by honeybees was 19, 9, 10, 16 and 30 per cent respectively as compared to those fruits which developed from open pollinated flowers. Thus, in self-incompatible varieties like Royal Delicious and Red Delicious where there was no fruit set at all in the control experiment, the fruit quality was significantly better in the fruits from honeybee pollinated flowers as compared to the fruits from open pollinated flowers (P<0.01).

ECO-PHYSIOLOGY OF *PLECTRANTHUS* SPP.: A MAJOR SOURCE OF HONEY IN NORTHERN INDIA

A major problem for keeping bees for pollination is that once the bloom of the crop of interest is over, the bees are left with considerably reduced floral resources. The problem can be circumvented by providing alternate forage source. In the Himachal and Kashmir regions of Northern India, *Plectranthus* spp., a small shrub belonging to the family Labiatae is an excellent source of nectar for honeybees. Three common species of this plant found in this region are *P. rugosus*, *P. coetsa* and *P. gerardianus*. *A. cerana indica* make good stores of honey from the white flowers of this plant and, however, there are contradictory reports in the literature about the preference of *A. mellifera* for this plant as a major honey source. In the present investigation, detailed studies on the eco-physiology of *Plectranthus* spp. as a major source of honey in Northern India are being made.

Floral data on different phenotypic characters revealed that the average number of flowers per plant is 61±0.82. Time taken for bud development and opening of flowers is about 6 days. Mean number of branches per tree is 10±0.79 and average number of flowers per branch is 6±0.69 flowers. Total sugar concentration was found maximum at 0800 hours in *P. rugosus* (39.77±0.26 μg/flower), *P. gerardianus* (29.88±0.37 μg/flower) and *P. coetsa* (27.74 μg/flower). Thereafter, the total sugar concentration decreases with time and it is minimum at 1700 hours in all three species of this plant.

The sugar concentrations in other important wild honey plants of these regions are also maximum at 0800 hours. For example, concentrations were 25.18±0.33, 23.8±0.27, 19.97±0.14, 19.73±0.77,

17.06±0.69 and 15.93±0.68 in *Prunus padam, Adhatoda vasica, Princepia utilis, Rosa moschata, Berberis* sp. and *Rubus lasiocarpus* respectively. Thereafter, in all these species the sugar concentrations decrease with time reaching minimum at 1700 hours.

Comparative foraging behaviour data reveals that *A. cerana* spends 5.18 seconds per flower and visits 8.38±0.97 flowers per minute. This species touches 5.12±0.78 stigmas per visit and peak hours of foraging activities are between 0900 and 1000 hours. Thus, the peak period of foraging activity coincided with the time when maximum concentrations of sugar are present in the nectaries of *Plectranthus* spp. When alternate forage sources are available, *A. mellifera* does not prefer to forage on this plant and even under controlled conditions, the foraging efficiency of this exotic species is much less than *A. cerana*.

LABORATORY AND FIELD STUDIES ON THE EFFECT OF BIOCIDES ON INSECT POLLINATORS

Broad spectrum biocides, besides protecting agricultural crops, also play a negative role in the destruction of predators, parasites and insect pollinators. At present in India, sumithion, metacid and metasystox are being used widely on apple trees to control blossom thrips. They are applied more or less during bloom and are rated as toxic to honeybees.

Apple scab, caused by *Venturia inaequalis*, has gradually spread to all the apple growing areas of Himachal Pradesh (India), in spite of the high mountain barriers. In 1983, the severity of the disease was such that the State Government destroyed 70,000 tonnes of the total production of 2,55,875 tonnes (figures from State Department of Horticulture). Therefore, the use of fungicides has become necessary as these chemicals act as protectors against this disease. Other insecticides, fungicides and herbicides are also coming into use in orchard management, and attention needs to be paid to the effects of these on insect pollinators.

In the present research project, some laboratory studies on the toxicity to *A. cerana* and *A. mellifera* of various biocides used in apple orchards in Himachal Pradesh have been undertaken. Further, the effects of their use in the field are also being investigated. So far, we have determined the LD_{50} values of the following fungicides by using probit analysis statistical methods: LD_{50} values of Foltaf (80% WP), Bevestin (50% WP) and Dithane M-45 (75% WP) for *A. cerana* are 5.25, 2.09 and 3.39 μg/bee respectively and these values for *A. mellifera* are 9.12, 6.92

and 6.46 μg/bee respectively.

According to the International Commission of Bee Botany, the chemicals with LD_{50} values between 2 and 11 are moderately toxic and should be used with care. It is also interesting to note that LD_{50} values for *A. cerana* are significantly lower than *A. mellifera* suggesting that the former species of honeybee is less tolerant to the effect of these fungicides than the latter.

CHAPTER 17

COMPARATIVE ASSESSMENT OF HONEYBEES AND OTHER INSECTS WITH SELF-POLLINATION OF SARSON (*BRASSICA CAMPESTRIS*) IN PESHAWAR

B.M. KHAN and M.I. CHAUDHRY

ABSTRACT

Self-pollinated sarson plants (covered with muslin netting) produced 26.46 to 34.34 (mean 28.68) grams of seed per plant while honeybee pollinated and non-*Apis* insect pollinated plants yielded 67.2 to 90.02 (mean 74.37) grams and 41.72 to 56.35 (mean 48.42) grams per plant, respectively. The increase in seed yield due to insect pollination was 159.31% in the case of honeybee pollinated plants and 68.8% in non-*Apis* insect pollinated plants. Besides producing increased yield, insect pollination caused formation of well-shaped, larger grains and more viable seed than the self-pollinated plants.

INTRODUCTION

Pollination is an important component of one of the essential inputs (quality seed, fertilizer and irrigation) for better and higher production and is indispensable in oil seed, fruit and vegetable seed production. According to Howard *et al.* (1915), mustard flowers open between 0900 hours and 1200 hours, and continue for three days. Mohammad (1935) reported that only 37 percent of bagged flowers were able to form fruit themselves compared to 100 percent in cross pollinated toria. Rahman (1940) has found 105 insect species, belonging to 55 families, pollinating *Brassica napus* and *B. campestris* of which honeybees, *Apis cerana* were predominating. According to Kremer (1945) most of the grain-producing crops require the service of insects for cross-pollination, out of which honeybees are the most satisfactory natural pollinator. Mustard is an excellent source of nectar and pollen for honey-bees (Pellett 1947). Sneep (1952) mentioned that better seed yield of brassica crops can be obtained from honeybee pollination in greenhouses. Priestley (1954) tried successfully the use of bees as pollina-tors in greenhouses and obtained better results. Sampson (1957) showed that compatibility varies with species, cultivar, and even with the age of the plant. Eckert (1959) reported that heavy pollens are carried by insects, mostly honeybees, while light ones by wind. Latif *et al.* (1960) reported that *A. indica* (*cerana*) were able to increase the yield of

brassica crops by about 100 percent. Olsson (1952) obtained a setting of 64.7 percent of the flowers, with 2.46 seeds per fruit, and 1.75 g per fruit with bees excluded, but with bees present these values were increased to 95.3, 4.08, and 2.69, respectively, more than doubling the total production. Koutensky (1959) also showed that the seed yield of white mustard was increased by 66 percent with honeybee pollination. Varieties of the polish rape are almost completely cross-pollinated (Anonymous 1961). Wind can carry pollen grains from one plant to another but insect pollinators, principally honeybees, ensure complete pollination. Free and Spencer-Booth (1963) found that bees more than doubled seed production of *Brassica alba*. Pritsch (1965) also obtained significantly better yields of white mustard in cages with bees than in cages where bees were excluded. Free and Nuttal (1968) stated that *Brassica* plants caged with honeybees produced 13 percent more seed than those without bees. According to Cook (1972), legumes, brassica and sunflower are greatly benefited from honeybee visitation. Free and Williams (1973) reported that cross-pollination is essential when producing crops that are self-sterile cultivars for hybrid seed. Howard (1975) reported that more than 80 percent of all pollination required for setting of fruit and seed crops is accomplished through honeybees. Shahid and Mohammad (1976) obtained the lowest yield from the raya plants (*Brassica* sp.) covered with polythene bags than the plants left open under natural conditions. McGregor (1976) has listed 53 crops dependent upon or greatly benefited by insect pollination in the USA. Kauffeld and Nelson (1982) obtained higher yields of cucumber foraged by *Apis mellifera* and the cucumber fruits were well-shaped and larger in size. Parker (1983) reported that there are about 95 crop species, grown in the USA, which are dependent upon or greatly benefited from insect pollination. Tanda (1984) reported that honeybee pollination increased the boll retention by 25-51 percent and improved the quality of cotton. William (1985a) reported that honeybee pollination played a vital role in the production of over US $95 million worth of horticultural crops in North Carolina in 1983. William (1985b) reported that honeybee pollination was indispensable in cucumber. Khan *et al.* (1986)

TABLE I. Comparative effect of insect pollination and self-pollination on fruit formation of sarson (means followed by different letters are significantly different, p<0.001).

Treatment	Average seed bearing fruits per plant in				Mean fruits per plant
	R_1	R_2	R_3	R_4	
Honey bee pollinated	760	664	940	1086	862.50a
Other insect pollinated	540	496	626	705	591.75b
Self-pollinated	442	428	450	512	458.00c

stated the honeybees are physically well suited and "flower constant", that is visiting only one kind of flower at a time either for nectar or pollen collections.

Keeping in view the paramount economic importance of honeybees in crop pollination, experiments were carried out at Peshawar to evaluate the role of honeybees in pollination of sarson (*Brassica campestris* L.) which occupied 41.995 hectares and yielded 21,749 tonnes of sarson seed during 1981-1982 (Siddiq *et al.* 1981-82).

MATERIALS AND METHODS

The experiment was conducted at Badaber Mera, at a distance of 26 km from the NWFP Agricultural University, Peshawar in order to avoid honeybees' routine visitation during 1986-87 with the following parameters:

T1 = Pollination by honeybees
T2 = Pollination by non-*Apis* insects
T3 = Pollination without insect pollinators

The crops were sown on 25-10-1986 in an area of half a hectare. Two meter wide border lines were discarded on all four sides of the field and the central area was divided into four replications. From each replication, three plants were taken at random and tagged as T1, T2 and T3 for observation. The T3 plant in each replication was covered with muslin cloth supported by four sticks fixed in soil around the plant in order to avoid pollinators. T2 plants were left uncovered for non-*Apis* pollinators in each replication. T1 plants were covered with muslin cloth supported by four sticks fixed in soil around the plant for introduction of honeybees in each replication. When the crop started blooming (5 percent), ten honeybee foragers of *A. mellifera* were released in each T1 enclosure in the morning and were recollected at dusk for putting in the respective hive. The process was repeated until the shedding of petals. The total number of fruits formed and grain weight per plant were recorded at maturity.

RESULTS AND DISCUSSION

The data given in Tables I and II indicate that, on the whole, higher numbers of fruits and seed weight per plant were obtained from the plants pollinated by insects than self-pollinated. The plants pollinated by honeybees and non-*Apis* pollinators produced 74.37 g and 48.4 g seed respectively as compared to 28.68 g obtained from non-pollinated plants. The study signifies that if oilseed crops such as sarson are adequately provided with honeybee colonies (3 to 5 colonies per hectare) for pollination at the inception of flowering then the yield can be increased tremendously. The non-*Apis* pollinators such as bumble bees, alkaline bees, solitary bees and other insects are not adequate in terms of numbers and timing to forage on the whole crop during the blossom period. On the other hand, these are not physically suited to ensure 100% pollination. One of the main reasons for their reducing numbers is pesticide poisoning due to their indiscriminate and irrational use. Honeybees are the only efficient and effective pollinators which can be readily hired and placed just at the right time of crop blooming with the required population to ensure pollination. During observations, it was also noted that the retention and size of the fruits were greater in the insect pollinated plants than self-pollinated ones. The number of fruits per plant was more, that is 862.50 and 591.75, borne by the *Apis* and non-*Apis* pollinated plants respectively, than the non-pollinated plants which produced only 458.00 fruits as detailed in Table I.

Thus, the data indicate that sarson is basically an insect-pollinated crop, with ample pollen and nectar to attract honeybees. It was observed that repeated visits of bee foragers are beneficial. Thus, an ample supply of bees should be present (3 to 5 colonies per hectare).

The results of the study also tally with the findings of the previous workers reviewed above. The data was analyzed and found to be highly significant as shown in Tables I and II.

TABLE II. Comparative effect of insect pollination and self-pollination on seed setting and yield of sarson (means followed by different letters are significantly different, p<0.001).

Treatment	Average seed weight per plant per replication (grams)				Mean seed weight per plant	% increase over self-pollinated
	R_1	R_2	R_3	R_4		
Honey bee pollinated	67.20	60.48	79.80	90.02	74.37a	159.31
Other insect pollinated	44.80	41.72	50.82	56.35	48.42b	68.83
Self-pollinated	27.44	26.46	28.49	34.35	28.68c	-

The observations on the pollination and fruit formation in sarson were compiled for each treatment and replication. The data so collected were analyzed and are presented in Table I. As seen from Table I, the average seed-bearing fruits per plant were 664 to 1086 (mean 862.5) in the honeybee pollinated plants, 496 to 705 (mean 591.75) in non-*Apis* insect pollinated plants and 428 to 512 (mean 458) in self-pollinated plants. Analysis of variance indicates the difference of seed-bearing fruits is significant among the replications but the difference among treatments is highly significant. The fruit formation is maximum (862.5) in honeybee pollinated plants followed by non-*Apis* pollinated plants (591.75) and the least number of fruits (458) in self-pollinated plants. It is quite evident that insects helped in pollination and formation of fruits in sarson, *B. campestris* L.

The observations on seed weight per plant in each treatment and replication were compiled. The data were analyzed and are presented in Table II. The comparison of data revealed that mean seed weight per plant was 74.37, 48.42 and 28.68 grams in honeybee pollinated plants, non-*Apis* insects pollinated plants and self-pollinated plants respectively. The difference in seed yield among the treatments is highly significant (Table II).

The increase in yield of sarson seed due to insect pollination over self-pollination was recorded to be 159.31% and 68.83%, respectively, in honeybee pollinated and non-*Apis* insects pollinated plants.

The honeybee pollinated brassica plants have shown 159.31% increase in seed yield as compared to 100% increase shown by Latif *et al.* (1960), 66% reported by Koutensky (1959) and 13% by Free and Nuttal (1968).

It has been established that insects help in pollination of sarson plants and increase seed yield. The non-*Apis* pollinators also showed significantly more fruit formation and seed yield but their number being not enough to cover the entire plant population. Thus the maximum effect is not realized. This contention has been proved by releasing honeybee foragers which caused complete pollination and increased yield by 159.31%. It is therefore desirable that honeybees may be deployed for pollination of brassica crops for realizing maximum seed yield.

REFERENCES

Anonymous. 1961. Production of rape in western Canada. Technical Bulletin No. 1020, p. 9, cal. 1961, Canada. Department of Agriculture (C.D.A.) Ottawa, Ontario.

Cook, V.A. (1972). Honey bee pollination of legumes, brassica and sunflower. New Zealand Beekeepers 34(4): 24-27.

Eckert, J.E. 1959. Honey bee in crop pollination. California Agriculture Experimental Extension Service. No. 32.

Free, J.B. and P.M. Nuttal. 1968. The pollination of oil seed rape (*Brassica napus*) and behaviour of bees on the crop. Journal of Agricultural Science, 71(2): 91-94.

Free, J.B. and Y. Spencer-Booth. 1963. The pollination of mustard by honey bees. Journal of Apicultural Research, 2: 69-70.

Free, J.B. and I.H. Williams. 1973. The pollination of hybrid Kale *Brassica oleracea*. Journal of Agricultural Science, 81(3): 557-559.

Howard, C. 1975. The hive and the honey bee. Dadant publication. Hamilton, Ill. 62341. USA, pp. 275-286.

Howard, A., G.L.C. Howard, and A.R. Khan. 1915. Studies in Indian oil seeds, safflower and mustard. Indian Department of Agriculture Memorial Botanical Series, 7: 237-272.

Kaufield, K.M. and J. Nelson. 1982. Production of fruits from picking fyneious cucumber with honey bee foraging period, *Apis mellifera*. Entomological Science, 17(4): 471-478.

Khan, B.M., M. Shahid and M.I. Chaudhry. 1986. Effect of honey bee pollination on the fruit setting and yield of loquat. Pak. G. For., 36(2): 73-77.

Koutensky, J. 1959. The pollination effect of the honey bee (*Apis mellifera* L.) on the increase in rape and white mustard yields per hectare. Ceskoslov. Akad. Zemedel, red, sbon. Rostlinna Vvvoba, 32(4): 571-582 (in Czech) AA. 441/631.

Kremer, J.C. 1945. Influence of honey bee visits on radish seed yield. Michigan University Agricultural Experimental Station Bulletin, 27: 413-420.

Latif, A, A. Qayum and M. Abbas. 1960. The role of *Apis indica* in the pollination of toria (*Brassica napus*) and sarson (*B. campestris*). Bee World, 41(11/12): 283-286.

McGregor, S.E. 1976. Insect pollination of cultivated crop plants. Agricultural Handbook No. 496: 226-228.

Mohammad, A. 1935. Pollination studies in toria (*Brassica napus*) and sarson (*B. campestris*). Indian Journal of Agricultural Science, 5: 125-154.

Olsson, G. 1952. (Investigations of the degree of Cross pollination in white mustard and rape). Severig. Utradesforen. Tidskr., 62(4): 311-322. (In Swedish, English summary).

Parker, F.D. 1983. Pollination and non-*Apis* pollination. Lecture National Beekeeping training course held at NARC, Islamabad.

Pellett, F.C. 1947. American Honey Plants. Ed. 4. Orange-Judd Publishing Co., Inc. New York. 467 pp.

Priestley, G. 1954. Use of honey bees as pollinator in unheated glass houses. N.J.I. Sci. Techno., 36(3): 232-236.

Pritsch, G. 1965. Increasing the yield of oil plants by using honey bees. Ved. Prace Vxykum. Ustav: Vecelar CSAZY, 4: 157-163. (In German) AA 770/66.

Rahman, K.A. 1940. Insect pollination of toria (*B. napus*) and sarson (*B. campestris*) at Faisalabad. Indian Journal of Agricultural Science, 5(2): 135-145.

Sampson, D.R. 1957. The genetics of self and cross-incompatibility in *Brassica oleracea*. Genetics, 42: 252-263.

Shahid, K. and L. Mohammad. 1976. Role of insects in pollination of Raya (*B. juncea*) flowers. Pak. Agr. Sci., xiii(i): 65-72.

Siddiq, M. and Fazli Subhan. 1981-1982. Agriculture in Figures. Agricultural Research Institute Tarnab Peshawar, pp. 95-98.

Sneep, J. 1952. Selection and breeding of some brassica plants. Proceedings of the XIIth International Hot. Congress. pp. 422-426.

Tanda, A.S. 1984. Bee pollination increases yield of 2 interplanted varieties of Asiatic cotton. American Bee Journal, 124(7): 539-540.

William, G.L. 1985a. Pollination of horticultural crops in North Carolina. American Bee Journal, 125(2): 127-130.

William, G.L. 1985b. Successful cucumber production will continue to depend on honey bees in the near future. American Bee Journal, 125(9): 623-625.

Yakovlera, L.P. 1975. Utilization of bees for pollination of entomophilous form crops in USSR. Proceedings of the III International Symposium on Pollination 1974: pp. 199-208. (French, German summaries).

CHAPTER 18

COMPARATIVE STUDY ON POLLINATION EFFECT OF HONEYBEE SPECIES *APIS CERANA* AND *APIS MELLIFERA* ON THE FRUIT YIELD OF TORIA (*BRASSICA NAPUS*) IN PESHAWAR, PAKISTAN

B.M. KHAN

ABSTRACT

Self-pollinated toria plants produced few toria fruits (vegetable pods) of small size weighing 1.225 kg while *Apis cerana*, *Apis mellifera* and non-*Apis* pollinated toria plants yielded 15.25, 1.50 and 7.25 kg respectively.

INTRODUCTION

Insects play a significant role in the fertilization of flowers but the indiscriminate and treadmill use of pesticides reduced the number of various pollinators tremendously. Pollination is an important link in fertilization, a complex process resulting in the production of vegetables, fruits, and seeds of flowering crops. Mohammad (1935) reported that only 37% of bagged flowers were able to form pods themselves compared to 100% pod formation occurring in cross-pollinated toria (*Brassica napus*). Rahman (1940) has found 105 insect species belong to 55 families pollinating toria and sarson (*Brassica campestris*) of which honeybees, *Apis cerana indica* were predominating. According to Kremer (1945), most grain-producing crops require the service of insects for cross-pollination, of which honeybees are the most satisfactory pollinators. Sneep (1952) mentioned that better yield of brassica crops can be obtained from honeybee pollination in greenhouses. Sampson (1957) showed that compatibility varies with species, cultivar, and even with age of the plant. Eckert (1959) reported that heavy pollens are carried by insects, mostly honeybees, while light ones by wind. Latif *et al.* (1960) reported that *A. cerana indica* were able to increase the yield of brassica crops by about 100 per cent. Howard (1975) reported that more than 80% of all pollination required for setting of fruit and seed crops is accomplished through honeybees. McGregor (1976) has listed 53 crops dependent upon or greatly benefited by insect pollination in the USA. Kauffeld and Nelson (1982) obtained higher yields of cucumber, foraged by honeybees and the cucumber fruits were well-shaped and larger in size. Parker (1983) reported that there are about 95 crop species, grown in the USA, which are greatly dependent on insect pollination. William (1985) reported that honeybee pollination is indispensable in cucumber production.

MATERIALS AND METHODS

The experiment was conducted at Kagawald (near Badaber) at a distance of 22 km from the North West Frontier Province Agricultural University, Peshawar, Pakistan during 1983-84 with the following parameters:

T1 = Pollination accomplished by *A. cerana*
T2 = Pollination accomplished by *A. mellifera*
T3 = Pollination accomplished by non-*Apis* pollinators
T4 = Selfing

The crop was sown on 15-2-1983 in an area of one acre under local cropping patterns. The field was divided into four replications. Within each replication, two plants were taken at random and tagged as T1, T2, T3 and T4 for observations. Before the opening of the flower, the T1, T2 and T4 tagged plants were covered with muslin cloth supported by four sticks fixed in soil around the flowering portion of the plants in order to avoid the visitation of nontarget pollinators through the experiment. The T3 tagged plants were left uncovered for natural pollinators in each replication. At the opening of the first flowers, five foragers of *A. cerana* and five foragers of *A. mellifera* were released in each T1 and T2 enclosures respectively in the morning and these foragers were set free at dusk to fly back to their respective colonies. This process was repeated until the end of the toria season. During the season, the toria fruits at market size and maturity were picked routinely and their respective weights were regularly recorded until no more fruit setting.

RESULTS AND DISCUSSION

The data given in Table I indicate that higher toria fruit yields were obtained from the plants tagged as T1, T2 and T3 than the plants tagged as T4 which were selfed. The plants of T1 and T2 pollinated by

TABLE I. Comparative effect of *Apis* species pollination and self-pollination on the toria fruits (fresh vegetable pods) yield per plant (means followed by different letters are significantly different, p<0.001).

Treatment	Average toria fruit yield per plant per replication in kg				Mean yield per plant in kg	% increase over selfed (hand) pollinated
	R1	R2	R3	R4		
Apis cerana pollinated	13	18	18	14	15.25a	1144.8973
Apis mellifera pollinated	12	11	12	10	11.50a	838.7755
Non-*Apis* pollinated	6	6	8	9	7.25b	491.8367
Selfed/hand pollinated	1.0	1.7	0.9	1.3	1.225c	-

honeybees gave higher yields than the plants of T3 left open to the natural pollinators (non-*Apis*). Toria fruit yields of 15.25 kg and 11.50 kg per plant were obtained from the plants pollinated by *A. cerana* and *A. mellifera* respectively whereas the plants pollinated by non-*Apis* insects yielded 7.25 kg per plant. This shows that either the non-*Apis* pollinators such as bumble bees, alkaline bees, solitary bees and other insects and mites are not available in adequate enough numbers to meet the crop pollination requirements or their synchronization of visiting hours and flower blooming is poor. Thus, this study further opens new horizons to elaborate more intensively in order to make sure that the pollination in this case is indispensable under local conditions. Such as in the United States, for increased yield production of some cucumber varieties, honeybee pollination is compulsory (Kauffeld and Nelson 1982). Moreover, the non-*Apis* pollinators are not physically suited to ensure 100% pollination for most of the crops. Pesticide poisoning takes a heavy toll of the non-*Apis* pollinators whereas the beekeeper can shift his apiary to a safer place, if informed earlier of the spray operation schedule. Honeybee colonies are movable and can be readily hired at the right time for crop pollination at nominal rates. These encouraging results signify that crop production can be improved and increased through the honeybees, particularly in fruit, vegetable, clover, and oil crops.

REFERENCES

Eckert, J.E. 1959. Honeybees in Crop Pollination. California Agricultural Experimental Station Extension Service No. 32.

Howard, C. 1975. The Hive and the Honey Bee. Dadant and Sons publication, Hamilton, Ill 62341, USA. pp. 275-286.

Kauffeld, N.M. and J. Nelson. 1982. Production of

fruits from picking ganacious cucumber with honey bees foraging period. Entomological Science, 17(4): 471-478.

Kremer, T.C. 1945. Influence of honey bees visits on radish seed yield. Michigan Agricultural Experimental Station Quarterly Bulletin, 27: 413-420.

Latif, A., A. Qayum and M. Abbas. 1960. The role of *Apis indica* (*cerana*) in the pollination of toria and sarson. Bee World, 41(11/12): 283-286.

McGregor, S.E. 1976. Insect Pollination of Cultivated Crop Plants. Agricultural Handbook No. 496, pp. 226-228.

Mohammad, A. 1935. Pollination studies in toria (*Brassica napus*) and sarson (*B. campestris*). Indian Journal of Agricultural Science, 5(2): 125-154.

Parker, F.D. 1983. Pollination and non-*Apis* pollination. Proceedings of the national beekeeping training course, held in March, 1984 at NARC, Islamabad, Pakistan.

Rahman, K.A. 1940. Insect pollination of toria (*Brassica napus*) and sarson (*B. campestris*) at Faisalabad. Indian Journal of Agricultural Science, 5(2): 135-145.

Sampson, D.R. 1957. The genetics of self and cross-incompatibility in *Brassica oleracea*. Genetics, 42(3): 252-263.

Sneep, J. 1952. Selection and breeding of some *Brassica* plants. Proceedings of the XIIth International Horticultural Conference, pp. 422-426.

William, G.L. 1985. Successful cucumber production will continue to depend on honeybees in the near future. American Bee Journal, 125(9): 263-265.

CHAPTER 19

PATTERNS OF FORAGING AND HONEY PRODUCTION FOR *APIS CERANA* IN BANGLADESH

S.M.A.L. DEWAN and R.J. PAXTON

INTRODUCTION

Agriculture is important to the economy of Bangladesh and to the livelihood of most of its people. It has been estimated that the agricultural rural poor could increase their family income by 10-30% if they were to practise beekeeping (Kevan 1983; Mohammad 1984). These estimates assume that a suitable flora exists in agricultural areas and that a surplus of honey can be extracted from managed hives of the indigenous honeybee, *Apis cerana*.

Bangladesh consists predominantly of alluvial deposits in the flat flood plains of large rivers (Johnson 1982). Most of the available land is devoted to agriculture with 80% given over to the growing of rice (Rashid 1978) from which bees can obtain little or no forage. There is only a short history of beekeeping in Bangladesh (Kevan 1983) and so it is not known how suitable most of the country is for beekeeping.

By keeping a few colonies of bees at an apiary for 2 or 3 years, it is often considered (e.g. Singh 1962) that one can evaluate the beekeeping potential of the site. This chapter documents the foraging and honey production of *A. cerana* over 2 years in an attempt to evaluate the beekeeping potential of typical agricultural land in Bangladesh.

METHODS

Five apiaries were located in a 50 kilometre radius of Dhaka in lowland agricultural land dominated by the growing of rice. Two hives of *A. cerana* were established at each apiary in Newton hives (which are suitable for lowland *A. cerana*, Singh 1962). During unsuitable periods of the year, the bees absconded from the hives and more bees had to be introduced using either established wild colonies or swarms. From July 1985 to June 1987, each apiary was visited every two weeks. The colonies were inspected and surplus honey was extracted and weighed. In addition, 15-minute counts were made at around 10:00 a.m. at one of the hive entrances of the number of bees entering the hive, both with and without pollen. The hive observations commenced in September 1985. Bees returning to their hive were classified as nectar foragers and

pollen foragers depending on whether or not pollen was attached to their corbiculae. An examination of the crop contents of returning foragers would be required to tell precisely whether or not a forager was collecting nectar (Erickson *et al.* 1973).

This chapter forms part of an in-depth study which aims to determine the potential of beekeeping in rice-growing areas of Bangladesh. Others studies will cover the floral resources and their utilization by bees (Day in preparation; Dewan in preparation).

RESULTS

Patterns of foraging across a year

Figures 1-5 show the pattern of foraging for pollen and nectar at the five sites across two years. For all sites, there is a peak in foraging during the months of December, January and February. The peak in foraging occurs a little later in the winter of 1986/1987 than in 1985/1986, perhaps reflecting subtle climatic variations between years.

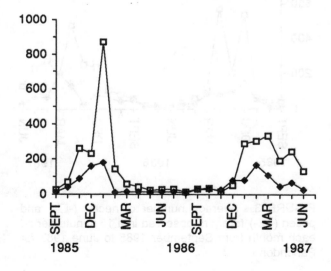

FIGURE 1. Average number of nectar (-□-) and pollen (-♦-) foragers observed in a 15 minute period each month from September 1985 to June 1987 for Jhitka.

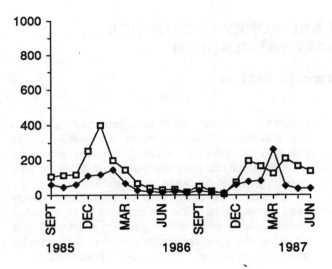

FIGURE 2. Average number of nectar (-□-) and pollen (-◆-) foragers observed in a 15 minute period each month from September 1985 to June 1987 for Manikgonj.

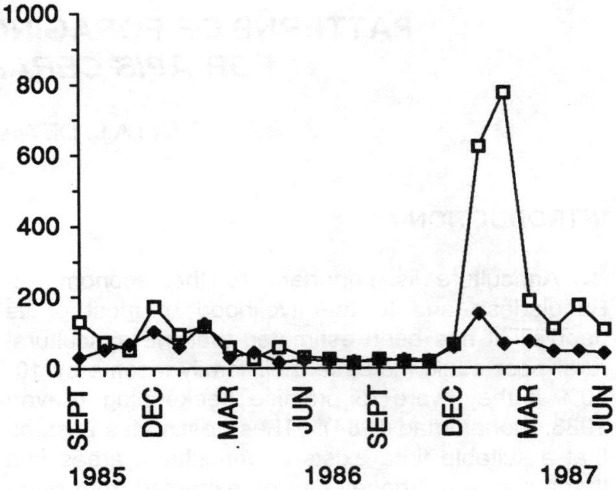

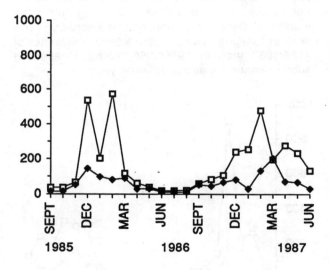

FIGURE 3. Average number of nectar (-□-) and pollen (-◆-) foragers observed in a 15 minute period each month from September 1985 to June 1987 for Panchdona.

For all sites, there is a positive correlation between pollen collection and nectar collection (P<0.05) (Table I). Roughly 72% of all returning bees were considered to be carrying nectar and 28% were carrying pollen.

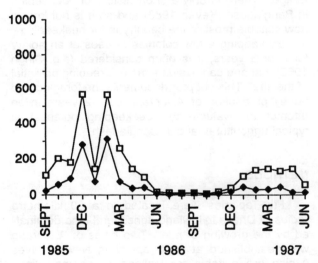

FIGURE 4. Average number of nectar (-□-) and pollen (-◆-) foragers observed in a 15 minute period each month from September 1985 to June 1987 for Sardagonj.

FIGURE 5. Average number of nectar (-□-) and pollen (-◆-) foragers observed in a 15 minute period each month from September 1985 to June 1987 for Sonargaon.

Patterns of honey production across a year

Figures 6-10 show the pattern of honey production per colony per month at the five sites across two years. Surplus honey is produced mainly in the months of January and March, reflecting the pattern

TABLE 1. The correlation between nectar and pollen foraging across all months of data collection (n=20) for all 5 sites.

Name of Site	Correlations coefficient - r	Significance
Jhitka	0.809	P < 0.001
Manikgonj	0.533	P < 0.05
Panchdona	0.593	P < 0.01
Sardagonj	0.580	P < 0.01
Sonargaon	0.964	P < 0.001

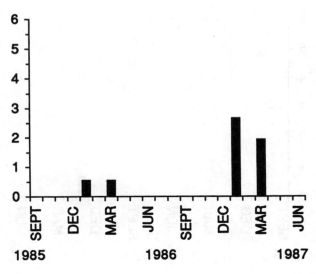

FIGURE 7. Weight of honey (kg) extracted per colony for each month from July 1985 to June 1987 for Manikgonj.

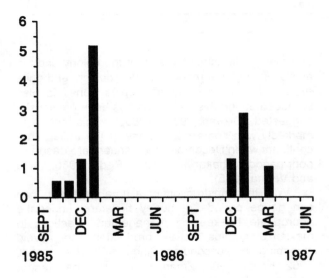

FIGURE 6. Weight of honey (kg) extracted per colony for each month from July 1985 to June 1987 for Jhitka.

of foraging. There is a strong positive correlation between the total amount of foraging at all sites and the total amount of honey produced per month at all sites (r=0.567, n=22, P<0.01). There is a trend for honey to be produced slightly later in the spring of 1987 compared to 1986, also reflecting the foraging data.

Annual honey production

There is much variation between sites in the total amount of surplus honey produced per colony per year (Table II). Some sites, such as Jhitka and Panchdona, averaged over 6 kg of honey per colony per year whereas colonies at Sardagonj averaged less than 1 kg of honey per colony per year. There

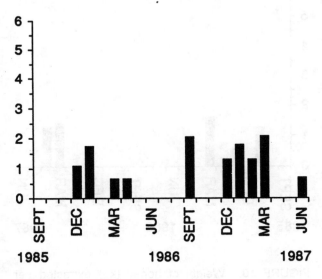

FIGURE 8. Weight of honey (kg) extracted per colony for each month from July 1985 to June 1987 for Panchdona.

was little difference between years in the total amount of honey produced per colony (Student t=0.720, n=5, n.s.).

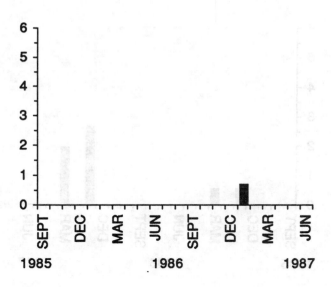

FIGURE 9. Weight of honey (kg) extracted per colony for each month from July 1985 to June 1987 for Sardagonj.

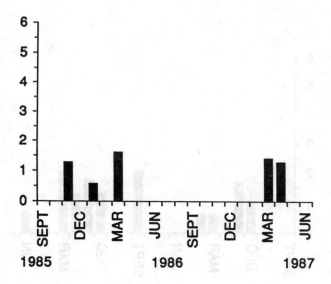

FIGURE 10. Weight of honey (kg) extracted per colony for each month from July 1985 to June 1987 for Sonargaon.

DISCUSSION

It is clear from the data that the majority of foraging by *A. cerana* in rice growing areas of Bangladesh occurs during the winter months. Patterns

TABLE II. The average honey production per colony per year for all 5 sites.

Name of Site	July 1986 to June 1986	July 1986 to June 1987	Average of both years
Jhitka	7.30	5.50	6.40
Manikgonj	1.00	4.50	2.75
Panchdona	3.68	8.88	6.28
Sardagonj	0.00	0.63	0.31
Sonargaon	3.38	2.63	3.00
Average for all sites	3.07	4.43	3.75

of foraging will reflect the size of the colony and the availability of floral resources. In addition, and quite expectedly, the majority of surplus honey is also produced during this period, as has been previously suggested (Dewan 1984, 1985). This contrasts markedly with some other areas of the Indian sub-continent when December and January are dearth or poor periods (Thakar *et al.* 1962; Reddy 1980; Mattu and Verma 1985).

With the construction of a floral calendar, one can gauge periods of honey flow and undertake appropriate beekeeping management practices to maximize surplus honey production, and avoid swarming and absconding (Singh 1962; Thakar *et al.* 1962; Kevan 1984; Zmarlicki 1984). The present study provides a calendar for appropriate beekeeping management in rice growing areas of Bangladesh but does not identify those floral sources which contribute to the honey surplus. It is often considered that forest trees, the wide variety of vegetation around villages and crops of mustard (*Brassica* spp.) provide much of the floral resources for bees in Bangladesh (Nash and Murrell 1981; Kevan 1983; Dewan 1984, 1985). Our preliminary observations suggest that *Brassica napus* provides a large honey surplus in the winter months, as it does for *A. mellifera* in other parts of the world (Williams 1980; Crane *et al.* 1984). Studies of the plants visited by bees and of the pollen types in the pollen loads and of the pollen in surplus honey of the bees will reveal the major floral resources (Day in preparation; Dewan in preparation).

Factors which influence the proportion of foragers that collect pollen include hive stimuli and the species of plant upon which bees are foraging. Across 2 years and at 5 different sites, 28% of foragers collected pollen. This relatively great emphasis on pollen collection by *A. cerana* may be typical for tropically evolved honeybees (Danka *et al.* 1987).

The variability that was found between the 5 sites in the average honey production per colony probably reflected the relative abundance of major honey plants at the different sites. Again, a knowledge of such plants will provide the information necessary to enable one to predict the suitability of sites for beekeeping.

Singh (1962) reports that between 1.4 to 2.3 kg of honey can be obtained from wild colonies of *A. cerana* living at low altitudes, compared with an average of 10 to 15 kg per annum in managed colonies. Others (Dewan 1984; Mohammad 1984) have suggested that similar amounts could be obtained from *A. cerana* colonies in Bangladesh. The colonies, used in the trials described here, only produced around 4 kg of honey per colony per year. In addition, some of the colonies absconded during unfavourable periods and had to be replaced with colonies collected from the wild. Set against this, the colonies of the present study were frequently manipulated. This would have disturbed them and could have resulted in lowered honey yields and absconding (Singh and Sharma 1943; Singh 1962). In well managed colonies sited in a suitable apiary with appropriate floral resources, 10 kg of honey per colony per year would probably be an attainable average yield. A figure of this magnitude should be used by those calculating the potential immediate benefits of beekeeping to rural poor in Bangladesh. This study suggests that some rice growing areas of Bangladesh are suitable for beekeeping.

CONCLUSIONS

In rice growing areas of Bangladesh, greatest foraging activity by *A. cerana* colonies was seen during the winter months of December to February. Most surplus honey was extracted during, or soon after, this time. *B. napus* is probably a major nectar source in such agricultural areas. Some locations would be favourable for beekeeping and it would seem that an average of 10 kg of honey per colony per year would be attainable.

ACKNOWLEDGEMENTS

Many thanks to Dr. Nicola Bradbear, Prof. John Free and Rosemary Day for their generous help and advice and to NORAD for financial support.

REFERENCES

Crane, E., P. Walker and R. Day. 1984. Directory of important world honey sources. I.B.R.A., London.

Danka, R.G., R.L. Hellmich, T.E. Rinderer and A.M. Collins. 1987. Diet-selection ecology of tropically and temperately adapted honey bees. Animal Behaviour, 35: 1858-1863.

Dewan, S.M.A.L. 1984. Apiculture in Bangladesh. Proceedings of the Expert Consultation on Beekeeping with *Apis mellifera* in Tropical and Sub-Tropical Asia. F.A.O., Rome. pp. 131-140.

Dewan, S.M.A.L. 1985. Honeybees, plants and beekeeping in the integrated rural developments in Bangladesh. Proceedings of the 3rd International Conference on Apiculture in Tropical Climates. I.B.R.A., London. pp. 123-135.

Erickson, E.H., L.O. Whitefoot and W.A. Kissinger. 1973. Honey bees: a method of delimiting the complete profile of foraging from colonies. Environmental Entomology, 2: 531-535.

Johnson, B.L.C. 1982. Bangladesh. Heinemann Educational, London.

Kevan, P.G. 1983. The potential for beekeeping in Bangladesh. A.S.T./C.I.D.A. Report.

Kevan, P.G. 1984. Bee botany: pollination, foraging and floral calendars. Proceedings of the Expert Consultation on Beekeeping with *Apis mellifera* in Tropical and Sub-Tropical Asia, F.A.O. Rome. pp. 51-55.

Mattu, V.K. and L.R. Verma. 1985. Studies on the annual foraging cycle of *Apis cerana indica* F. in Shimla Hills of North West Himalayas. Apidologie, 16: 1-18.

Mohammad, A. 1984. Economic impact of beekeeping: a case study of Bangladesh. Proceedings of the Expert Consultation on Beekeeping with *Apis mellifera* in Tropical and Sub-Tropical Asia, F.A.O., Rome. pp. 111-121.

Nash, W.T. and D.C. Murrell. 1981. Beekeeping in Bangladesh. American Bee Journal, 121: 352-356.

Rashid, H.E. 1978. Geography of Bangladesh. Westview Press, Boulder, Colorado.

Reddy, C.C. 1980. Observations on the annual cycle of foraging and brood rearing by *Apis cerana indica* colonies. Journal of Apicultural Research, 19: 17-20.

Singh, S. 1962. Beekeeping in India. Indian Council of Agricultural Research, New Delhi.

Singh, S. and P.L. Sharma. 1943. Absconding among Indian bees, *Apis indica*. Indian Bee Journal, 5: 98-101.

Thakar, C.V., V.V. Diwan and S.R. Salvi. 1962. Floral calendar of major and minor bee forage plants in Mahabaleshwar Hills (Western Ghats). Indian Bee Journal, 24: 4-6.

Williams, I.H. 1980. Oil-seed rape and beekeeping, particularly in Britain. Bee World, 61: 141-153.

Zmarlicki, C. 1984. Evaluation of honey plants in Burma - a case study. Proceedings of the Expert Consultation on Beekeeping with *Apis mellifera* in Tropical and Sub-Tropical Asia, F.A.O., Rome. pp. 57-76.

SECTION V: AFFLICTIONS AND PROTECTION

CHAPTER 20

VIRUSES OF *APIS CERANA* AND *APIS MELLIFERA*

DENIS L. ANDERSON

INTRODUCTION

Viruses, unlike bacteria, lack the ability to multiply independently. Instead their infectious particles must enter living susceptible cells and use the cell's molecular machinery to make replica copies of themselves. An infected cell may eventually die or become damaged by the replicating virus thereby releasing thousands of infectious virus particles which are capable of subsequently infecting other living susceptible cells and individuals. These virus particles are some of the smallest infectious agents known. Most can only be clearly seen when highly magnified by an electron microscope.

Insect viruses are classified according to physical and physico-chemical properties of their particles and to whether or not their particles become incorporated into crystalline inclusion bodies (polyhedra) during replication (Mathews 1982). The physical structure of many insect virus particles is relatively simple; the simplest particle is little more than a strand or core of genetic nucleic acid surrounded by a protective coat of protein. The nucleic acid from different insect viruses may contain either the sugar ribose (ribonucleic acid = RNA), or deoxyribose (deoxyribonucleic acid = DNA). The protective protein coat consists of repeated copies of a single or several smaller proteins. Antibody molecules, Immunoglobulin G's (IgG's), that react specifically with antigenic regions on the exposed surfaces of coat proteins, and which are used in serological tests for identifying viruses, may be obtained from the blood serum of rabbits and other animals that have been injected with purified preparations of virus particles.

Only three viruses have been isolated from the Eastern hive bee *Apis cerana* F., compared with 13, not including serologically related strains, from the European honeybee *Apis mellifera* L. This difference probably reflects the greater effort given to isolating and studying viruses of *A. mellifera* rather than a difference in host susceptibility. Two of the three viruses of *A. cerana* are related to viruses of *A. mellifera*. Hence, other viruses related to viruses of *A. mellifera* may yet be found in *A. cerana*. In this chapter I briefly describe the known viruses of *A. mellifera* before describing aspects of the three known viruses of *A. cerana* and methods by which these and other viruses of *A. cerana* may be isolated

and identified. Comprehensive reviews of all these viruses are given by Bailey (1981, 1982).

VIRUSES OF *APIS MELLIFERA*

Most of the viruses of *A. mellifera* were first isolated at Rothamsted Experimental Station in Britain, where all the known viruses of *A. cerana* were also first isolated. Their particles are non-occluded and replicate, either experimentally or in nature, in tissues of larvae, pupae, or adults, or only adults. Some physico-chemical properties of their particles are given in Table I.

Several viruses of *A. mellifera* exist as infections of seemingly healthy bees. These inapparent infections may persist in individual bees and colonies for long periods of time producing small numbers of virus particles and causing no obvious harm. However, they have the 'latent' ability to develop into acute infections in which they rapidly produce large numbers of virus particles and kill many bees and sometimes even whole colonies. Inapparent virus infections are far more common in colonies than acute infections and an individual bee may be inapparently infected with several viruses simultaneously (Bailey *et al.* 1979; Bailey *et al.* 1981a; Bailey 1981, 1982; Dall 1985; Hornitzky 1987; Anderson and Gibbs 1988, 1989).

a. Viruses that multiply in all life stages of *Apis mellifera*

Most of the viruses that multiply in tissue of larvae, pupae and adult worker bees are picornavirus-like in that their particles are isometric in shape and approximately 30 nm in diameter (Table I).

Acute bee paralysis virus

Acute bee paralysis virus has been reported in bees from Britain (Bailey *et al.* 1963), Europe (Bailey 1965; Ball and Allan 1988), Australia (Reinganum 1969), Belize (Bailey *et al.* 1979), USSR (Batuev 1979; Bailey 1981) and New Zealand (Anderson 1988). It commonly exists as an inapparent infection of seemingly healthy bees and has not been reported to be associated with mortality of bees in Britain (Bailey and Gibbs 1964; Bailey 1982) or New Zealand (Anderson, D.L., unpublished results). However,

161

it kills larvae, pupae and adult bees in colonies in the USSR, Belize and Germany, but only in association with the parasitic mite *Varroa jacobsoni* (Bailey *et al.* 1979; Batuev 1979; Bailey 1982; Ball 1985; Ball and Allan 1988). Recent evidence suggests that the mites' feeding behaviour activates replication of the virus in inapparently infected adult bees. The mite is also thought to transmit the virus directly from adult bees to pupae and indirectly to larvae by contaminating larval food (Ball and Allan 1988).

Arkansas bee virus and Egypt bee virus

Little is known of the life history of these two viruses. Arkansas bee virus was first detected as inapparent infections of healthy bees in Arkansas, USA (Bailey and Woods 1974), but high concentrations of the virus have subsequently been found in dead bees from dwindling colonies in California, USA (Bailey 1981). Egypt bee virus has only been found in honeybees from Egypt (Bailey *et al.* 1979).

Black queen cell virus

This virus has been detected in Britain (Bailey and Woods 1977b), North America (Bailey 1981), Belize, Papua New Guinea, Australia (Bailey *et al.* 1979; Anderson 1983; Hornitzky 1987), Fiji (Anderson 1990) and New Zealand (Anderson 1988). It is an extremely important but yet much understudied virus.

Black queen cell virus commonly infects adult bees mostly during spring and usually in association with the microsporidian pathogen *Nosema apis* (Bailey *et al.* 1983a; Anderson 1988). The virus also infects prepupae and pupae of queen bees after they become sealed in their cells. Infected queen prepupae first turn pale yellow and develop a tough 'sac-like' skin, resembling prepupae that have died of sacbrood. Their decomposing remains darken and stain the cell walls almost black. Infected queen larvae are mostly found in queenless colonies used to raise queen cells. In New Zealand many seemingly healthy adult queen bees have been found to be infected with the virus (Anderson, unpublished results). Thus the virus may be transovarially transmitted.

In Australia, at least, black queen cell virus also commonly kills prepupae of worker bees (Anderson 1983; Hornitzky 1987). Dying worker prepupae first turn pale yellow and develop a tough 'sac-like' skin (Anderson, unpublished observations). The virus has also been isolated in high concentrations in adult worker bees (Anderson, unpublished results; Bailey *et al.* 1981a).

Chronic bee paralysis virus

Chronic bee paralysis virus is the major cause of paralysis of adult bees. It was first isolated from adult bees in Britain (Bailey *et al.* 1963), but has subsequently been found in bees worldwide (Bailey 1981). The virus multiplies mostly in the heads of infected workers (Bailey *et al.* 1968), but also infects other parts of the body (Bailey 1976). It also infrequently multiplies in old pupae in the late stages of development (Bailey 1981; Bailey *et al.* 1981a) and will readily multiply experimentally when injected into younger pupae (Bailey and Woods 1977b).

According to Bailey (1975), infected adult bees show two distinct 'types' of symptoms designated Type 1 and Type 2. Bees with Type 1 symptoms show abnormal trembling of wings and body, are flightless and crawl on the ground outside the hive, have bloated abdomens, huddle at the top of the colony and have partially dislocated wings. They usually die within a few days. Bees with Type 2 symptoms are able to fly when first infected, have bodies that are shiny, greasy, hairless and black and hence appear small, are hindered from returning to the colony by guard bees, and are attacked and nibbled by other bees in the colony. In New Zealand many naturally infected adult bees from severely affected colonies have been found to display a combination of Type 1 and 2 symptoms (Anderson, unpublished observations).

Evidence suggests that chronic bee paralysis virus is transmitted between individuals in a crowded colony via the epidermal cytoplasm that becomes exposed when hairs of trichogens are nibbled by other bees (Bailey *et al.* 1983b).

Chronic bee paralysis associate virus

This is one of the smallest viruses known (Table I). It has only been reported from Britain where it is consistently associated with infections of chronic bee paralysis virus (Bailey *et al.* 1980a). Its particles will not multiply experimentally when injected alone (Bailey 1981) and their nucleic acid shows relationships with the nucleic acid of chronic bee paralysis virus particles (Overton *et al.* 1982). Hence chronic bee paralysis associate virus may be a satellite of the paralysis virus. Bailey (1981) suggests it may be of some significance in, or a reflection of, the defense mechanisms of individual bees against paralysis. The virus is more commonly isolated from queen bees than from worker bees (Bailey *et al.* 1980a).

Kashmir bee virus

This virus was first isolated from *A. mellifera* pupae that had been experimentally inoculated with extracts of *A. cerana* adults from Kashmir (Bailey and Woods 1977b). Strains of that virus were subsequently discovered in *A. mellifera* in Australia (Bailey *et al.* 1979). Since the virus had not been detected

TABLE I. Properties of viruses of the European honey bee, *Apis mellifera* and the Eastern hive bee, *Apis cerana*.

Host	Virus	Virion size (nanometers)	Virion symmetry	S20W (Svedbergs)	Buoyant density in CsCl (g/cm³)	Number of structural proteins	Molecular weights of structural proteins (Kd)	Nucleic acid strandedness
	Acute bee paralysis	30	Isometric	160	1.37	2	23.5,31.5	ssRNA
	Arkansas bee	30	"	128	1.37	1	41.0	"
	Egypt bee	30	"	165	1.37	3	24.9,30.0,41.0	"
	Black queen cell	30	"	151	1.34	3	29.0,32.0,34.0	"
	Chronic bee paralysis	20 x 30-65	Anisometric (ellipsoidal)	82,97-106,110-124,125-136	1.33	1	23.5	"
	Chronic bee paralysis associate	17	Isometric	41	1.38	1	15.0	"
Apis mellifera	Kashmir bee (NSW strain)	30	"	172	1.37	3	44.5,35.4,24.9	"
	Kashmir bee (Queensland 1 strain)	30	"	172	1.37	3	38.8,32.9,24.8	"
	Kashmir bee (Queensland 2 strain)	30	"	172	1.37	3	40.3,36.4,25.2	"
	Kashmir bee (South Australian strain)	30	"	172	1.37	3	44.3,35.6,25.0	"
	Sacbrood	30	"	160	1.35	3	25,28,31.5	"
	Bee virus X	35	"	187	1.35	1	52.0	"
	Bee virus Y	35	"	187	1.34	1	50.0	"
	Cloudy wing	17	"	49	1.38	1	19.0	"
	Filamentous	150 x 450	Brick-shaped	ND*	1.28	~12	13.0-17.0	dsDNA
	Slow bee paralysis	30	Isometric	172-178	1.37	3	27.0,29.0,46.0	ssRNA
Apis cerana	Apis iridescent	150	Isometric	2216	1.32	ND	ND	ssDNA
	Kashmir bee (Indian strain)	30	"	172	1.37	3	24.5,37.3,41.1	ssRNA
	Thai sacbrood	30	"	160	1.35	3	30.0,34.0,39.0	"

* ND = Not determined

References: Bailey 1981; Bailey and Woods 1974, 1977a; Bailey *et al.* 1963, 1964, 1968, 1976, 1979, 1980a, 1980b, 1981b; Ball *et al.* 1985; Clarke 1977, 1978.

in Britain, and the Australian isolates were different strains, Bailey *et al.* (1979) suggested that Kashmir bee virus may have originated in *A. cerana* and spread to *A. mellifera* in Australia, possibly by way of another insect species common to Asia and Australia such as *Trigona* species. However the virus could not be isolated from *T. carbonaria* colonies in Australia (Anderson and Gibbs 1982), and has more recently been detected in bees from Fiji (Anderson 1990), New Zealand (Anderson 1985, 1988) and Canada (Anderson 1985).

In Australia and New Zealand, Kashmir bee virus exists commonly as inapparent infections of seemingly healthy bees (Dall 1985; Hornitzky 1987; Anderson and Gibbs 1988, 1989). The virus particles will not multiply to detectable levels when experimentally fed to adult bees but do, and at a much faster rate than other viruses, when injected (Bailey 1981; Anderson and Gibbs 1988). Evidence suggests the virus exists mostly as an inapparent infection of bee guts causing no obvious harm but occasionally causes mortality in association with other bee pathogens, such as *N. apis* (Anderson 1988) and the bacterium *Melissococcus pluton* (Hornitzky 1981).

Sacbrood virus

Sacbrood virus was one of the first viruses isolated from *A. mellifera* (Bailey *et al.* 1964) but has subsequently been reported in bees worldwide (Bailey 1981). It causes sacbrood disease of larvae, mainly during spring and early summer (White 1917; Bailey 1967) but also infects adult bees modifying their foraging behaviour and reducing their life-span (Bailey and Fernando 1972).

Two-day-old larvae are most susceptible to sacbrood, but they do not begin to show signs of the disease until they become prepupae, that is, about 6 days after becoming infected. First their unshed final larval cuticle becomes a transparent 'sac' and fluid accumulates between this and the epidermis (Fig. 1a). Then beginning at the head and spreading posteriorly, their body colour gradually changes from a pearly white to pale yellow. Shortly afterwards, they die stretched on their backs with their heads pointing towards the cell cappings (Fig. 1b). Their bodies eventually dry to dark brown 'gondola'-shaped scales, which are easily removed from the cell and in which the sacbrood virus particles (Fig. 1c) become non-infectious (White 1917). Nurse bees often remove larvae from their cells that are in the early stages of infection or that have recently died giving capped brood a 'spotty' or 'peppered' appearance (Bailey *et al* 1964; Bailey 1969; Anderson and Gibbs 1989).

There are two main lines of thought as to the cause of the fluid-filled 'sac' that forms around the

larvae with sacbrood (Fig. 1a). One hypothesis is that sacbrood virus damages part of the larval brain and corpora allata upsetting the production of molting and juvenile hormones in such a way that larvae cannot cast off the final skin (Bailey 1970). The second hypothesis is that sacbrood virus damages dermal glands preventing the production of chitinase, the enzyme which is responsible for breaking down the skin. Hence ecdysial fluid lacking chitinase builds up under the skin giving it a 'sac-like' appearance (Fernando 1972; Bailey 1976). The ecdysial fluid in the 'sac' has been found to contain much infectious virus (Fernando 1972).

Sacbrood virus multiplies in several body tissues of larvae (Lee and Furgala 1967) and in head glands of adult bees (Bailey 1969). A single infected larva contains enough particles to infect all the larvae of more than 1,000 colonies (Bailey 1981), but in most colonies sacbrood remains uncommon. This is probably due, in part, to two inherited, behavioural traits which enable worker bees to limit the spread of the disease. One of these traits is that larvae, in the early stages of infection are recognized and removed from the colony by nurse bees before they have produced large concentrations of infectious particles in their bodies (Anderson and Gibbs 1989). The other is that nurse bees do not remove dead larvae until at least 3 weeks after they have died, when the virus particles in them have become non-infectious (White 1917). When both of these strategies fail, nurse bees become infected. They soon cease eating pollen, rearing brood, and attending to queens or drones. They also try to forage sooner. However, even in these infected foraging workers the spread of the virus appears to be restricted by subtle, virus induced changes. For instance, the infected adults die sooner than healthy bees and show altered foraging behaviour by collecting mainly nectar, not pollen. The few infected bees that do collect pollen contaminate their loads with sacbrood virus by way of secretions from the mandibular and hypopharyngeal glands (Bailey and Fernando 1972; Fernando 1972). This altered behaviour probably limits the spread of the disease because nectar, as opposed to pollen that is collected by infected bees, usually contains fewer infectious particles than are required to infect a susceptible larva (Bailey *et al.* 1964).

Sacbrood virus is thought to persist from year to year in adult bees, in which it multiplies without causing symptoms (Bailey 1969). Drones, robbing bees or 'drifting' bees may transmit the virus between colonies.

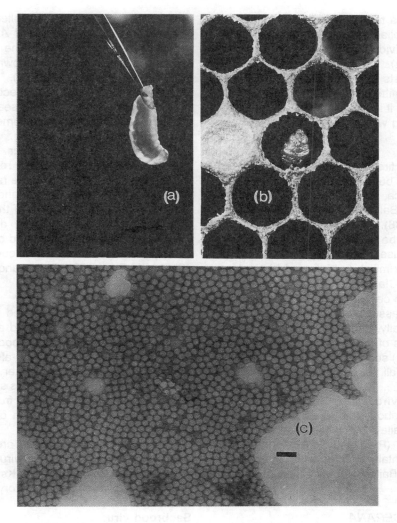

FIGURE 1. The 'skin' of *Apis mellifera* prepupae with sacbrood develops into a fluid-filled 'sac' (a). These prepupae die stretched on their backs with their heads pointing upwards toward the cell cappings (b). Sacbrood virus particles highly magnified by an electron microscope (c). Bar = 100 nm.

b. Viruses that multiple only in adults of *Apis mellifera*

Five viruses are known to multiply in only adult bees and interestingly, their particles are mostly different in shape and size from the particles of those viruses that infect all life stages of bees.

Bee virus X and Bee virus Y

Bee virus X has been isolated in England (Bailey 1981), New Zealand (Anderson 1988) and Fiji (Anderson 1990). It is distantly related serologically to bee virus Y (Bailey *et al.* 1980b). The virus is often found in association with the protozoan bee pathogen *Malpighamoeba mellificae*, and like that pathogen is probably transmitted by faecal contamination (Bailey 1981).

Bee virus Y has been detected in England, North America, Australia (Bailey *et al.* 1980b), New Zealand (Anderson 1988) and Fiji (Anderson 1990). The virus invariably multiplies only in adult bees that are infected with *N. apis* (Bailey *et al.* 1983a).

The particles of bee virus X and Y will only multiply experimentally when given in food to adult bees. Bee virus X significantly reduces the life-span of the bees it infects (Bailey 1981).

Cloudy wing virus

Like chronic bee paralysis associate virus, cloudy wing virus is one of the smallest known insect viruses (Table I). It has been detected in Britain, Egypt, Australia (Bailey *et al.* 1980a; Hornitzky 1987) and New Zealand (Anderson 1988). The wings of infected bees often show a marked loss of transparency, but this is not a reliable symptom (Bailey 1982; Hornitzky 1987). Individuals die soon after becoming infected (Bailey 1982).

Evidence suggests that cloudy wing virus is airborne, being transmitted when bees are closely confined. In England it is associated with mortality of whole colonies during winter (Bailey 1982).

Filamentous virus

This virus was first discovered in the United States (Clarke 1977) but has since been detected in Britain, North America, Australia, Japan, the USSR and New Zealand (Bailey and Milne 1978; Bailey 1982; Anderson 1988). Its large particles contain DNA and can just be seen by light microscopy. Sometimes they cause the usually clear blood of adult bees to appear milky, but infected bees show no other symptoms (Clarke 1978).

Like black queen cell virus and bee virus Y, the filamentous virus is associated with infections of *N. apis* and experimentally, it infects bees most readily when fed with spores of that pathogen (Bailey *et al.* 1983a). Bailey (1982) suggests the filamentous virus is the commonest of all the bee viruses.

Slow bee paralysis virus

Little is known about this virus. It has been detected in Britain (Bailey 1982), Fiji (Anderson 1990) and Western Samoa (Reid and Bettesworth 1988). Adult bees experimentally injected with the virus die after about 12 days (Bailey 1982).

VIRUSES OF *APIS CERANA*

The viruses of *A. cerana*, like the viruses of *A. mellifera*, are non-occluded. Some physico-chemical properties of their particles are given in Table I.

Apis iridescent virus

Apis iridescent virus is the only iridovirus of Hymenoptera. It has only been found in sick adult bees from colonies in Northern India and Kashmir (Bailey *et al.* 1976; Bailey and Ball 1978).

Naturally infected adult bees are said to become inactive and cluster together in small groups on the outer or inner hive walls, combs and bottom boards. They also lose their ability to fly and are commonly found crawling on hive parts (Kshirsagar *et al.* 1975; Shah and Shah 1976; Bailey and Ball 1978). The virus multiplies in fat bodies, ovaries and most other organs of susceptible bees forming cytoplasmic crystalline aggregates which reflect blue-violet or green light. In severely infected bees whole coloured tissues can be seen with the naked eye (Bailey and

Ball 1978). The virus multiplies when fed to, or injected into, adult workers of *A. mellifera*, but not when injected into larvae of the wax moth *Galleria mellonella* in which all other known insect iridoviruses will multiply (Bailey *et al.* 1976).

Many adult bees may become infected in a single bee colony and as the disease progresses, the queen bee is thought to become infected, thereby reducing her rate of egg-laying. Death of the whole colony may follow (Kshirsagar *et al* 1975; Singh 1979). Colonies have been reported to become infected during summer and the rainy season (Kshirsagar *et al.* 1975; Bhambhure and Kshirsagar 1978).

Many important aspects of the life cycle of *Apis* iridescent virus are yet to be discovered, but the virus is probably not transmitted by the tracheal mite *Acarapis woodi* with which it is commonly associated (Shah and Shah 1977; Bailey and Ball 1978).

Kashmir bee virus

This virus was first isolated in association with *Apis* iridescent virus from dead adults of *A. cerana* from Kashmir (Bailey and Woods 1977b). It has subsequently been detected alone and in large concentrations in adult worker bees from India (Bailey *et al.* 1979). The virus is serologically related to strains of Kashmir bee virus from *A. mellifera* and also has physical properties in common with those strains (Table I).

Many *A. cerana* colonies are claimed to have been killed by Kashmir bee virus in northern and western India (Bhambhure and Kshirsagar 1978), but nothing is known of the life history of the virus.

Sacbrood virus

Sacbrood virus was first isolated from *A. cerana* larvae from Thailand by Bailey *et al.* (1982). It became known as 'Thai sacbrood virus' because the physical properties of its particles differed from those of sacbrood virus of *A. mellifera*. The Thai sacbrood virus strain has not been recorded from *A. mellifera*, but has been isolated from *A. cerana* larvae in several Indian states (Kshirsagar *et al.* 1981, 1982; Bailey *et al.* 1982: Kshirsagar and Phadke 1984), suggesting it may be a strain specific to *A. cerana*.

Thai sacbrood virus causes sacbrood of *A. cerana* larvae. The symptoms shown by diseased larvae are identical to those described above for *A. mellifera* larvae with sacbrood (Kshirsagar *et al.* 1982), except that Thai sacbrood virus is reported to be more virulent than sacbrood virus of *A. mellifera* (Morse 1982; Kshirsagar and Phadke 1984). Severely infected *A. cerana* colonies are reported to desert their hives leaving behind infected and dead brood (Kshirsagar *et al.* 1982).

Little is known of the maintenance and spread of

Thai sacbrood virus within and between colonies. Studies directed at these aspects seem warranted if control measures are to be devised. At the present time no cure of Thai sacbrood is known, although in India heavily infected brood and adult bees are sometimes killed to reduce the spread of the disease and hive parts are cleaned for reuse by washing with bleaching powder dissolved in water (Kshirsagar *et al.* 1982). It may also be possible to breed bees that are genetically resistant to Thai sacbrood virus though this would be an ongoing process.

IDENTIFYING AND ISOLATING VIRUSES OF *APIS CERANA*

The techniques used to identify and isolate viruses of *A. mellifera* may also be used for identifying and isolating viruses of *A. cerana*. In developing identification techniques it is usually necessary to work with purified preparations of virus particles and, as large numbers of virus particles become lost during the purification procedure, the viruses must be propagated beforehand.

Methods for extracting and purifying most bee viruses have been described by Bailey (1981). The extraction procedure involves grinding bees in a suitable buffer and solvents and filtering through muslin. Such preparations are then clarified by low and high speed centrifugation. Further purification using density gradients is usually necessary to obtain virus preparations that are suitable for antiserum production. This general extraction and purification procedure can easily be modified and improved if necessary.

No alternative host or susceptible cell line has been found for propagating bee viruses. Hence, bee viruses must be propagated in bees, some of which are already inapparently infected with several other viruses (Anderson and Gibbs 1988). Nevertheless, most bee viruses can be propagated by injection into young (white-eyed) pupae or by injection into, or feeding to, young adult bees (Bailey and Woods 1977b).

Diluted semi-purified virus extracts are best injected into white-eyed pupae or adult bees through a dorso-lateral abdominal intersegmental membrane using a sterile 25-30 gauge needle connected by a bacteriological filter (0.22 μm) to a micrometer syringe (Anderson and Gibbs 1988). Pupae suitable for injection can be easily located amongst sealed brood by removing their wax cappings. Each pupa is then carefully withdrawn from its cell using bent forceps to grip behind the head vertices. Young bees are best obtained as they hatch from their cells. They may be kept in small cages supplied with water

and a 60% sugar solution. Usually young adult bees do not need to be anaesthetized prior to injection but if they need to be anaesthetized it is best to use carbon dioxide gas from a pressurized cylinder, passing the gas through water to remove harmful frozen particles of solid carbon dioxide. Inoculated pupae are best incubated at 30°C or 35°C in a container with filter paper wetted with 12% glycerol to humidify the air, until they become moribund or die. It is usual for the eye colour of virus-infected pupae to remain undeveloped or to turn red before the eye colour 'shatters'. Inoculated adults are also best incubated at 30°C or 35°C in a dry environment in small cages supplied with water and a 60% sucrose solution.

Antibodies against highly purified preparations of virus particles are readily produced in rabbits by immunizing each with three 1.0 ml injections of purified virus particles over an 8-week period. The first injection is intramuscular, using virus particles emulsified in Freund's complete adjuvant and the others are intravenous using only virus particles. Blood samples may be removed from the ear vein of each rabbit 1-2 weeks after the final injection and the serum separated from clotted blood. This serum, which contains virus specific antibodies, may then be used in serological tests to detect and identify viruses.

Several serological techniques have been compared for identifying and detecting bee viruses (Anderson 1984). However, an effective and relatively simple and inexpensive technique is the immunodiffusion test described by Mansi (1958). In this test, wells of about 4 mm in diameter are punched in a 0.75% agar or agarose in a hexagonal pattern with a central well, all wells about 2 mm apart. A suitable dilution of antiserum is placed in the central well and virus 'test' extracts in surrounding wells. The gel is incubated for about 12 hours at room temperature in a moist environment then examined for the formation of precipitin lines (Fig. 2) which indicates that virus antigens and their specific antibodies have reacted. The immunodiffusion test is also useful for determining whether viruses are serologically related (Fig. 2). A suitable agar can be prepared in 50 mM potassium phosphate buffer, pH 6.7, containing 5 mM sodium ethylene diaminetetra-acetate (EDTA) and 0.2% sodium azide, but Bailey (1981) reports that the best agar for Thai sacbrood virus is obtained by adding 1 to 2% sodium chloride to this formulation.

CONCLUSIONS

It is likely that many viruses of *A. cerana* are yet to be discovered. Of the three known viruses it ap-

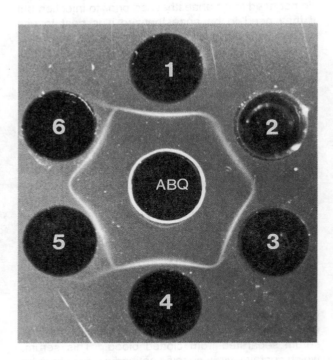

FIGURE 2. Precipitin line formation in a gel diffusion test using a black queen cell virus antiserum (ABQ) and black queen cell virus particle isolates (1-6). Complete fusion of neighbouring precipitin lines (as seen between isolates 3 and 4) indicates the virus isolates have antigenic sites in common with each other and are therefore serologically indistinguishable strains. Partial fusion of neighbouring precipitin lines associated with spur formation (as seen between isolates 4 and 5) indicates that the virus isolates have some uncommon antigenic sites and are serologically distinct strains.

pears as though Thai sacbrood virus is the most common and causes the greatest damage, apparently more so than sacbrood virus does in *A. mellifera* colonies. However, there is much speculation about the impact and effects of Thai sacbrood virus on colonies and much detailed research is needed.

Studies to determine whether the parasitic mite *V. jacobsoni* can transmit and enhance the effects of viruses of *A. cerana* seem warranted since that mite has been shown to transmit and activate replication of inapparent acute bee paralysis virus in *A. mellifera* colonies in Europe (Ball and Allan 1988).

Finally, studies comparing the viruses of the different *Apis* species will enhance our understanding of the origin and evolution of bee viruses and may assist in developing general control measures.

REFERENCES

Anderson, D.L. 1983. Viruses of honeybees in north eastern Australia. The Australasian Beekeeper, 84(11): 219-222.

Anderson, D.L. 1984. A comparison of serological techniques for detecting and identifying honeybee viruses. Journal of Invertebrate Pathology, 44: 233-243.

Anderson, D.L. 1985. Viruses of New Zealand honey bees. The New Zealand Beekeeper, 188: 8-10.

Anderson, D.L. 1988. Pathologist's report. The New Zealand Beekeeper, 199: 12-15.

Anderson, D.L. 1990. Pests and diseases of the honey bee (*Apis mellifera* L.) in Fiji. Journal of Apicultural Research, 29(1): 53-59.

Anderson, D.L. and A.J. Gibbs. 1982. Viruses and Australian native bees. The Australasian Beekeeper, 83(7): 131-134.

Anderson, D.L. and A.J. Gibbs. 1988. Inapparent virus infections and their interactions in pupae of the honey bee (*Apis mellifera* Linnaeus) in Australia. Journal of General Virology, 69: 1617-1625.

Anderson, D.L. and A.J. Gibbs. 1989. Transpuparial transmission of Kashmir bee virus and sacbrood virus in the honey bee (*Apis mellifera*). Annals of Applied Biology, 114: 1-7.

Bailey, L. 1965. The occurrence of chronic and acute bee paralysis viruses in bees outside Britain. Journal of Invertebrate Pathology, 7: 167-169.

Bailey, L. 1967. The incidence of virus diseases in the honey bee. Annals of Applied Biology, 60: 43-48.

Bailey, L. 1969. The multiplication and spread of sacbrood virus of bees. Annals of Applied Biology, 63: 483-491.

Bailey, L. 1970. Virus diseases of the honey bee. *In*: Report of the Rothamsted Experimental Station for 1970, Part 2. pp. 171-183.

Bailey, L. 1975. Recent research on honeybee viruses. Bee World 56(2): 55-64.

Bailey, L. 1976. Viruses attacking the honey bee. Advances in Virus Research, 20: 271-304.

Bailey, L. 1981. Honey Bee Pathology. Academic Press, New York and London. 124 pp.

Bailey, L. 1982. Viruses of honeybees. Bee World, 63(4): 165-173.

Bailey, L. and B.V. Ball. 1978. *Apis* iridescent virus and 'clustering disease' of *Apis cerana*. Journal of Invertebrate Pathology, 31: 368-371.

Bailey, L. and E.F.W. Fernando. 1972. Effects of sacbrood virus on adult honey-bees. Annals of Applied Biology, 72: 27-35.

Bailey, L. and A.J. Gibbs. 1964. Acute infection of bees with paralysis virus. Journal of Insect Pathology, 6: 395-407.

Bailey, L. and R.G. Milne. 1978. Filamentous virus particles in honey bees in Britain. Journal of Invertebrate Pathology, 32: 390-391.

Bailey, L. and R.D. Woods. 1974. Three previously undescribed viruses from the honey bee. Journal of General Virology, 25: 175-186.

Bailey, L. and R.D. Woods. 1977a. Bee Viruses. In The Atlas of Insect and Plant Viruses. K. Maramororosch (ed.), Academic Press, New York, London. pp. 141-156.

Bailey, L. and R.D. Woods. 1977b. Two more small RNA viruses from honey bees and further observations on sacbrood and acute bee-paralysis viruses. Journal of General Virology, 37: 175-182.

Bailey, L., A.J. Gibbs and R.D. Woods. 1963. Two viruses from the adult honey bee (*Apis mellifera* Linnaeus). Virology, 21: 390-395.

Bailey, L., A.J. Gibbs and R.D. Woods. 1964. Sacbrood virus of the larval honey bee (*Apis mellifera* Linnaeus). Virology, 23: 425-429.

Bailey, L., A.J. Gibbs and R.D. Woods. 1968. The purification and properties of chronic bee paralysis virus. Journal of General Virology, 2: 251-260.

Bailey, L., B.V. Ball and R.D. Woods. 1976. An iridovirus from bees. Journal of General Virology, 31: 459-461.

Bailey, L., J.M. Carpenter and R.D. Woods. 1979. Egypt bee virus and Australian isolates of Kashmir bee virus. Journal of General Virology, 43: 641-647.

Bailey, L., B.V. Ball, J.M. Carpenter and R.D. Woods. 1980a. Small virus-like particles in honey bees associated with chronic paralysis virus and with a previously undescribed disease. Journal of General Virology, 46: 149-155.

Bailey, L., J.M. Carpenter, D.A. Govier and R.D. Woods. 1980b. Bee virus Y. Journal of General Virology, 51: 405-407.

Bailey, L., B.V. Ball and J.N. Perry. 1981a. The prevalence of viruses of honey bees in Britain. Annals of Applied Biology, 97: 109-118.

Bailey, L., J.M. Carpenter and R.D. Woods. 1981b. Properties of a filamentous virus of the honey bee (*Apis mellifera*). Virology, 114: 1-7.

Bailey, L., J.M. Carpenter and R.D. Woods. 1982. A strain of sacbrood virus from *Apis cerana*. Journal of Invertebrate Pathology, 39: 264-265.

Bailey, L., B.V. Ball and J.N. Perry. 1983a. Association of viruses with two protozoal pathogens of the honey bee. Annals of Applied Biology, 103: 13-20.

Bailey, L. B.V. Ball and J.N. Perry. 1983b. Honey-bee paralysis: its natural spread and its diminished incidence in England and Wales. Journal of Apicultural Research 22(3): 191-195.

Ball, B.V. 1985. Acute paralysis virus isolates from honey bee colonies infested with *Varroa jacobsoni*. Journal of Apicultural Research, 24(2): 115-119.

Ball, B.V. and M.F. Allan. 1988. The prevalence of pathogens in honey bee (*Apis mellifera*) colonies infested with the parasitic mite *Varroa jacobsoni*. Annals of Applied Biology, 113: 237-244.

Ball, B.V., H.A. Overton, K.W. Buck, L., Bailey and J.N. Perry. 1985. Relationships between the multiplication of chronic bee-paralysis virus and its associate particle. Journal of General Virology, 66: 1423-1429.

Batuev, Y.M. 1979. [New information about virus paralysis]. Pchelovodstvo, 7: 10-11. In Russian.

Bhambhure, C.S. and K.K. Kshirsagar. 1978. Occurrence of bee viral disease in *Apis cerana indica* F. in Maharashtra area (India). Indian Bee Journal, 40: 66.

Clarke, T.B. 1977. Another virus in honey bees. American Bee Journal, 117: 340-341.

Clarke, T.B. 1978. A filamentous virus of the honey bee. Journal of Invertebrate Pathology, 32: 332-340.

Dall, D.J. 1985. Inapparent infection of honey bee pupae by Kashmir and sacbrood bee viruses in Australia. Annals of Applied Biology, 106: 461-468.

Fernando, E.F.W. 1972. Sacbrood: a virus disease of the honey bee. Ph.D. Thesis, Faculty of Science, University of London. 150 pp.

Hornitzky, M.A.Z. 1981. The examination of honey bee virus in New South Wales. The Australasian Beekeeper, 82(11): 261-262.

Hornitzky, M.A.Z. 1987. Prevalence of virus infections of honeybees in eastern Australia. Journal of Apicultural Research, 26(3): 181-185.

Kshirsagar K.K. and R.P. Phadke. 1984. Occurrence and spread of Thai sacbrood disease in *Apis cerana*. In Proceedings of the Third International Conference on Apiculture in Tropical Climates, Nairobi, 1984. pp. 149-151.

Kshirsagar, K.K., D.B. Mahindre, S.R. Salvi and M.C. Mittal. 1975. Occurrence of a viral disease in Indian hivebee *Apis cerana indica* F. A preliminary report. Indian Bee Journal, 37: 19-20.

Kshirsagar, K.K., V.V. Diwan and R.K. Chauhan. 1981. Occurrence of 'sac brood' disease in *Apis cerana indica* Fab. Indian Bee Journal, 43: 4.

Kshirsagar, K.K., U.C. Saxena and R.K. Chauhan. 1982. Occurrence of sac brood disease in *Apis cerana indica* F. in Bihar, India. Indian Bee

Journal, 44: 8-9.

Lee, P.E. and B. Furgala. 1967. Electron microscopic observations on the localization and development of sacbrood virus. Journal of Invertebrate Pathology, 9: 178-187.

Mansi, W. 1958. Slide gel-diffusion precipitation test. Nature (London), 181: 1289.

Mathews, R.E.F. 1982. Classification and Nomenclature of Viruses. Fourth Report of the International Committee on Taxonomy of Viruses. Karger. 199 pp.

Morse, R.A. 1982. Bee disease consultancy in Nepal. Report to Food and Agriculture Organization of United Nations, Rome, Italy. 5 pp.

Overton, H.A., K.W. Buck, L. Bailey and B.V. Ball. 1982. Relationships between the RNA components of chronic bee-paralysis virus and those of chronic bee-paralysis virus associate. Journal of General Virology, 63: 171-179.

Reid, G.M. and D. Bettesworth. 1988. A Survey of Honey Bee Diseases and Pests in Western Samoa. Ministry of Agriculture and Fisheries Report. 48 pp.

Reinganum C. 1969. In: Victorian Plant Research Institute Report, 5: 28.

Shah, F.A. and T.A. Shah. 1977. Virus associated with crawling disease of Kashmir bees. British Bee Journal, CV: 73.

Shah, T.A. and F.A. Shah. 1976. An unknown adult honeybee disease. British Bee Journal, CIV: 38.

Singh, Y. 1979. Iridescent virus in the Indian honey bee *Apis cerana indica* F. American Bee Journal, 119: 398.

White, G.F. 1917. Sacbrood. Bulletin of the U.S. Department of Agriculture, No. 432:1-55.

CHAPTER 21

PARASITISM AND REPRODUCTION OF *VARROA* MITE ON THE JAPANESE HONEYBEE, *APIS CERANA JAPONICA*

T. YOSHIDA, M. SASAKI, and S. YAMAZAKI

INTRODUCTION

Although *Apis cerana* is thought to be the original host of *Varroa jacobsoni* (Koeniger and Koeniger 1985), the parasitic incidence on *A. cerana* was low and no notable damage was reported in Sri Lanka (Koeniger *et al.* 1981) and in Japan (Ritter *et al.* 1980). In the reported literature, female adult mites reproduced only in drone cells and there were neither nymphs nor eggs within the worker cells. This was thought to be the major reason why the parasitism of *Varroa* in *A. cerana* is maintained at a low level.

In colonies of *A. cerana japonica* (one of the northern subspecies of *A. cerana*), we were able to observe:

1. The parasitism in natural colonies which are isolated from *Apis mellifera*.
2. Mite reproduction within worker cells in an observation hive.
3. Abnormally high parasitic incidence of drone cells in a worker-laying colony.

MATERIALS AND METHODS

Natural colonies

Apis cerana japonica (ACJ) colonies, reared in traditional style without any frame, were chosen from different localities in Ehime prefecture, Shikoku island. Adult workers (30~330 each) were collected from 26 such colonies in June, 1984, and the rate of parasitism by *Varroa* was checked. In March, 1985, nest debris on the bottom of the hives was sampled from 20 colonies and the number of dead adult female mites in the debris was counted.

Worker cells

When an ACJ colony in a glass observation hive absconded due to a shortage of stored honey on 14 July 1985, all (n=433) sealed worker cells (no drone cells) were checked for *Varroa* mites. Since the number of brood cells was limited, the infestation should have been concentrated in these cells. Developmental stages of the worker pupae were classified according to Rembold *et al.* (1980). Number, sex, and stages of mites were also identified according to Ifantidis (1983). Young (newly emerged) adult female mites could be recognized from the mother mite by body colour.

Drone cells

When a natural nest constructed under the floor of Komagatake Shrine, Yamanashi prefecture was collected in July 1985, 700 sealed drone cells were examined. The colony was queenless and all sealed cells were drones (no worker brood) because of worker-laying.

RESULTS AND DISCUSSION

Low parasitic incidence in natural colonies

No mite was found on adult workers collected from 26 natural colonies in several localities, all of which had been reared in traditional hives and the majority of which had long been isolated from *A. mellifera*.

To get more information about the presence or absence of *Varroa* mites in the native, original host species, we further investigated the nest debris from 20 of these colonies (Table I). The debris (10 to 200 g/colony) was collected carefully from the bottom of hives (under the natural combs). The main debris might have piled up during the cold season just before collection because it appeared fresh. But, much older debris was also included because of infestation by *Achroia innotata* which is common in the debris of ACJ (Okada 1985). Carcasses of *Vespa mandarina* and *Acherontia styx crathis* were also found.

In ACJ colonies located 200 to 500 m (within drift or robbing range) from *Varroa*-infested *A. mellifera* hives, some newly fallen-down mites were observed by bimonthly monitoring throughout the winter (unpublished). Thus, the small number of mites found in the debris of these ACJ colonies suggests that ACJ could become a host but it is highly resistant. This is consistent with the fact that only one female adult *Varroa* was reported from a survey of native ACJ in Tshishima island, 129°N, 34°E, which is approximately 100 km north of the main island of Japan and which has been isolated for decades from *A. mellifera* (Hara 1980).

TABLE I. Number of dead mites detected in nest debris piled on the floor of natural colonies of *Apis cerana japonica*.

Colony No.	Weight of nest debris (g)	No. of mites
1	14	0
2	32	0
3	53	0
4	64	2
5	110	2
6	58	0
7	32	3
8	31	1
9	23	10
10	48	1
11	50	0
12	106	0
13	34	5
14	21	0
15	233	0
16	110	7
17	73	0
18	122	2
19	130	0
20	72	1

Possible reproduction in worker cells

Parasitic incidence on worker pupae of an absconded ACJ colony at the different developmental stages is shown in Table II. Of all 433 cells, only eight (1.9%) were invaded; five of these had off-spring. Three female (numbers 1, 6, and 7) out of the eight had not laid any eggs. Importantly, new female adults were found in cell numbers 4 and 8; one had just emerged within the cell, and the body of the other young one was only lightly pigmented. Male adult mites were found in three cells.

The brood temperature in an ACJ colony is usually maintained at 34° to 35°C even in a glass observation hive, and the sealed period for workers is normally 11 to 12 days (unpublished data). Although the body temperature of the developing worker pupae may be somewhat lower than normal, reproduction of the next generation of *Varroa* is possible in worker cells. A cell temperature of 32°C, for example, may be cold enough to delay the hosts' development, but may still be warm enough for the parasite's normal development.

Multiplication in a summer worker-laying colony

A queenless colony with laying worker consisting of approximately 7,000 workers, 1,200 drones, and 700 drone pupae in worker cells was examined. The parasitic incidence for adults was 5.3% (21/389) for workers and 10% (7/70) for drones. Of the 700 drone cells, 269 (38.4%) cells were invaded. An average of 6-9 dark-brown (aged) and 2-3 pale or reddish brown (young) female adult *Varroa* were detected in the cells containing late-stage ACJ pupae (Table III). Some of the dark-brown female mites may

TABLE II. *Varroa* mites in worker cells in *Apis cerana japonica*.

Cell no.	Stage	Egg	Protonymph ♂	Protonymph ♀	Deutonymph ♂	Deutonymph ♀	New Adult ♂	New Adult ♀	Old Adult	Total
1	Dark brown-eye pupa (dbe)								1*	1
2	Dark brown-eye pupa		1			2	1		1	5
3	dbe, lightly-pigmented thorax pupa	1	1						1	3
4	dbe, lightly-pigmented thorax pupa		1			2	1	1	1	6
5	Unemerged adult					1	2			3
6	Unemerged adult								1*	1
7	Unemerged adult								1*	1
8	Unemerged adult	1					1	1	1	4

* No offspring observed.

Data were obtained from 433 brood cells left after colony absconded on 14 July 1985. No mites were found in the other 425 cells.

TABLE III. Examination of drone brood in *Apis cerana japonica* for *Varroa* mites.

Stage	No. of cells examined	No. of infested cells (%)	% of cells with new offspring							
			Egg	Protonymph		Deutonymph		New adult		Old adult [a]
				♂	♀	♂	♀	♂ [a]	♀ [a]	
Spinning larva	12	7 (58)	0	0	0	0	0	0	0	100 (1.4)
Prepupa	131	50 (38)	46	2	18	0	0	0	0	100 (1.7)
White-eye pupa	23	3 (13)	67	67	67	0	33	0	0	100 (1.0)
Pink-eye pupa	34	6 (18)	100	50	83	33	50	0	0	100 (1.2)
Red brown-eye pupa	71	10 (14)	60	10	60	40	90	50 (1.2)	30 (1.7)	100 (2.8)[b]
Dark brown-eye pupa (dbe)	63	15 (24)	47	0	47	20	93	93 (1.4)	80 (2.4)	100 (3.6)[b]
Dbe, lightly-pigmented thorax pupa	78	24 (31)	9	0	25	8	88	100 (1.1)	100 (2.1)	100 (4.7)[b]
Dbe, medium-coloured thorax pupa	72	31 (43)	3	0	10	0	74	100 (1.1)	100 (2.7)	100 (6.4)[b]
Dbe, dark thorax pupa	101	58 (57)	0	0	3	2	21	100 (1.6)	100 (2.6)	100 (8.7)[b]
Unemerged adult	115	65 (57)	0	0	2	0	5	100 (1.3)	100 (2.0)	100 (8.3)[b]

[a] Average no. of mites/infested cell
[b] Aged new adult(s) may be included

have been young but they could not be distinguished. New adult mites appeared at the red-brown eye stage of their ACJ hosts or later. Eggs were found from the ACJ pre-pupal stage (46%), and, after the ACJ white-eye stage, 100% of ACJ pupae permitted reproduction of the mites. This contrasts with the workers (Table II). The trend to earlier emergence of male adults is the same as that of *A. mellifera* (Ifantidis 1983).

This unusually high incidence of parasitism can be explained as follows (Fig. 1): Since the number of drones was about 15%, the queen might have been lost at the end of the swarming season (around June). At that time, *Varroa* density would have reached the highest level of the year, although it would be significantly lower than that in *A. mellifera*. If the colony had been a normal queen-right colony, the density would have declined gradually because no, or very little, drone brood is produced after the swarming season. In this particular case, however, laying workers continued to produce a lot of drone brood. This permitted a second distinct multiplication

of the mite and resulted in the observed unusually high incidence in ACJ. This implies that ACJ drone brood is favourable from both nutritional and sense-physiological points of view as a mite host and quite different from the worker brood which is resistant to *Varroa* by both inhibition of oviposition and short sealed period.

How does *Varroa* survive in *Apis cerana japonica* colonies?

It is worth clarifying how the population of *Varroa* is held far below the economic injury level in colonies of ACJ. The candidate mechanisms are tentatively summarized as follows:

1. *Varroa* completes generations even on worker pupae as suggested by Table II, although workers are capable of keeping the mite population very low. The *Varroa* may reproduce only if they invade peripheral brood cells which have a longer sealed period (Tsuruta *et al.* 1989; our unpublished data for ACJ). There is also 1-2 days variation in the sealed brood period of *A.*

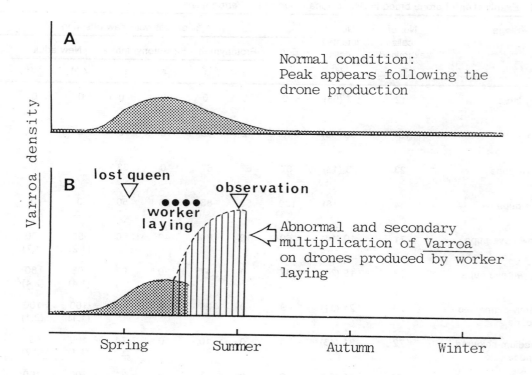

FIGURE 1. Estimated annual fluctuation of *Varroa* density in normal (A) and abnormal (B) *Apis cerana japonica* colonies.

cerana indica (Kapil 1959). The facts that 3 out of 8 females remained in brood cells without oviposition (Table II), and that ACJ worker pupae attracted fewer mites than males or *A. mellifera* worker pupae in a choice experiment in petri dishes (unpublished), indicate the role of a chemical factor(s) in the low incidence.

2. Drone brood is just as favourable for *Varroa* even in ACJ, because of a long sealed period and its palatability (Sasaki 1989). Usually, however, there are no or very limited brood cells in the colony during autumn-winter. *Varroa* may survive and reproduce in these rather exceptional drone cells at a very low multiplication rate. These drone cells are produced by normal queens. This seems at least partially due to the fact that the cell size dimorphism (worker vs. drone) is not clearly evolved in ACJ. Abnormal multiplication may occur in colonies of laying workers as shown in Table III, and the dying colony may serve as a source of dispersion of *Varroa* to other normal colonies.

3. Female *Varroa* may survive for a long time and wait for spring in reproductive diapause. We do not have positive data for this assumption but the possibility should not be excluded.

REFERENCES

Hara, A. 1980. On an exoparasitic mite of honeybee, *Varroa jacobsoni* Oudemans. Honeybee Science, 1(1): 17-20. (In Japanese)

Ifantidis, M.D. 1983. Ontogenesis of the mite *Varroa jacobsoni* in worker and drone honeybee brood cells. Journal of Apicultural Research, 22(3): 200-206.

Kapil, R.P. 1959. Variation in the developmental period of Indian bee. Indian Bee Journal, 21: 3-6 and 26.

Koeniger, N. and G. Koeniger. 1985. Change of host by parasitic mites in Asia after a new honeybee species is introduced. Proceedings of the Third International Conference on Apiculture in Tropical Climates, Nairobi, 1984. pp. 160-162.

Koeniger, N., G. Koeniger and N.H.P. Wijayagunasekara. 1981. Beobachtungen über die anpassung von *Varroa jacobsoni* an ihren natürlichen wirt *Apis cerana* in Sri Lanka. Apidologie, 12(1): 37-40.

Okada, I. 1985. The Japanese honeybee in nature. Iden, 39(10): 58-68. (In Japanese)

Rembold, H., J.P. Kremer and G.M. Ulrich. 1980. Characterization of postembryonic developmental stages of the female castes of the honey bee, *Apis mellifera* L. Apidologie, 11(1): 29-38.

Ritter, W., T. Sakai and K. Takeuchi. 1980. Entwicklung und Bekämpfung der Varroatose in Japan. Diagnose und Therapie der Varroatose. Apimondia Pr., Bukarest. p. 69-71.

Sasaki, M. 1989. The reason why *Apis cerana japonica* is resistant to *Varroa* mite. Honeybee Science, 10(1): 28-36. (In Japanese)

Tsuruta, T., M. Matsuka and M. Sasaki. 1989. Temperature as a causative factor in the seasonal colour dimorphism of *Apis cerana japonica* workers. Apidologie, 20: 149-155.

CHAPTER 22

MITES ATTACKING HONEYBEES AND THEIR CONTROL IN PAKISTAN

RAFIQ AHMAD

There are three species of mite pests of honeybees in Pakistan. These are acarine mite (*Acarapis woodi*), *Tropilaelaps* mite (*Tropilaelaps clareae*) and *Varroa* mite (*Varroa jacobsoni*). In addition, *Neocypholaelaps indica* has also been recorded feeding on pollen in the hive. These are distributed almost throughout Pakistan.

ACARINE MITE

A. woodi is an exotic parasite. It was introduced in infested swarms of the oriental bee, *Apis cerana* migrating from Indian Kashmir to Azad Kashmir during April-May, 1981. This mite was detected in the oriental bee colonies in Pakistan for the first time in November, 1981.

In Pakistan, most commercial beekeepers move their oriental bee colonies to Swat Valley for the *Plectranthus* honey flow in August every year. The infested oriental bee swarms from Kashmir were also taken to that area. There were more than 10,000 colonies of *A. cerana* (from various parts of Pakistan) in Swat Valley during September-October, 1981. The few infested colonies acted as starters for spreading this disease. Later on, the apiaries were shifted from Swat back to their original areas, spreading the disease in their respective locations until the situation became out of control. Some Folbex was imported for control of the mite, but it was expensive and beekeepers could not afford to use it. Thus, among commercial beekeepers, 10,000 colonies succumbed to the attack of the acarine mite during 1981-83. During this period, the disease also infected bee colonies in the traditional hives (wall hives, log hives, pitcher hives, and hollow portions of the trunks of trees) throughout the range of this bee in Pakistan and destroyed about 95% of the colonies by 1983.

The commercial beekeepers who lost their colonies started beekeeping with the occidental bee (*Apis mellifera*). As the honey yield of *A. mellifera* is much higher than that of *A. cerana*, almost all of them completely dispensed with keeping the latter bee.

To document the recovery of populations of the oriental bee from the acarine mite infestation, the mortality in the colonies of this bee was studied in a small valley in the Marghalla Hills during 1983-87. In this valley, the beekeepers had 88 colonies in traditional hives in 1982. Some colonies died of the disease and the number was reduced to 38 colonies in January, to 9 colonies in December, 1983, and to 2 colonies in March, 1984. These colonies produced swarms and their number increased to 11 colonies in May, 1984. Of these, 5 colonies died of disease and 6 survived by February, 1985. There were about 22 colonies in the same valley in May, 1985 and 11 colonies in February, 1986. The number increased to 32 colonies in February and 42 colonies in June, 1987, indicating a gradual recovery of the oriental bee from the infestation caused by acarine disease.

The oriental bees usually produce up to 9 swarms in the spring in some areas, in the spring and autumn in other areas, and in the spring and winter in still other areas. Some valleys in which the oriental bee was almost completely destroyed by the acarine disease in Pakistan now have fairly good numbers of colonies. In this way, the oriental bee in traditional hives is recovering from the acarine epidemic by natural selection without human efforts.

Studies were made to determine any possible change in the morphological characters involved during the development of resistance to acarine disease. There is some evidence of difference in size and number of some setae around the tracheal openings possibly indicating that these check the entry of the mite into the tracheae of the bees to some extent.

A. woodi has also destroyed a considerable number of the rock bee (*Apis dorsata*) colonies in some areas where the oriental bee and the rock bee overlap in distribution. The rock bee colonies became infected with acarine mite as a result of robbing the oriental bee colonies. The rock bee colonies migrate 3-5 times a year, depending on the availability of flora and there are a few areas where both species overlap in distribution. In the migrating rock bee colony, the individual bees affected by acarine mite get tired after a short journey and failed to keep pace with the flying speed of the healthy bees. The diseased bees are isolated and suffered mortalities. Thus, this mite could not become a serious pest of the rock bee colonies in the plains of Punjab and Sind which are far away from the range of the oriental bee.

Acarine mite also attacks the occidental bee, but

in strong and well-managed colonies it is a pest of little importance.

VARROA MITE

V. jacobsoni attacks the oriental and occidental bees in Pakistan. After the introduction of the occidental bee in 1977, the Varroa mite became a serious pest of this bee and destroyed a considerable number of colonies within a few years. Keeping in view the serious losses caused by this mite, studies on its control were initiated in 1979.

Sun heat treatment

It is usually very hot in most parts of Punjab in May and June with maximum temperature occasionally reaching 42-44°C at mid-day for a short time during these months. Infested colonies of the occidental bee were shifted to the central Punjab and placed in the Daffar Forest area. There was a shortage of flora and the infested colonies were almost broodless. At mid-day, the top covers of infested colonies were replaced with a glass slab covered with black cloth. The colony temperature rose to 46-47°C within 15-20 minutes when the ambient temperature was 41-43°C. A paper having a layer of powdered sulphur was placed on the bottom board and covered with a wire mesh to protect the bees from coming in contact it. The colonies were thus treated for about half an hour at 45-47°C three times in 10 days. The mites lost their grip on the honeybees at 46-47°C and fell down onto the powdered sulphur through the wire mesh. After each treatment, the papers along with sulphur and mites were removed from the hives. This treatment proved successful except that it resulted in the loss of some bees and some queens greater than one year old due to sun heat. However, the young queens survived the sun-heat treatment hazards.

Biological control

The Varroa mite has been associated with the oriental bee for the last thousands of years. Biological control agents such as parasites, predators, and pathogens have been reported to keep several insect and mite pests' populations below the economic threshold. It was, therefore, considered that attempts may be made for biological control of this mite infesting the occidental bee colonies. Because both the new and old hosts of the mite were present in Pakistan, efforts were made to transfer any possible parasite or pathogen directly from the oriental bee to the occidental bee colonies instead of isolating them and developing techniques for their mass-multiplication. The oriental bee and occidental bee colonies

were kept side by side except in swarming season. The sealed queen cells of the occidental bee were successfully introduced into the oriental bee colonies and several colonies of the latter bee were converted into that of the former bee. This practice was followed by many beekeepers to raise the numbers of high honey-yielding occidental bee colonies. Thereafter, the Varroa mite population started declining and decreased to such an extent that after 2-3 years it was difficult to collect a sufficient sample of this mite within a reasonable time. Several U.S. and European scientists have examined these apiaries and have reported that the Varroa mite is not a problem in Pakistan.

Two different viruses have been isolated from the oriental bee and the Varroa mite in Pakistan. It is possible that these viruses and some other pathogens may be infecting this mite and keeping it under control. Further studies are being conducted to isolate the pathogens from this mite in different ecological areas.

Ruttner (1983) has mentioned two hypotheses about this mite. The first hypothesis has been based on the findings of Bailey (1981) and Bretschko (1980, 1983). According to this hypothesis the parasite does not kill its host and finally an equilibrium of the Varroa mite in the colony is reached at a level which does not harm the host. This hypothesis is not accepted by most of the world scientists except for a few Asian workers. According to the second hypothesis advanced by Grobov (1976) and accepted by most of the European scientists, all races of the occidental bee are easily infested by the Varroa mite and if any colony receives no assistance or control measures, it will die at last. The author of this chapter is of the opinion that both hypotheses are correct under their respective situations. The first hypothesis is sound in the presence of an effective biological control agent as in Pakistan while the second hypothesis is acceptable to all because of the absence of effective biological control agents of the mite in Europe and several other countries.

Further studies on the natural enemies of the Varroa mite may facilitate isolation of the pathogen responsible for keeping the mite populations below economic threshold. Such a pathogen, after isolation, can be used for biological control of this mite. The most productive locations for such natural enemies seem to be northern areas of Pakistan and some parts of Afghanistan.

There are more than 400 examples of biological control of insect and mite pests and diseases recorded from various parts of the world (DeBach 1964; Huffaker and Messenger 1976). According to a report of the U.S. Department of Agriculture, some bacteria (Bacillus spp.) and viruses have been developed as biological insecticides for the control of insect pests (Anonymous 1978). Studies on the mite along these lines in its distribution area where it is not a pest may yield some other pathogens suitable for biological control of the mite in various parts of the world.

TROPILAELAPS MITE

This mite attacks the small bee (*Apis florea*), oriental bee, occidental bee, and rock bee throughout their ranges in the country. The mite infestations were higher in drone brood than in worker brood and also in the occidental bee than in the oriental bee colonies.

The infested colonies were treated with powdered sulphur ('amlasar') at the rate of 12 g per colony by dusting 4 g of powder on the frames' top bars, by impregnating the cloth covering the frame with 4 g of powder and spreading 4 g of powder on butter paper at the bottom board. Three treatments of 12 g of sulphur at 15 day intervals proved very useful in controlling the mite populations in the apiaries.

REFERENCES

Anonymous. 1978. Biological agents for pests control - status and prospects. Report of a special study team coordinated by the Office of Environmental Quality Activities, USDA, Super. Document, U.S. Government Printing Office, Washington, D.C. 138 pp.

Bailey, L. 1981. Honeybee Pathology. Academic Press, London. 124 pp.

Bretschko, J. 1980. Verlauf des Varroabefalls innerhalb einer Vegetationsperiode auf verschiedenen Bienenstanden der Station-Apicole, Dr. Schroder in Tunesien. Symposium Oberursel, pp. 100-107.

Bretschko, J. 1983. Varroatose auch ein problem der Bienenpflege. Bienervater, 2: 48-54.

DeBach, P. 1964. Biological Control of Insect Pests and Weeds. Reinhold Publishing Corp. 844 pp.

Grobov, O.F. 1976. Varroasis in bees. Symposium Sofia. pp. 46-90.

Huffaker, C.B. and P.S. Messenger. 1976. Theory and Practice of Biological Control. Academic Press, London. 788 pp.

Ruttner, F. 1983. Varroatosis in honeybees: Extent of infestation and effects. pp. 7-13. *In*: Proceedings of meeting of EC Experts on *Varroa jacobsoni* Oud. affecting honeybees. Commission of European Communities, Directorate-General Information, Market and Innovation, Luxembourg.

CHAPTER 23

TESTING OF ACARICIDAL FUMIGANTS FOR THE CONTROL OF TRACHEAL MITE DISEASE OF HONEYBEES IN PAKISTAN

B.M. KHAN and M.I. CHAUDHRY

INTRODUCTION

The honeybee may have been the first arthropod to have its maladies recorded. Tracheal mite, generally known as acarine disease, is the most destructive endoparasite of young adult honeybees. This mite, *Tarsonemum woodi* Rennie, described by Rennie *et al.* (1921), later changed to *Acarapis woodi* (Rennie) by Hirst (1921), is microscopic. Its minute size enables it to enter through the prothoracic spiracles and invade the tracheal system of young bees of age less than 12 days (Eckert and Shaw 1974).

Prior to 1980, *A. woodi* had not been reported as a parasite of honeybees in Pakistan; but its presence in the neighbouring countries of India, Afghanistan and the USSR had always posed the threat of its introduction at any time. In India, Singh (1957) reported its presence on *Apis cerana*, which might have migrated into Pakistan carried by man himself. Subsequent to the Soviet intervention in Afghanistan in 1979, the Afghan refugees brought their colonies of *Apis mellifera* to Pakistan in 1980 along with their belongings and livestock. Scattered settlements of these refugees, and their migration of mite-infected colonies to follow the honey flow not only introduced this mite to Pakistan, but also caused quick dispersal and out-break of acarine disease in Pakistan in 1982-83. This brought about 85% and 70% mortality in the population of *A. cerana* and *A. mellifera*, respectively. N.W.F. Province, being the base for most refugee populations, suffered the most: All apiaries were hard hit and *A. cerana* colonies completely perished on account of this disease.

Jeffree (1959) reported acarine disease as the most serious problem in some states of America. Adam (1968) reported that almost all the honeybee colonies on the British Isles perished in 1904 due to the great malady called the "Isle of Wight disease", and later it swept away 90% of the colonies during 1913. Morgenthaler (1951) and Morse (1978) reported that tracheal mite is a serious major pest among other acarine mites of honeybees. Woyke (1984a,b) reported 90% mortality of the *A. mellifera* colonies in Afghanistan due to acarine disease.

Illingworth (1928) applied Frow treatment of nitrobenzene mixture to control the acarine disease but its application promoted robbing. Frala (1950) applied hydrochloric acid in the Frow treatment during the broodless period. Atwal and Sharma (1970) recommended the use of methyl salicylate, menthol and chlorobenzilate separately for the control of the parasitic mites. Methyl salicylate (oil of wintergreen) has been found fairly effective in the control of these mites by Eckert and Shaw (1974). Grobov (1976) reported at least eight materials used in European countries against mites but none proved effective. Morse (1978) reported several miticides including chlorobenzilate (Folbex), phenothiazene, naphthalene, tobacco and sulfur as potential fumigants for the control of the tracheal mite disease but none of these has been adopted universally. Khan *et al.* (1986) found the use of Folbex fumigant strip in combination with the dequeening treatment very useful for control of tracheal mite.

MATERIALS AND METHODS

The trials were conducted in the apiaries at Badaber Agricultural University and Islamia College, Peshawar during the year 1984-85. The following acaricidal fumigants were tested:

1. Folbex - one strip per week.
2. Perizin - 25 ml per week.
3. Frow mixture - 5 ml per week.

For Folbex treatments, a shallow super was placed in each hive without frames. The treatment was applied after closing the entrance at dusk when the bees had stopped foraging and were all back in the hive. The colonies were kept warm to avoid clustering of bees. The Folbex strip was fixed to the underside of the top inner cover in the middle with the help of a drawing pin, leaving the strip hanging downwards in the empty super. The lower end of the strip was ignited to glow and give off fumes. The top cover was replaced tightly to avoid leakage. An hour after the treatment, the entrance was opened but the empty super was removed at daybreak. Subsequent treatments were repeated the same way.

Frow was prepared by mixed nitrobenzene, safrol oil and petrol in the ratio of 2:1:2 and 5 ml of the mixture was poured on the flannel pad which was fixed on the underside of the top inner cover.

181

TABLE I. Comparative % reduction in acarine disease in honeybees.

Treatment	After 2 weeks	After 4 weeks	After 6 weeks	% Mite in microscopic test
Folbex strip	50	100	colonies normal	nil
Perizin	42	75	no paralysis	10
Frow mixture	36	64	-do-	16
Check	75	100	colonies perished	100

Ten ml of Perizin was mixed in 500 ml of distilled water and 25 ml of the mixture was sprinkled, with the help of an atomizer, on the hive frames starting from one end to the other.

In the check treatment, one teaspoon of luke-warm distilled water was sprinkled over the frames.

The observations were recorded on the number of paralysed honeybee workers in each colony at the start of the experiment and at intervals of two weeks. To ascertain the results, microscopic examination of prothoracic tracheae of the workers was also carried out after 42 days of the treatment. The mite-infected tracheae were clearly seen congested while the healthy ones gave a shining appearance.

RESULTS AND DISCUSSION

The data based on the observations recorded 2, 4, and 6 weeks after treatment are presented in Table I. It is quite evident that acarine disease was reduced considerably after 2 weeks in all the treated colonies compared to a 75% increase in disease in the check treatment. After 4 weeks, 100%, 75% and 64% of the disease was wiped out from the colonies treated with Folbex, Perizin, and Frow mix, respectively. One hundred percent of the colonies treated with Folbex became normal after 6 weeks, and disease was also completely controlled in Perizin and Frow treated colonies, although 10% and 16% of the bees harboured stages of the mite which disappeared in a few days without causing any paralysis. The colonies in check completely perished due to the disease.

In order to ascertain the comparative efficacy of the acaricides, the data were statistically analyzed for significance (Table II). Folbex proved better than Frow mixture and Perizin but the difference with Perizin was not significant. Perizin and Frow mixture were clearly better than check but were not significantly different from one another.

CONCLUSION

Folbex strip treatment controlled acarine disease in honeybees up to 50% within 2 weeks and completely wiped out the disease in 4 weeks, allowing the colonies to function normally in 6 weeks. Perizin and Frow mixture treatments took 6 weeks to completely control the disease whereas the colonies in the check treatment perished altogether in 4-6 weeks.

REFERENCES

Adam, Brother. 1968. Isle of Wight or acarine disease; its historical and practical aspects. Bee World, 49(1): 6-18.

Atwal, A.S. and O.P. Sharma. 1970. Acarine disease of adult honey bees: prevention and control. Indian Farming, 20: 39-40.

Eckert, J.E. and F.R. Shaw. 1974. Beekeeping. Macmillan Publishing Co. Inc., New York. pp. 374-377.

Frala, F. 1950. Treatment of acarine disease with hydrochloric acid. Bee World, 33: 161-162.

Grobov, O.F. 1976. Varroa disease in honey bees. Apiacta, 11: 145-148.

Hirst, S. 1921. On the mite (Acarapis woodi Rennie) associated with Isle of Wight bee disease. Annals and Magazine of Natural History, 7: 509-519.

Illingworth, L. 1928. The Frow treatment of acarine disease. Bee World, 9: 176-177.

Jeffree, E.P. 1959. The World distribution of acarine disease of honey bees and its probable dependence of meteorological factors. Bee World, 40: 4-15.

Khan, B.M., M.I. Chaudhry and P. Khawja. 1986. Acarine disease of honey bees and its control in NWFP. Pakistan Journal of Forestry, 37(2):109-114.

TABLE II. % Reduction in disease in honeybees in different acaricidal treatments after 2 weeks.

Replication	Folbex	Perizin	Frow Mix	Replication Total
1	44	39	32	115
2	56	44	41	141
3	40	38	34	112
4	60	47	37	144
Treatment total	200	168	144	512
Mean	50	42	36	

CV	DF	SS	MS	F value
Replication	3	283.33	94.445	6.392
Treatment	2	394.67	197.335	13.354**
Total	11	766.67	69.697	4.716
Error	6	88.66	14.777	-

LSD = 8.45

Means in ascending order	Frow Mix	Perizin	Folbex
	36	42	50

Underlines show nonsignificant at 5%

Morgenthaler, O. 1951. Some problems of acarine disease. Scottish Beekeeper, 1951 (Nov.): 1-3.

Morse, R.A. 1978. Honey Bee Pests, Predators, and Disease. Cornell University Press. Ithaca, New York. pp. 197-209.

Rennie, J., P.B. White, and E.J. Harney. 1921. Isle of Wight disease in hive bees. Trans. Royl. Soc. Edinb., 52:IV(29): 737-779.

Singh, S. 1957. Acarine disease in Indian honey bee (*Apis indica* F.). Indian Bee Journal, 19: 27-28.

Woyke, J. 1984a. Beekeeping in Afghanistan. Proc. Expert Consult. Beekeeping with *Apis mellifera* in Tropical and subtropical Asia, FAO Rome, pp. 124-130.

Woyke, J. 1984b. Honey bees disease situation in Afghanistan. American Bee Journal, 125(7): 497-499.

CHAPTER 24

CURRENT STATUS OF PESTS AND DISEASES OF THE HONEYBEE, *APIS CERANA* F. IN PENINSULAR MALAYSIA

MOHAMED RANI YUSOF and ROHANI IBRAHIM

INTRODUCTION

Currently, the major pests of the honeybee, *Apis cerana*, in Malaysia are the asiatic mite, *Varroa jacobsoni*, the wax moths (the greater wax moth, *Galleria mellonella* and the lesser wax moth, *Achroia grisella*), the predatory wasps, *Vespa tropica tropica* and *V. affinis indonesiensis* and ants, especially the red ant (krengga), *Oecophylla smaragdina*. Cockroaches, lizards, spiders and frogs are considered minor pests. No disease has so far been confirmed, although previous reports have indicated that a disease outbreak occurred in bee colonies located in Kampung Lubok Darat, in the district of Batu Pahat in Johore. However, the nature of disease was not described (Chan and Alias 1982). The wax moth, *G. mellonella*, is considered as the most important pest of bees in Malaysia (Mardan and Osman 1980).

THE ASIATIC MITE, *VARROA JACOBSONI*

V. jacobsoni, a pest of concern to beekeepers throughout the world (Ritter 1981), has been found infesting bee colonies in many localities in Peninsular Malaysia (Fig. 1). Our studies have shown that the severity of mite infestation in these localities varies with the mean number of mites per drone cell varying from 0 to 4.7. An infestation of more than four mites per cell causes the formation of deformed wings and legs in drone bees (Fig. 2). These drones fail to emerge from the cells. Correlation analysis on the data shows that a significant ($P \leq 0.01$) negative correlationship between the number of mites (T_h) and weight of drone bees (W_o) with $R_{Wo,Th} = -0.5149^{***}$ (N = 236). Their relationship is significant and can be expressed by a quadratic regression equation as follows:

$$W_o = 0.106 - 0.008T_h + 0.0003T_h^2$$
R square = 33.29%
F. model = 58.15^{**} ($P \leq 0.01$)
CV = 22.69%

The mean number of mites found on healthy drone bees is significantly ($P \leq 0.01$) lower (1.47 mites) than that found on deformed bees (8.14 mites). Consequently, mean body weight of healthy bees is significantly ($P \leq 0.01$) higher (0.0913 g) than that of deformed bees (0.0593 g). There is a significant ($P \leq 0.01$) negative correlationship between number of mites (T_h) and weight of healthy drones (W_h) with $R_{Wh,Th} = -0.2349^{**}$ (N = 131). Their relationship as shown by regression analysis is significant and their relationship can be expressed by a quadratic regression equation as follows:

$$W_h = 0.096 - 0.039T_h + 0.021T_h^2 - 0.004T_h^3 + 0.0002T_h^4$$
R square = 12.16%
F model = 4.361^{**} ($P \leq 0.01$)
CV = 22.24%

The body weight of deformed drones bees can be as low as less than 0.02 g or they can be comparable to the weight of healthy bees (0.09 g). Since deformed bees are unable to fly, and mate with virgin queens at critical times, a low drone population caused by high mite infestation could result in unmated and inadequate mating of queens, and eventually the weakening of bee colonies.

The current control method involves the removal of unnecessary drone cells after the queen has been mated.

WAX MOTHS (THE GREATER WAX MOTH, *GALLERIA MELLONELLA* AND THE LESSER WAX MOTH, *ACHROIA GRISELLA*)

Observations made during hive inspection have shown that the greater wax moth, *G. mellonella*, is more commonly encountered than the lesser wax moth, *A. grisella*. They are usually found on the bottom boards of more than 90 percent of hives, surviving on wax droppings from the colonies. When colonies become weakened during rainy periods or as a result of pesticide poisoning, exposed combs not guarded by the bees are quickly infested by wax moths. The wax moths subsequently destroy the combs by feeding and burrowing through them. The infestation then can quickly spread throughout the colony and cause it to abscond.

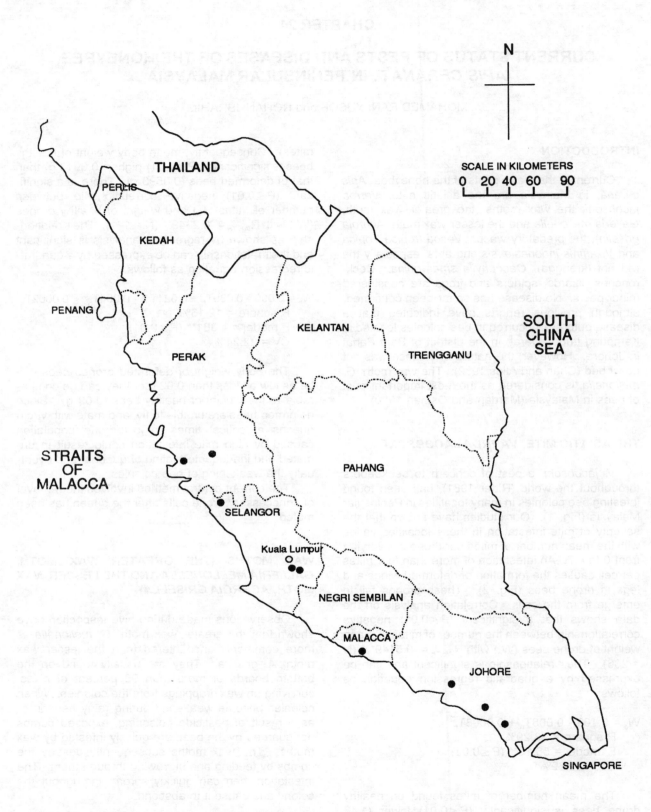

FIGURE 1. Occurrence of *Varroa jacobsoni* Oud. in some localities in Peninsular Malaysia (●).

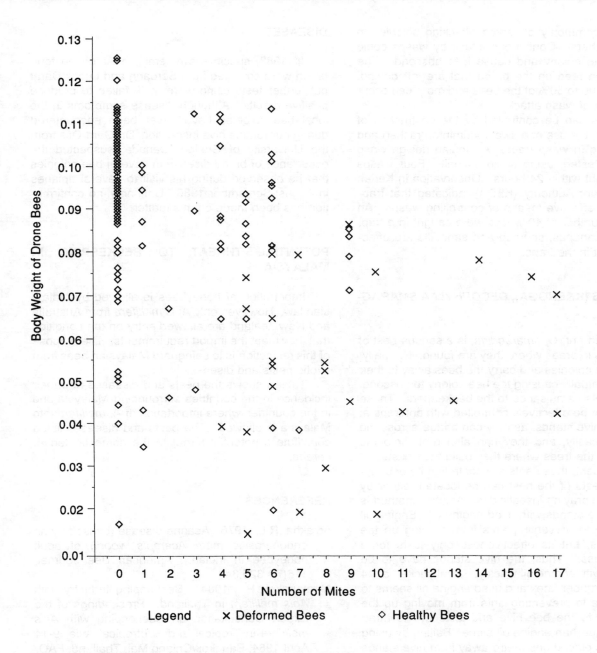

FIGURE 2. Effect of mite infestation on body weight of drone and formation of bees.

The removal of exposed combs to a moth-proof place and sweeping the bottom board clean of wax droppings during routine hive inspection have been found to effectively control wax moth infestations.

Experiments conducted in the laboratory using *Bacillus thuringiensis* at a concentration of 1 part B.t. to 19 parts water showed that the product is effective against only the greater wax moth. The lesser wax moth, *A. grisella* is not susceptible. However, the product has not been tested in the field.

PREDATORY WASPS, *VESPA AFFINIS INDONESIENSIS* AND *VESPA TROPICA TROPICA*

In most areas, the predatory wasps are commonly found in most areas foraging for nectar from flowers and feeding on overripe and rotten fruits. They occur seasonally in Malaysia, and in the apiary are not a nuisance during dry periods when food is abundant. However, during rainy periods and after fruit season, especially in September and October, they are commonly observed attacking colonies in large numbers. Continuous attack by wasps could weaken the colony and cause it to abscond. The wasps then feed on the brood that are left behind. Losses of up to 50% of the bees and more can occur as a result of wasp attack.

Wasps can be controlled by the destruction of their nests, the use of a swat (badminton racket) and by trapping in wasp traps. An Indian design wasp trap was tested, using squid as bait. Four wasps were caught within 24 hours. Observation in Kedah Development Authority (KEDA) indicated that trapping is an effective means of controlling wasps. An average number of 40 wasps were caught in a trap. Overripe bananas, soursop and sapodilla are effective as bait in the traps.

RED ANTS (KRENGGA), *OECOPHYLLA SMARAGDINA*

The red ant, *O. smaragdina*, is a serious pest of honeybees in areas where they are found. Normally, they attack colonies and carry the bees away to their nests, eventually causing the bee colony to abscond. They are also a nuisance to the beekeepers. These ants cannot be effectively controlled with ant traps at the leg of hive stands, as they can bridge across the gap very easily, and they can also drop onto the hives from the trees where they build their nests.

At present, these ants are controlled by destroying their nests (if the nest can be located) either by burning or spraying insecticides. Another method is to paint hive stands with used engine oil. Engine oil is effective in preventing ants from moving up the hive stands, but its effectiveness only lasts for a week or less. Thus, the hive stands have to be repainted with engine oil weekly. Local sticker, a 1:4 mixture of rubber latex and used engine oil seems to be effective in preventing ants from moving up the hive stand to the bee hive and lasts two to three weeks longer than engine oil alone. Baiting by using beef bones placed one metre away from hive stands can be an effective temporary measure for attracting ants away from bee hives.

MINOR PESTS

There is no research work done on minor pests in Malaysia. However, our past experience shows that most of these pests can be easily controlled by reducing the hive entrance and by killing them during routine hive inspection.

DISEASES

In 1983, specimens resembling American foulbrood were collected from Serdang and Lubok Darat but further tests using warm milk failed to produce positive results. Although disease symptoms in the local bee colonies have never been encountered during our routine hive inspection, Dr. Gard Otis from the University of Guelph, Canada, suspected the occurrence of brood disease in several bee colonies that he observed during his visit to several apiaries in August-September 1986. Until now, no confirmation has been made on this matter.

POTENTIAL THREAT TO BEEKEEPING IN MALAYSIA

Importation of honeybees is allowed by Malaysian law. However, only *Apis mellifera* from Australia and New Zealand are allowed entry on the condition that they meet the import requirements. The purpose of this restriction is to safeguard Malaysian bees from exotic pests and diseases.

Table I shows the pests and diseases and their incidence in the countries surrounding Malaysia and in the countries where importation of *A. mellifera* into Malaysia is allowed. The pests and diseases listed constitute a potential threat to the domesticated *A. cerana*.

REFERENCES

Adlakha, R.L. 1976. Acarine disease (caused by an endoparasitic mite, *Acarapis woodi*) of adult honeybee in Indian. American Bee Journal, 116(7): 325,344.

Akratanakul, P. 1984. Beekeeping industry with *Apis mellifera* in Thailand. Proceedings of the Expert Consultation on Beekeeping with *Apis mellifera* in Tropical and Subtropical Asia, 9-14 April 1984, Bangkok/Chiang Mai, Thailand, FAO.

Bailey, F. 1985. Beekeeping in Australia. William Heinemenn, Australia. pp. 109-129.

Bailey, L. 1974. An unusual type of *Streptococcus pluton* from the Eastern hive bee. Journal of Invertebrate Pathology, 23: 246-247.

Bailey, L. 1976. Viruses attacking the honeybee. Advances in Viruses Research, 20: 271-304.

Bailey, L. 1984. Viruses of honeybee. Bee World, 63(4): 165-173.

Bailey, L., B.V. Ball and R.D. Woods. 1976. An iridovirus from bee. Journal of General Virology,

TABLE I. Pests and diseases of honeybees in the countries surrounding Malaysia.

Name of pests/diseases	Country	Honeybee species	References
American foulbrood	Thailand	*Apis mellifera*	Akratanakul (1984)
	Burma	*A. mellifera*	Zmarlicki (1984)
	India	*A. cerana*	Sekariah and Seth (1959)
	Australia	*A. mellifera*	Bailey (1985), Rhodes and Goebel (1986)
	New Zealand	*A. mellifera*	Winter (1980)
European foulbrood	Thailand	*A. mellifera*	Akratanakul (1984)
	India	*A. mellifera*	Bailey (1974), Kshirsagar and Godbole (1974)
		A. cerana	Bailey (1974), Kshirsagar and Godbole (1974), Thakar (1976)
	Australia	*A. mellifera*	Bailey (1985), Rhodes and Goebel (1986)
Sacbrood	India	*A. cerana*	Kshirsagar *et al.* (1981), Kshirsagar (1982)
	Pakistan	*A. mellifera*	Rafiq (1984)
	Australia	*A. mellifera*	Rhodes and Goebel (1986)
Thai sacbrood	Thailand	*A. cerana*	Bailey (1982)
	India	*A. cerana*	Bailey (1982)
	Nepal	*A. cerana*	Bailey (1982)
Kashmir bee virus disease	India	*A. cerana*	Bailey (1982)
	Australia	*A. mellifera*	Rhodes and Goebel (1986)
Apis iridescent virus disease	India	*A. cerana*	Bailey *et al.* (1976), Bailey (1982), Kshirsagar *et al.* (1975), Shah and Shah (1981)
Bee paralysis	Hong Kong	?	Gochnauer (1978)
	Australia	*A. mellifera*	Bailey (1976), Gochnauer (1978)
	New Zealand	*A. mellifera*	Winter (1980)
Acarine disease	India	*A. cerana*	Dhaliwal *et al.* (1974), Adlakha (1976), Thakar (1976)
	Japan	?	Delfinado (1963)
Nosema disease	India	*A. cerana*	Singh (1975), Thakar (1976), Kshirsagar (1982)
	Bangladesh	*A. cerana*	Nezza *et al.* (1983)
	Australia	*A. mellifera*	Bailey (1985)
Neocypholaelaps mite	India	*A. cerana*	Kshirsagar (1968)
	Pakistan	*A. cerana*	Delfinado-Baker and Baker (1983)
	Nepal	*A. cerana*	Baker and Delfinado (1976)

31: 459-461.

Baker, E.W. and M.D. Delfinado. 1976. Notes on the bee mite *Neocypholaelaps indica* Evans. American Bee Journal, 116(8): 384,386.

Chan, H.H. and Md. Alias Azizol. 1982. A report presented at the MDF committee meeting in Kuala Lumpur.

Delfinado, M.D. 1963. Mites of the honeybee in South East Asia. Journal of Apicultural Research, 2(2): 113-114.

Delfinado-Baker, M. and E.W. Baker. 1983. A new species of *Neocypholaelaps* (Acari.: Amerosei-idae) from brood combs of the Indian honeybee. Apidologie, 14(1): 1-7.

Dhaliwal, H.S., S. Srivastava and P.L. Sharma. 1974. Some biological observations on the mite, *Acarapis woodi* Rennie infesting honeybees, *Apis cerana indica* F. Current Science, 43(23): 750-752.

Gochnauer, T.A. 1978. Viruses and rickettsiae. *In*: Honeybee pests, predators, and diseases. R.A. Morse (ed.). Cornell University Press, Ithaca, U.S.A. Chapter 2, pp. 23-42.

Kshirsagar, K.K. 1968. Further observations on phoretic bee mites *Neocypholaelaps indica* (Evans). Indian Bee Journal, 30(2): 68-69.

Kshirsagar, K.K. 1982. Current incidence of honey-bee diseases and parasites in Indian. Bee

World, 63(4): 162-164.

Kshirsagar, K.K. and S.H. Godbole. 1974. Indian *Streptococcus pluton*. Indian Bee Journal, 36(1/4): 39.

Kshirsagar, K.K., D.B. Mahindre, S.R. Salvi and M.C. Mittal. 1975. Occurrence of a viral disease in Indian hivebee, *Apis cerana indica* F.: a preliminary report. Indian Bee Journal, 37(1/4): 19-20.

Kshirsagar, K.K., V.V. Diwan and R.M. Chauhan. 1981. Occurrence of sacbrood disease in *Apis cerana indica* Fab. Indian Bee Journal, 43(2): 44.

Makhdzir, b. Mardan and Mohd. Shamsuddin B. Osman. 1980. Beekeeping in coconut smallholdings in Pontian, Johore, West Malaysia. Proceedings of the Second International Conference on Beekeeping in Tropical Climates, New Delhi, India.

Nessa, Z., M.A. Muttalib and A. Begum. 1983. A preliminary study on *Nosema* disease of honeybee and its control. Proceedings of the Second International Conference on Apiculture in Tropical Climates, Feb. 19 - Mar. 4 1980, New Delhi, India, pp. 457-460.

Rafiq, A. 1984. Country status report on beekeeping. Proceedings of the Export Consultation on Beekeeping with *Apis mellifera* in Tropical and Subtropical Asia, 9-14 April 1984, Bangkok/Chiang Mai, Thailand, FAO.

Rhodes, J. and R. Goebel. 1986. Diseases of honeybees, the importance of correct diagnosis. Queensland Agricultural Journal, March - April 1986: 71-74.

Ritter, W. 1981. *Varroa* disease of honeybee, *Apis mellifera*. Bee World, 62(4): 141-153.

Sekariah, P.C. and R.N. Seth. 1959. Studies on the bacterial flora of the intestinal tract of the honeybee (*Apis indica*). II. On the occurrence of *Bacillus thuringiensis* Berliner in the foulbrood of honeybees in India. Indian Veterinary Journal, 36(1): 19-23.

Shah, F.A. and T.A. Shah. 1981. *Apis* iridescent virus. Indian Bee Journal, 43(2): 44-45.

Thakar, C.V. 1976. Practical aspects of bee management in India with *Apis cerana indica*. *In*: Crane, E. Apiculture in Tropical Climates. International Bee Research Association, London. pp. 47-49.

Winter, T.S. 1980. Beekeeping in New Zealand. Bulletin 267, Ministry of Agriculture and Fisheries New Zealand, pp. 137-149.

Zmarlicki, C. 1984. Beekeeping with *Apis mellifera* and mite control in Burma. Proceedings of the Expert Consultation on Beekeeping with *Apis mellifera* in Tropical and Subtropical Asia, 9-14 April 1984, Bangkok/Chiang Mai, Thailand, FAO.

CHAPTER 25

THE PRESENT SITUATION OF BEE DISEASE IN BEEKEEPING WITH *APIS CERANA* IN CHINA

FANG YUEZHEN

In China, beekeeping practice dates from ancient times. Culture of the Chinese bee (*Apis cerana*) began as early as the fourteenth century when many households started traditional beekeeping.

At present, there are about 800,000 colonies of *A. cerana* in China (comprising about 40-50% of total colonies) using movable frame beehives and adopting new techniques in management. They are mostly distributed south of the Yang-tse River and in the southwest mountainous regions. Stationary and short distance migratory beekeeping is practised.

PRESENT BEE DISEASES AND PESTS IN *APIS CERANA*

The European honeybee (*Apis mellifera* L.) was brought into Asia in the twentieth century by beekeepers, and certain of the diseases of *A. mellifera* began to infect the Asiatic bee species. In the past decade, sacbrood and foulbrood diseases caused havoc with local beekeeping when they entered the *A. cerana* population. Later, diseases such as amoeba and nosema affected *A. cerana* more severely than *A. mellifera*.

SACBROOD DISEASE

A. cerana is more susceptible to sacbrood disease than *A. mellifera*. In 1971, it was first found in *A. cerana* in Guangdong province, and afterwards the Fujian, Jiangxi, Yunan, Sichuan, and Anhui provinces reported great losses of *A. cerana*. Today, sacbrood disease has spread throughout China.

In 1983-1984, our research group in Beijing isolated a strain of sacbrood virus from *A. cerana*. When the extract of larvae with Chinese sacbrood virus (CSBV) was fed to healthy worker larvae, they showed typical sacbrood disease symptoms. The Chinese sacbrood virus contained isometric particles about 30-nm in diameter. The viral capsid protein was composed of three major species of polypeptide (mol. wt. 27×10^3, 29×10^3, 39×10^3) and one species of single-strand RNA. The serological property is not very similar to that of sacbrood virus coming from *A. mellifera*.

The difficult part of controlling CSBV disease is that currently there are no remedies to control it effectively. However, more recently, beekeepers have recommended that requeening the infected colony with young queens three times a year, or caging the queen could be used effectively.

At this time, there is the possibility of selecting and breeding strains of *A. cerana* with a strong tendency to resistance to sacbrood virus, and using them to establish SBV resistant stock. By years of selecting resistant strains, such colonies are able to check the disease. For instance, with this disease under control, the Fujian and Guangdong provinces have been able to develop and boost the production of *A. cerana* up to 100,000 colonies.

EUROPEAN FOULBROOD AND AMOEBA DISEASES

European foulbrood and amoeba disease are a serious threat to the beekeeping industry in south China. By 1962, European foulbrood had been discovered in the plain areas of southeast China. This disease can be treated by application of antibiotics in combination with good management.

In China, the amoeba disease and nosema disease of the Chinese bee (*A. cerana*) was reported in 1984 from the centre of Fujian province. These diseases have a spring peak in March or April in south China.

Control of amoeba disease is currently based on hygiene and disinfection of equipment. Chemicals have been found to control amoeba and nosema diseases in *A. cerana*, and the effective drugs are Flagyl and citric acid in sugar syrup. They are effective against *Malpighamoeba mellificae* and *Nosema apis*.

ASIATIC BEE MITES RESISTANCE BY *APIS CERANA*

There are two species of mites in China, *Varroa jacobsoni* which naturally parasitizes *A. cerana* and *Tropilaelaps clareae* which parasitizes *A. dorsata*. Both infest *A. mellifera*, but the Asian honeybee, *A.*

cerana, has evolved mechanisms to maintain the mite infestation at low levels.

In the summer of 1985, we cooperated with Dr. Y.S. Peng in China to conduct a research project investigating the host-parasite relationship between the Chinese honeybee (*A. cerana*), the European honeybee (*A. mellifera*), and their external parasite *V. jacobsoni*. The research project has for the first time shown that the Asian honeybee has a behavioural adaptation whereby the parasitic mites are effectively removed from the hosts and discarded outside the bee hives. Observations also indicate that *A. cerana* can detect and recognize the mite as a pest. A comparative study conducted at the same time showed that the European honeybee performed similar grooming behaviour, however it had much lower success in mite removal.

TACTICAL AVOIDANCE OF ATTACKING WASPS

There are many species of wasps in China. The important ones are: *Vespa mandarina* Smith, *V. bicolor* Fabricius, *V. basalis* Smith, *V. tropica baematodes* Bequaert, *V. ducalis* Smith, and *V. affinis*. All of these Vespids are formidable predators of the honeybee. Worker bees are usually attacked by wasps while foraging in the field and at the hive entrance as well. However, Chinese bees (*A. cerana*) are active and fast-flying and can tactically avoid the wasps' attacks. European bees (*A. mellifera*) appear less able to avoid and retreat from an attacking wasp.

CHAPTER 26

HONEYBEES IMPORTATION PROCEDURES: THE EXAMPLE OF PENINSULAR MALAYSIA

CHAN JENN KWANG

INTRODUCTION

Importation of honeybees that are not indigenous to any country may pose the threat of introducing exotic pests and diseases that may endanger local and national apiculture. Live honeybees imported into Peninsular Malaysia are subjected to regulations of the Plant quarantine Act, 1976. Quarantine procedures adopted by the Department of Agriculture (DOA) in Malaysia are the front line defense approach towards any accidental introduction of exotic pests and diseases of honeybees. Such quarantine requirements illustrate a practical approach to avoiding potential problems in the future. The Malaysia example may be useful to other countries or regions.

BACKGROUND

Importation of the European honeybee, *Apis mellifera*, started as early as the 1960's and continues today. However, the quantity involved is small and importations occur only sporadically (Table I). Consignments, shipped by air, are usually purchased from countries like Australia, Taiwan, England and India by local hobbyists or private entrepreneurs. On arrival at designated entry points, such as international airports, consignments of bees are inspected by quarantine officials and subsequently released to the importers if they do not contravene any regulations.

The purchase of *A. mellifera* colonies at high prices by a few individuals still persists because of their interest generated while studying abroad, and the notion that imported bees are superior to the local bees. So far, these apiaries have been unable to sustain their activities beyond a 3-year period. Their failure can be attributed to poor management practices, ravages of pests and diseases, poor adaptation to the local environment, and genetic problems in reproduction caused by the small genetic pool available (Mardan 1984).

Common diseases associated with the European honeybees such as American foul brood, European foul brood, sac brood, viral diseases, and tracheal mites are still absent in Malaysia. The cross-infect-ability of these easily transmitted diseases to the native honeybees of Malaysia is not well known and the ramifications not understood (Kevan 1987). Hence, if introductions are considered as an option, quarantine or certification of disease-free status or both is called for. It is within this context that members of the Malaysian Bee Research and Development Team (MBRDT) met with officials of the Plant Quarantine Section in late 1985 to review and upgrade quarantine procedures. Presently, importations of live honeybees into Malaysia are limited to being from countries like Australia and New Zealand which are relatively disease-free.

IMPORTATION PROCEDURES

Live honeybees imported into Malaysia fall within the 5th section of the Plant Quarantine Act which states that:

Eighth Schedule
[Regulation 5(4)]
The importation into a component region of any beneficial organisms is prohibited except under a permit contained in the Eighth Schedule issued by the Director in accordance with the regulations and subject to such conditions as the Director may, by endorsement on the permit, impose.

This section of the Act refers to importation of beneficial organisms and other stipulated materials that may only be imported through appointed entry check points (Department of Agriculture, 1986). Within the Department of Agriculture Malaysia, the Plant Quarantine is responsible for all procedures related to honeybee importation. The procedures are as follows:

Import permit

It is mandatory for an importer to apply for permission to import honeybees from the Plant Quarantine office in Kuala Lumpur. An application for importation (Appendix I) goes through a series of steps before an import is approved (Fig. 1). The completed application form will contain the following information:

TABLE I. Importation of *Apis mellifera* into Peninsular Malaysia (1980-1987).

Year	Source	Quantity	No. of Importers
1980	Australia	7 colonies	1
1981	Australia	25 nuclei hives 4 colonies	2
1982	Taiwan	30 colonies 14 colonies	2
1983	Australia	160 colonies	6
1984	Australia Taiwan India	10 colonies 5 colonies 4 colonies	3
1985	Australia	24 colonies 20 queens	2
1986	Australia	72 nuclei hives 30 colonies	2
1987	Australia	60 (application only, not imported)	2

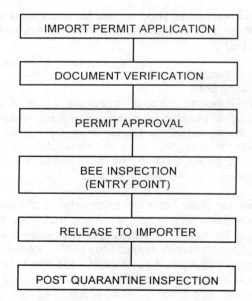

FIGURE 1. Process in live honeybee importation in Peninsular Malaysia.

(a) Name, address, telephone of importers.
(b) Type of bees and quantity
(c) Country of origin
(d) Proposed entry points
(e) Means of transport
(f) Expected date of arrivals

A processing fee of R$5.00 is levied per application. If an application is approved, an import permit is issued with the condition that the imported honeybees be accompanied by certification from a competent authority that they are healthy and free from pests and diseases.

Attached to the import permit are additional conditions imposed by the plant quarantine authorities as recommended by MBRDT.

Arrival notification

The importer of any bee consignment is obligated to notify the Plant Quarantine authority in Kuala Lumpur by means of a manifest, commercial invoice, and relevant documents as to the expected time, date and port of entry. This information facilitates inspection and examination of live bee consignments on arrival at designated entry points.

Entry points inspection

Under present arrangements, inspection officers, appointed by the Director-General of Agriculture, in collaboration with appointed members of the MBRDT are responsible for implementing bee inspection at approved entry points.

Air-flown bee consignments are subject to customs clearance before quarantine procedures are carried out.

Bee inspection involves the inspection of accompanying documents, escape-proof containers, ·live bees, quantity and contents.

If the imported consignments do not conform to specifications stipulated in the import permit, they are detained and promptly destroyed. If they conform, they are released to the importers.

Post-entry inspection

Post-entry inspections are conducted on imported honeybee colonies at the importer's apiary. The objective of these inspections by quarantine officials and MBRDT members is to monitor and diagnose any symptoms of exotic pests and diseases after the honeybees have been released in their new environment. These inspections are normally carried out at 3 week, 3 month and 6 month intervals.

During these inspection visits, colonies are checked at random. Observations are made on colony strength, comb development, and egg-laying pattern. Adult bees are examined and bee larva samples are also taken for subsequent laboratory testing.

DISCUSSION AND SUGGESTIONS

The Malaysian bee quarantine procedures are not as elaborate and stringent as compared to those found in the United States and other countries. The government adopts a cautious stand towards bee importation, taking into cognizance the limited resources that are available, the low volume of imports, and the situation of the bee industry today. As the bee technology in Malaysia becomes more sophisticated, additional provisions can be recommended to be included in the Plant Quarantine Act 1976 to provide further protection against the introduction of pests and diseases.

In order for the bee quarantine system to be more effective, the development of expertise in bee pathology in the Plant Quarantine Section must be a priority. Laboratory facilities to screen disease pathogens and pests need to be established at designated entry points. The current arrangement of inter-dependence of expertise between DOA and the MBRDT is far from satisfactory because the enforcement responsibilities lie with the DOA.

The phytosanitary certificate is a vital document that must accompany each bee consignment to be imported. Quarantine officials rely on this endorsement by a competent authority before making other necessary inspections and before releasing the bee consignment to the importer. There have been cases where the authenticity of certification is questionable, especially when endorsement has been by non-government agencies. Therefore, there should be reliable guidelines for reference by importing coun-

tries in order to facilitate bee quarantine procedures in that country.

Lastly, inter-regional cooperation on matters relating the quarantine aspects of honeybee importation, incidence of disease outbreak, and a constant exchange of information on pests and diseases of quarantine interest need to be encouraged so the bee industries of the surrounding region can be safe-guarded from the ravages of pests and diseases.

CONCLUSION

The quarantine procedures for imported honey-bees being enforced at present are by no means adequate for a complete quarantine against the prevention of the entry of exotic diseases and pests into this country. Given the resources that are available and the status of an emerging honeybee industry, the present system appears to be adequate for the present and meets quarantine requirements of Malaysia. Thus, our experience of involving bee biologists and quarantine officials in the process of importing honeybees is working quite well. That approach, together with the example of Malaysian regulations, may assist other countries in developing policy for importing beneficial insects in general.

REFERENCES

Department of Agriculture. 1986. Plant Quarantine Act 1976. Agricultural Pests and Noxious Plants (Import & Export) Regulations 1981 and Agricultural Pests and Noxious Plants (Imports & Export) (Amendment) Regulations 1986.

Mardan, M. 1984. Current status, problems, prospects and research needs of *Apis mellifera* in Malaysia. (FAO, 1984).

Kevan, P.G. 1987. The European honeybee and its proposed introduction into Malaysia for pollination of mango: An ill-founded proposal. (Department of Environmental Biology, University of Guelph, Canada, 1987).

APPENDIX I. Facsimile of Permit to Import Beneficial Organism used in Malaysia.

(Permit valid for one consignment only)

(Pertanian 105)

Serial No. **No. 000000**

DEPARTMENT OF AGRICULTURE, MALAYSIA

PERMIT TO IMPORT BENEFICIAL ORGANISM

Plant Quarantine Regulations 1981

(Regulation 5 (4))

*Permit No.*_____

*Name and address of consignee*_____

*of*_____
(address)

_____

_____

*Name and address of consignor*_____

*of*_____
(address)

_____

_____

*Permission is granted to the consignee to import*_____

_____ *contained in the Schedule hereto through*

_____
(appointed entry check-point)

This permit is issued subject the following conditions:

(1) Import Licence is to be sought from the relevant Ministry.

(2) A copy of this Import Permit must be sent to the consignor and must accompany the consignment.

(3) The consignment is subject to inspection prior to clearance by the Customs.

(4) This Import Permit is valid until the _____ for one consignment only.

APPENDIX I. - continued.

(5) *The consignment must be accompanied by a phytosanitary certificate or a statement from the official Plant Protection Service or a relevant research agent of the country of origin bearing the following certification:*

    (a) Treatment _____

        _____

        _____

        _____

    (b) Other declarations _____

        _____

        _____

(6) *Further conditions* _____

    _____

    _____

    _____

    _____

    _____

    _____

    _____

Schedule

Description	Quantity	Country of Origin

Date of issue _____

_____

Director-General of Agriculture,
Peninsular Malaysia

L-J.P.N.,K.L.

CHAPTER 27

USE OF PESTICIDES AND BEE POLLINATION FOR CROP YIELD
WHY AND HOW?

R.C. SIHAG

Use of pesticides is the most effective method of crop protection against pests and diseases, and the use of bee pollinators ensures cross-pollination and helps increase the hybrid vigour of seeds. Both practices can be complementary to each other, but most pesticides, especially insecticides, are hazardous to bees and kill them, thus indirectly causing heavy crop losses. To simultaneously allow for the use of pesticides and the safety of bee pollinators, an integrated pesticide-pollination approach is needed. Such an approach is described in this chapter. Readers are also directed to "Pest Control Safe for Bees: A Manual and Directory for the Tropics and Subtropics" (Adey et al. 1986).

WHY THE USE OF PESTICIDES IN AGRICULTURE?

Many efforts have been made by the agricultural scientists and plant breeders to evolve pest- and disease-resistant cultivars (Frey and Browning 1971; Beck and Maxwell 1976; Russell 1978; Hill and Waller 1982; Singh 1986). However, the resistance often lasts only for a short period, and after some time these cultivars become pest-disease susceptible again (Hill and Waller 1982; Fenemore 1984). If the pests or diseases are not properly managed, they cause severe damage to the crop plants, resulting in heavy crop reduction (Smith et al. 1976; Sihag 1987). Seed yield from 6-7 times higher has been reported in pest and disease protected crop plants compared with those on which pests and diseases were not controlled (Sihag 1987). Thus, pest and disease control of crops is essential for higher seed yields.

To obtain higher crop yields if long-term resistance cannot be achieved, two main pest control measures are used, biological control and chemical control. The combination of both methods is Integrated Pest Management (IPM) and has gained in popularity and use, even though it is more complex. Much effort has been made in the field of biological control of pests (Wilson and Huffaker 1976; Coppel and Mertins 1977; DeBach 1979; Klassen 1981; Bosch et al. 1982; Yeargan 1985). Although some success has been achieved for a few pests, many require chemical control as the most effective

method of crop protection (Wilson and Huffaker 1976; Klassen 1981; Hill and Waller 1982).

WHY THE USE OF BEE-POLLINATORS IN AGRICULTURE?

Bees and flowering plants are interdependent, forming a mutually compatible system (Kevan and Baker 1983). In this system, bees derive their nourishment in the form of nectar and pollen, and flowers receive the benefit of pollination. The system goes well if the participating organisms complement each other in these functions. Evolution of several barriers by plants like self-incompatibility, protogyny, and protandry, make cross-pollination essential and plants' dependence on pollinators more obligatory (Chapter 11; Frankel and Galun 1977; Faegri and van der Pijl 1979). Agricultural crop plants are no exception. Cross-pollination of flowers of entomophilous crops by insects is the most effective and cheapest method of increasing yield (Free 1970; McGregor 1976; Sihag 1985a, 1985b, 1985c, 1986). Bees constitute a major group of insect pollinators. Honeybees, leaf cutter bees, orchard bees, bumblebees, and a few other species are especially valuable as they are easily manipulated by agriculturalists (Todd and McGregor 1960; Jay 1986; Richards 1987; Torchio 1987). The efficiency of bee pollination is manifested not only through increase in yield but also by the improvement in crop quality through heterosis (Mel'nichenko 1976). While visiting thousands of flowers and transferring pollen from flower to flower, bees provide the most favourable conditions for selectivity of pollen which helps increase viability and absolute weight of seeds, so improving their germination and seedling strength (Hawthorn et al. 1956; Kurennoi 1971; Kozin 1976; Bisht et al. 1980). In several crops, from 1.8 to 40 times higher seed yield has been observed in some bee-pollinated plants than those where bees were completely excluded. In the absence of the bees, very low seed yield was observed in several self-sterile and self-incompatible crops (Sihag 1987). Chapter 14 amplifies the reasons why bee-pollination plays a great role in agriculture and is essential for higher seed yield, especially in entomophilous crops.

INTERACTION OF PESTICIDES AND BEE-POLLINATORS AND EFFECT ON CROP PRODUCTION

The indiscriminate or careless use of pesticides for plant protection in modern agriculture has severely threatened the integrity of the bee-flower mutualistic system. This is because the pesticides used are generally hazardous to bees (Johansen 1963, 1965, 1966a, 1966b, 1972, 1977; Johansen et al. 1965; Johansen and Eves 1967; Anderson and Atkins 1968; Atkins et al. 1970; Anderson et al. 1971; Johansen and Brown 1972; Kevan 1974, 1975; Kevan and Collins 1974; Kevan and Laberge 1979; Wood 1979) and cause large-scale mortality of bee pollinators. The bee poisoning takes place either because of direct field application of pesticides or bringing in of poisoned nectar and pollen to the hive or nest. Direct exposure to insecticidal sprays causes heavy mortality of the foragers of natural as well as managed bee pollinators (Kevan and Collins 1974; Kevan 1975; Kevan and Laberge 1979).

Some pesticides persist in the pollen and nectar and, at high enough concentrations, also cause mortality of the foragers and brood. The residues of pesticides at lower concentrations in pollen and nectar are transported in the hive or nest (Johansen 1972; George and Rincker 1982; Tasei and Carre 1985; Tasei et al. 1987) and these accumulate in the bodies of developing larvae, ultimately proving hazardous.

The net result is that indiscriminately used pesticides drastically reduce the number of natural and managed bee-pollinators (Kevan 1975; Johansen 1977; Logan and Schofield 1984), ultimately resulting in heavy crop reductions and affecting the economic returns of agricultural crops on a global scale (Kevan 1977; Kevan and Opperman 1980; Crane and Walker 1983; Sihag 1990). This is obviously the opposite of what crop protection seeks to achieve. Recent estimates from India on seed yields of several crops reveal that complete absence of bee pollination caused loss of economic returns from 235 to 1290 dollars per ha (Sihag 1987, 1988). The effect is similar with complete absence of pest management where losses from 185 to 1160 dollars per ha in different crops has been estimated (Sihag 1990). The effect of bee pollination or pesticides alone on the seed yield is significant (Sihag 1987, 1990), but when combined together, the two treatments act in a synergistic way, the effect of which is much greater than merely additive. In India, as in other parts of the world, bee poisoning has increased several fold with greater use of insecticides and other chemicals during the last twenty years, and insect pollination has become a more critical problem. In the absence of natural pollinators, the growers have to rent honeybee colonies in order to obtain good yields. However, honeybees are not the best pollinators of some crops like alfalfa (Medicago sativa L.), sunflower (Helianthus annuus L.) and several others (Parker and Frohlich 1983; Sihag 1983a, 1983b, 1983c, 1983d, 1986; Torchio 1987). Thus, although both pesticides and bee-pollination are essential components of modern agriculture and can be complementary in increasing the seed yield, proper integration of pesticide use and pollinator management is required to ensure higher seed yield.

BEE POISONINGS, DETECTION AND PREVENTION

Most honeybee poisonings occur when insecticides are applied to crops during their blooming period, or during the blooming period of other plants near the treated crops. Apart from direct applications of pesticides to blooming plants, the hazard of bee poisoning can occur if spray or dust pesticides drift in the air from adjacent crops, if cover plants are incidentally sprayed (a problem in orchards), if pesticides remain as residues on plants which bees use, if pesticides are collected instead of pollen (e.g. as dusts) by bees, or if bees drink or come into contact with water, nectar or pollen contaminated with pesticides.

Most beekeepers discover that their bees have been poisoned when they find heaps of dead bees in front of the hives. However, if beekeepers regularly visit their hives, they may also see changes in the bees' behaviour. Typical symptoms of poisoning are stupefaction, paralysis, and disorganized behaviour patterns. Sometimes the bees regurgitate the contents of their honey crops and become wetted, especially when organophosphate insecticides are the cause. Bees that cannot fly (crawlers) and walk as if chilled are symptoms typical of carbaryl (Sevin) poisoning.

Within the hive, the communication and orientation dance language may be distorted. The queen may be affected in various ways and lose her ability to produce an even pattern of egg laying as well as her chemical influence over the hive. She may be superseded long after the poisoning event occurred.

The most important part of preventing bee poisonings is co-operation between beekeepers, growers, and pesticide applicators. Uninformed growers and careless applicators must bear the responsibility for many bee poisonings. Beekeepers must also accept their responsibility of informing neighbours of the whereabouts and value of their bees. It is important for all parties to realize that pest control programmes often can be modified to minimize their hazard to bees. Beekeepers and growers involved in pollination arrangements should be especially concerned about understanding the consequences of pesticide use.

The second important step in preventing bee poisonings is knowing the pesticides and using them safely. Read the label because if the chemical is hazardous to bees or to pollinators on blooming crops the label will state that. Seed treatments are considered to have a low relative toxicity to bees primarily because it is unlikely that bees will encounter such formulations; however, it is important that they are handled in a safe manner. There is no excuse for the misuses of pesticides.

In general, the following recommendations apply to applications. Pesticides that are hazardous to bees should not be applied on blooming crops. Note that this includes cover plants and adjacent blossoming plants. Pesticides posing a lesser hazard to bees should be used whenever a practical choice is possible. Emulsifiable liquid formulations and those with stickers are less hazardous than wettable powders or dusts. Granular formulations are also relatively safer. In contrast, aerial application usually poses a greater risk to bees because of the greater amount of spray drift. Applications should be timed to minimize the hazard, for example late in the evening or early in the morning, when bees are not foraging. These times also coincide with the lowest windspeeds and convection and so minimize spray drift. Unused pesticides should be disposed of in an environmentally safe manner.

Beekeepers should act to minimize their risk. They should choose apiary sites that are least likely to be affected by pesticide applications or drift. They should learn about pest problems and pest control programs for each crops grown in the area of the apiaries and work with local growers towards mutually advantageous co-operation. Apiary pesticides should be used with care (e.g. for wax moth and mite control, etc.). Beekeepers should take action to protect bees from pesticide applications by: (a) determining the kind of pesticide to be used, the nature of its application, and the potential hazard to bees; (b) then, if appropriate, before pesticide application, removing the bees to a safe location; or (c) covering hive entrances with wet burlap early in the morning before spraying commences, and keep covered for 6 to 12 hours, leaving the corners open for ventilation; completely remove at the end of the period when the insecticide has had time to dry. Both means of protection are not easily accomplished, disrupt the bees, and cost in terms of hive productivity - growers and applicators need to be aware of this.

If the bees are poisoned, it may be possible to collect clean, large samples as soon as possible, one sample per hive, into polyethylene bags, label them as to location, date, and pesticide(s) suspected of causing the poisoning, seal the bags and quickly freeze the samples at as cold a temperature as possible for analysis.

HOW TO INTEGRATE PESTICIDES AND BEE-POLLINATION?

The indiscriminate use of pesticides has occurred too often in modern agriculture and the importance of bee-pollinators has been neglected relative to its importance. This is particularly true in tropical and sub-tropical developing countries where pest problems are enormous and many people are illiterate. This is even observed with plant breeders who resist every argument other than those related to the genetic recombination and selection of crop varieties. In order to increase productivity, along with pest-management, bee pollination should be given equal importance as a factor in agricultural production. The bees can be saved by providing them with functional protection through the use of repellents individually or in combination with pesticides (Shaw and Bourne 1944; Atkins et al. 1975a, 1975b; Moffett and Morton 1975; Atkins 1981; Mahavir 1982). However, efforts so far made in this direction by several workers have yielded little success (Jones 1952; Johansen 1953, 1966b; Palmer-Jones et al. 1957; Laere and Gillard 1960; Atkins et al. 1975a, 1975b; Gupta 1987a, 1987b; Gupta and Kapil 1983; Gupta and Mohla 1986; Reith et al. 1986).

Many pesticides have been identified as highly toxic, moderately toxic, or safe to European honeybees (*Apis mellifera*), however few data are available for *Apis cerana* (Crane 1993; Crane and Walker 1993). The selection of non-toxic or moderately toxic pesticides is the best way to save the bees from their demise. However, the bees can also be protected even against the highly toxic pesticides by adopting an integrated pollination-pest management practice (Fig. 1). The practice will involve sufficient understanding of the foraging behaviour of bees (Kapil et al. 1971) and using this knowledge as the basis for pesticide application. A time lag provided between bee foraging and pesticide application would ensure the safety of bees. The use of safe insecticides or moderately toxic ones in the latter scheme would be additionally advantageous.

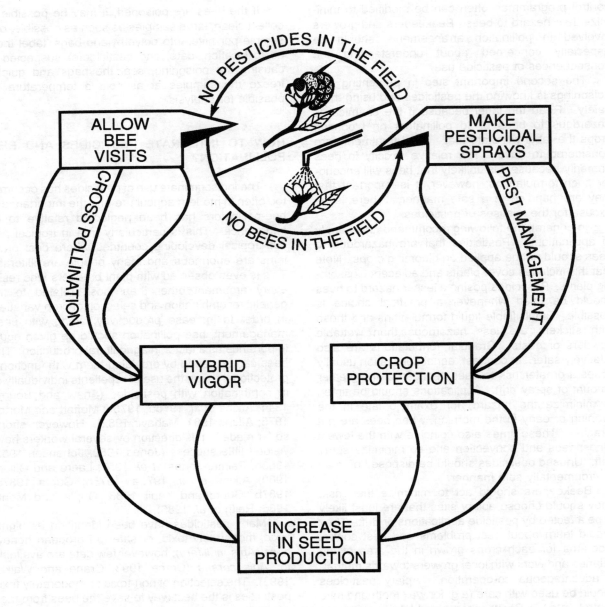

FIGURE 1. A schematic model explaining the integrated approach involving application of pesticides for the management of crop pests and utilization of bee pollinators for cross-pollination and hybrid vigour. The net result is an increase in the seed production. The model documents a time lag between the two practices, which should ensure the safety of bees from the pesticides.

ACKNOWLEDGEMENTS

The author wishes to thank Drs. R.B. Mathur and R.C. Mishra for general and typing facilities. The article was written under the project C(a)Zoo-2-N.P. Agric. (Commit) sponsored by the State Government of Haryana.

REFERENCES

Adey, M., P. Walker and P.T. Walker. 1986. Pest Control Safe for Bees: A manual and directory for the tropics and subtropics. Hill House, Gerrards Cross, UK, International Bee Research Association. 224 pp.

Anderson, L.D. and E.L. Atkins. 1968. Pesticides usage in relation to beekeeping. Annual Review of Entomology, 13: 213-238.

Anderson, L.D., E.L. Atkins, H. Nakakihara and E.A. Greywood-Hale. 1971. Toxicity of pesticides and other agricultural chemicals to honeybees: field study. University of California Agriculture Extension, AXT-251, 8 pp.

Atkins, E.L. 1981. Repellents reduce insecticidal kills of honeybees. Proceedings of 28th International Beekeeping Congress, Acapulco, pp. 305-310.

Atkins, E.L., L.D. Anderson, H. Nakakihara and E.A. Greywood-Hale. 1970. Toxicity of pesticides and agricultural chemicals to honeybees: laboratory studies. University of California Agriculture Extension, M-16, 25 pp.

Atkins, E.L., R.L., MacDonald and E.A. Greywood-Hale. 1975a. Repellent additives to reduce pesticide hazards to honeybees: field tests. Environmental Entomology, 4: 207-210.

Atkins, E.L., R.L. MacDonald, T.P. McGovern, M. Beroza and E.A. Greywood-Hale. 1975b. Repellent activities to reduce pesticide hazards to honeybees: laboratory testing. Journal of Apicultural Research, 14: 85-97.

Beck, S.D. and F.G. Maxwell. 1976. Use of plant resistance. In: Theory and Practice of Biological Control. Huffaker, C.B. and Messenger, P.S. (Eds.), Academic Press, pp. 3-15.

Bisht, D.S., M. Naim and K.N. Mehrotra. 1980. Studies on the role of honeybees in rape seed production. Proceedings of the Second International Conference on Apiculture in Tropical Climates, New Delhi, pp. 491-496.

Bosch, R. van den, P.S. Messenger and A.P. Gutierrez. 1982. An introduction to Biological Control. Plenum Press, New York, 247 pp.

Coppel, H.C. and Mertins, J.W. 1977. Biological Insect Pest Suppression. Springer-Verlag, Berlin, 314 pp.

Crane, E. 1993. Current status of research on Asian honey bees. In: Asian Apiculture. L.J. Connor, T. Rinderer, H.A. Sylvester, and S. Wongsiri (eds.). Wicowas Press, Cheshire, Conn. pp. 19-42.

Crane, E. and P. Walker. 1983. The Impact of Pest Management of Bees and Pollination. International Bee Research Association, England, pp. 107 + appendices.

Crane, E. and P. Walker. 1993. Bibliography on Asian honey bees 1979-1991. In: Asian Apiculture. L.J. Connor, T. Rinderer, H.A. Sylvester, and S. Wongsiri (eds.). Wicowas Press, Cheshire, Conn. pp. 647-680.

DeBach, P. 1979. Biological Control by Natural Enemies. Cambridge University Press, 323 pp.

Faegri, K. and L. van der Pijl. 1979. The Principles of Pollination Ecology. Pergamon Press, 291 pp.

Frankel, R. and E. Galun. 1977. Pollination Mechanisms, Reproduction and Plant Breeding. Springer-Verlag, Berlin, 281+ xi pp.

Fenemore, P.G. 1984. Plant Pests and their Control. Butterworths and Company Limited, London, 280 pp.

Free, J.B. 1970. Insect Pollination of Crops. Academic Press, London, 544 pp.

Frey, K.J. and J.A. Browning. 1971. Breeding crop plants for disease resistance. In Mutation Breeding for Disease Resistance. Proceedings of Panel on Mutation Breeding for Disease Resistance, Food and Agriculture Organization/International Atomic Energy Agency, pp. 45-54.

George, D.A. and C.M. Rincker. 1982. Residues of commercially used insecticides in the environment of Megachile rotundata. Journal of Economic Entomology, 75(2): 319-323.

Gupta, M. 1987a. Efficacy of ketones on the foraging behaviour of Apis florea F in field conditions. Apidologie, 18(2): 121-128.

Gupta, M. 1987b. Essential oils: a new source of bee repellents. Chemistry and Industry, 2 March 1987: 162-163.

Gupta, M. and R.P. Kapil. 1983. Olfactory response of Apis florea F. to some repellents in semi-field conditions. Proceedings of 5th International Symposium on Pollination, Versailles, pp. 65-78.

Gupta, M. and R.S. Mohla. 1986. Aliphatic straight chain ketones as potential bee repellents. Chemistry and Industry, 5 May 1986: 327-328.

Hawthorn, L.R., G.E. Bohart and E.H. Took. 1956. Carrot seed yield and germination as affected by different levels of insect pollination. Proceedings of American Society of Horticultural Science, 67: 384-389.

Hill, D.S. and J.M. Waller. 1982. Pests and Diseases of Tropical Crops. Longman, London, 175 pp.

Jay, S.C. 1986. Spatial management of honeybees on crops. Annual Review of Entomology, 31: 49-65.

Johansen, C.A. 1963. The effect of pesticides on the alfalfa leaf cutting bee. Washington State Agricultural Experimental Station Circular, 418, 12 pp.

Johansen, C.A. 1965. Bee poisoning versus clover red weevil control in white-dutch-clover grown for seed. Journal of Economic Entomology, 58: 372-386.

Johansen, C.A. 1966a. Solving bee poisoning problems on legume seed crops. American Bee Journal, 106: 128-129.

Johansen, C.A. 1966b. Digest on bee poisoning, its effects and prevention. Bee World, 47: 9-25.

Johansen, C.A. 1972. Toxicity of field-weathered insecticide residues to four kinds of bees. Environmental Entomology, 1: 393-394.

Johansen, C.A. 1977. Pesticides and pollinators. Annual Review of Entomology, 22: 177-191.

Johansen, C.A. and F.C. Brown. 1972. Toxicity of carbaryl contaminated pollen collected by honeybees. Environmental Entomology, 1: 385-386.

Johansen, C.A. and J.D. Eves. 1967. Toxicity of insecticides to the alkali bee and the alfalfa leaf cutting bee. Washington State Agricultural Experimental Station Circular, 475, 100 pp.

Johansen, C.A., M.D. Levin, J.D. Eves, W.R. Forsyth, M.B. Busdicker, D.S. Jackson and L.I. Butler. 1965. Bee poisoning hazards of undiluted malathion applied to alfalfa in bloom. Washington State Agricultural Experimental Station Circular, 455, 10 pp.

Johansen, P. 1953. Pestox III and bees. Bee World, 34: 8-9.

Jones, C.D.C. 1952. The response of honeybees to repellent chemicals. Journal of Experimental Biology, 29: 372-386.

Kapil, R.P., D.P.S. Lamba and H.S. Brar. 1971. Integration of bee behaviour with aphid control for seed production of Brassica campestris var. toria. Indian Journal of Entomology, 33: 221-223.

Kevan, P.G. 1974. Pollination, pesticides and environmental quality. Bio Science, 24: 198-199.

Kevan, P.G. 1975. Forest application of the insecticide Fenitrothion and its effect on wild bee pollinators (Hymenoptera: Apoidea) of lowbush blueberries (Vaccinium spp.) in southern New Brunswick, Canada. Biological Conservation, 7: 301-309.

Kevan, P.G. 1977. Blueberry crops in Nova Scotia and New Brunswick - Pesticides and crop reductions. Canadian Journal of Agricultural Economics, 25(1): 61-64.

Kevan, P.G. and H.G. Baker. 1983. Insects as flower visitors and pollinators. Annual Review of Entomology, 28: 407-463.

Kevan, P.G. and M. Collins. 1974. Bees, blueberries, birds, and budworms. Osprey, Newfoundland Natural History Society Newsletter, 5: 54-62.

Kevan, P.G. and W.E. Laberge. 1979. Demise and recovery of native pollinator populations through pesticide use and some economic implications. Proceedings of the IVth International Symposium on Pollination. Maryland Agricultural Experimental Station Special Miscellaneous Publication, 1: 489-508.

Kevan, P.G. and E.B. Opperman. 1980. Blueberry production in New Brunswick, Nova Scotia and Maine: a reply to Wood et al. Canadian Journal of Agricultural Economics, 28(1): 81-84.

Klassen, W. 1981. The role of biological control in integrated pest management system. In: Biological Control in Crop Production, Papavizas, G.C. (Ed.), Allanheld, Osmun Publishers, Granada, pp. 433-445.

Kozin, R.B. 1976. Effect of bee pollination on the yield of agricultural crops. In: Pollination of Entomophilous Agricultural Crops by Bees, Kozin, R.B. (Ed.), Amerind Publishing Co. Pvt. Ltd., New Delhi, India, pp. 61-63.

Kurennoi, N.M. 1971. Effect of bee population rates on yield and quality of coriander seeds. Proceedings of 23rd International Beekeeping Congress, pp. 512-516.

Laere, O.V. and A. Gillard. 1960. The use of repellents against bees. Parasitica, 15: 53-70.

Logan, J.W.M. and P. Schofield. 1984. The Environmental Effects of Insecticides on Non-target Organisms in Tropical and Sub-tropical Developing Countries. Tropical Developmental Research Institute Publication, London, U.K.

Mahavir. 1982. Olfactory physiology of Apis florea F. with reference to repellents. Ph.D. Thesis, Haryana Agricultural University, Hisar (India), 168 pp.

McGregor, S.E. 1976. Insect Pollination of Cultivated Crop Plants. Agriculture Hand Book No. 496, Agriculture Research Service, United States Department of Agriculture, 411 pp.

Mel'nichenko, A.N. 1976. Role of insect pollinators in increasing yields of agricultural plans. In: Pollination of Entomophilous Agricultural Crops by Bees, Kozin, R.B. (Ed.), Amerind Publishing Col. Pvt. Ltd., New Delhi, India, pp. 1-14.

Moffett, J.O. and H.L. Morton. 1975. Repellency of surfactants to honeybees. Environmental Entomology, 4: 780-782.

Palmer-Jones, T., I.W. Forster and G.L. Jeffrey. 1957. Effect on honeybees of Rogor and Endothion applied from the air as sprays to Brassicas: trial of M.G.K. repellent 874. New Zealand Journal of Agriculture Research, 2: 463-480.

Parker, F.D. and D.R. Frohlich. 1983. Hybrid sunflower pollination by manageable composite specialists: the sunflower leafcutter bee (Hymenoptera: Megachilidae). Environmental Entomology, 12(2): 576-581.

Reith, J.P., W.T. Wilson and M.D. Levin. 1986. Repelling honeybees from insecticide treated flowers with 2-heptanone. Journal of Apicultural Research, 25(2): 78-84.

Richards, K.W. 1987. Alfalfa leafcutter bee management in Canada. Bee World, 65(4): 168-178.

Russell, G.E. 1978. Plant Breeding for Pest and Disease Resistance. Butterworths, London, 485 pp.

Shaw, F.R. and A.I. Bourne. 1944. Observation on bee repellents. Journal of Economic Entomology, 37: 519-521.

Sihag, R.C. 1983a. Life cycle pattern, seasonal mortality, problem of parasitization and sex ratio pattern in alfalfa pollinating megachilid bees. Zeischrift fur angwandte Entomologie, 96(4): 368-379.

Sihag, R.C. 1983b. Foraging behaviour and pollination ecology of different bee pollinators in relation to cultivated cruciferous crops. Proceedings of 29th International Apiculture Congress, Budapest, pp. 334-335.

Sihag, R.C. 1983c. Foraging behaviour and pollination ecology of different bee pollinators in relation to cultivated umbelliferous crops. Proceedings of 29th International Apiculture Congress, Budapest, pp. 335-336.

Sihag, R.C. 1983d. Foraging behaviour and pollination ecology of different bee pollinators in relation to onion crop. Proceedings of 29th International Apiculture Congress, Budapest, p. 336.

Sihag, R.C. 1985a. Floral biology, melittophily and pollination ecology of cultivated cruciferous crops. In: Recent Advances in Pollen Research, Varghese, T.M. (Ed.), Allied Publishers, New Delhi, pp. 241-268.

Sihag, R.C. 1985b. Floral biology, melittophily and pollination ecology of cultivated umbelliferous crops. In: Recent Advances in Pollen Research, Varghese, T.M. (Ed.), Allied Publishers, New Delhi, pp. 269-276.

Sihag, R.C. 1985c. Floral biology, melittophily and pollination ecology of onion crop. In: Recent Advances in Pollen Research, Varghese, T.M. (Ed.), Allied Publishers, New Delhi, pp. 277-284.

Sihag, R.C. 1986. Insect pollination increases seed production in cruciferous and umbelliferous crops. Journal of Apicultural Research, 25(2): 121-126.

Sihag, R.C. 1987. Effect of pesticides and bee-pollination on seed yield of some crops in India. Journal of Apicultural Research, 27(1): 49-54.

Sihag, R.C. 1990. Some economic estimates of use of pesticides and bee pollination for crop yield. (submitted)

Singh, D.P. 1986. Breeding for Resistance to Diseases and Insect Pests. Springer-Verlag, Berlin, 222 pp.

Smith, R.F., J.L. Apple and D.G. Bettrell. 1976. The origin of integrated pest management concept. In: Integrated Pest Management, Apple, J.L. and Smith, R.F. (Eds.), Plenum Press, New York, pp.

1-16.

Tasei, J.N. and S. Carre. 1985. Effects du traitment de luzerne en fleurs (Medicago sativa L.) avec de la deltamethrine et de la phosalone sur l'abeille solitaire: Megachile rotundata F (Hym., Megachilidae). Acta Oecologica: Oecologica Applicata, 6(2): 165-173.

Tasei, J.N., S. Carre, P.G. Bosio, P. Debrey and J. Hariot. 1987. Effects of the Pyrethroid insecticide, WL85871 and phosalone on adults and progeny of the leaf-cutting bee Megachile rotundata F., pollinator of lucerne. Pesticide Science, 21: 119-128.

Todd, F.E. and S.E. McGregor. 1960. The use of honeybee in production of crops. Annual Review of Entomology, 5: 265-278.

Torchio, P.F. 1987. Use of non-honey bee species as pollinators of crops. Proceedings of the Entolological Society of Ontario, 118: 111-124.

Wilson, F. and C.B. Huffaker. 1976. The philosophy, scope and importance of biological control. In: Theory and Practice of Biological Control, Huffaker, C.B. and Messenger, P.S. (Eds.), Academic Press, pp. 3-15.

Wood, G.W. 1979. Recuperation of native bee populations in blueberry fields exposed to drift of fenitrothion from forest spray operations in New Brunswick. Journal of Economic Entomology, 72(1): 36-39.

Yeargan, K.V. 1985. Alfalfa: Status and current limits to biological control in the eastern U.S. In: Biological Control in Agriculture IPM System, Hoy, M.A. and Herzog, D.C. (Eds.), Academic Press, pp. 521-536.

SECTION VI: MANAGEMENT, ECONOMICS, AND HONEY PRODUCTION

CHAPTER 28

MANAGEMENT PRACTICES AND MIGRATORY BEEKEEPING

C. CHANDRASEKHARA REDDY

EARLY BEEKEEPING AND MANAGEMENT

The exploitation of bees in India is of great antiquity, being known since prehistoric times. The use of honey for religious and medicinal purposes is also ancient and well known but its consumption as food is a recent development (Ransome 1937; Muttoo 1944, 1956; Singh 1962; Joshi and Godbole 1970). India has been traditionally an agricultural country and 80 percent of its population lives in villages. In this context, beekeeping has gained importance as an agricultural activity and has been inextricably linked with rural life.

Beekeeping in India was established as a modern industry only after the invention of movable frame hives in 1882 and the transfer of this technology to India (Singh 1983). In India, the beekeeping industry evolved from different bases and practices and fits under various categories of rural activity: e.g. village cottage industry, agro-based rural industry, forest-based industry, decentralized industry, subsidiary part-time industry, and also as a profitable hobby.

It was only in the latter part of the 19th century that some steps were taken to modernize beekeeping in parts of the country. In this context, beekeeping is a scientific method of conservation and rearing of bees for production of honey, wax, royal jelly, pollen, bee venom, and pollination of crop plants. The theory of beekeeping management is simple but its practise requires keen observation and close attention. Beekeeping is practised under wide agro-climatic conditions in the plains, and hills up to 2,700 m A.S.L. (Melkania et al. 1983) and modern methods of collection, processing, storage and marketing of honey and wax are in place.

MODERN BEE MANAGEMENT PRACTICES

Modern beekeeping was introduced throughout India by the pioneering efforts of Khadi and the Village Industries Commission and a community of progressive beekeepers practising commercial beekeeping has gradually emerged. Modern beekeeping techniques, which were originally developed in countries such as the U.S.A., the U.K., and West Germany have been adopted and modified to suit local conditions and special requirements in India. Recognition of regional differences in the flora and environment has resulted in appropriate techniques to capture, establish, and manage bee colonies in different seasons and for different purposes. Some of the important modern management practices used with Apis cerana indica, and their role in the growth of the beekeeping industry, are discussed here in detail.

Hive/Equipment Management

The primitive hives such as log hives, wall hives of clay pots, wicker hives, and box hives were widely used by early beekeepers (Shah 1975). Though the invention of movable frame hives by L.L. Langstroth in 1881 marked the beginning of modern beekeeping, the traditional way of beekeeping is still widespread throughout the country and modern methods are still unknown in some remote parts of India. Increased application of technology to beekeeping and honey handling has led to the development of sophisticated and specialized bee equipment. Different types of hives and their shapes have been used in the development of beekeeping techniques. The variety, and/or lack of availability of bee equipment together with insufficient expert guidance in beekeeping have been constraints to the development of the industry. Bee hives have undergone a series of changes and modifications mainly for easier manipulation of colonies under local beekeeping conditions. As a result, many sizes of bee boxes, hive stands, and honey extractors have been developed and the management of the colonies along modern lines with this equipment has been hampered. Now, a standard beekeeping kit, which includes state-of-the-art standardized beekeeping equipment and other equipment for the management of an apiary of five colonies is being used widely (Table I).

To develop the standard kit, experiments were carried out to determine the appropriate sizes and designs of bee hives for the plains and hills, and also for different ecotypes of bees (Table II). A typical bee box consists of one bottom board, one brood chamber with frames, one super chamber with frames, one crown board, one roof, one division or dummy board, and one queen gate. Any bee hives with 8-10 frames were found to be bigger than necessary, reflecting the egg-laying capacity of the queen, which is around 400 eggs a day (Mahindre

TABLE I. Standard apiary kit for beekeeping with *Apis cerana indica*.

1.	Standard bee hive
2.	Bee stand
3.	Ant wells
4.	Feeders
5.	Bee veil
6.	Hive tool
7.	Swarm net
8.	Queen gate
9.	Queen excluder
10.	Nucleus boxes
11.	Carrying cages
12.	Honey extractor
13.	Honey bottles
14.	Comb foundation
15.	Books and periodicals

1983). Use of the proper size of hive, determined on the basis of egg-laying capacity of the queen bee and utilization of space for brood rearing and storing of honey, can ensure, with careful management, the survival of the bees throughout winter and summer, both in the plains and hills.

Seasonal management

The success of beekeeping depends on the proper manipulation of the apiary during different seasons. Generally, colonies should not be exposed to hot sun, rain, and severe cold. In India, where temperate, tropical, sub-tropical, arid, and semi-arid climates can be found, management techniques tailored to these conditions are necessary.

Summer Management: During the summer, colonies should be kept in the shade and the hive entrance should be to the lee of hot winds. Wet gunny cloth can be kept on top of the hive to keep it cool. A source of water for the bees must be provided in the apiary to keep hive temperature (32-36°C) and humidity (40-60%) in the range required by the bees.

Monsoon Management: Management for control of wax moth is important during this season because shade and dampness are favourable to their attack. A strong colony with all the combs covered with bees can successfully repel wax moth attack. Timely removal of all combs is recommended as they become empty or devoid of bees.

Winter Management: During winter, starvation should be prevented by providing concentrated feed which provides the energy the bees need to regulate hive temperature. The colony may be covered with tar paper leaving an adequate opening at the entrance and also at the ventilation hole of the top cover. Special arrangements are required to protect bees from severe cold, especially in northern and mountain regions. Beekeepers usually feed and build up their colonies in spring to make good any winter losses.

Swarm control

Swarming should be controlled to keep colonies strong and also to assure a high yield of honey. The swarming season is usually from February to April but occurrence of swarms several times a year is not uncommon. Various measures have been suggested for control of swarming. Weekly inspection during swarming season is necessary to monitor conditions in the colony. Splitting of colonies is sometimes very successful. The removal of queen cells also prevents swarming. Prevention of swarming by the use of a queen gate has been highly successful and is widely practised. Methods to control swarming vary from area to area and no one standard method is suitable to all areas. Breeding for less swarming tendency is also helpful and has proven successful for some beekeepers.

Increasing colony numbers

Beekeepers can increase the number of colonies they have by swarm or colony capture or splitting strong colonies.

Colony uniting

Colony uniting is practised widely. The time and frequency of uniting are highly variable. Depending on the conditions and needs of a colony, the following methods of uniting colonies, as recommended by Johansson and Johansson (1976a) have been commonly used: Uniting two or more colonies, combining small colonies into one larger colony, uniting a colony without a queen to one with a queen, uniting a colony with laying workers to a queen right colony, and uniting a swarm to an established colony. The splitting of colonies is done in both the plains and hills, depending on the type of bee forage, nature of habitat, and season. Swarm capture is relatively simple. Once a swarm has been located it can be enticed or knocked into a catching box for transport, or directly into an empty hive. Similarly, wild colonies can be collected directly from their natural hive, or

TABLE II. Type of bee box recommended for beekeeping with *Apis cerana indica* for different regions of India.

Type of bee box	Area
1. I.S.I. 'A' with not less than 8 frames	Kerala, Tamilnadu, Karnataka, Andhra Pradesh, Pondicherry, Maharashtra, Goa, Gujarat, Madhya Pradesh, Rajasthan, Orissa, Tripura and Plain districts of West Bengal, Bihar, Uttar Pradesh, Assam, Arunachal Pradesh, Nagaland, Manipur, Haryana, Punjab and Himachal Pradesh
2. I.S.I. 'B' with not less than 8 frames	Hill districts of West Bengal, Punjar, Himachal Pradesh, Haryana, Assam, Uttar Pradesh and also the Hill areas of Arunachal Pradesh, Meghalaya, Manipur, Nagaland and Mizoram
3. Langstroth Box with 8 to 10 frames	Jammu and Kashmir state and adjacent regions

from bait hives set out to entice them to establish. Splitting requires a little more finesse. Strong colonies can be divided by removing half the brood and the bees covering the comb to a new hive body. It is important that both splits have eggs so that the queenless split can raise a new queen.

Requeening or queen renewal

A prolific, laying queen is absolutely necessary to keep the colony strong. A good population of industrious workers is vital for high yields of honey, wax, services pollination better, and also offers protection against pests and diseases. Thus, the economy of the colony and of beekeeping depends upon the performance of the queen. The sure way for a common beekeeper to get the desired results is by requeening at the proper time. Generally, fertile queens lay eggs quite reliably for two years but changing queens annually is always profitable. The egg-laying capacity of queen bees is comparatively less in the second year than the first (Naim 1983). Annual renewal of the queen bee is practised by most of the beekeepers in different parts of the country, especially in the plains. The most active

period of egg-laying is from April to June when temperatures are between 37° and 40°C (Naim 1983).

Queen rearing

Little work has been done in genetically improving the performance of *A. cerana indica*. There is an urgent need and great demand for improved bee stock. Improved stock coupled with better management can only lead to better profitability in beekeeping. Attempts to improve the egg-laying capacity of queen bees through selective breeding using instrumental insemination has been initiated in several places but the results have not been commercialized. Rearing queen bees with good qualities such as gentleness, industriousness, resistance to diseases, and absence of absconding has been successfully carried out by researchers and progressive beekeepers. Queen production on a large scale by grafting techniques, is common and practised by commercial beekeepers for sale of queens and package bees for pollination services. Queen rearing is demonstrated by many educational centres catering to the beekeeping industry.

Honey production

Honey producing abilities of bees differ from colony to colony, even under identical conditions. The national average honey yield per colony at present is about 6 kg/year (Fig. 1) but many progressive beekeepers have been extracting up to 80 kg by practising modern management (Shah 1975).

For extraction of honey from comb, the type of extractor and filters have been standardized. The methods of pooling, processing, and storing honey have also been worked out. Before the honey flow, beekeepers build colonies by uniting weak colonies, by supplementary feeding, and also by using comb foundation sheets. During the honey flow, one to three supers are added depending on its rate and duration. Many beekeepers extract honey more than once a year. Multiple extraction of honey is possible only by management techniques such as migratory beekeeping, cultivation of bee plants, supplementary feedings, queen renewal, and use of comb foundation sheets. Usually monsoon, spring, and summer are the periods of honey extraction. The time of honey harvest depends on the type of bee forage, the duration of flowering crop, and abundance of nectar.

Comb foundation

Use of comb foundation sheets saves honey and time for worker bees and ultimately, the beekeeper. Different types of comb foundation sheets made of wax and also plastic (Weiss 1983) are widely used.

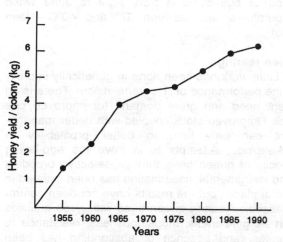

FIGURE 1. Honey yield of *Apis cerana indica* per colony during the period 1955-1990.

The shape, size, and method of their use have been standardized. Many beekeepers harvest more honey as a result of increased use of comb foundation sheets. The acceptance of both wax and plastic foundation sheets by the bees has been an encouraging development.

Supplementary feeding

Different types and concentrations of sugar (25 to 67% W/W) are recommended, and are widely used, for feeding bees at different times of year and for different purposes following the formulations of Johansson and Johansson (1976b, 1977). Supplementary feeding is done when bad weather prevents bees from foraging, during the periods of dearth, at the time of establishment of swarms, splits, package bees, when weak colonies are united, during queen rearing, and also at the time of inspecting colonies. It is also done to stimulate brood rearing to increase the colony population. Feeders which go in the hive and open air feeders are used.

Bee plant propagation

The beekeeping industry depends on the exploitation of the nectar/pollen resources of the flowering plants (Suryanarayana *et al.* 1983) by the bees. Continuous sources of pollen and nectar are essential for the success of beekeeping. Bees may get forage during a crop season and naturally starve during the remaining period, if no other nectar and pollen sources are available. During these dearth periods, the population of bees greatly decrease. As an alternative to supplementary feeding during dearth, beekeepers may provide supplementary bee forage near the apiary by planting various bee plants

which flower throughout the year. This would be particularly helpful if done on a large scale. It is also necessary to take up large scale afforestation with bee plants and establishment of social forestry and farm forestry in and around the apiary, in fallow agricultural lands, around farms, and near forests. Social and farm forestry assumes special significance in rural programmes, particularly integrated rural development (Mohana Rao and Suryanarayana 1983). Propagation of bee plants, in addition to sustaining large numbers of bee colonies and increasing the income of the beekeeper, also provides gainful employment to local people. Important bee plants yielding pollen and nectar have been catalogued for different areas together with duration of flowering and methods of propagation. The lists of such bee plants may run into hundreds.

Bee pollination

In India, beekeeping has been practised almost only for honey production. The role of bees as crop pollinators has been largely unrecognized and a vast potential in using bees to augment national income through increased crop yield has been wasted. It is well known that bees are the first and foremost insect pollinators. The intensive interaction between bees and flowering plants was undoubtedly an integral part of the evolution of flowering plants. Many oil seed, vegetable, pulse, legume, fodder, plantation, and orchard crops depend on honeybees for pollination. To improve the rate of seed setting and quality and also to produce hybrid seeds on a large scale, honeybees for pollination are absolutely necessary. Bees, through pollination, not only enrich the beekeeper with honey but may also provide income through pollination services. Also, income derived by a farmer/beekeeper by way of increased crop yield from bee pollination is much higher than the value of honey harvested. The rate of increase in crop yield as a result of bee pollination has been estimated to range from 30 percent to an astounding 3000 percent. As a result of the green revolution and because of increased demands for hybrid seeds, the Government of India has taken several measures to implement bee pollination on a large scale throughout the country. Certainly, beekeeping should be considered as an integral part of agriculture and its role in pollination must be developed at a faster rate.

Safeguard of bees against insecticide poisoning

Use of insecticides to control pests on agricultural and horticultural crops has been steadily increasing. The pesticides applied to the crops not only kill the harmful pests but also seriously affect non-target beneficial insects, like honeybees. The indiscriminate use of pesticides poses a serious hazard to populations of honeybees. Information on the relative toxicity of various commonly used pesticides to honeybees is available and categorizing them as highly toxic, moderately toxic, and relatively non-toxic. Bee losses caused by pesticides can be minimized by developing appropriate preventative measures. Avoiding application of pesticides during the flowering period of a crop or when bees are foraging on flowers, use' of low toxicity pesticides, and prevention of bees foraging on the pesticide treated flowers by closing the gate of a hive or by shifting the colonies far away from the place of pesticide application are some of the important measures. Use of repellents in order to prevent the bees from coming in contact with treated flowers has also been investigated, but with questionable success. If preventative measures are observed strictly by beekeeper, farmer, pesticide manufacturing companies, and government, the loss of bees to pesticides can be minimized.

Migratory beekeeping

The migration of bees is not a new phenomenon. Even under natural conditions, tropical bees are known to leave their established nests and move to new foraging places. As geography, topography, and climate are highly variable in India, bee flora is not available uniformly in all areas. Varying agro-climatic conditions and changing cultivated crop patterns are very common resulting in temporal changes in availability of flora. Any change in the availability of bee flora seriously affects beekeeping, and as a result, migratory beekeeping has become one of the most important management practices of modern apiculture in India. Migratory beekeeping was first introduced in North India in 1939 (Muttoo 1952). It has since been practised by all the Government Centres, Sub-centres, and beekeepers, and some of the important migratory schedules for different regions have been worked out.

Bee colonies can be shifted from a place of dearth to a place of plenty in an effort to obtain better bee forage. Colonies may be moved either by local or long distance migration. For commercial beekeeping, colonies have to be migrated three times a year, with a migration to hills during spring and to plains during winter and rainy seasons. The period of migration to the hills is used for colony multiplication and the migrations to the plains are used for honey production. Migration of colonies to lower altitudes during October to January for wintering and to higher altitudes during the months of February to October for honey flow has also been widely practised in different regions.

ADVANCED BEE MANAGEMENT

Management of pests and diseases

Like other species of *Apis*, the Indian honeybee is not free from pests and diseases. However, the damage caused to Indian honeybees by pests and diseases is not very severe when compared to other honeybee species.

Pests: Among all the known pests of the Indian honeybee, the most destructive, both in live colonies and in stored equipment, is the wax moth, *Galleria mellonella* L. The nature of the damage, the incidence of infestation, and control by physical, chemical and biological methods are well known. As a method of control, destruction of infested combs has been widely practised in India (Singh *et al*. 1983). Other pests such as wasps, ants, lizards, and frogs also cause considerable damage to bees. Placing bee hives on stands off the ground and above the ground vegetation and keeping water either in the cups or ant wells at the base of the hive help to prevent the damage caused by ants and other pests.

Diseases: The occurrence and present distribution of bee diseases in India has been reported (Kshirsagar 1983). All known brood diseases such as American foul brood, European foul brood, sac brood, and adult bee diseases such as *Nosema*, acarine mite, and clustering diseases have been reported in different parts of India. Fortunately, the damage caused to Indian bees by these diseases has not yet reached a severe stage.

Management practices to control different diseases have been standardized, including manipulations and control measures. Keeping colonies strong, destruction of natural pests and infested combs, fumigation of colonies, and adoption of hygienic methods of management are some of the important measures followed by most beekeepers to control pests and diseases. Obtaining disease-resistant strains through selective breeding is the only permanent solution and this aspect has been undertaken by various research institutions, including the universities.

Management of bee education

Techniques for beekeeping have become more specialized and also mechanized. As a result, modern beekeeping has become highly technical, and a scientific knowledge of different subjects of science and technology is essential. Unfortunately, many beekeepers of India are not educated and are not in a position to understand the scientific basis of beekeeping. This is one of the reasons responsible for the lack of development in beekeeping and also for not practising modern beekeeping.

Research and development: Research in Indian beekeeping has begun only recently. There is a vast potential for qualitative improvement in the industry through the application of modern beekeeping technology. India has the third largest community of scientists and technologists in the world. Applying the fruits of science and technology for the development of rural areas is of paramount importance. Universities and research institutions need a new direction in research programmes and the Central Bee Research Institute and its centres in different parts of the country should be strengthened to take up research on different aspects of apiculture. In addition, universities and other agricultural institutions should also take up research and teaching of apiculture. Standardization of management practices, beekeeping equipment, quality control, breeding of good strains, control of pests and diseases, and evaluation of bee plants are some of the areas of beekeeping which require immediate attention.

Training: The progress of beekeeping is very much dependent on the type of personnel involved. The efficiency of beekeepers has to be increased so that one can manage more hives and, with the same conditions, the honey yield per hive can easily be increased. Increased efficiency of management during the past fifty years has resulted in the upward trend in honey yield per hive.

Training of beekeepers in the modern methods of bee management and beekeeping technology is needed immediately. Practical training centres should be established in each region so that all beekeepers, whether employed or unemployed, can be trained in beekeeping techniques and management practices. Practical demonstrations of the modern methods and technology to beekeepers have been conducted in different centres located in different parts of the country. Different courses such as apiarist courses, fieldman's courses, beekeepers summer courses, and refresher courses have been offered to progressive beekeepers in different centres established by Khadi and Village Industries Commission and Khadi and Village Industries Board.

Extension: The present beekeeping technology and management practices available in India are of the most advanced in tropical regions of the world (Thakar 1976). In spite of this, many of the modern beekeeping techniques and practices are still unknown to many village beekeepers. Therefore, a programme of extension disseminating current apicultural technology should be launched immediately through training camps, exhibitions, practical demonstrations, and discussions. The extension units should be adequately supplied with beekeeping equipment, models, charts, and literature in local languages to effectively promote bee information.

This will keep beekeepers abreast of the latest developments in beekeeping, and prevent deteriorating trends. Audio-visual aids should also be used for the education of the beekeepers and farmers. Mass education coupled with mass communication is necessary to spread modern beekeeping throughout India. There can be no innovative change unless there is a closer co-operation among the scientific institutions, bee equipment manufacturing units, training and extension units, marketing firms, and beekeepers.

SCOPE AND FUTURE PLANS

There is a vast scope for qualitative improvement in the bee industry through modern beekeeping technology. Beekeeping by its very nature is a highly technical and scientific activity and involves simultaneous attention to the diverse scientific fields of entomology, botany, pathology, genetics, chemistry, behaviour, engineering, physiology, and management (Thakar 1976). The growth and development of beekeeping has been very slow because of the vast area and the multitude of beekeepers involved. Beekeeping is not developed uniformly in all regions, and many potential areas remain unexploited for no apparent reason. Commercial beekeeping has yet to gain momentum. Though beekeeping is a many facetted activity, the value of many aspects like bee pollination, wax production, medicinal properties of honey, and dietary importance of honey have yet to be realized. The yield of honey for a colony per year is extremely low, but there is a tremendous potential to increase production by applying the right technology and sound management. The present yield of 6 kg of honey per colony could easily be raised to 10 kg within a short span of time by judicious management. Tropical countries like India have an advantage over other countries because of the rich variety of flora, and the suitable climates for beekeeping almost throughout the year.

Considering the availability of 60 million hectares of forest and 50 million hectares of land under the cultivation of pulses, orchards, and other crops useful to bees for honey production and requiring pollination, the existing number of colonies is meager. There is a great scope for increasing the number of colonies to 100 million, both for honey production and for pollination.

Bee research in India has yet to gain momentum. There is an urgent need to improve the quality of *A. cerana indica*, particularly its egg-laying capacity. Greater emphasis should be placed on developing suitable and productive strains through selective breeding. The management practices should be standardized for different regions including the hills, plains, and forest regions. Migratory beekeeping should be accelerated both in quality and quantity to increase the production of honey and yield of crops. Establishment of bee houses, bee parks, bee nurseries, and bee research and training centres would speed up development of beekeeping to a large extent. Live demonstrations of various bee techniques to beekeepers and standardization of bee equipment would also stimulate modern beekeeping, especially among village beekeepers.

ACKNOWLEDGEMENTS

The author expresses his thanks to Mr. M. Shankar Reddy, Research Assistant, Department of Zoology, Bangalore University, Bangalore, for his help and assistance and Mr. R. Ravikumar, Junior Research Fellow, Department of Zoology, Bangalore University, Bangalore, for his help in the preparation of manuscript.

REFERENCES

Johansson, T.S.K. and M.P. Johansson. 1976a. Uniting colonies. Bee World, 57(3): 96-100.

Johansson, T.S.K. and M.P. Johansson. 1976b. Feeding sugars to bees. 1. Feeders and syrup feeding. Bee World, 57(4): 137-143.

Johansson, T.S.K. and M.P. Johansson. 1977. Feeding sugars to bees. 2. When and how to feed. Bee World, 58(1): 11-18.

Joshi, C.G. and N.N. Godbole. 1970. The composition and medical properties of natural honey as described in Ayurveda. Indian Bee Journal, 32(3-4): 77-78.

Kshirsagar, K.K. 1983. Diseases of bees in India. Indian Bee Journal, 45(2-3): 39;42.

Mahindre, D.B. 1983. Queen rearing in Apis mellifera. Indian Bee Journal, 45(2-3): 75-76.

Melkania, N.P., U. Pandey, and T. Sharma. 1983. Apiculture in rural Himalayas: Existing status, problems and strategies for development. Indian Bee Journal, 45(2-3): 67-68.

Mohana Rao, G. and M.C. Suryanarayana. 1983. Potentialities for bee pollination of crops in U.P. Indian Bee Journal, 45(2-3): 58-61.

Muttoo, R.N. 1944. Beekeeping in India: Its past, present and future. Indian Bee Journal, 6(3-4): 54-77.

Muttoo, R.N. 1952. Migratory beekeeping in Kuman hills. Indian Bee Journal, 14(1-2): 18-21.

Muttoo, R.N. 1956. Facts about beekeeping in India. Bee World, 37: 125-133; 154-157.

Naim, M. 1983. The queen bee of Indian Apis cerana and its effects on colony performance. Indian Bee Journal, 45(2-3): 69-70.

Ransome, H.M. 1937. The Sacred Bee in Ancient Times and Folklore. George Allen & Unwin Ltd., London. 308 pp.

Shah, F.A. 1975. Some facts about beekeeping in Kashmir. Bee World, 56(3): 103-108.

Singh, B.P., R.P. Phadke, and M.C. Mittal. 1983. Beekeeping potential and pattern of management in Uttar Pradesh. Indian Bee Journal, 45(2-3): 35;37.

Singh, S. 1962. Beekeeping in India. Indian Council of Agricultural Research, New Delhi. 214 pp.

Singh, Y. 1983. Beekeeping in Uttar Pradesh - A review. Indian Bee Journal, 45(2-3): 84-91.

Suryanarayana, M.C., G. Mohana Rao and R.P. Phadke. 1983. Plant propagation, beekeeping and pollination. Indian Bee Journal, 45(2-3): 64-66.

Thakar, C.V. 1976. Beekeeping technology: Its pace and plans. Indian Bee Journal, 38(1-4): 23-28.

Weiss, K. 1983. Experiences with plastic combs and foundation. Bee World, 64(2): 56-62.

CHAPTER 29

BEE MANAGEMENT AND COMPANY MANAGEMENT

BÖRJE SVENSSON

INTRODUCTION

Honeybees behave differently in different parts of the world. They vary in characteristics such as rate and timing of nest build-up, honey collection, swarming, etc. Natural conditions such as flora and climate as well as the human apicultural infrastructure also vary a lot. Peasants have different educational levels, technical experiences and financial resources in different places. Government policies also differ in different countries.

In addition, beekeeping has become a complicated activity because of the variety of different technical solutions concerning beehive design and management. The solutions are often diffused in inappropriate ways: some methods and some equipment are being used in some places and situations where actually completely different solutions would be more appropriate.

All of the above factors form a complex interrelationship which influences the choice of bee management and company management and thus also the rate of success in a particular operation. Crane (1984) has stressed the importance for a global strategy to coordinate the spread of information and knowledge on the complex science of beekeeping. This short chapter is a small attempt to simplify the discussion about the choice of bee management and technology under different conditions.

Hypothetical situations in three different countries have been chosen in order to exemplify the discussion.

DEFINITIONS

With **bee management**, I mean a complete system which includes the whole range of operations from starting up as a beekeeper to finally handing over the product(s) to the processor or consumer. I also enclose the choice of equipment and tools in this definition.

With **company management**, I mean the way of organizing work with a specific beekeeping unit, the relationship between beneficiaries and including eventual work with processing, marketing, and distribution of the product(s).

The choice of bee management also has implica-

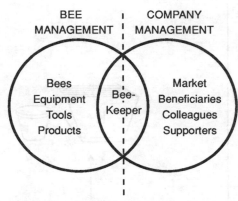

FIGURE 1. Interrelationship between bee management and company management.

tions for the choice of company management or level of cooperation between beekeepers and vice versa (Fig. 1).

CHOICE OF BEE MANAGEMENT AND TECHNOLOGY

Before I present the three examples from different countries, I would like to explain what I mean by **appropriate technology** in a schematic diagram (Fig. 2). This diagram is an attempt to illustrate the process of technology development for:

a) a country or a region as time goes by and development from traditional to modern beekeeping takes place.

b) an individual beekeeper as he gradually gains more and more experience and improves his investment capacity.

The diagram could, of course, have been made much more complicated, but I have chosen to illustrate the two main development alternatives as I see them at present:

1. Low cost and simple top-bar hives.

2. Expensive and advanced movable-frame hives.

The situation is in reality not so simple - it is, in fact, multidimensional because other factors such as local materials, traditions, taboos, market demand, international influence, bee diseases and pests also impinge on the choice of bee management and technology.

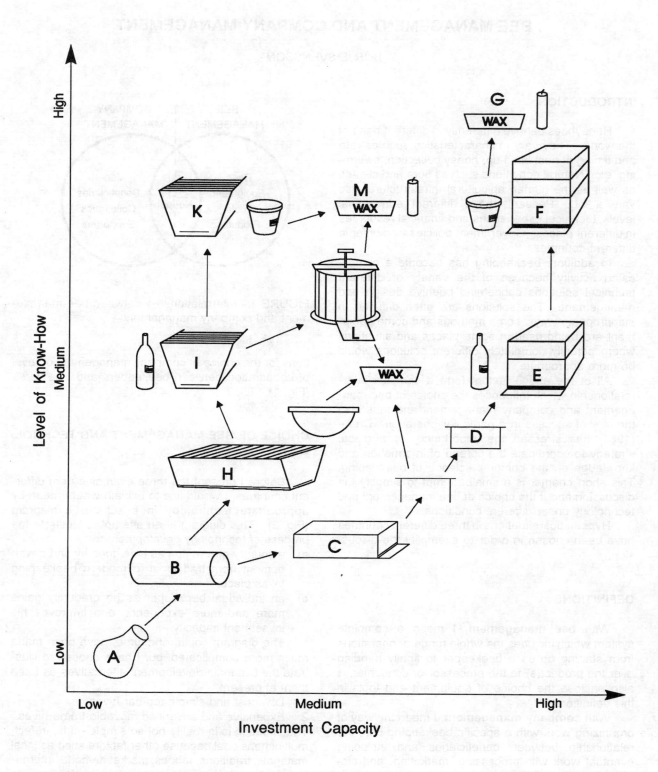

FIGURE 2. Schematic diagram illustration of a discussion around appropriate beekeeping technology.

It is possible to elaborate a great deal on this diagram, but I leave it to the readers to compare it with their own experiences and to think of ways to develop the discussion around this diagram further.

THREE EXAMPLES

I have chosen to exemplify the discussion around the choice of bee management and company management through three different hypothetical cases in three countries with completely different conditions. The countries are Nicaragua (Svensson 1985), Gambia (Svensson unpublished) and Bangladesh (Svensson 1988) and the discussion is summarized under the headlines:
- present bee management
- present company management
- possible steps in technology development and company development (illustrated with letters A,B,C,D, etc. in Fig. 2).

Nicaragua
Present bee management: The natural conditions for beekeeping are very good but the Africanized honeybees have caused a lot of trouble both to beekeepers and the public. The bees are managed extensively in Langstroth standard hives. Only honey is produced and is mostly packed in barrels.

Present company management: Government policy, land reform and the limited resources for development are favourable for cooperation among peasants (1988). Beekeeping development is supported by the Development Banks and beekeepers' associations are young and weak. The market is fairly developed (Fig. 3).

Possible development steps: No further investment into beehives or equipment is needed until the present problems have been technically solved. Instead, I propose research and training for better bee management, product quality and for product diversification. Also, cooperation towards better product marketing is recommended. Therefore, in Figure 2, I suggest a development from a low level of know-how to a higher level, but continuing with the same equipment (from E to F and G).

Gambia
Present bee management: The melliferous flora is highly suitable but other factors are causing great troubles for modern movable-frame hive beekeeping. The traditional beekeeping is almost forgotten but many experiments with modern beekeeping systems are going on. The honey quality is low.

Present company management: The traditional lifestyle and lack of government or organizational initiatives is making cooperation difficult at present. The potential market for honey sales at the many tourist hotels is great (Fig. 4).

Possible development steps: First of all, a standardized system for top-bar beekeeping is needed with careful instructions for small-scale or medium-scale family beekeeping (H). Then, improved methods for hand-pressing of honey and melting of beeswax should be introduced (I). Then development can continue with further training towards mechanical honey pressing (L) or product diversification (K) and distribution to tourists. Forming local associations of beekeepers is also desirable.

Bangladesh
Present bee management: *Apis cerana* honeybees are managed in movable-frame hives (Newton) with poor results. Bee management is highly influenced by *Apis mellifera* technology which causes great problems with absconding, swarming, waxmoths, and poor honey quality. The beekeepers are generally very poor and have received inappropriate training. Bee colonies are scarce.

Present company management: Because of lack of government involvement, a large number of small organizations are engaged in beekeeping development, but with little cooperation. The organizations have given intensive support to small-scale family beekeeping. Some of the organizations also support the formation of groups of villagers or beekeepers. The honey market is good and production is low (Fig. 5).

Possible development steps: First of all, I suggest organizational changes. The organizations involved in beekeeping development should start cooperating and coordinating their efforts. Secondly, I suggest a step away from the present beekeeping technology and instead, central development of appropriate hive design and simple bee management. In the diagram, I suggest going back from the present situation (E) to single box hives (C), top-bar hives (H) or even simple kinds of cylindrical hives (B). Only when the beekeeping system is successful, will development of honey extraction, honey quality or marketing be meaningful. Wax collection should be started immediately (N).

REFERENCES

Crane, E. 1984. Tropical apiculture and the need for a global strategy. IBRA. pp. 27-32.
Svensson, B. Personal notes from Gambia 1979 and 1986.

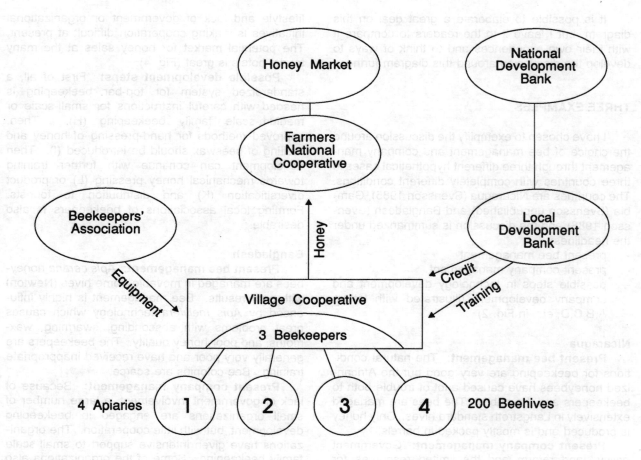

FIGURE 3. Company management in Nicaragua.

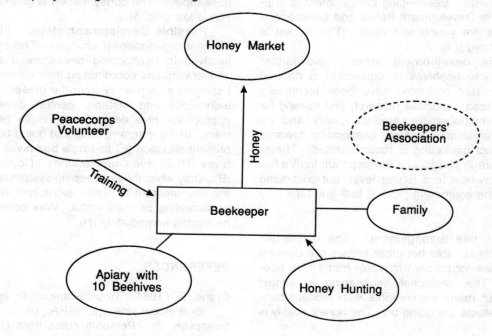

FIGURE 4. Company management in Gambia.

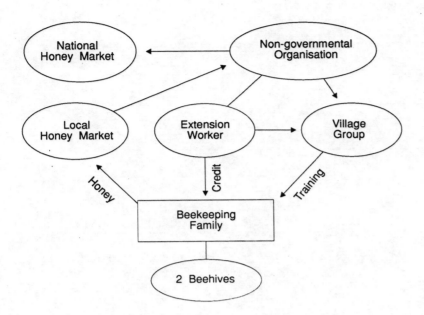

FIGURE 5. Company management in Bangladesh.

Svensson, B. 1985. National Beekeeping Program,
     Nicaragua, Evaluation report 1980-1984 with
     future recommendations. Sala.
Svensson, B. 1988. Beekeeping Technology in
     Bangladesh - A description of past and present
     situation with suggested modifications. 2nd
     edition. Sala.

CHAPTER 30

FORAGING RANGE FOR *APIS CERANA* AND ITS IMPLICATIONS FOR HONEY PRODUCTION AND APIARY MANAGEMENT

P.G. KEVAN, R.W.K. PUNCHIHEWA, and C.F. GRECO

The concept of carrying capacity is well understood by ecologists. It refers to the size of population which a given area can support. If populations of a particular organism exceed the carrying capacity of their area something must give. In diverse ecosystems, ecologists have noted various effects of overloaded environments. The most catastrophic event is mass starvation by which the population is reduced to levels which the environment can support. Very often, the population is reduced below that level and rebounds, only to be stricken again. Such oscillating populations are well known to economic entomologists (Huffaker and Rabb 1984). Another event which may bring relief to a population of organisms stressed by having exceeded the carrying capacity of its environment is departure, or migration (Johnson 1969). Organisms which behave this way are also well known to ecologists.

In considering honeybees, the matter of absconding is frequently discussed. There are various reasons for absconding, but one of the prime ones is lack of sufficient food (nectar or pollen) in the vicinity of the hives. Absconding and migration may be closely linked in respect of their causes, but we make a distinction in that absconding may take place at any time and under any conditions of stress, including paucity of resources whereas migration is more predictable as to time and conditions. Thus, we know that *Apis dorsata* has an annual migratory habit which takes it from areas which will become impoverished in terms of food availability and relatively harsh conditions for living (i.e. the tall tree forests in the rainy seasons). This bee migrates before conditions deteriorate to cause starvation. The bees move to another habitat where resources are increasing in their seasonal abundance. There are other examples of bees following the blooming seasons on annual back and forth migrations in the tropics (e.g. in Kenya (Kigatiira 1984) and by *A. dorsata* (Koeniger and Koeniger 1980)) which is sometimes called "seasonal absconding".

There have been indications that *Apis cerana* is migratory in some areas. Little is known about this activity, whether it is characteristic of some biotypes of the bee or is really absconding behaviour. If the activity is characteristic of a certain biotype, annual migration may be difficult, if not impossible for

beekeepers to control. If the activity is absconding then beekeepers must manage their bees and apiaries so that the bees remain where they are wanted and produce honey. There are a number of insects that are known to have migratory and nonmigratory biotypes in the same species (see Johnson 1969). In some, the differences in behaviour are genetically controlled but in others the environment and hormones play an important role.

The foregoing aside, it is well known that *A. cerana* has a high propensity for absconding and that this behaviour is a major concern to beekeepers managing this species. The importance of scarcity of resources in causing absconding and the concept of carrying capacity clearly coincide. What is not so obvious is that the two ideas require some understanding of what is scarcity to the bees. To understand that, one must consider two important ecological components of foraging:

1. The foraging range, the energetic requirements of the bees and the colony, and
2. The productivity of resources within the foraging range.

We present two models, based on the idea expressed in Figure 1 that shows that if the foraging range is constant (small for *A. cerana* but larger for *Apis mellifera*, see below) and the population becomes large (as with more hives per apiary), the carrying capacity (plane of nectar availability) of the foraging area becomes exceeded and resources depleted to scarcity, even if there are plentiful resources just beyond that area. Under those constraints, honeybees could not be expected to store honey. Our model also embraces the converse, small populations and relatively abundant resources in that same foraging range, in which the maximum amount of honey the bees could store is stored and honey crops are the greatest. In the latter, some amount of resource may remain un-harvested by bees so that the foraging range is underutilized from the perspective of honey production.

The foraging range of *A. cerana* in Sri Lanka has been worked out by Punchihewa *et al.* (1985) on the basis of the dance communication and distance over which they forage at feeding stations. In general, it appeared that foragers did not travel further than 500 m and preferred to remain within 100 m of their hives

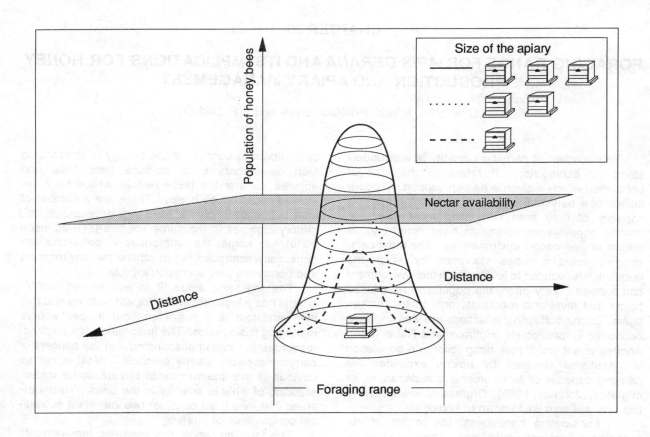

FIGURE 1. This simple diagram illustrates the effect of adding hives to an apiary. The foraging range of all the bees in the apiary is within the same radius, thus as the number of hives increases, the population of bees dependent on the resources in the foraging range increases proportionately. The amount of resources, however, remains constant as represented by the plane of nectar availability. Thus, if the apiary is too crowded with respect to the resource availability, then the carrying capacity of the foraging range is exceeded and the bees do not have sufficient forage for sustenance and certainly not enough for the beekeeper to harvest.

(Fig. 2). Thus, we may calculate foraging areas of about a maximum of 75 ha and generally about 3 ha. In the temperate part of its distribution, *A. cerana*'s foraging range is greater (see Verma 1990). However, the foraging range of *A. mellifera* is much more extensive, at 5 km or more and generally within 500 m from the hive, encompassing about 8,000 ha to 75 ha (see Winston 1987; Seeley 1985; Vickery 1991). For our purposes we have used 75 ha for *A. cerana* and 8,000 ha for *A. mellifera* as representing the range within which about 90% of the foragers are active (Punchihewa *et al.* 1985; Seeley 1985).

In general, it may be considered that a colony of bees requires large amounts of sugar for its activities and maintenance. Only after those needs have been met can sugar be stored as honey. For colonies of *A. mellifera* in summer in temperate countries it has been estimated that a given colony requires about 40 kg sugar for general activities and colony mainte-

nance (Winston 1992). We can use proportionately smaller figures for *A. cerana* to compensate for the smaller size of the colonies and their lesser energy demands and proportionately larger figures for their year-long activity in tropical and subtropical environments and estimate that 10-20 kg would be needed. We stress that these figures are highly approximate and that actual values are not available. Through these assumptions, it can be seen that the availability of nectar over the foraging range of a single colony must be 10-20 kg of sugar per season. It is a simple matter to multiply the requirements for more colonies.

As noted, only after the colonies' daily needs are met can honey be stored. Thus, if a beekeeper operates an apiary of 10 hives of *A. cerana*, the productivity of nectar available to honeybees in the 75 ha foraging range for all colonies must exceed 100-200 kg of sugar before any can be stored. Only

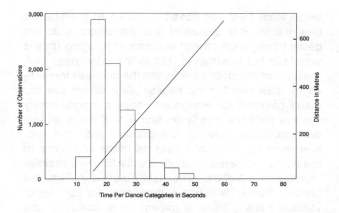

FIGURE 2. Natural foraging range for *A. cerana* in Sri Lanka shown by the frequency of dance-time categories (bar graph) and the corresponding distances they represent (oblique line). The most common dance time category is 15 to 20 seconds which corresponds to a distance of about 100 meters to the favoured source of forage (from Punchihewa *et al.* 1985).

the excess sugar is stored as honey so that becomes divided among the colonies. If this excess is to be about 10 kg of honey per colony, then the 200-300 kg of sugar in nectar would have to be produced in the foraging range. Considering that most nectar is secreted at about 20% to 30% sugars, although that found in the flowers may be much richer as a result of evaporation of water, 1 to 1.5 metric tonne of nectar available to honeybees must be secreted by the flowers within 500 m of the apiary per season. This amount does not consider the nectar required by the myriad of other insects (butterflies, moths, wasps, flies, beetles) and flower visitors (birds and bats), beneficial and pestiferous (Kevan 1986), in the same area.

There are few data on nectar secretion rates per unit area. Shuel's (1992) summarized data on nectar sugar yields from temperate regions indicate that for various plants, nectar production is highly variable from year to year and between locations. Figures range from a few kg/ha to over a tonne, but the mean is about 260 kg/ha/plant species. Given that the plants studied have only a short flowering period of about 3 weeks each and are among the most highly regarded honey plants, and in their immediate vicinity (field or stand) they are the only plant to bloom profusely, it is reasonable to suggest total productivity in the area is similar at 0.25 tonne/ha/season. For the tropics and subtropics, data have not been gathered, but we can use a similar figure in our calculations to reflect the longer,

but generally less intense, blooming season, the lesser prevalence of massively blooming herbaceous species, and the idea that plants have only a single bloom per year.

If we assume (1) that the levels of nectar sugar productivity given above are representative, (2) that a colony of *A. mellifera* uses 3 to 4 times the amount of sugar that it stores, and (3) that a colony can store about 25 kg honey/season, then we arrived at a figure for the carrying capacity of about 2 colonies/ha. This figure is not unreasonable in the area of a blooming crop, and is a little low by comparison with most figures given for servicing crop pollination (McGregor 1976). However, the foraging range of *A. mellifera*, at 5 km from the hive, encompasses about 80 square km, or 8,000 ha. Clearly, stocking densities of bees in a given area of 10 km by 10 km could not be 20,000 colonies. In general, it is estimated that apiaries should be managed with no more than 20-40 hives and established at 5 km apart in highly agricultural lands of southern Ontario in eastern Canada. Thus, a factor of 1/100 might be reasonable for the practicalities of honey production and carrying capacity.

Honeybees are known to vary genetically in terms of their hoarding activity and honey production (Page and Laidlaw 1992). This is also true of *A. cerana*, but few data, and those mostly anecdotal, are available. If an apiary has colonies with a high propensity for hoarding, then honey yields should be high. However, if there are too many hives, i.e. not enough resources to satisfy the hoarding behaviour of the bees, the honey yields would be sub-maximal as proportionately more nectar sugar is consumed in the colonies' activities and maintenance.

From the above, we can model this system using a Lotka-Volterra approach with a matrix of mutual effects among colonies:

$$dNg/dC = Ng(\beta_{Ng/C} + \sum \alpha_{ij} Ng_j)$$ [1]

where dNg/dC is nectar (honey) gathered per apiary, Ng_i or Ng_j is nectar gathered by colony i or j in the foraging range of the apiary, $\beta_{Ng/C}$ is the per colony rate of decrease (increase) of Ng, α_{ij} is the per colony effect of colony j on colony i, and C is number of colonies.

Although this is a simple model with assumptions derived from the theory of competition in ecology (May 1976), it is sufficiently general to be a first approximation. Because our chapter is not intended to model any specific production system, there is little reason to add specific processes and/or mechanisms. Figure 3 presents the outcome of this model.

However, the basic mechanism that describes the natural economics of honey production from the

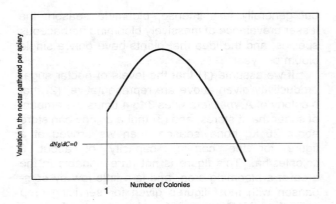

FIGURE 3. A Lotka-Volterra representation of the change in the amount of nectar, surplus to the needs of daily maintenance of the colonies, gathered per apiary according to its size in terms of the number of colonies. At the start, the carrying capacity of the foraging range is underutilized with a single (the start of the curve) or very few colonies maximizing their nectar gathering capabilities. As the number of colonies increases so does the amount of nectar gathered for the entire apiary. This trend continues until the colonies start to compete for the available nectar. Then, the trend of increasing honey (=surplus nectar) production slows and becomes reversed. For a while, honey yields per apiary remain high, but efficiency is lost. Eventually, when the apiary is too crowded and the carrying capacity for colony sustenance and honey crop is exceeded, finally the colonies decline in strength as nectar accumulation falls below that needed for colony maintenance.

perspective of the bees and their environment can be expressed clearly as follows:

$$Hpotmax = Ng_*Sc - (m + a) \qquad [2]$$
$$A(Hpotmax) = A(Ng - (m + a)) - V \qquad [3]$$

where *Hpotmax* is the potential maximum amount of sugar that could be stored as honey by a given hive or colony in an apiary, *Ng* is nectar gathered by a given colony in the foraging range of the apiary, *Sc* is the sugar concentration in nectar, *m* is sugar used in colony and individual maintenance, *a* is sugar used in colony activity such as foraging, etc., *A* is the number of colonies in the apiary, *V* is the nectar consumption by other inhabitants of the range, and *A(Hpotmax)* is the apiary yield of honey.

But, the amount of nectar available within the foraging range of the apiary is finite, so that *A(Hpotmax)* must have a maximum value. Figure 4 presents these relationships in which the colonies' demands for daily maintenance are 3 times and 4

times what they can possibly store. In the straight line graphs, it is assumed that the colonies do not detract from each others' success in foraging (this is simplistic but illustrative), but in the curvilinear plot, the level of competition between the colonies increases as their number increases. After there are too many colonies for maximum honey storage, honey storage declines rapidly (in fact 3 or 4 times as fast per additional hive by comparison with the pre-maximum numbers of hives) as more and more of the nectar gathered is used directly for daily maintenance and activities. The rising curves in Figure 4 present the trends in honey production for apiaries of various sizes. Thus, a maximum is achieved and production from apiaries that are slightly smaller than the maximum is equal to that from slightly over-stocked apiaries. From an operational viewpoint, a beekeeper should prefer fewer hives than more because of the extra trouble of husbandry and extraction, etc. without compensatory returns. Certainly, once the apiary is definitely too large, honey crops decline even more rapidly than in individual hives.

Unfortunately, the approach to the natural economics of honey production we have used is complicated in the world of honeybees and has not been taken in apicultural research. Thus, few data are available to provide approximations of most of the variables. Some are presented above, mostly as "guesstimates" and for the sake of illustration.

If we consider comparing apiaries and foraging ranges of *A. mellifera* and *A. cerana*, we arrive at some interesting conclusions. Taking the body size of *A. mellifera* as 1, and that of *A. cerana* as 0.5, and then the colony sizes as 40,000 *vs.* 7,000 respectively (Seeley 1985) and foraging areas of 8,000 ha (i.e. a range 5 km) *vs.* 75 ha for the two species respectively, we come to a value of 5 bees/ha for *A. mellifera* but about 90 bees/ha for *A. cerana*. Recognizing the difference in biomass of bees to be supported, which includes foragers and nest bees, the ratio come out to about 9:1 hives of *A. mellifera:A.cerana* per apiary. If we use the smaller ranges of 75 ha for *A. mellifera* and 3 ha for *A. cerana*, the relative numbers of bees comes to 530 *vs.* 2,300 bees/ha, or a ratio of 3:1 hives per apiary. Thus, we tentatively suggest that, until real data are available for representative regions, that the rules of thumb developed for apiary size for profitable honey production with *A. mellifera* can be used for *A. cerana*. Our conclusion is that apiaries of *A. cerana* should be small, containing 1 to 5 hives, and that they should be spaced about 0.5 to 1 km apart, depending on the nectar resources available.

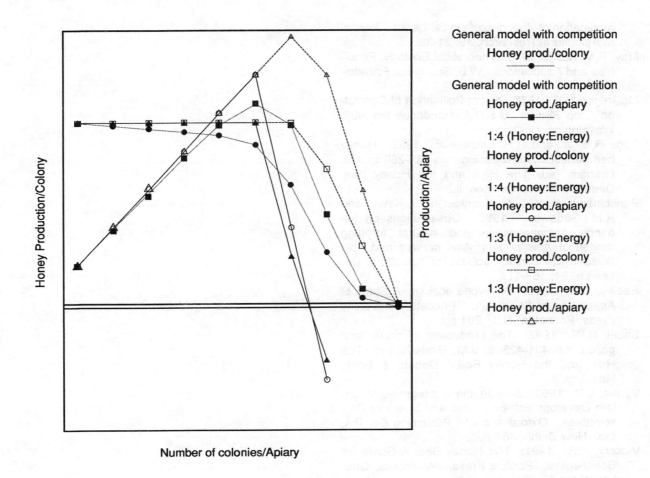

Number of colonies/Apiary

FIGURE 4. A simple representation of the honey production per colony and per apiary as the size of the apiary increases. The ratio of honey stored to nectar gathered (in terms of amount of sugar) are presented at 1:4 and 1:3. The lines which start horizontally correspond to the left-hand vertical axis as honey production per colony and production per apiary is given by the lines which start sloping upward. The left-hand and right-hand axis have relative scales of 1:3. While the number of colonies per apiary is small, each colony maximizes its nectar accumulation and honey production (horizontal lines). As the number of colonies rises above a certain threshold, they start to compete and share resources. This results in a decline in nectar accumulation. Thus, while the number of colonies is low relative to the resources available in the foraging range, the honey production per apiary rises proportionately, but once the colonies start to compete, efficiency of honey production declines even though total production may continue to increase. This effect is shown by the rising lines which reach a maximum. Once the carrying capacity (for nectar for sustenance and surplus for honey) for the foraging range is reached, the honey crops decline rapidly at a slope equivalent to the ratio of honey stored to nectar gathered in terms of sugar content.

REFERENCES

Huffaker, C.B. and R.L. Rabb (Eds). 1984. Ecological Entomology. J. Wiley & Sons. New York. 844 pp.

Johnson, C.G. 1969. Migration and Dispersal of Insects by Flight. Methuen & Co., Ltd., London.

Kevan, P.G. 1986. Pollinating and flower visiting insects and the management of beneficial and harmful insects and plants. pp 439-452 *In* M.Y. Hussein and A.G. Ibrahim (Eds), Biological Control in the Tropics. Universiti Pertanian Malaysia, Serdang, Selangor.

Kigatiira, I.K. 1984. Aspects of the ecology of the African honeybee. Ph.D. dissertation, Cambridge University, England. 182 pp.

Koeniger, N. and G. Koeniger. 1980. Observations and experiments on migration and dance communication of *Apis dorsata* in Sri Lanka. Journal of Apicultural Research, 19: 21-39.

May, R.M. (Ed.). 1976. Theoretical Ecology: Principles and Applications. W.B. Saunders, Philadelphia.

McGregor, S.E. 1976. Insect Pollination of Cultivated Crop Plants. U.S.D.A. Handbook No. 496. Washington, D. C.

Page R.E. Jr. and H.H. Laidlaw Jr. 1992. Honey bee genetics and breeding. pp 235-260 *In* J.M. Graham (ed) The Hive and the Honey Bee. Dadant & Sons, Hamilton, Ill.

Punchihewa, R.W.K., N. Koeniger, P.G. Kevan and R.M. Gadawski. 1985. Observations on the dance communication and natural foraging ranges of *Apis cerana*, *Apis dorsata* and *Apis florea* in Sri Lanka. Journal of Apicultural Research, 24: 168-175.

Seeley, T.W. 1985. Honeybee ecology: A Study of Adaptation in Social Life. Princeton University Press, Princeton, N.J. 201 pp.

Shuel, R.W. 1992. The production of nectar and pollen. pp 401-425 *In* J.M. Graham (ed) The Hive and the Honey Bee. Dadant & Sons, Hamilton, Ill.

Verma, L.R. 1990. Beekeeping in Integrated Mountain Development: Economic and Scientific Perspectives. Oxford and IBH Publishing Co. Pvt. Ltd., New Delhi. 367 pp.

Vickery, V.R. 1991. The Honey Bee: A Guide for Beekeepers. Particle Press, Westmount, Quebec, Canada. 240 pp.

Winston, M.L. 1987. The Biology of the Honey Bee. Harvard University Press, Cambridge, Mass. 281 pp.

Winston, M.L. 1992. The honey bee colony: Life history. pp 73-93 *In* J.M. Graham (ed) The Hive and the Honey Bee. Dadant & Sons, Hamilton, Ill.

CHAPTER 31

ECONOMICS OF BEEKEEPING IN DEVELOPING COUNTRIES

BÖRJE SVENSSON

INTRODUCTION

When working as a consultant and beekeeping advisor in developing countries, I often have to find arguments for investments in beekeeping development. I am often in the position of having to address donor agencies, development organizations, or private companies, trying to convince them what an excellent opportunity beekeeping is for people of low income.

From the works of IBRA (Crane and Drescher 1982; Bradbear 1984) and FAO (Kevan *et al.* 1984; Puri 1984), lists of advantages for beekeeping among poor people in developing countries can be quoted. These major arguments in favour of beekeeping development can be summarized as follows:

1. Beekeeping is suitable to poor landless people.
2. There is no competition for resources between beekeeping and other rural activities.
3. Beekeeping is a simple and cheap technology.
4. Beekeeping improves pollination.
5. Beekeeping generates self-reliance.
6. Beekeeping is suitable in family production.
7. Beekeeping has a low and flexible labour demand.
8. Beekeeping can stimulate cooperation activities.
9. Beekeeping leads to improved income distribution.
10. Beekeeping means a broadened food basis.

These kinds of lists are very important to show to local decision-makers and other people involved in rural development projects. They will understand that beekeeping can be one of the best ways to create new income-generating alternatives for poor people. They will also realize that beekeeping will help to fulfil the goals of rural development such as:
- improved income distribution
- break-up of present socio-economic structures
- people's participation in rural development
- build-up of new resources and production potentials.

ECONOMIC BENEFITS - THEORETICAL ASSUMPTIONS

The above-mentioned arguments would be even more convincing if combined with reliable calculations of the economic benefits of beekeeping to rural people. It is then important to start with the fundamental condition that such calculations must be applicable to real life, and that practical results should come close to calculated expectations.

Very few such calculations are available. However, Ali Mohammad, CIDA Agricultural Sector Team in Dhaka, Bangladesh tried to make a cost-benefit analysis for beekeeping in a case-study from Bangladesh (FAO 1984, 1987). His calculations are based on a limited survey of beekeepers within the BIA programme in Bangladesh. I have tried to translate his figures from local currency to US dollars (Table I). The per colony cost and return calculation indicates a net return of about $28 per year. Furthermore, his cost-benefit analysis for a ten-year project with 10 beehives indicates a positive result already during year two. His risk analysis and later recalculations based on more realistic figures still indicate a good net return from years 3, 4 or 5.

The net return per colony in the Mohammad analysis is approximately equal to 15-20% of the annual family income among rural landless people in Bangladesh. A 10-hive operation would even create a steady income from only part-time work which exceeds the present average yearly family income. However, according to my experiences from Bangladesh, this study is a desk-product based on theoretical assumptions rather than the already existing beekeeping system. The calculation is based on an ideal situation that does not yet exist. If beekeeping was already this profitable in Bangladesh, an expanding and profitable honey industry would surely be on its way. This is evidently not the fact!

I would like to describe the basic assumptions of the Mohammad analysis as follows:
- High cost alternative
- Advanced technology
- Intensive management
- Large scale
- Capital easily available
- Easy access to market
- Access to land and buildings
- Access to beekeeping supplies

These assumptions would be more relevant for another country with well educated and relatively rich beekeepers than for Bangladesh. The calculations by Mohammad are a mixture of unrealistic in-

TABLE I. Economic benefits from beekeeping in Bangladesh based on theoretic assumptions (After Mohammad in FAO, 1984 and 1987).

Cost and return per bee colony

Costs	Lifetime	US $
Beebox	10 years	1:06
Bees	10 years	0:30
Knife	4 years	0:15
Queen gate	2 years	0:30
Comb foundation sheets	2 year	0:45
Bee veil	3 years	1:51
Queen excluder	5 years	0:91
Extractor	5 years/10	0:60
Labour cost	1 hr/wk	2:36
Total		7:64

Returns		
Honey, 15 kg		27:27
Beeswax, 1/4 kg		0:45
Bee venom		0:76
Pollen		0:76
Royal jelly		0:45
Sale of bees		3:00
Sale of queens		3:00
Total		35:69
Net return per colony	US $	28:05

formation and exaggerated expectations that will only cause confusion to anyone involved in practical beekeeping.

ECONOMIC BENEFITS - PRESENT SITUATION

The present beekeeping system in Bangladesh is far less successful than indicated by Mohammad. The present beekeeping technology in Bangladesh with suggested modifications has been described by Svensson (1988).

A study of the average costs and returns among beekeepers within the Proshika program gives a completely different picture as shown in Table II. The output is very low due to several technical problems and the costs are comparatively high due to the choice of advanced equipment and a relatively short pay-off time (2-4 years). Hence, in the average case, there is no net profit at all until the credit has been fully repaid after about 5 years.

Evidently, the beekeepers are not successful at present. Many colonies are dying or disappearing every year, loan repayment rate is very low, and beekeepers are not keen at all to expand their beekeeping activities. If foreign aid was not available, I assume that beekeeping initiatives would very soon be terminated.

However, we must not get pessimistic because of this analysis. Instead, I suggest a discussion around alternative ways for beekeeping development that in reality lead to profitable investments and a self-expanding industry. One such alternative way is suggested in the following section.

ECONOMIC BENEFITS - A FUTURE ALTERNATIVE

This alternative suggestion is a hypothetical system for appropriate beekeeping in Bangladesh that does not yet exist. This alternative is aimed at the poorest, landless people with a low educational level. I also assume that the rural malnutrition, poor markets, and lack of infrastructure will lead to local

TABLE II. Economic benefits from beekeeping in Bangladesh based on the present situation among the PROSHIKA programme members (After Svensson 1988).

Cost and return per bee colony.

Costs		US $
Beebox, queen gate and access to a honey extractor (Credit: $ 21:00/4 years)		5:25
Project fee (= service charge)		3:00
Interest for loan		1:80
	Total	10:05

Returns		
Honey, 4 kg	Total	10:00

Net return per colony:	
Year 1-4, deficit	- 0:05/year
After year 5, profit	+ 7:00/year

TABLE III. Economic benefits from beekeeping in Bangladesh based on a hypothetical future alternative.

Cost and return per bee colony.

	US $	
Costs	Year 1	Year 2
Top bars and local materials	3:00	0
Bees	3:00	0
Filter Cloth	0:60	0:30
Sugar	1:50	1:50
Credit cost (10% interest rate through assistance project)	0:80	0:18
Total	8:90	1:98
Returns		
Honey, 4 kg	12:00	12:00
Beeswax, 1/4 kg	2:40	2:40
+ Money lender interest rate substitution (14:40 x 150%) x 4 months per year	7:20	7:20
Total	21:60	21:60
Net return per colony US $	12:70	19:62

consumption of honey. I also assume that beeswax will have a value thanks to central marketing activities.

When summarizing the basic assumptions in this alternative, we will find that they are almost completely opposite to the Mohammad alternative. Assumptions in a future alternative are:
- Minimum cost involvement
- Local materials and simple methods
- Extensive (minimum) management
- Small scale
- High capital costs
- Low honey quality
- Lack of supporting resources

The costs can be kept at a minimum by using local materials such as straw or bamboo and hive designs such as single box hives or top bar hives. The honey return will not be more than 4 kg per hive per year which is equal to the actual honey production. The net return in my future alternative is only US $12-15, but this is still very good compared to the average annual family income of approximately $150 (Table III).

This additional income from beekeeping could be especially valuable because of the low input needed and the low risk involvement. It is important to keep investments down and to limit the risks of failure if poor landless people on the limits of survival are to get interested at all. Also, it is necessary to show a

net profit in the first year because this type of people will have difficulty trusting in expected future incomes from present investments.

On the other hand, poor people will judge the benefits of their investment in other ways compared to the economic specialist. For instance, in the case of Bangladesh, the conditions are very extreme because of the enormous dependency of poor people on money-lenders and landowners for their annual survival. Capital interest rates are often above 150% per year and more than 60% of the population is landless. Having a small amount of interest-free income at the right time of year may save a family from total dependency on the landowner. I have tried to include the value of such a benefit in Table III (Money-lender interest substitution).

CONCLUSION

This chapter is a small attempt to present and compare a few alternative benefit analyses of beekeeping economy in a developing country. There is a great need for locally adapted analyses like these in order to popularize beekeeping among rural development people, and in order to improve feasibility studies before investments in beekeeping development take place. The socio-economic effects of different beekeeping systems should also be studied in detail before a choice of appropriate technology takes place. Beekeeping can be very profitable for poor people, but expectations must be correct!

REFERENCES

Birgegård, L-E. 1980. Manual for the analysis of rural underdevelopment. Swedish University of Agriculture, Uppsala.

Bradbear, N. 1984. Promoting Beekeeping in Rural Economics. FAO, Bangkok. pp. 102-110.

Crane, E. and W. Drescher. 1982. Technical Co-operation Activities: Beekeeping, A Directory and Guide. GTZ, Eschborn.

Jones, T. 1984. Closing Address: The Future. IBRA, Nairobi. pp. 261-264.

Kevan, P.G., R.A. Morse and P. Akratanakul. 1984. Apiculture in Tropical and Sub-Tropical Asia with Special Reference to European Honey Bees and Development Programmes. FAO, Bangkok. pp. 10-33.

Mohammad, A. 1984. Economic Impact of Beekeeping: A Case Study of Bangladesh. FAO, Bangkok. pp. 111-122.

Mohammad, A. 1987. Beekeeping for Profit in Developing Countries: A Bangladesh Case Study. FAO Agriculture Service Bulletin 68. Rome.

Puri, S. 1984. Opening Ceremony - Speech. FAO, Bangkok. pp. 6-9.

Svensson, B. 1988. Beekeeping Technology in Bangladesh - A description of past and present situation with suggested modifications. 2nd edition. Sala.

CHAPTER 32

REMOVING WATER FROM HONEY[1]

EVA CRANE

1. GENERAL INTRODUCTION

The information here applies to honey from either *Apis cerana* or *Apis mellifera*, and some of it could be applied to honey from *Apis dorsata* and *Apis florea*.

In *Honey: a comprehensive survey* (1975), Townsend contributed a chapter on processing and storing liquid honey (2-7 below), and Dyce one on controlled granulation referring especially to *A. mellifera* honey in temperate climates. *Bees and beekeeping: science, practice and world resources* (Crane 1990) gives a general account of these subjects, with more attention to other species of *Apis*.

Once honey has been made and stored by bees kept in hives, the most usual system for handling it comprises the following stages. All except 1, 7 and 9 involve *processing*, i.e. handling honey in such a way that its physical or chemical properties are purposely altered, temporarily or permanently, in order to facilitate handling or to improve certain qualities of the honey.

1. Clearing bees from the honey supers, or framed combs to be harvested, and taking them to the honey house or other place where the honey can be extracted from them. This is the last *beekeeping* operation.
2. Warming the combs to 32°-35°C.
3. Uncapping the combs, and dealing with the cappings.
4. Extracting the honey from the combs in a centrifuge.
5. Straining the honey.
6. In large processing plants in some countries, flash-heating and pressure-filtering.
7. Storing the honey in bulk containers.
8. If desired, initiating controlled granulation, on a large or small scale, then storing.
9. Bottling in retail containers.

In all processing of honey, including its flow through pipes, pumps and strainers, the honey should be held at temperatures below 40°C, or ideally below 35°C, as in the hive. At lower temperatures its rate of flow would be unnecessarily slow. At higher temperatures the honey may be damaged in various ways which are referred to below. Higher temperatures are often used in large processing plants, e.g. (at stage 6) between 62.8°C and 65.5°C to kill yeasts and thus control fermentation. In any such excessive heating, both heating and cooling must be as rapid as possible, to minimize the period at high temperatures. If honey is subjected to direct heat, fructose in it is likely to 'burn', and the flavour of the honey is impaired for this reason.

Because honey is hygroscopic, it should not be exposed to humid air - with a relative air humidity above 60% - at any temperature (Martin 1958). If the water content of honey is to be reduced, this is done during stage 2 or between stages 5 and 7.

During handling and processing, honey should not be in contact with the human body, or with metals that can react with it, or with surfaces such as unglazed earthenware that can absorb dirt, or with any contaminating substance.

2. OPTIONS FOR REDUCING THE WATER CONTENT OF HONEY

Figure 1 summarizes options that may be available for removing water from honey.

In temperate zones, the sealed combs of honey (usually still in their supers) are warmed to 32°C to 35°C before extraction; this is the highest safe temperature, and at 38°C combs full of honey may start to break down. If it is necessary to remove water from the honey, the easiest and least damaging way is to pass warm dry air over the combs at this stage (Section 3 below). A large extracting unit incorporates a thermostatically controlled 'warm room' where supers are held.

For several decades, methods have also been explored for removing excess water from bulk liquid honey after extraction from the combs. For reasons set out in Section 4a (below), beekeepers in many parts of southeast Asia habitually use single-box hives and remove honey combs from them, instead of using honey supers above a brood box for each hive, as is customary in most of the world. They extract the honey from combs a little at a time, and

[1]Prepared at the request of the Advanced Course and Workshops (Resolution II R1).

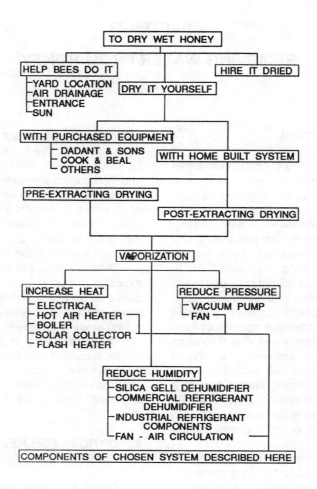

FIGURE 1. Options for removing water from honey (Paysen 1987).

replace the combs in the hive straight away, so pre-extraction removal of water from honey is impossible. This chapter is occasioned by the apparent lack of, and need for, satisfactory methods for removing water from extracted honey, i.e. methods that do not damage the honey, and that use only low-cost equipment.

3. REDUCING THE WATER CONTENT OF HONEY BEFORE EXTRACTION

Beekeepers who use honey supers on their hives normally remove water from the honey (if necessary) while the sealed combs are still in the supers in the warm room. Water can evaporate through the cell cappings, as these are not completely impermeable.

Removal of water from honey in the combs has been practised at least since 1940. Air, dried with a dehumidifier and then heated, is blown through the stacks of supers in the warm room; the colder this air is before it is heated, the more moisture it can take up from the honey. The warm moist air leaving the supers, and carrying off the excess water, is pumped out by exhaust fans. Stephen (1941) made a detailed study of the process and of ways of increasing its efficiency. Passing air at 38°C over combs reduced the water content 4 or 5 times as rapidly from un-capped as from capped combs (Townsend 1975). Marletto and Piton (1976) developed a rather sophisticated enclosed system for removing water from combs of honey in 90 supers, arranged in 9 stacks. Paysen (1987) built a warm room in which half the heat required for warming and drying the honey is collected in solar panels.

Murrell and Henley (1988) give much quantitative information on the removal of water from combs of honey taken from hives incompletely capped, as is now customary in Saskatchewan, Canada. They emphasize the need to maintain a relative humidity in the warm room below 58%, by adjusting the air flow using (a) exhaust and circulation fans, a dehumidifier with a humidistat, and (b) a heat supply which is connected to a thermostat set at the temperature desired. A table sets out programmes for removing e.g. 45 kg water from 160 supers, or 180 kg from 640 supers, in 24 or 36 hours; it is necessary to use different regimes by day and by night, because outside air temperature and humidity differ.

4. THE NEED TO REDUCE THE WATER CONTENT OF HONEY AFTER EXTRACTION

Before discussing the dehydration of honey, it is useful to examine where and why such a relatively energy-intensive operation is necessary. If the need for it could be obviated, honey production should become more effective for the beekeepers concerned.

Table 13.22A (Crane 1990) includes the following entries for the water content of honey:
- lowest water content commonly recorded   13%
- maximum for complete safety from fermentation (Lochhead 1933)   17%
- working maximum for safety from fermentation (Killion 1975)   18.6%
- maximum for safety from fermentation if the yeast count is less than 1/g (Lochhead 1933)   19%
- maximum in European Community Directive, and in proposed World-wide Standard (Codex Alimentarius Commission, 1983/84)   21%
- reported values at high atmospheric humidities in the tropics (for honey in capped cells)   up to 28%

Section 13.2 (Crane 1990) defines honey, and Section 13.21 explains the enzymatic processes by which honeybees and some other social insects are able to convert nectar and honeydew into honey. The sugar composition of the resulting honey is such that the total sugar content can become very high, and the water content low enough to *prevent fermentation of honey* during storage in the nest or hive. Table I here converts refractive index to water content, for honeys containing between 13% and 40% water, and indicates the necessary temperature correction.

Most honeys with a water content too high to ensure safety from fermentation (and even too high for the proposed World-wide Standard mentioned above) are produced in hot, humid regions of south-

east Asia. This high water content of the honey is a major constraint to the development and improvement of beekeeping there. Coupled with it is a wide acceptance of fermented honey, whereas in most of the world honey that is properly produced and treated, by its very nature *does not ferment*. In some areas, what is sold as honey is outside both definitions of honey in Section 13.2 (Crane 1990).

4a. Factors leading to the harvesting of honey with a high water content
Constraints to the production of honey safe from fermentation include the following, of which those in the first group are much in need of detailed study.
1. Causes likely to be outside the beekeeper's control:
   - high atmospheric humidity and temperature
   - honey flows from certain plants (e.g. rubber)
   - flows at certain seasons of the year, or in certain years
   - species of bee used
2. Beekeeper's failure to provide proper conditions for the bees:
   - inappropriate hives, e.g. too small, necessitating removal of honey before it is sealed (see below); or not allowing adequate ventilation
   - inappropriate siting of hives (e.g. without a clear air flow around them)
3. Inappropriate beekeeping management:
   - removing honey before it is sealed (but see Murrell and Henley 1988)
4. Inappropriate treatment of honey taken out of the hive:
   - exposure to humid atmosphere.

With regard to species of bee, figures quoted for the water content of individual *A. cerana* honeys (Crane 1975) vary from 14.3% to 28.4%; those in Table 13.2A (Crane 1990) for *A. mellifera* honeys range from 13.4% to 26.6%. In Yucatán, Mexico, Weaver and Weaver (1981) recorded the water content of honeys from *Melipona beecheii* and from European *A. mellifera* as 26%-27% and 19%-21%, respectively; they say that the former 'does not spoil'. It seems likely that the higher acidity of honeys from stingless bees, and probably also of those from tropical *Apis* species, protects them from the action of harmful micro-organisms at somewhat higher water contents than that of honey from temperate-zone *A. mellifera*.

Factors 2 to 4 are considered by Crane (1990). With regard to 2, in parts of southeast Asia, beekeepers use a movable-frame hive consisting of only one (deep) box, holding 10 to 16 combs, without honey supers; the system seems to have originated in China. Throughout a flow, combs containing nectar

TABLE I. Refractive index (RI) and water content of honeys containing from 13% to 40% water. If the refractive index is measured at a temperature higher than 20°C, add 0.00023 per degree C above 20°C to the reading, before using the Table. Figures between 13% and 22% are from White (1975b); between 22% and 40% from White *et al.* (1988).

Water (%)	RI	Water (%)	RI	Water (%)	RI
13.0	1.5044	18.0	1.4915	22.0	1.4815
13.2	1.5038	18.2	1.4910	23.0	1.4789
13.4	1.5033	18.4	1.4905	24.0	1.4763
13.6	1.5028	18.6	1.4900	25.0	1.4740
13.8	1.5023	18.8	1.4895	26.0	1.4717
14.0	1.5018	19.0	1.4890	27.0	1.4693
14.2	1.5012	19.2	1.4885	28.0	1.4670
14.4	1.5007	19.4	1.4880	29.0	1.4647
14.6	1.5002	19.6	1.4875	30.0	1.4624
14.8	1.4997	19.8	1.4870	31.0	1.4600
15.0	1.4992	20.0	1.4865	32.0	1.4577
15.2	1.4987	20.2	1.4860	33.0	1.4554
15.4	1.4982	20.4	1.4855	34.0	1.4531
15.6	1.4976	20.6	1.4850	35.0	1.4509
15.8	1.4971	20.8	1.4845	36.0	1.4487
16.0	1.4966	21.0	1.4840	37.0	1.4665
16.2	1.4961	21.2	1.4835	38.0	1.4443
16.4	1.4956	21.4	1.4830	39.0	1.4421
16.6	1.4951	21.6	1.4825	40.0	1.4299
16.8	1.4946	21.8	1.4820		
17.0	1.4940	22.0	1.4815		
17.2	1.4935				
17.4	1.4930				
17.6	1.4925				
17.8	1.4920				

and honey (whether sealed or not) are removed, centrifuged, and replaced in the hive; alternatively this is done to all combs. Reasons stated for using a single box include:

- colonies do not thrive as well in supered hives
- in smaller colonies, mite control is more effective with brood and honey in the same box
- such hives are easier to handle, with the transport available
- capital is not available to buy supers
- out-of-hive comb storage is very difficult because of wax moths
- for the honey flow, many small colonies are preferred to fewer larger ones, on a variety of grounds:
  - they thrive better
  - they are easier to manage
  - the total honey yield is higher
  - the system increases the sugar allocation to

the beekeeper (e.g. in Vietnam).

For southeast Asia in general, investigations are needed to establish: (a) the exact conditions that give honey containing too much water, in relation to constraints 1 to 4 above; (b) the best ways of changing conditions that can be changed. For countries using a single-box hive in the way referred to, an enquiry should be made into the validity of the stated reasons for its use, and some alternative system developed in which *sealed* honey can be harvested, that is practicable in the circumstances in which the beekeepers have to work.

4b. Possible intermediate and high technology methods for reducing the water content of extracted honey

In this section, reduction of water content by 1% means e.g. from 20% to 19%, or from 17% to 16%. Operations to obtain honey with an acceptably low water content, and safe from fermentation, start in the apiary; hives must be provided with adequate ventilation, and sited so that there is a clear air flow around them. However, in humid areas of tropical Asia there are reports of sealed honey produced by good beekeeping that contains up to 28% water. Many beekeepers in these areas do not use separate honey supers, so the honey combs cannot be treated before extraction. Methods are therefore widely sought for reducing the water content of honey (dehydrating it) after extraction, and in view of the lack of collected information, the subject is discussed here in some detail.

Reverse osmosis, or ultrafiltration, can reduce the water content of some solutions by forcing water under high pressure through a membrane within the liquid to be concentrated. However, the method does not seem to be practicable for honey, which has a very high sugar content. Madsen (1974) gives a general discussion of reverse osmosis.

In order to remove water from the bulk liquid honey after extraction, therefore, the water must be evaporated from the honey surface. Evaporation of water at any temperature removes part of the volatile components of honey, and hence impairs the aroma and flavour of the honey. So any heating of honey (and volatilization) must be closely controlled. Honey must not be 'boiled' to evaporate water from it, as the high temperatures would destroy enzymes, burn fructose, and remove volatiles. Evaporation can, however, be speeded up by:

- a good air circulation in which dry air is constantly passed over the honey surface (absorbing water vapour), and then removed
- increasing the surface area of the honey in contact with the dry air
- increasing the honey temperature, to 35°C for an extended period, or to higher temperatures by flash-heating methods
- making the air flow relatively drier by increasing air temperature, or decreasing air pressure.

In a preliminary study, Fix and Palmer-Jones (1949) investigated the 'settling out' of honeys of different densities which occurs in storage tanks except at high temperatures; honey with the highest water content forms a layer at the top. After trials, they built a commercial 'tank drying room' holding 2.3 tonnes of honey; hot air was circulated through the room to maintain the temperature at 36°C, and the relative humidity was 40%. The procedure reduced the water content of the honey, but was less effective than treatment of honey before extraction.

4c. Evaporating water from an increased surface area of honey

Under normal atmospheric pressure the rate of evaporation is increased by increasing the rate of air flow over the honey, by reducing the relative humidity of this air, and by increasing the temperature of the honey and its surface area in contact with the air. However, systems have been developed for reducing the water content of honey in which the humidity of the air is not reduced before it is passed over the honey. Maxwell (1987) in the USA only heats the honey, in a simple home-made system, before blowing air at room temperature (13°C) over it. Honey from a 300-kg drum, heated by an immersed hot water pipe, is pumped to a warmed evaporating tray 0.6 x 1.2 m, which slopes down at 20° to a chute delivering the honey to another drum. Honey in the tray flows in a layer about 4 cm deep, and is kept at 32°C-35°C; two fans blow air over its surface (Fig. 2). The water content of the honey was reduced from above 19% to 18% in under 2 hours, after 2 or 3 passages through the system. Kuehl (1988) uses a series of sloping trays made of expanded metal screen, with a fan heater.

Where the relative humidity of the air is high, pre-heating of the air is necessary to increase its capacity to absorb water. Especially in the humid tropics, with relative humidity above 80% and high atmospheric temperatures, air should be pre-dried by air conditioners or air dehumidifiers that cool the air and thus condense water vapour from it. The colder the dry air before it is warmed to pass over the honey, the more water it can remove from the honey.

Small-scale dehydration systems for honey were designed in humid regions of southeast Asia in the late 1980s (Wakhle et al. 1988). An experimental system developed in Vietnam by Mulder increases the honey surface by allowing the honey to trickle down under gravity (Fig. 3). A cabinet contains a stack of 10 horizontal trays (35 x 65 cm), mounted 7 cm apart, each with an array of 2-mm holes perforated all over it, 1 per cm^2. Heated air is blown into the cabinet by a fan on the left; on the right is the air outlet, 15 x 35 cm. Honey is poured on to the top tray and trickles down through all 10 trays into a honey container below the cabinet. After a series of 8 trickling cycles, the water content of 20 kg of honey was reduced from 26% to 21%; one cycle lasted a little more than 10 minutes. The relative humidity of the outside air was 85%, and the temperature of the honey was kept below 40°C.

Platt and Ellis (1985) patented a system (and refer to earlier patents) in which water is evaporated from honey in a horizontal drum fitted with a rotating shaft along its axis. The shaft carries with it a series of discs or other surfaces having a large area. As the shaft rotates, honey is picked up from the bottom of the drum and spreads in a thin film over the surfaces. Air at 40°C to 75°C is blown along the drum

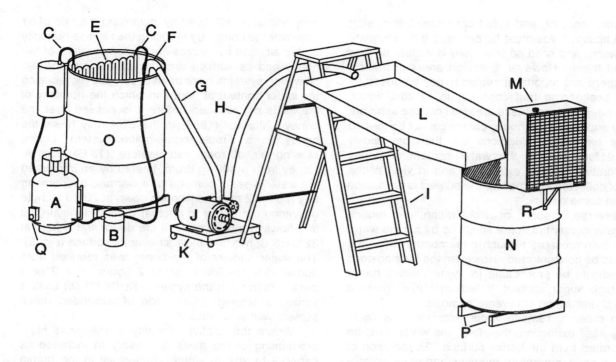

FIGURE 2. Simple batch-system for removing water from honey, used in the USA (Maxwell 1987).

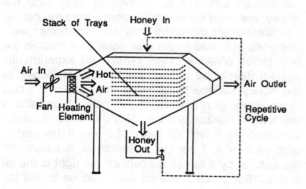

FIGURE 3. Experimental design for low-cost removal of water from extracted honey, used in Vietnam.

from a fan at one end, and carries evaporated water through the air outlet at the other end. A research prototype, said to be expensive, has been operated in Sumatra, Indonesia (Platt 1988), in a project referred to by White *et al.* (1988). I have seen a somewhat similar system in Malaysia. The drum was about 70 cm long and 30 cm in diameter; air at 70°C was blown in, and the temperature of the honey was raised to 50°C.

A much larger evaporator has been built in the USA by Paysen (1987), who uses solar heat. Honey cascades in thin streams over the edge from one to another of 24 large trays; their combined area is 360 m². The exit-edges of the trays are cut and bent so that the honey runs out in many thin streams. Paysen is very satisfied with the unit's performance; 57 tonnes of honey passing through it lost 0.6% of water (the required amount) in 30 hours; this is equated to 3.6% per hour per drum of honey (300 kg) (Fig. 4).

Mannheim and Passy (1974) published a useful general discussion on commercial continuous-flow methods for concentrating liquid food products by removing water from them. For liquids that are not heat-sensitive, evaporation temperatures of 70°C-90°C may be applied. For those (like honey) that are heat-sensitive, thin-film evaporators are used, either at or below atmospheric pressure. Such evaporators are manufactured with a tubular or conical evaporating surface, which may be stationary but usually rotates; one that is effective with viscous liquids is the Centri-Therm made in Sweden (Alfa-Laval 1988-a), which can operate at either atmospheric or a reduced pressure (see 4d below). Figure 5 indicates the mechanism. Honey is led through tubes on to a steam-heated conical surface that rotates at a high speed, where it spreads out into a film no more than

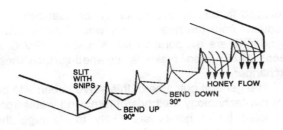

FIGURE 4. Cutting and bending tray edge (Paysen 1987) so that the honey runs out in thin streams (instead of sheets, which billow in the wind).

0.1 mm thick; the film is forced by centrifugal force to the outer edge of the surface, whence the honey is pumped out of the centrifuge and immediately to a cooler.

The honey is in contact with the steam-heated surface for only about 1 second, but this is enough to evaporate water, the water vapour being drawn off through the central column under a partial vacuum, and condensed. Volatile substances evaporated from the honey can to some extent be condensed separately from the water and recombined with the honey output. The rate of evaporation of water can be controlled by the rate of honey flow, the vacuum pressure, and the centrifuge speed. Use of a Centri-Therm for honey is planned in Indonesia, and it is expected to evaporate 50 kg of water per hour (Akratanakul 1988).

4d. Evaporating water from honey under low pressure

Vacuum (actually low-pressure) systems for evaporating water from honey are used, or being considered for use, in Asia, but they are expensive, and so are their operating costs; they are not part of intermediate technology. They incorporate a vacuum pump connected to the air space of a container in which water is evaporated from the honey, evaporation being accelerated by constant circulation of air at low pressure across the turbulent honey surface, and subsequently through a condenser. Such systems can operate even without enlarging the honey surface, although this is not efficient. They have the great advantage that they function at low honey temperatures, but water is lost more rapidly if the temperature is higher.

Volatile substances give honey its aroma, and part of its flavour. There is a detrimental loss of these substances when water is evaporated from honey, according to the increase in temperature and decrease in pressure; volatiles with low boiling points are lost most readily. Girotti et al. (1977) refer to

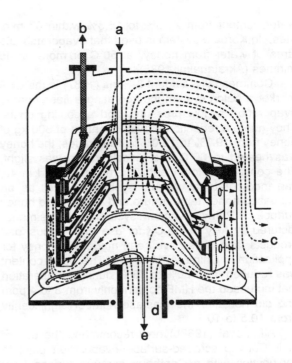

FIGURE 5. Vertical section through the Centri-Therm Evaporator (Alfa-Laval 1988a). a - Process liquid in; b - Concentrate out; c - Vapour to condenser; d - Steam in; e - Steam condensate out. Steam is admitted through the hollow spindle (d) to the jacket surrounding the cone stack and thence to the insides of the cones, where it is condensed by the liquid passing on the other side of the cone walls. As soon as condensate droplets form, they are flung by centrifugal force to the upper inside surface of the cone and travel down this surface, escaping back into the steam jacket through the same holes by which the primary steam entered. The condensate runs down the walls of the steam jacket to a paring channel at the bottom, from which it is removed by a stationary paring tube (e) mounted inside the hollow spindle.

loss of volatiles when honey is dehydrated at low pressure; on the other hand, Tabouret (1977) did not find any loss in flavour and aroma.

Experimental low-pressure plants were developed in New Zealand during the 1950s (Paterson and Palmer-Jones 1954, 1955; Roberts 1957), and later in the USA, also France (Tabouret 1977) and the USSR (Stirenko 1983). Tabouret (1977) used a pressure of 680 mm of mercury (0.92 bar, $9.2 \times 10^4 N/m^2$) for 45 litres of honey heated on average to 63°C. This reduced the water content from 20.4% to 16.0% within 90 minutes. At 68°C, using atmospheric pressure (760 mm mercury), he could reduce the water content from 21.3% to 15.8% within 37 minutes. In Korea a system is used that evaporates 200 litres of water from honey, at 50°C or more, in 45 minutes (Akratanakul 1988).

Commercially, Dadant & Sons (1987) in the USA market a batch system incorporating a flash heater, evaporation at low pressure, and a cooling chute. They quote a reduction of water content of 300 kg of honey from 19.2% to 18.0% in 45 minutes; the honey was heated to 66°C and discolouration was slight. The continuous-flow Centri-Therm, described in 4c, can incorporate a vacuum system, as well as an increased honey temperature and an enlarged honey surface. A Paravap vacuum system (Fig. 6) is manufactured by APV in the UK for use with various food products, and trials have been made with honey for application in China (APV 1988). The water content was reduced from 30% to 18%, during an operation that increased the HMF content only from 3 to 4 ppm and did not alter the diastase number significantly (from 10.5 to 10.3).

Alfa-Laval (1988b) now recommend the use of their Convap scraped-surface evaporation plant in conjunction with a Contherm scraped-surface heat exchanger (1988c). In the evaporator, rotating blades

are used to scrape 'sticky, lumpy, or heat-sensitive products' from the heated inner wall of the vacuum cylinder where evaporation takes place. APV Crepaco (1988) also make a scraped-surface heat exchanger.

The general outcome of this survey seems to be that low-technology methods of removing water from extracted (bulk) honey are likely to damage the honey, and that high-technology systems - which may do less damage - are so expensive as to be out of proportion to the value of the product. I therefore reiterate what was said earlier in this chapter that attention should be concentrated on the list of 'Factors leading to the harvesting of honey with a high water content' (Section 4a). Most of the factors relate to beekeeping management, and ways of dealing with some are already known. Where further information is needed before remedial action can be taken, this should be sought. Where the water content of honey harvested is then still too high, excess water should be removed while the honey is still in the combs; this necessitates the use of separate honey supers, or some other system yet to be devised.

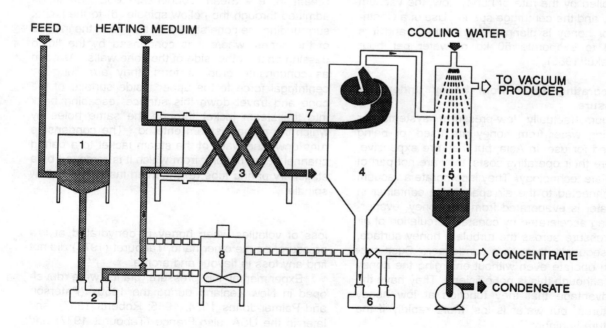

FIGURE 6. Paravap Evaporator system (APV 1988).

1. balance tank
2. feed pump
3. heat exchanger
4. separator
5. condensor
6. product (honey) pump
7. orifice plate
8. pressurized recirculation vessel

5. HEATING HONEY TO KILL YEASTS, AND OTHER METHODS OF PREVENTING FERMENTATION

The risk of honey fermentation depends on the water content and yeast count of the honey, its natural granulation behaviour, and the processing, if any, it undergoes before storage. In commercial processing plants, honey is usually heated to 60°C or above *to kill yeasts* in it. This is commonly referred to as pasteurization, but the purpose of the process with honey is quite different from that with milk, which is pasteurized to reduce the number of micro-organisms that are harmful to human health, such as *Bacillus tuberculosis*. Milk must be held at a temperature between 62.8°C and 65.5°C for 30 minutes, but the same temperature applied for a much shorter period to honey kills yeasts in it, and thus inhibits fermentation during storage. White (1975c) quotes the following times necessary to kill yeasts in honey at different temperatures:

Temperature	60°C	63°C	66°C	68°C
Time (minutes)	22	7.5	2.8	1.0

The heating also dissolves any small crystals that might promote granulation.

Honey is damaged in various ways if heated above 35°C or 40°C (Townsend 1975; White 1975a). Nair and Chitre (1980) published a report on heating *A. cerana* honey to 63°C-68°C, and cooling it again as rapidly as possible. In continuous-flow systems a tubular heat-exchanger may be used, in which the heating water and the cooling water pass through a revolving coil. Larger systems use a plate-type heat-exchanger, in which the honey flows in a very thin layer through the plates. Townsend (1975, 1978) gives details of the commercial processes, and Bryant (1987) describes a smaller plant built by a New Zealand beekeeper that processes 2.5 tonnes an hour. Tabouret (1980) made an extensive study on the ways in which the honey is affected, and Tabouret and Mathlouthi (1972) tabulated the HMF content of the honey before and after treatment in a plate-type heat-exchanger processing up to 600 kg an hour, and also before and after 30 and 60 days' storage.

Honey that has been 'flash-heated' to a pasteurizing temperature is usually pressure-filtered while it is still at the high temperature, or even after heating it further, to 77°C. The honey is forced through a filter-press of diatomaceous earth, which removes material that would pass through a strainer, such as pollen and colloids, and small air bubbles. Townsend (1978) recommends using a temperature of 79°C, for 4 minutes only, then filtering or straining at this temperature.

Pasteurizing and pressure-filtering constitute the most cost-effective bulk treatment of honey, but flavour and aroma are impaired. The resultant honey is very clear (transparent), and is likely to remain liquid. In some countries, such honey competes well with clear syrups and jellies on supermarket shelves, and it has a long shelf life without granulating.

Small-scale trials have been made in Malaysia, using a microwave oven to heat 250-ml lots of *A. cerana* honey containing 21.3% water, to 71°C for 100 seconds, to destroy yeasts and inhibit fermentation during storage (Ghazali *et al.* 1987).

Liebl (1977) reported the inhibition of fermentation and granulation by subjecting honey, held at temperatures from 10°C to 38°C, to ultrasound (18 to 20 kHz) for less than 5 minutes. Kaloyereas and Oertel (1958) used ultrasound (9 kHz) for 15-30 minutes to delay granulation. They and Townsend (1975) refer to some further methods.

ACKNOWLEDGEMENTS

Much of this report has been written in close consultation with Vincent Mulder, KWT Committee of Science and Technology for Vietnam, IMAG, Netherlands, and I much appreciate his collaboration. Thanks are also due to the International Food Information Service (IFIS), which provided many of the references quoted.

REFERENCES

Akratanakul, P. 1988. Personal communication.

Alfa-Laval. 1988a. Centri-Therm: ultra-short-time evaporator for heat-sensitive liquids. (Lund, Sweden: author).

Alfa-Laval. 1988b. Contherm scraped-surface heat exchanger. (Lund, Sweden: author).

Alfa-Laval. 1988c. Convap scraped-surface evaporation plant. (Lund, Sweden: author).

Apicultura & Polinização. 1989. A desumidificação do mel no Brasil. Apicultura & Polinização, 6(31): 27-29.

APV. 1988. Personal communication.

APV Crepaco. 1988. Vertical scraped surface heat exchangers. (Chicago: author) 4 pp. Section Bull. D-1-350.

Bryant, T. 1987. Honey filtration unit. New Zealand Beekeeper, 196: 25-26.

Codex Alimentarius Commission. 1983/84. Proposed draft Codex Standard for Honey (Worldwide Standard). Rome: FAO/WHO, CX/PFV 84/13, also Revisions ALINORM 85/20, Appendix IX, Appendix X.

Crane, E. (ed.) 1975. Honey: A Comprehensive

Survey. (London: Heinemann).

Crane, E. 1990. Bees and Beekeeping: Science, Practice and World Resources. (Oxford: Heinemann Newnes).

Dadant & Sons. 1987. [System for reducing the water content of honey.] American Bee Journal, 127(4): 272.

Dyce, E.J. 1975. Producing finely granulated or creamed honey. In: Honey: a comprehensive survey. E. Crane (ed.). Chapter 10, pp. 293-325.

Fix, W.J. and T. Palmer-Jones. 1949. Control of fermentation in honey by indirect heating and drying. New Zealand Journal of Science and Technology A, 31(1): 21-31.

Ghazali, H.M., R.M. Hamidi and T.C. Ming. 1987. Effects of microwave heat-treatment on the quality of starfruit honey. Annual Report of the Malaysian Beekeeping Research and Development Team. pp. 14-21.

Girotti, A. and 3 others. 1977. Honey production and extraction. Apiacta, 12(4): 49-53.

Kaloyereas, S.A. and E. Oertel. 1958. Crystallization of honey as affected by ultrasonic waves, freezing and inhibitors. American Bee Journal, 98(1): 442-443.

Killion, C.E. 1975. Producing various forms of comb honey. In: Honey: a comprehensive survey. E. Crane (ed.). Chapter 11, pp. 307-313.

Kuehl, L.J. 1988. Apparatus for removing moisture from honey. U.S. Patent 4,763,572. 7 pp.

Liebl, D.E. 1977. Method of preserving honey. US Patent 4,050,942. 1 p.

Lochhead, A.G. 1933. Factors concerned with the fermentation of honey. Zentralblatt für Bakteriologie, Parasitenkunde II Abt., 88: 296-302.

Madsen, R.F. 1974. Membrane concentration. In: Advances in preconcentration and dehydration of foods. A. Spicer (ed.). (London: Applied Science Publishers). pp. 251-301.

Mannheim, C.H. and N. Passy. 1974. Non-membrane concentration. In: Advances in preconcentration and dehydration of foods. A. Spicer (ed.). (London: Applied Science Publishers). pp. 151-193.

Martin, E.C. 1958. Some aspects of hygroscopic properties and fermentation of honey. Bee World, 39(7): 165-178.

Marletto, F. and P. Piton. 1976. Impianto per la disidratazione del miele mediante ventilazione. Apicoltore Moderno, 67(3): 81-84.

Maxwell, H. 1987. A small-scale honey drying system. American Bee Journal, 127(4): 284-286.

Murrell, D. and B. Henley. 1988. Drying honey in a hot room. American Bee Journal, 128(5): 347-351.

Nair, K.S. and R.G. Chitre. 1980. Effect of moisture and temperature on the multiplication of honey fermenting yeasts in Indian honeys. Indian Bee Journal, 42(2): 39-47.

Paterson, C.R. and T. Palmer-Jones. 1954. A vacuum plant for removing excess water from honey. New Zealand Journal of Science and Technology A, 36(4): 386-400.

Paterson, C.R. and T. Palmer-Jones. 1955. Vacuum plant for removing excess water from honey. New Zealand Journal of Agriculture, 90(6): 571-578.

Paysen, J. 1987. A method of drying honey on a commercial scale. American Bee Journal, 127-(4): 273-283.

Platt, J.L. and J.R.B. Ellis. 1985. Removing water from honey at ambient pressure. US Patent 4,536,973. 6 pp.

Platt, J.L. 1988. Personal communication.

Roberts, D. 1957. A plant for treating honey by the vacuum process. New Zealand Beekeeper, 19(3): 31-35.

Stephen, W.A. 1941. Removal of moisture from honey. Science in Agriculture, 22(3): 157-169.

Stirenko, V.V. 1983. [Method for processing honey.] USSR Patent SV 1 009 401 A. In Russian.

Tabouret, T. 1977. Vacuum drying of honey. Apiacta, 12(4): 157-164.

Tabouret, T. 1980. Contribution à l'étude fondamentale de la pasteurization du miel et des solutions aqueuses sursaturées de D-glucose. Université de Dijon, Thèse pour...Docteur.

Tabouret, T. and M. Mathlouthi. 1972. Essais de pasteurization du miel. Revue Française d'Apiculture, (299, 300): 258-261; 301-304.

Townsend, G.F. 1975. Processing and storing liquid honey. In: Honey: a comprehensive survey. E. Crane (ed.). Chapter 9, pp. 269-292.

Townsend, G.F. 1978. Preparation of honey for market. (Ontario Ministry of Agriculture and Food), rev. ed.

Wakhle, D.M., K.S. Nair and R.P. Phadke. 1988. Reduction of excess moisture in honey - I. A small scale unit. Indian Bee Journal, 50(4): 98-100.

Weaver, N. and E.C. Weaver. 1981. Beekeeping with the stingless bee Melipona beecheii, by the Yucatecan Maya. Bee World, 52(1): 9-18.

White, J.W. 1975a. Composition of honey. In: Honey: a comprehensive survey. E. Crane (ed.). Chapter 5, pp. 157-206.

White, J.W. 1975b. Physical characteristics of honey. In: Honey: a comprehensive survey. E. Crane (ed.). Chapter 6, pp. 207-239.

White, J.W. 1975c. Honey. In: The hive and the honey bee. Dadant & Sons (ed.). Chapter 17, pp. 491-530.

White, J.W., J.L. Platt and G. Allen-Wardell. 1988. Quality control for honey enterprises in less-developed areas: an Indonesian example. Bee World, 69(2): 49-62.

CHAPTER 33

MARKETING PURE BEES HONEY IN SRI LANKA

G.D. WILSON

INTRODUCTION

There are those who feel that marketing receives too much emphasis, subscribing to a theory that a better product is all one needs for successful selling...that people wanting to buy will come to you if you have the best product. Emerson wrote: "if a man...make a better mouse trap...the world will beat a path to his door".

As marketing experts Professors McCarthy and Shapiro (1975:4) point out, "The mouse trap theory probably was not true in Emerson's time, and it certainly is not true to-day". They suggest that many "better mouse trap factories" will be idle, gathering cobwebs, if the better mouse trap is not properly marketed.

WHAT DOES "MARKETING" MEAN?

Marketing is traditionally divided into two categories:
. Macro Marketing, which focuses on the marketing of an entire economy, examining how well it functions and how efficiently it performs.
. Micro Marketing, by contrast, looks at the individual organization within the larger economic system. In the apicultural industry, it encompasses the performance of all business activities that direct the flow of pure bees honey from the farmer to the consumer in order to both satisfy consumer needs and provide additional income for the producer.

This chapter is confined to Micro Marketing as it applies to pure Sri Lankan bees honey but the general approach is probably applicable through much of the developing world in regard to honey and products of cottage industries.

There is a common misconception that selling (moving the product) is the sole marketing activity. This misinterpretation should be corrected, for marketing normally begins with the consumer, not the producer. Marketing goals should influence decisions on what product is to be produced, the places where it is to be marketed, the price at which it must be sold, and the type of promotion that is needed to assist sales.

In the field of education we are all familiar with the '3 R's: Reading, 'Riting and 'Rithmatic. In the field of marketing we have the '4 P's:
. Product
. Place
. Promotion
. Price
The four 'p's make up the market mix.

PRICE

Classic marketing strategy requires that Product be considered first, because how the customer views the product has an immediate bearing on the other 'P's (Place, Promotion, and Price). However, the Sri Lankan Honey Production Project's objective necessarily is to provide income (selling price less expenses) to farmers for the one honey product they have. Therefore, purchase price from the farmer, and selling price to the distributor or retailer must be considered first.

In the marketing of a toy, for example, price calculations could result in a decision that profit margins cannot be achieved, and the toy, however appealing, should not be produced. But in the case of honey, the necessity of marketing an existing product requires priority determination of price, so that appropriate markets can be targeted, i.e. consumers who can afford the price that ensures cost recovery plus a profit margin.

Product quantity is a factor in establishing price. In Sri Lanka, notwithstanding previous data indicating that a well maintained colony of *Apis cerana* could yield 15-20 kg, and that with proper hive management yield could be raised to 20-30 kg, an analysis revealed that the national average annual yield is 1.6 kg, with high productivity areas yielding 2.7 kg, and low productivity areas yielding 0.6 kg.

Subsequent economic modelling determined that the purchase price from the farmer had to be a minimum of Rs.65/- per kg to ensure at least cost recovery (Table I).

Five different pricing constructions are available:
1. Honey Project to consumer
2. Honey Project to retailer to consumer
3. Honey Project to distributor to retailer to consumer

TABLE I. Economic modelling to profitability in Sri Lankan apiculture.

		Number of Colonies		
		1	3	5
Capital Costs				
Hive	Rs.	150	450	750
Extractor	Rs.	275	275	275
Smoker	Rs.	95	95	95
		520	820	1,120
Recurrent Costs				
Depreciation (10 year)			82	112
Interest at 10%		52	82	112
		104	164	224
Revenue				
1.6 Kg @ Rs. 65/-		104	328	448
Profit		Nil	164	224

One Sri Lankan Rupee = US$ 0.325 (January 1988)

4. Honey Project to distributor to stockist to consumer
5. Honey Project to Ayurvedic Corporation (producers of indigenous medicines)

Taking the last first, the Ayurvedic Corporation, which manufactures indigenous medicines, requires ten metric tons of honey annually. In Sri Lanka ayurvedic medicines are credited with curing a multiplicity of ailments, from asthma to heart disease. Despite the preference for using local honey as the base for Sri Lankan medicines, the history of adulteration by honey hunters and bee farmers led to all the Ayurvedic Corporation's honey being imported from Australia, duty free. In 1987, the landed Colombo price of Australian honey was Rs. 39.44 per kg! Because our purchase price from the farmer is Rs. 65, sales to the ayurvedic market initially were not possible.

Rural folk cannot afford the price of bottled honey so the target market in our first year of marketing had to be the middle income and upper middle income consumers located in major centres. Our competition for this market is imported honey that retails through supermarkets in the price range of Rs. 160 per kg to Rs. 217 per kg, bottled in 450 gram glass containers.

Pricing must be related to cost, but it must also

be sensitive to demand, which can be calculated from import data. In Sri Lanka, in the years 1985-86, imports averaged 20,000 kg. The pricing strategy in 1987-88 is as follows:

		Rs/kg
Honey Project to consumer 100%*		111
Honey Project to retailer	100% + 10%	122
Retailer to consumer	100% + 10% + 20%	147
Honey Project to distributor	100% + 10% - 18%	100

PRODUCT

The product, to be marketed successfully, must be appropriate to the target market, satisfying a consumer need or desire, so product planning should incorporate the following:

- quality
- packaging
- brand establishment

Quality

In June of 1987 we participated in an agricultural exposition in the city of Colombo that was sponsored by the Women's Chamber of Commerce. Located in the city, it mainly attracted consumers of our target market, the middle and upper-middle income segment. In discussions with them, it quickly became evident that quality must be our main focus. These consumers have a long-standing mistrust of bees' honey because of adulteration.

To overcome this resistance, and to safeguard against adulteration, the Department of Agriculture's Agricultural Instructors and Village Instructors personally supervised the on-site extraction or the collecting of honey comb cut from the super directly into large polyethylene bags we supplied. It was necessary to cut out some comb as many farmers' frames were not extractable. Purchase of honey from feral colonies was discouraged, and a price differential of Rs. 5 per kg was given to encourage extraction and better quality product. Cut comb honey was chopped, strained, placed in settling tanks, and finally strained through nylon mesh. It was, nevertheless, inferior to extracted honey in clarity.

Tests for addition of sucrose and water were also made when the honey was brought to the honey house by the Agricultural Instructors or Village Instructor.

Granulation is a major problem. *Eucalyptus robusta* honey, because of a high dextrose to water or levulose percentage, granulates within two months. To control granulation, the honey is bottled, sealed and stored without labels. Immediately prior to shipment the sealed bottle is heated in water to

60° for thirty minutes, then labelled. We recommend to our customers that they purchase no more than a two-month supply and clear it from their shelves before re-ordering.

Packaging

In planning marketing strategy one carefully matches the package offered to target market preferences and needs. Packaging is a key part of marketing and doubts as to its importance can be answered by a look at the perfume industry's products. A better bottle, or label, may help a market newcomer to compete with established competitors.

In order to compete with imported honey, we packed the Project's honey in 450 gram glass bottles with metal Omnia lids. These lids are sealed, but not re-sealable once the bottle is opened by the customer. Honey is also packed in jars with a screw top lid and a protective foil inner seal. A tamper-proof seal is essential to assure customers of purity.

Our label, designed by an advertising agency and offset printed on quality art paper in three bright colours, features a representation of a friendly honeybee. It prominently displays the brand name and the Project source and describes the contents as "Pure Bees Honey". The term 'honey' is commonly used in Sri Lanka for treacle from the treacle palm so we must specify bees' honey. Assurance of quality is also prominently stated as "Bottled according to strict purity and hygienic standards by the Canada-Sri Lanka Honey Project, Bandarawela".

Because the Sri Lankan customer believes that crystallized honey is (a) inferior, (b) adulterated, and (c) "gone back to sugar", a small label printed in black and white is affixed to the back of the bottle stating that "Pure wholesome bees' honey may crystallize. Warm this bottle in water to restore to a liquid."

Branding

The establishment of a brand name and reputation gives consumers quality assurance, and may help bring the producer a higher price. This is important, because maintaining quality does have a cost, but it also has the benefit of assisting sell-through.

A good brand name should be:
. simple and easy to read; short is best;
. easy to identify and remember (alliteration helps);
. easy to pronounce, preferably with an appealing sound;
. free of negative aspects; (for instance, 'Buzzy Bee' is great alliteration and onomatopoeia, but lots of people don't like the buzzing of bees, and it won't sell honey!).

The choosing of a brand identification may be as much an art as a science; no empirical determination can be expected. The Honey Project's brand name is "Bobby Bee", selected to appeal to our target market and meet the criteria above. A native brand name such as "Sri Bee" appealed to me, but was rejected because the targeted Sri Lankan consumer has a preference for imported product, which signifies quality, and a resistance to local product which may be adulterated.

PLACE

Honey must be available to the customer at the right time and the right place to encourage purchase. For example, a customer would not expect, or be prepared to purchase honey in a hardware store or theatre.

Place decisions are concerned with the location of marketing facilities and the selection of specialists, including transportation and storage agencies, distributors, stockists and retailers.

The product route from producer to consumer may be direct, or it may involve middlemen who act as channels in getting the right product to the target market. Direct channels are the simplest for small amounts of produce, and often are referred to as "farm gate". Farm gate channelling in Sri Lanka is traditional, but unsatisfactory because of problems of product quality, pricing promotion and distribution. These problems have kept sales of bees' honey static at a low level, making beekeeping a marginal proposition. Farm gate selling does, however, offer the potential to maximize profit.

The insertion of middlemen such as the distributor, stockist and retailer has an adverse effect on the income of the Honey Project, but brings increased sales, and overcomes problems of customers' uncertainty about and so resistance to farm-gate quality.

Four channels of distribution are available:
. Farmer to consumer;
. Farmer to Honey Project to consumer;
. Farmer to Honey Project to retailer to consumer;
. Farmer to Honey Project to distributor to retailer to consumer.

Each channel, in progressive order, has greater sales potential, but smaller return to the Honey Project. The farmer, however, is assured of a constant selling price by the Project.

The Honey Project has elected to employ a multi-channel system, in that it uses all channels, which could sometimes be resented by established middlemen who do not appreciate competition from their own suppliers. Prior to the marketing of a given year's honey, a decision must be made to continue or discontinue the multi-channel system.

In some countries, a target market may be an export market. Then the Place category becomes much more complicated because the entire process of taking honey to the target market - wherever it is - is part of Place. But exports are one problem Sri Lanka does not have.

PROMOTION

Promotion can include any effort that helps publicize and sell-through the product, anything that brings the product to the attention of the target market in a positive way. It involves positioning the honey in such a way that people are encouraged to buy it, and may include special displays, special prices, personal product promotion in direct selling, or an advertising campaign aimed at a mass audience. It is important to identify and know the target market before planning a promotional activity, and then to follow through in planned stages that build a momentum of product awareness in potential customers.

Early in projects, advertising would likely be far too expensive a promotional tool, whereas in Sri Lanka our display at Agromart gave us very direct and positive contact with customers (personal selling), and opportunity to distribute relatively inexpensive hand-out promotional brochures (personal selling), and a bonus of free advertising through media coverage of the fair (mass selling).

Our modest marketing efforts have been received by the customer with enthusiasm because we have positioned correctly the right Product in an appealing package, in the right Place, at the right Price, with appropriate Promotional publicity.

I think it also may have something to do with the support Sri Lankans given a local product of quality entering into competition with imports.

THE NEXT STEPS

Sri Lankan experiences from the first marketing year indicate that projects should progress by:
1. Making the flow of money from the Project to the selling farmer easier, reducing the number of handling officers involved;
2. Supporting our quality efforts by widening the price difference of comb and extracted honey to encourage the use of community owned extractors;
3. Meeting specific needs of our target market by packaging in a 450 gram screw top bottle with

protective inner foil seal, and expand our target market by packaging in 2 ounce bottles with Sinhala and Tamil labels to serve the ayurvedic market;
4. Increasing product appeal by solving the granulation problem;
5. Beginning the process of privatizing our honey marketing.

REFERENCES

McCarthy, E.J. and S.J. Shapiro. 1975. Basic Marketing. Irwing-Dorsey, Georgetown.

SECTION VII: DEVELOPMENT

CHAPTER 34

INTEGRATING SCIENCE AND DEVELOPMENT
TO SUCCESSFUL APICULTURE

P.G. KEVAN

BEEKEEPING - GENERAL INFORMATION

Beekeeping is a form of animal husbandry and has gone through some major developments in the last 130 years. The main aim of beekeeping is the production of honey, although nowadays bees are kept for crop pollination in many areas. Other traditional bee products are beeswax, used in polishes, cosmetics, sealants and candles; propolis or bee glue, used in the production of drugs and ointments due to its bacteriostatic properties; royal jelly, a highly valued food in many countries, especially the Far East; and bee venom, used for production of anti-allergic substances and for cure of rheumatism and arthritis. Pollen is also collected from bee hives by use of a pollen trap which removes the pollen pellets from the baskets on the hind legs of bees. The collected pollen pellets are used as natural food, rich in protein, vitamins, and possessing anti-allergenic properties.

Modern beekeeping relies on "movable-frame" hives. This system works on the basis of wooden boxes which can be stacked. They are without tops or bottoms and are placed on a bottom board and covered by a lid over the top. The size of the cavity can be expanded and contracted to meet the needs of the bee colony housed within. Each box, called a super, contains a number of frames. Some hives are not stacking, they are single boxes with a lid. The frames are the most important component. They are made of wood and consist of a top bar which is more or less square in cross section, except for a lug at each end. The lug rests on a shelf cut out of the top of each end of the box or super. Side bars are attached to the top bar and a bottom bar is attached to the ends of the side bars. These bars support the comb. In some hive designs the side and bottom bars are not used and may be replaced by other means of supporting the comb (e.g. Kenya Top Bar hive). The whole frame is suspended by the lugs in the super. Frequently, wax foundation, a sheet of beeswax cut to the size of the inside of the frame, is used in each frame. The foundation is impressed with hexagons, the size of honeycomb cells. Bees build their comb on this foundation. However, bees often build a comb without a foundation. A completed super or box will contain a series of frames with or without foundation, spaced so that the bees will not build combs between the frames, nor use propolis to fasten them, yet being wide enough to allow them free passage. This space is the "bee-space" and its discovery was the crucial step leading to the design of modern bee hives. The bee-space is different for different species and races of bees.

The bees use the comb they build for laying eggs, rearing the larvae through to adulthood and for foods, pollen and honey. While brood rearing usually takes place in the lower to middle part of the hive or comb, honey is stored in the upper part.

Movable frames of comb can be easily pulled out of hives and inspected or, if filled with honey, they can be removed for extraction. The extraction of honey by rotary extractors does minimal damage to the comb in the frame, which when empty is replaced for the bees to re-use. Furthermore, movable frames make access to the hives very easy for inspection of brood, the queen's performance, colony development and general health, and for diseases and for application of medication if needed.

All species of honeybees have much the same social system. There is a single egg-laying queen, as well as a large number of worker bees which are under-developed and sterile females (the sting is a modified ovipositor) who nurse the brood, tend the hive, guard the entrance and forage for nectar and pollen (the food for the colony and its brood). It is processed nectar which is removed as honey. Males are present in smaller numbers and at particular times of the year, or under undesirable circumstances (e.g. poor queen). These drones are usually fed by the workers and have as their main function mating and insemination of the queens.

Standard textbooks and manuals describe bee biology and management well and readers are referred to these through this book. Particularly valuable is the book on beekeeping with the Asiatic hive bee by Punchihewa (1995).

ADVANTAGES OF DEVELOPMENT AID IN BEE-KEEPING

The arguments for apicultural aid programmes in developing nations are clearly stated by Drescher

251

and Crane (1982). We paraphrase them here for easy reference.

1. Beekeeping can be done by small holders and landless peasants. For these people, any source of additional income or food that does not require land is important. Beekeeping occupies very little space and hives can be placed on non-agricultural field edges, forests and waste land.

2. Beekeeping does not compete for resources with other agricultural endeavours. Furthermore, it produces food from otherwise unattainable sources (i.e. nectar and pollen) and supplements agricultural productivity through pollination. Many forests and non-agricultural lands have a good honey flora.

3. Beekeeping is not expensive to implement and the basic management techniques are quite simple. Thus, rural people can become involved with little financial outlay and a small amount of instruction. We will return to this point later on for further discussion.

4. Bees, while they forage for pollen and nectar for themselves, bring about or improve the level of pollination of both agricultural and other plants. In this way, the quantity and quality of many crops, oil seeds, vegetables and fruits are improved. Recently there has been an increased interest in bees as crop pollinators in the tropics and sub-tropics. This speaks well for the diversification of diet for peoples in the developing world.

5. A beekeeper has developed a knowledge and skill which is rewarding and helps generate self-reliance.

6. The whole family can become involved since the work can be done at home by men, women or older children.

7. The amount of time involved can differ according to the beekeeper's interest for leisure time, part-time or full-time involvement. No matter at which level of intensity a beekeeper operates, a cash crop can be harvested.

8. Professional and social interactions, as well as mutual benefits, can be stimulated by beekeepers forming local associations in which bees and equipment can be bought, sold or traded, hive products marketed and successes and problems discussed.

9. Further advantages can be itemized for the socio-economic impact of beekeeping. For example, successful beekeepers raise their socio-economic standing in areas with subsistence agriculture.

10. Beekeepers broaden the food basis of the local population at large, not just with hive products, but also through improved pollination of crops.

11. The manufacture of the basic beekeeping equipment such as hives, frames, smokers, extractors, containers, and clothing can stimulate the activities of local craftspeople. Even the first steps in honey and beeswax processing can be done locally with only little technical equipment.

12. Quality beeswax fetches a high price on world markets, is easily transported and requires no containers. The scope for this hive product in Asia has not been explored. Lastly, and perhaps most important, is the fact that subsistence farmers in developing countries can substantially supplement the family income, sometimes even doubling it. This means the family will have a higher standard of living.

Large scale commercial and cottage level beekeeping operations result in many of the same advantages, but the impact of each may be somewhat different. The large scale or commercial operation will generate employment for a few people involved as full-time beekeepers or as seasonal labour. Commercial operations could stimulate spare-time and part-time beekeeping, although normally the process is reversed.

The relative merits of cottage industry and large scale operations need to be examined in the context of the needs, potential and resources of the region being considered.

OBJECTIVES AND JUSTIFICATION

The principal objective of apiculture development should be to establish a self-perpetuating beekeeping industry. The principal objective can be broken down into the following components: research, training, production, marketing and associations. The objective of the research component is to innovate and protect beekeeping in the fields of bee management, pathology and parasitology, bee botany for honey and pollination, hive and equipment design for local conditions, bee genetics and selection of harder working, less aggressive and more reliable bees, and honey and bee products' standards. The objectives of training are to educate local personnel to undertake meaningful research and to implement the results of the research, to train professional apiarists who extend the educational process to potential and practicing beekeepers in villages and who are available for advice and encouragement to local beekeepers, to train and encourage local beekeepers in bee biology, bee management, bee product handling and association information. The objective of the production phase is to produce good quality honey and other bee products in order to satisfy local and national demands and ultimately export demands.

Marketing requires standardization of the quality of honey and bee products, their being properly and reliably labelled and their reaching the consumer at competitive prices so that the beekeepers reap most of the benefit. The formation of associations of beekeepers can fulfil those objectives, as well as provide standardized and well tested equipment at fair prices. Associations also are useful for the exchange of beekeeping information between beekeepers, apiarists and researchers.

The upsurge in interest in beekeeping in the developing countries is a firm indication of improvements in the nutrition of the people in those countries. Bee products may not be consumed a great deal by the beekeepers themselves because the products are more valuable in trade, especially as specialty commodities (gourmet and medicine). Nonetheless, the income from beekeeping can be used for family improvement in diet, clothing, shelter, animal stocks, plantings and education. The interest in bees as pollinators indicates an increase in the variety of crops now being grown, especially of fruits, vegetables and oil crops. The diversification of agriculture, diet and personal opportunity, as evidenced through beekeeping, is a highly positive step at the grass roots level for improving the lot of many people in the developing nations.

ORGANIZATION OF BEEKEEPING AID PROGRAMMES

There are six components which must be balanced to promote agriculture in developing countries. These components are the same for all agricultural development, including beekeeping. They are:
1. Training.
2. Research and development.
3. Establishment of associations.
4. Manufacture and design of equipment.
5. Processing and marketing of products.
6. The role of governments and development agencies.

Figure 1 shows the interrelationship of these facets as they impinge on beekeeping.

It is clear that aid programmes in beekeeping must be aimed at establishing a viable industry, specifically for marginal farmers and landless people, but also in some instances at the larger scale commercial level. It is also clear that scientific underpinnings need to be established to develop, improve, nurture and protect that industry.

At present, scientific beekeeping is almost non-existent in many places, even though modern beekeeping is quite well established and accepted locally in others. However, as with any form of agriculture, beekeeping needs more than just bee farmers. Bees, like all domestic animals or plants, suffer from disease, predation, parasitism, drought, starvation and general adversity. As such, advances in beekeeping to circumvent adversity to control diseases, parasites and predators to improve the genetic lines of domesticated bees and to improve general management techniques should always be incorporated as quickly as possible into the industry. The part-time, i.e. cottage industry, or full-time beekeeper cannot be expected to innovate research and keep abreast of developments by himself, while at the same time dealing with day-to-day management of colonies. These beekeepers would not have sufficient experience to recognize new problems as they might arise (e.g. a new bee disease to the area).

Thus, there is a need for a scientific establishment to service beekeeping. As mentioned above, beekeepers cannot be expected to stay abreast of recent developments in apiculture or to recognize new problems as they might arise.

A well-staffed extension service is needed through which information can be disseminated directly by field officers or by newsletters or through local organizations. An extension service provides additional benefits, besides information and inspection services; it provides experts who visit beekeepers in the field. This is especially important in areas where there are few beekeepers as the expert represents an external source of encouragement and sustains interest, providing advice and assistance. Extension service would also be involved in training beekeepers at the beginning as well as more advanced levels (Figure 1).

Intimately linked with beekeeping in all countries where beekeeping is well developed are beekeeper associations. Extension personnel and professional apiculturalists usually take on leading roles in these associations, although they leave the administration of the associations to the general membership. These associations may organize training programmes, seminars, meetings, shops for honey sales and purchasing of equipment in bulk at reduced prices. They may also be involved in lobbying for beekeeping protection and support in their regions. These regional associations form an important hub of activity and coordination of general business and information regarding beekeeping (Figure 1).

The role of associations or other organizations in the marketing and processing of honey and in the manufacture, design and development of equipment must be firmly related to the scientific establishment. Honey must be marketed clean and free of contaminants such as cane sugar, syrups or pesticides. Equipment, especially hives and their comp-

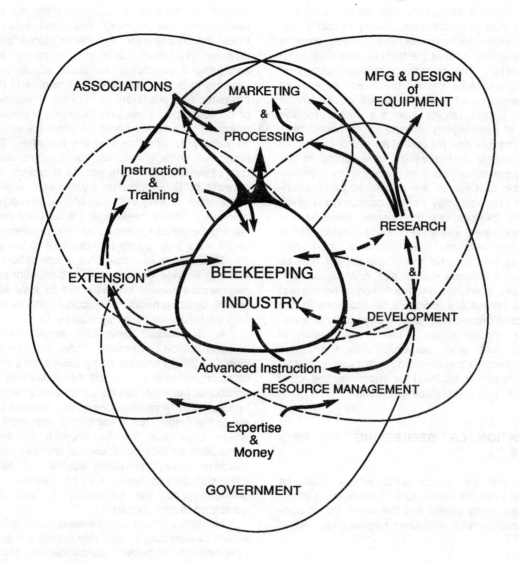

FIGURE 1. The components of beekeeping as a viable industry (from Kevan 1983).

onents, must be made to close tolerances based on the "bee-space". As improvements are discovered through research in honey processing or equipment design, they should be incorporated as quickly as possible into the industry at large (Figure 1).

Inasmuch as research and development and extension work require funds, it is likely to be necessary for the government to become involved. This can be either through the government's direct establishment of research and development laboratories and of extension services with an existing department or through the funding of an organization which can more adequately handle the specialized services required.

From the foregoing, one can see that a coordinated series of steps is needed so that development proceeds in as flexible a way as possible, while establishing beekeeping on a firm footing for the future. The steps are made on three fronts: training, physical facilities and associations. Table I presents the interrelation of these steps.

Training beekeepers has been a traditional approach of many well-meaning programmes and organizations in the developing world. Where training is not supported with the rest of the integrated package, beekeeping development usually fails or, at best, stagnates (there are numerous examples).

TRAINING

No agricultural development can proceed on a firm footing unless qualified personnel are present during and after development projects. A number of apicultural projects and others have run into considerable difficulty or failed after development funds have finished and expert personnel have left. This is mainly because of lack of adequately trained nationals who can carry out the project after the completion of external aid. It is not enough to train beekeepers. Apiculture, like any agricultural endeavour, requires a firm scientific basis, a technical foundation and a dedicated group of practitioners (beekeepers). Thus, training must include the following:

1. University level education to at least Masters' degree level for scientific and research staff. This will be done abroad. These people are the innovators and developers of the industry, researching and adapting practices to suit local conditions and changing demands. They should also be involved in the educational process themselves.
2. High level technical personnel are needed in support of the above and to assist, with the rest of the scientific and research staff, in extension education at advanced and intermediate levels, and in the duties of the intermediate technical personnel. These people should have a Bachelors' degree. This would be best done abroad, at least in part.
3. Intermediate level technical personnel are needed for routine work in apiculture throughout a developing nation. This involves disease diagnosis, bee product quality monitoring, extension education and general promotion of apiculture. Some of the training should be done abroad.
4. Lower level technical personnel are needed as extension personnel for demonstrations, teaching and general apicultural development. Training abroad would be useful.

The above represents what is needed for the establishment of core organization of a beekeeping institute. Training of more people at all levels is important so that colleges, universities and the like can develop apiculture programmes for the country or region.

Training is needed for serious, commercial beekeepers. This needs to be done at an advanced level and could be undertaken within the country as long as the personnel of the beekeeping institute were in place.

Training for part-time beekeepers is the backbone of the industry as it is in this category that cottage level beekeepers are placed. This requires a considerable outreach programme of quality instruction in the form of village level short courses to be put on by the personnel of the beekeeping institute.

REFERENCES

Drescher, W.R. and E. Crane. 1982. Technical Cooperation Activities: Beekeeping. A Directory and Guide. Deutsche Gesellschaft für Techuische Zusammenarbeit (GRZ) GmbH, Eschborn, Germany.

Kevan, P.G. 1983. The potential for beekeeping in Bangladesh. Unpubl. report to CIDA/AST, Dhaka. 30 pp.

Punchihewa, R.W.K. 1995. Beekeeping for honey production in Sri Lanka: Management of Asiatic hive honeybee *Apis cerana* in its natural tropical monsoonal environment. Sri Lanka Dept. of Agriculture, Peradeniya, Sri Lanka. 232 pp.

TABLE I. The components of a development programme in apiculture.

Step I:	Mission of experts to determine potential and existing facilities, expertise, interest for project formulation
Step II:	The programme (below)

TRAINING	FACILITIES	ASSOCIATIONS
Planning	**Planning**	**Planning**
1. Train personnel to start: - training others - supervising others - developing facilities	1. - classrooms - demonstration station - workshop for equipment manufacture - small processing facility - transport	1. Establish 1 or 2 local associations for: - bee product processing - bee product marketing - equipment supply and/or manufacture - social events
2. Train personnel for professional, in-depth apiculture expertise (M.Sc. degree or equivalent) for: - research - development - training others - supervising others Continue with step 1.	2. Laboratory centre: - diseases - bee botany - bee biology - bee products, nature and quality control Bee breeding centre: - for queen rearing - bee selection - providing bees Increase size of facilities in step 1	2. Continue with step 1 - expand
3. Continue with steps 1 and 2 to provide minimum critical mass of expertise in: - extension - research - development - leadership		3. Start national organizations with newsletter and publicity

CHAPTER 35

ROLE OF BEEKEEPERS IN PROMOTION AND POLICY

S.M.A.L. DEWAN

INTRODUCTION

Honey has been known to the people of tropical Asia, mainly as a medicine rather than as a food and gathering and hunting has been practised since time immemorial. There is widespread belief that nests of honeybees at a person's house brought luck. Those human interests in honey, and the livelihood of people who obtained honey, perhaps kept alive honey hunting and gathering activities into modern times. Those interests, arising from different viewpoints, have allowed for a modern thinking which has given rise to various beekeeping projects in the region.

In most countries, projects started with feasibility studies and progressed from these. For example, a pilot project was undertaken for Beekeeping in Bangladesh in 1976-1977 with financial help from the Canadian International Development Agency (CIDA), through the programme of Canadian Universities Services Overseas (CUSO). The experience of the pilot project was positive, promising and encouraging. Once reassured about the feasibility of beekeeping in Bangladesh, Research and Demonstration Centres (RDC) were established at the most suitable and potentially productive locations in many parts of Bangladesh. Basic techniques, such as (a) capturing of wild bee colonies of *Apis cerana*, hiving and managing them following modern methods of beekeeping, (b) observing the honey plants in those areas and the foraging behaviour of *A. cerana* as well as of *Apis dorsata* and *Apis florea*, (c) observing the bees' activities in the colony in relation to their growth and management, (d) observing the carrying capacity of the land for beekeeping in those areas, (e) evaluating honey production, and (f) judging the interest of local people as potential beekeepers, were carried out in those centres. All of these aspects have been studied and, based on the findings, the following objectives have been considered to be important in the promotion and development of beekeeping in Bangladesh, as anywhere else:

1. To introduce beekeeping in a disciplined and organized manner to the people of Bangladesh, especially to rural men and women.
2. To show that honey can be a source of income generation so as to help the people to improve their standard of living, and be a source of food so as to help to alleviate malnutrition.
3. To use the honeybees in planned pollination to help increase food production through the services of cross-pollination in all agricultural and horticultural fields.
4. To undertake appropriate measures to improve the quality of the indigenous honeybees, especially *A. cerana*, and to emphasize the need for continuous research on the subject of apiculture as and when necessary, and
5. To keep up the training and extension efforts while maintaining an awareness of the development of beekeeping technology globally.

Based on the above broad objectives which apply to apicultural development in tropical and subtropical Asia in general, we confirmed our approach to involve **Training**, **Extension**, **Marketing**, and **Applied Research**. These components, once conceptualized and institutionalized, were used to found and establish the Bangladesh Institute of Apiculture (BIA), a non-governmental organization, to be fully engaged in the promotion and development of scientific beekeeping in Bangladesh. In this chapter I want to discuss the components mentioned above in which the beekeepers have an important role in promoting technology and aiding in the formulation of national, regional and local policies.

TRAINING

It is well known that training is a medium for dissemination and advancement of knowledge in any subject. Training is most effective if there is participation by the trainees, namely potentially new beekeepers. Trainers in Bangladesh usually work in their own rural areas, especially in the capturing and hiving of wild honeybee colonies. This provides opportunity for demonstrations on beekeeping and welcomes villagers' curiosity in a situation with easy and broad opportunity for communication on beekeeping know-how, its usefulness in development in general, and as a part of family productivity in particular. The villagers' presence, attention and observation of the work and the ease of handling bees helps motivate them and convinces them of their own potential capabilities. Thus, some become eager to take up beekeeping.

Although that is not the conventional way of motivating people in development efforts, it has proven appropriate to apply this new system. The method has overcome the idea that beekeeping requires a high level of technology and investment and demonstrated its feasibility as an economically viable enterprise, especially for the rural poor. In considering the potential of beekeeping, as well as the increasing interest of the rural poor, organized training has been planned.

Beekeepers training course (BTC)

The Beekeepers Training Course for the rural illiterate people has been of two weeks' duration and follows a practically oriented syllabus that starts with capturing of wild bee colonies of A. cerana, then hiving them, followed by instruction and demonstration of routine management, with care and attention, through to honey production. By 1988, nearly 1,500 rural poor have been trained and they are keeping approximately 3,000 bee colonies in Bangladesh. In addition to beekeepers course, a Fieldman Training Course was organized for extension workers, with refresher courses on various special subjects as and when necessary.

Technical follow-up

In Bangladesh, the introductory two-week training course has not been enough for people to practise beekeeping independently. It has not been possible to demonstrate many of the technical aspects of beekeeping while training in progress. Shortcomings in training have been observed later, mainly by extension personnel while visiting beekeepers to see their progress. Thus, the Technical Follow-up Programme was developed and conducted as an ongoing process for the six months following the training course and after the beekeeper had started activity. The multifarious benefits of the follow-up showed its value and that without it, beekeeping could not be successful and expeditiously introduced in the rural areas. In Bangladesh, follow-up programme was of four visits in the first month, two in the second and third months, and one in the fourth, fifth, and sixth months.

The follow-up allowed the transfer of technology to the beekeepers to enable them to practise independently. Furthermore, by monitoring beekeepers it was discovered that honey production had risen to 12 kg/colony/year, the average in 1988.

THE CONCEPT OF A BEEKEEPERS' ASSOCIATION

Technical follow-up was found to be highly valuable as it made the technology easier for novice beekeepers to understand and practise. It also made beekeepers consider the value of their activity to their family income. Further, it provided opportunity for sharing experiences and encouragement. Through particular successes achieved by the individual beekeepers, it seemed appropriate to bring them together to understand the importance of sharing technical knowledge and information both on problems and prospects. Thereby they could develop common goals while reminding themselves to keep up beekeeping as a low-cost, productive activity. In some places, monthly meetings were arranged to discuss various points of beekeeping. Especially important have been discussions of individuals' problems and of marketing honey as a collective problem. Out of the discussions, which have been dubbed "one-day monthly training", the idea of a Beekeepers' Association originated. In Bangladesh, the Association has become defined as organized and disciplined groups of beekeepers in rural areas. Another aim of the Associations is to present practically oriented instruction and discussion with extension agents and so advocate the promotion of scientific beekeeping. Others are invited to participate and learn how they might increase their family income through beekeeping. Associations can also ensure quality control of honey (yet to reach a satisfactory standard) as well as its marketing.

RELATIONSHIP BETWEEN THE BEEKEEPERS AND THE BEEKEEPERS' ASSOCIATION

Beekeepers are the individual practitioners and the Associations are their organizations which honour and encourage their efforts for their eventual economic uplift. The beekeepers have felt that they are becoming technically unified for a common good. Accordingly, they have continued to promote continuous development of their Associations, so that they can derive the maximum benefit. They sell their products, mainly honey, through Associations at a fixed price determined by them depending on the grade of honey, (i.e. moisture content, sources of honey and period of collection). As the Associations sell honey, they keep a small levy for their operation. This type of marketing facility has encouraged beekeepers to produce more and more honey. In 1988, one beekeeper was selling about 15 to 20 kg of honey at the average rate of 80 Taka per kilogram. The Associations were selling it at 90-100 Taka per kilogram. In 1988, there were Associations, with a total of 1500 registered beekeepers, distributed throughout the rural areas in Bangladesh. The members pay a small monthly subscription regularly to generate a fund for their Association.

THE ROLE OF THE GROUP LEADER

Without active members, an organization is meaningless. An organization that is well established has an infrastructural set-up and good network and brings benefits to its members. In Bangladesh, as elsewhere, beekeepers have embraced these ideas. In Bangladesh, some Associations divided into several groups of 10-15 members headed by a leader. The group leader's responsibilities have been in coordinating technical knowledge among fellow beekeepers and facilitating supply of some equipment that could be used by all the beekeepers (e.g. honey extractors, queen excluders, queen cages, etc.). The group leaders of each Association meet twice a month at the regional Research and Demonstration Centre (RDC) of the Bangladesh Institute of Apiculture (BIA) to discuss and share their experiences and learn from each other (Fig. 1). The fortnightly meetings of the group leaders have been coordinated by the Extension Workers of BIA. At these meetings, the group leaders may bring the honey purchased from the beekeepers to the Association for processing, bottling, labelling, and finally marketing. All the group leaders of all the Associations under one regional Research and Demonstration Centre have met once every three months to participate in broader discussion so as to disseminate knowledge and information. I coordinated such meetings in the presence of the staff of the Research and Demonstration Centre there. This chain of responsibility functions effectively because it promotes togetherness, follow-up, mutual feedback, and learning, thereby aiding a combined role for the socio-economic development and promotion of apiculture in the area. Indeed, it has also been observed that beekeepers' enthusiasm and responsibility have increased, so enabling them to maintain high standards of their own work. Friendly competition has automatically originated.

THE ROLE OF THE RESEARCH AND DEMONSTRATION CENTRES

In Bangladesh, the Research and Demonstration Centres are modest, yet important. They provide regional central locations where extension workers and beekeepers can meet and share information. They provide a site for beekeepers' meetings and instructional sessions with extension personnel. They also provide a place for research activities to be conducted. Thus, investigators, whether they are

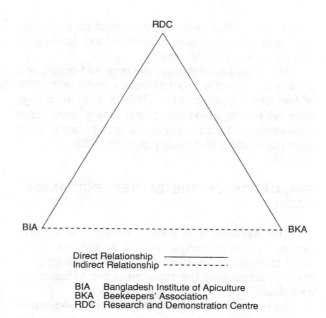

FIGURE 1. Flow sheet showing coordination of the Bangladesh Institute of Apiculture with the Regional Development Centres and the Beekeepers' Associations. BIA - Bangladesh Institute of Apiculture; RDC - Research and Demonstration Centre; BKA - Beekeepers' Association.

professional scientists, extension officers, or beekeepers, have bases of operation. They have proven useful in co-ordinating and conducting feasibility studies and honey plant surveys. More such facilities are needed through the country.

SELECTION OF THE PRESIDENTS AND THEIR ROLE TOWARDS THE BEEKEEPERS' ASSOCIATION

Honey production on a competitive basis is becoming popular among the beekeepers. The beekeeper of a particular Association who can maintain his bee colonies at a required level and can produce the highest amount of honey per colony is encouraged to be the president of the association in the following year. Further, it has been arranged that the highest producer among all the presidents of all the Associations would be sent abroad to a nearby country, to observe their beekeeping efforts and learn from their experiences. From this system, significant positive changes took place; competition tended to keep bee colonies at a high standard and enabled almost all beekeepers to produce more honey. This encouraged further care in practise and gave rise to the habit of selling honey at the Associations. Such successes further helped bring attention to groups and new areas where extension and training in apiculture were badly needed.

Many beekeepers have become self-reliant and earn a significant amount of money, even up to 80% of the family cash income. This is a great change from when the beekeepers and others considered beekeeping to be an unimportant activity ranked third after handicrafts and poultry (Kevan 1983).

EVALUATION OF THE BEEKEEPERS' ASSOCIATION

The Association is a new concept and the only one of its kind in Bangladesh. It was introduced in 1983 to help the beekeepers to create self-employment. I summarize the situation of the Associations as follows:

1. All persons trained are the members registered in the Association after the completion of the training course.
2. They pay a small monthly subscription fee after an admission fee at the time of registration.
3. Through monthly meetings and members' direct participation, it has been possible to establish a two-way communication which ensures a regular flow of technical information so as to help increase confidence in beekeeping and advance skills.
4. Beekeepers sell their product, mainly honey, at the Associations and enjoy the facilities of a ready market and good price.
5. Various groups of members have been formed and these facilitate coordination of honey sales or availability of equipment.
6. Technical follow-up has been formulated and established to ensure efficient transfer of beekeeping technology.
7. Many of the developmental organizations have become interested in the system and have picked up, or are picking up, on the idea and model and trying to organize the same system within their own workplans.

SUPPORT SERVICE FACILITIES TO THE BEEKEEPERS' ASSOCIATION AND THE OTHER ORGANIZATIONS

The Bangladesh Institute of Apiculture (BIA) has been considered to be a pioneering centre in the promotion and development of apiculture in Bangladesh. Kevan (1983) commented that "Bees are an untapped resource in Bangladesh". This view has been proven by the BIA. BIA has developed a good

extension network for organizing Beekeepers' Associations. In addition, it has offered services to as many as fifty different organizations of local, national, government, semi-government, autonomous, and non-governmental organizations. A few of them are: Bangladesh Small and Cottage Industries Corporation, Bangladesh Agriculture Research Institute, Government of Bangladesh, Rural Advancement Committee (BRAC), Proshika, Gono Unnayan Prochesta. Among them, Proshika, Gono Unnayan Prochesta and BRAC have taken up an extensive beekeeping programme. It has been the intention of BIA to encourage other organizations to come forward and take up apiculture in the way demonstrated by those listed above.

QUEEN REARING, HONEY PLANTS, AND WAXMOTH CONTROL

With the increase in interest and with the increase in members of the trainees, three problems became acute, (1) the availability of wild honeybee colonies of A. cerana, (2) the pressure on the existing vegetation, thereby decreasing honey production, and (3) waxmoths. BIA initiated work in queen rearing, a honey plants propagation programme, and in waxmoth control.

Queen rearing
BIA started the queen rearing and colony multiplication programme only in 1987. The Doolittle method has been followed, using qualitative and quantitative methods of selection of honeybee colonies and grafting the larvae. About 60% success rate was achieved and the nucleus colonies so developed have been distributed to new beekeepers, mainly women. The bee colonies became strong enough to maintain seven brood combs. It has been planned to offer training in queen rearing and colony multiplication to interested beekeepers.

Bee plants and their propagation
Nectar and pollen sources are central for the growth and strength of the bee colonies as well as to honey production. Beekeepers in Bangladesh have understood the importance of a plant propagation programme in addition to improved and better colony management practices. The role of the beekeepers has been praiseworthy—they have started to propagate indigenous bee plants. They must keep in mind the honey flow seasons already known to them and the plants produced during the period to match with prevailing conditions. In Bangladesh so far, we have identified 75 different species of honey plants. We have a honey flow season beginning with September

to February as the major honey flow with a minor honey flow in March to May and a dearth period in June to August. To name a few of the indigenous plants and crops which are now considered as being of priority: *Moringa oleifera, Litchi chinensis, Citrus aurantifolia, Citrus grandis, Phoenix sylvestris, Ricinus communis, Zea mays, Cocos nucifera, Ziziphus mauritiana, Syzygium cumini, Justicia genederusa, Bombax malabaricum, Alstonia scholaris, Aegle marmelos, Azadirachta indica, Crataeva nurvala.* Further, beekeepers have become motivated to cultivate crops which are useful for pollen or nectar or both, e.g. *Brassica napus, Cucumis melo, Momordica charantia, Raphanus sativus, Musa paradisiaca, Momordica cochinchinensis, Cucurbita maxima, Allium cepa, Coriandrum sativum.* Not only that, they are conscious of the need not to destroy the wild plants and creepers having beekeeping value, e.g. *Dupatorium odoratum, Mikania scandens, Merremia hideracea, Coccinia cordifolia, Mimosa pudica, Polygonum orientale, Polygonum hydropiper, Amaranthus spinosus.*

Waxmoth control

The humidity in much of tropical and subtropical Asia is very high, reaching 90% or more at times. As a result, we have severe problems with waxmoth (*Galleria mellonella*). The damage to colonies by waxmoth reaches a peak in June, July and August. In the beginning, we used paradichlorobenzene (PDB) as a fumigant to eradicate waxmoths. The result was good but the chemical was expensive and difficult to obtain in Bangladesh. Therefore, we tried to find improved methods of colony management. We cleaned the bottom board every third day and so did not allow the waxmoth eggs to hatch. We also cleaned the other parts of the hive. We have been able to educate, demonstrate, and motivate our beekeepers to follow this system to get control waxmoths. Secondly, we have suggested that beekeepers try to keep their colonies queenright and strong so as to help the colony defend itself. Beekeepers, as being observed through the technical follow-up programme, do follow the system. As a result, absconding and deserting resulting from waxmoth infestation was reduced to 5% per year, which helped speed the technological advancement of beekeeping greatly.

RESEARCH AS A SUPPORT SERVICE TO TRAINING AND EXTENSION

Research is always needed to maintain the standard of any beekeeping programme. Research and its findings helps to keep a programme going,

suggests remedies to difficulties and problems and helps maintain a high competitive standard. Research is also needed for any newly introduced technology as in the case of beekeeping in Bangladesh. Scientific beekeeping, based on scientific knowledge and feasibility studies, has been introduced in Bangladesh. However, much remains to be discovered to enhance and encourage a more successful programme.

Although some of the plant species providing nectar and pollen are known, honeybees collect both nectar and pollen at times and from places when and where the source is unknown. Thorough knowledge of nectar and pollen sources can suggest which plant species are lacking in areas where beekeeping could be otherwise practised. Palynological and melissopalynological studies are needed to elucidate floral origins of honey and to start a broader and scientifically based programme of plant propagation. This needs to be combined and compared with observations on foraging preferences of *A. cerana* on flowers at different times of day and year.

To that end, I conducted a two-year programme of research on the honeybee flora and the behaviour of Bangladeshi honeybees *A. cerana, A. dorsata,* and *A. florea* (Dewan unpublished).

Socio-economic research in Bangladesh is planned with the aim of judging the role of beekeeping in the life of our people and in changing their standard of living. Research on marketing has also been planned. Costs of wood and other raw materials for the manufacture of beekeeping equipment are high and equipment design may not be the best for Bangladeshi conditions. To overcome these problems, research is planned to investigate other available raw materials to use in making less costly and better equipment.

ACKNOWLEDGEMENTS

I believe it is possible to conduct appropriate and applied research to aid the promotion and development of apiculture in Bangladesh to improve the life of the poor. In this connection, I want to express my humble gratitude to our generous donor agencies, the Canadian International Development Agency (CIDA), the Swedish International Development Authority (SIDA), the Royal Norwegian Development Corporation (NORAD), NOVIB of the Netherlands, OXFAM, EEC and the International Bee Research Association who generously provided and are providing funds for our endeavour to promote scientific beekeeping in Bangladesh.

I am sincerely grateful to Dr. Robert J. Paxton for reading this manuscript and suggesting improvements. I am thankful to Dr. R.S. Pickard, Head of the Bee Research Unit of the Department of Zoology, University College, Cardiff, United Kingdom for encouragement and granting leave to attend the advanced course.

Finally, I thank very sincerely Dr. Peter G. Kevan who kindly invited me to attend the conference. Further, I thank Dr. Syed Jalaluddin, Deputy Vice-Chancellor and Dr. Abdul Rahman Razak and the members of the organizing committee for their generous help, cooperation, and facilities offered to me.

Finally, I thank Mrs. Ab. Rahman Mohd. Ariffin for care and attention in typing the manuscript.

REFERENCES

Dewan, Syed Md. Abdul Latif. 1980a. Apiculture in Bangladesh - Management and Extension. *In* Proceedings of the Second International Conference on Apiculture in Tropical Climates. Indian Agricultural Research Institute, New Delhi, India. pp. 123-135.

Dewan, Syed Md. Abdul Latif. 1980b. The role of the central Bee Research Institute, in the process of development of beekeeping in Bangladesh. *In* Proceedings of the Second International Conference on Apiculture in Tropical Climates. Indian Agricultural Research Institute, New Delhi, India. pp. 24-28.

Dewan, Syed Md. Abdul Latif. 1981. Beekeeping: A self-employment and income generating source. Adab News, Vol. viii, No. 6.

Dewan, Syed Md. Abdul Latif. 1982. Beekeeping: An income generating source. The Bangladesh Observer, January 6, 1982, Dhaka, Bangladesh.

Dewan, Syed Md. Abdul Latif. 1984. Beekeeping in Bangladesh. *In* Proceedings of the Expert Consultation in Beekeeping with *Apis mellifera* in Tropical and Sub-tropical Asia. Bangkok/Chiangmai, Thailand, 9-14 April 1984. Rome, Italy, FAO.

Dewan, Syed Md. Abdul Latif. 1986. Report on the Farmer's training on Apiculture in Bangladesh. Bangladesh Agricultural Research Council and Bangladesh Institute of Apiculture, Dhaka, Bangladesh. pp. 1-41.

Dewan, Syed Md. Abdul Latif. 1987a. Beekeeping with *Apis cerana* in Bangladesh. Paper presented at the 31st International Apiculture Congress of Apimondia, Warsaw, Poland.

Dewan, Syed Md. Abdul Latif. 1987b. Beekeeping in Bangladesh and the role of the Bangladesh Institute of Apiculture. BIA, 23/12 Khiljee Road, Dhaka - 1207, Bangladesh.

Kevan, P.G. 1983. Potential for Beekeeping in

Bangladesh. Department of Environmental Biology, University of Guelph, Guelph, Ontario, Canada. Unpublished report to CIDA/AST Dhatia.

Murrell, D. and W.T. Nash. 1981. Nectar secretion by Toria (*Brassica campestris* L.V. Toria) and foraging behaviour of three species on Toria in Bangladesh. Journal of Apicultural Research, 20: 34-38.

Nessa, Z., Muttalib, M.A. and A. Begum. 1980. Waxmoth and its control in Bangladesh. Proceedings of the Second International Conference on Apiculture in Tropical Climates. Indian Agricultural Research Institute, New Delhi, India. pp. 461-465.

Paxton, R.J. and Syed Md. Abdul Latif Dewan. 1987. Foraging of *Apis* during winter in Bangladesh. Paper presented at the 31st International Apiculture Congress of Apimondia, Warsaw, Poland.

Zahurul Alam, M. and Gul-e Zannat. 1980. Apiculture in Bangladesh. Proceedings of the Second International Conference on Apiculture in Tropical Climates. Indian Agricultural Research Institute, New Delhi, India. pp. 83-86.

CHAPTER 36

BEEKEEPING WITH *APIS CERANA* - RESEARCH NEEDS AND PROBLEMS: THE EXAMPLE OF THE PHILIPPINES

ADELAIDA C. QUINIONES

INTRODUCTION

Beekeeping is not new in most countries of Asia, including the Philippines. As early as 1913, C.H. Schultz successfully introduced the Italian honeybee, *Apis mellifera* which flourished for some time (Gabriel 1981). Modern beekeeping, however, was introduced in the Philippines by the Bureau of Plant Industry shortly before World War II by importing several colonies of *A. mellifera* and conducting demonstrations showing the success of culturing imported bees under Philippine conditions, if properly managed.

The honeybee colonies were reared within the environs of the city of Manila to serve as sources of new colonies for honeybee enthusiasts. As a result, several hobbyists became beekeepers and founded apiaries, mostly in the suburbs of Manila. Unfortunately, the hives were destroyed during the war and those that survived were eventually wiped out when the American liberation forces, using airplanes and spray trucks, embarked on a methodical DDT-oil spray campaign to control flies and mosquitoes in Manila and neighbouring regions (Otanes 1950, 1952).

Revival of beekeeping was attempted again by the Bureau of Plant Industry after the war in 1955 through the ICA-NEC grant. Stocks of *A. mellifera* bees that were donated to the Bureau through the grant increased and were obtained by enthusiastic beekeepers. In 1969, about 72 beekeepers and 666 colonies were found in five cities and eighteen provinces in the Philippines (Pangga 1972). However, only ten out of the 72 beekeepers kept bees commercially in later years. This was attributed to the *Varroa* mite infestation (Delfinado 1963; Morse and Laigo 1969a) which became a serious problem, causing the abandonment of some apiaries.

Nevertheless, in 1980, more than 50 beekeepers in the country were reported to maintain over 2,000 hives of *A. mellifera*. Table I gives some information on the distribution of colonies in the Philippines where numbers are available. The increased number of beekeepers was attributed to the high market price of honey, which occurred as a result of the importation of mites that caused the upsurge of *Varroa* infestation. At present, the *Varroa* infestation re-

TABLE I. The distribution of honeybee colonies in the Philippines in 1980s.

Site	Number of colonies	
	A. mellifera	*A. cerana*
Luzon		
Benguet	150	
Ifugao	20	
Nunez, N.E. (CLSU)	15	9
Metro Manila area	500	
Laguna	100	200
Carute	200	
Batangas	150	20
Quezon	50	
Visayas		
Leyte, Biliron	10	
Mindanso		
Davai	300	
Bukiduos	20	
TOTAL	**1,515**	**229**

mains a challenge to beekeepers who are in the beekeeping business.

The foregoing discussion demonstrates that beekeeping in the Philippines is based on a technology generated for the management of the imported honeybee, *A. mellifera*. As a consequence, the potential of the native honeybee as a honey producer on a commercial scale has never been considered seriously, making it entirely unexplored. Although honey is a highly relished food because of its high food value and its many recognized uses, its production through domestic hiving of native honeybees has not been encouraged and supported by the government. This policy is surprising because the Philippines is a net importer of honey. A comprehensive survey of honey production in the Philippines by Cunanan (1981) showed that the total value of honey sold in Metro Manila was close to seven million pesos (Table II). This trend will increase as a consequence of decreased sugar production in the country.

TABLE II. Honey market survey by Cunanan (1981).

Source	Quantity (tons)	Value in million
Imports[1]	67	3.60
Honey from wild bees	20	1.62
Local apiaries[2]	70	230
Total		7.52

[1] Honey importing companies such as Long Distance Trading Import and Export, Malibay Commercial Company, Ongsit and Co. Import and Export, Sysu and Company Food Products, Wiltrate Enterprises, and Queen Bee.

[2] Estimated from 150 *Apis mellifera* and 1,500 *A. indica* colonies for an average of 40 kgs production per hive per year respectively.

SPECIES OF HONEYBEES

There are four species of honeybees belonging to the genus *Apis*, three of which are native to the Philippines. These are *Apis cerana indica* (F.) which are common in coconut groves, *Apis dorsata* F., giant honeybee or rock bee, and *Apis* (*Micrapis*) *florea*, the dwarf honeybee which was reported to be found only in Palawan (Morse and Laigo 1969a; Gabriel 1981) but was later discovered in the Mountain Province and in Mt. Makiling, Laguna (Cadapan *et al.* 1982). Of the three species, only *A. cerana* can be cultured inside a box and commercially managed.

Few beekeepers in the Philippines use the native bee for commercial honey production. Eroles (1979) and Summataro and Avitable (1978), under the supervision of Cadapan, reported that they successfully produced *A. cerana* in captivity. However, they did not elaborate on the number of colonies they produced and maintained afterwards. Later, Cadapan (1985) mentioned in his professional lecture at University of the Philippines at Los Baños (UPLB) that 50 *A. cerana* hives were found in the country in 1979 and these increased to 2,000 hives in 1982 from splitting the colonies and from domesticating abundant wild colonies.

Some years ago, Central Luzon State University (CLSU), located in Nueva Ecija province, started an apiary in the Pomology Project with six nuclei Italian colonies through Dr. A. Al-Azawi, a UNESCO-UNDFP Plant Protection expert. But the next year, the honeybee colonies were destroyed by a typhoon leaving only one colony. After the typhoon, the leader of the project in charge of the apiary was informed of a honeybee colony that sought sanctuary in one of the houses on the campus. Thinking that this was one of the colonies of Italian bees, he hunted it and boxed them in a Langstroth hive. The colony was found to be a colony of *A. cerana*. As a result of improper management, the honeybees, which were split into three colonies within a period of six months, slowly absconded. In 1981, when all the colonies were lost, the University bought 50 colonies of *A. cerana* from a beekeeper in Batangas, a province in southern Luzon. At this time, two entomologists joined the staff of the College of Agriculture and they took over the management of the apiary. No research was recorded and their activities were devoted to the production of bee colonies. When they left CLSU and joined another university in the Southern Philippines, the apiary management was again delegated to an agricultural technician. Again the colonies dwindled to 20 colonies by the next year. Some colonies absconded, reducing the colonies to five. The continuous spraying of insecticides in the vegetable projects surrounding the apiary must have led to further reduction of the colonies. This situation was compounded by the presence of numerous predators. Table III shows a list of species of birds, mites, insects, and animals prevalent in the region that eat honeybees. Similar problems were encountered and cited by other beekeepers in the country.

UNIVERSITY RESEARCH

Promoting beekeeping not only generates a sideline occupation for the farmers but also protects the wild honeybees and preserves useful trees that harbour their hives. In cooperation with the Bureau of Plant Industry, UPLB and CLSU at Muñoz, Nueva Ecija are conducting research pertaining to honeybees. The study on the biology, ecology, distribution, and production of the native honeybees in the Philippines was undertaken by Cadapan *et al.* (1982). In this study, they revealed the location preference and type of comb constructed by the native honeybee. They were found to construct multiple combs in sheltered places like houses, boxes, and tree holes regardless of the nature of the place and type of vegetation. No morphological and behavioural differences were observed among the colonies. A colony builds half-moon shaped combs under natural conditions, however, in a man-made box and frames with wax foundation, the honeybee workers construct a straight and regular comb.

Moreover, they also reported that the total developmental period of workers, drones and queens from the egg stage to pupal emergence was 18-19, 24

TABLE III. Predators and parasites of honeybees in the Philippines.

A. Birds
   1. *Merops philippinus linue* or blue-tailed or green-headed bee eater
   2. *Merops viridis americanus* or chestnut-headed bee eater
   3. *Chitura gigantea* or spine-tailed swift

B. Mites
   1. *Varroa jacobsonii* Oudemans
   2. *Tropilaelaps clareae*
   3. *Calorella obisae*

C. Spider
   1. *Argiope catenulata* or orb weaver

D. Other insects
   1. *Galleria mellonella* or wax moth
   2. *Vespa tropica deusta* or Vespid
   3. Red ants

E. Other animals
   1. Lizards
   2. Ducks (Mallard duck)
   3. Toads

and 15-16 days, respectively. Noting the daily activities of *A. cerana* workers, they observed that workers started very early (0500 h) and ended late (1900 h) with a peak between 0700 and 1000 h during sunny days. A colony containing an average of 5,000 workers produced as much as 1,753,80 g of honey and 129.10 g of wax per year even without feeding.

The lack of supply of queens is now alleviated with the mass queen rearing techniques by grafting (Quiniones 1984) and artificial insemination. Some beekeepers have undergone training in universities in Saudi Arabia, Australia, Israel and U.S. and are now in the business of selling grafted queens. The artificial production of queens during rainy season (September to October) was found possible in colonies with high worker/nurse bees populations (10,000) at temperatures of 26-28°C at 76-85% RH (Mataac 1984).

A comparative study of honey production by *A. cerana* and *A. mellifera* was also conducted by Cadapan *et al.* (1982). He found out that even without artificial feeding of a colony containing 5,000 workers, *A. mellifera* can produce over 15 times the amount of honey of *A. cerana* (Table IV). But this latter species was documented as the major pollina-

tor of various economic crops and an efficient pollen collector as well. It collected pollen mostly from coconuts (30.80%) and *Mimosa pudica* (23.44%), but 22.27% was collected from 15 other plant species. *A. mellifera* collected pollen from 12 species of plants.

The native honeybee is raised not only for its honey, wax and pollen, but also as a major pollinator of agricultural crops and other plants in the forest and pastures. Cadapan *et al.* (1982) reported an increase in mean yield of various crops to as much as 75.9-98.7% for cucurbits, 35% for cotton, 35-70% for coconut, 30% for sunflower, and 40% for cucumber. In a similar study, Doliente (1987) found out that caged cucumber plants (Pixie variety) with *A. cerana* had produced significantly higher mean number of fruits than the plants caged without bees. However, open field plots yielded the most (mean) number of fruits. When *A. cerana* colonies were used to pollinate three varieties of mungbean, namely Pagasa I, Pagasa II and Fatigue in open field and caged plots, Vitales (1984) observed that Pagasa I was the most frequently visited by the honeybees. As before, aged plants gave lower yield than open-pollinated plants.

Meanwhile, three species of mites, *Varroa jacobsonii* Oudemans, *Tropilaelaps clareae* Delfinado and Baker and *Calorella apisae* Rimando were found in colonies of honeybees (Sevilla 1963; Malabuyoc 1972). The two mites, *Varroa* and *Tropilaelaps* reduced bee colonies by directly feeding on the larvae and pupae. Mite populations had their peak in July. Though both species of mites commonly attack the native bees (*A. cerana* and *A. dorsata*), they do not cause as serious damage as when they attack *A. mellifera*. This was attributed by Cadapan *et al.* (1982) to the peculiar behaviour of adult *A. cerana* which actively remove mites from the body of other bees.

The introduction of Korean smoking paper in the Philippines for the control of *Varroa* mite was believed to have successfully reduced infestation of the colonies. But its prohibitive cost led to the seeking of alternative treatments. Powdered naphthalene balls + 50% sulfur powder placed at the bottom board over a sheet of paper was found effective and its cost is only 10% of the fumigation paper (Duatin and Cadapan 1984). Also, folbex + fresh leaves of plants with known insecticidal properties such as kakawate, *Gliceridia sepium* (Jacq.) Steud, Sambong, *Blumea balsamifera* Linn and Suag-kabayo, *Hyptis suaveolems* Poir and folbex showed some biological activity (Dumaguing 1985). *Varroa* mites succumbed to folbex, which gave the highest mean mites killed, followed by Suag-kabayo, kakawate, and sambong. Though the number of mites killed was 50% less than the folbex, the miticidal activity of fresh leaves

TABLE IV. Mean honey yield of honeybee species (January - April, 1981).

Species		Yield (kg)
Apis mellifera 14 frames		28
A. cerana	10 frames	2
A. dorsata	field	10
A. florea		no harvest

Source Cadapan (1984)

was demonstrated by the presence of dead mites on the bottom board three days after each application of the treatment.

Besides mites, unfavourable environmental conditions in the apiary such as excessive exposure to afternoon sun and frequent disturbance by natural enemies (lizards, wax moth, etc.) caused swarming and absconding (Cadapan *et al.* 1981). Since temperature in the broad hive regulates activities of the workers and that thermoregulation is most efficient during peak nectar flow and active brood rearing, it should be sustained because poor thermoregulation generally precedes absconding and swarming (Rabanal 1982).

POLLEN AND NECTAR SOURCES OF HONEY-BEES

During the 1800's, Huber proved that pollen was essential in the production of brood (Eckert 1942). In support of this, it has been established that the nectar and pollen supply directly affects the brood rearing capability of the colony. Since the amount of honey a colony can produce depends on the strength of the colony, greater production should be obtained from food sources which supply pollen as well as nectar. It is important, therefore, that the source of the food supply of the colony be known to beekeepers.

The pollen calendar is a measure of the potential seasonal value for brood rearing of a given area. In the Philippines, the pollen supply for apiaries located in Metro Manila and various provinces in the southern part of the country was studied by Payawal (1984). Figure 1 shows the major pollen sources and relative frequency of different pollen types from two apiaries in nearby Metro Manila. Four plant species were identified as major sources of pollen in the Manila area, namely *Muntingia calabura* L. (Ratiles 16%), *Leucaena leucocephala* (Ipil-ipil 39%), *Mimosa*

pudica L. (Makahiya 27.5%) and *Cocos nucifera* L. (Coconut 12%).

Other minor sources are from gramineae pollen, grains, legume pollen, *Areca* pollen, Verbenaceae pollen and Acanthaceae pollen. These occur sporadically in pollen samples. In an apiary in Makati, 57 plant species in 35 families were cited as pollen sources throughout the year. Eight of these plant species are the major pollen plants, namely *Muntingia calabura* (35.5%), *Mimosa pudica* (6%), *Leucaena leucocephala* (3%), *Erythrina* sp. (Eugenia 2%), Cucucurbitaceae type (3.5%), *Cocos nucifera* (coconut 5%), and *Illicium* sp., *Caesalpinia* sp., *Cadiosperemum* sp., Compositae pollen type.

TRAINING PROGRAMMES AND EXTENSION ACTIVITIES

A series of short summer courses from April 1979-83 was initiated at UPLB, Laguna by the staff of the Department of Entomology. A total of over 50 people from all over the country were trained in the basic skills for both *A. cerana* and *A. mellifera*. A seminar-workshop on beekeeping was also held at CLSU on March 10, 1973 to acquaint the University staff in extension and manpower development. Some farmers from the surrounding barrios attended and learned the importance of bees in crop pollination and the value of beekeeping as a source of livelihood. The workshop also provided an excellent venue for discussion and exchange of experiences among invited beekeepers and resource speakers. Subsequent training programmes have been continuously held every summer (March - April) by the Department of Crop Protection in cooperation with the Research and Extension Department. In fact, two batches of prospective farmer beekeepers from region 2 (Mountain Province) are scheduled to come to CLSU this summer (March - April, 1988) for training on beekeeping.

Other agencies of the government, like the Bureau of Animal Industry (BAI), joined the group of producers of *A. cerana* in 1981, and they started their own training programme for beekeepers in cooperation with the self-help (KKK) projects of Region IV.

In support of training programmes, the Philippine Beekeeping Manual, a monograph on *A. dorsata*, and a number of other publications (Morse and Laigo 1968a, 1968b, 1968c, 1969b) were produced. A sequel to these publications is a series of teaching modules on how to raise honeybees, prepared and published by Technology Resource Center Foundation Inc. in cooperation with the Correspondence School of the University of Life, Metro Manila. The

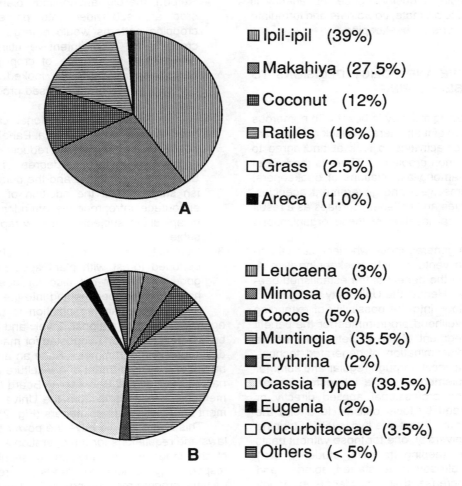

Ipil-ipil (39%)

Makahiya (27.5%)

Coconut (12%)

Ratiles (16%)

Grass (2.5%)

Areca (1.0%)

Leucaena (3%)

Mimosa (6%)

Cocos (5%)

Muntingia (35.5%)

Erythrina (2%)

Cassia Type (39.5%)

Eugenia (2%)

Cucurbitaceae (3.5%)

Others (< 5%)

FIGURE 1. The relative frequency of different pollen types from (A) Manila apiary, and (B) Makati apiary.

modules deal with topics such as: Beekeeping: An Introduction, The Bee Farm (Apiary), Operation and Maintenance of the Beefarm, Diseases and Pests of Honeybees, and the Products of Honeybees.

Also, beekeeping associations and cooperatives were organized to mutually help in selling their honeybee products and institute standardization of prices. To date, there are five registered beekeepers associations and cooperatives in the Philippines, namely Philippine Beekeepers Development Cooperative (PBDC), Metro Manila Beekeepers Association (MMBA), Philippine Beekeepers Association (MPA), Guenca Beekeepers "Samahang Kabuhayan ng Pioneer Beekeepers (SKPB) and Samahan ng Nagaalaga ng Pulot Pukyutan (The Beekeepers). The association/cooperatives publish journals of beekeeping and newsletters as sources of information on research and news about beekeeping activities of fellow beekeepers.

PROBLEMS AND CONSTRAINTS OF BEEKEEPING WITH *APIS CERANA*

1. Although *A. cerana* can now be raised in boxes, absconding and swarming of colonies are common.
2. Lack of management studies focusing on environmental factors and the effect of natural enemies on the economics of honeybee productivity.
3. Little trained manpower to do research, extension and production of honeybees.
4. Limited information on nectar and pollen sources for *A. cerana* during different seasons in different regions of the country.
5. Low honey yield in spite of supplemental feeding.
6. High cost of beekeeping equipment making it difficult for many beekeepers to get started.
7. Lack of government support for the promotion of

the beekeeping industry, hence, no agency is empowered to promote, coordinate and formulate laws/regulations on beekeeping.

ADMINISTRATIVE AND POLICY DECISIONS TO ENCOURAGE BEEKEEPING

The beekeeping industry is beset with numerous problems. On top of it all, there is a lack of organization/integration of activities to look at and agree to solutions of common problems. There is the lack of communication among associations of beekeepers, beekeepers themselves, and government agencies, and the universities and colleges, perhaps as a result of the geographical location of these organizations and apiaries.

However, in general, those who lack capital and are interested in venturing into beekeeping with *A. cerana* do not get the benefit of the established beekeeping industry. Hence, the University and government agencies look into the possibility of extending beekeeping to livelihood programmes for the benefit of the poorer segment of the society. A massive programme of dissemination of generated technologies (foreign and local) through regular and summer training was implemented. The interested farmer, entrepreneur, and professional applied directly or were recommended by local officials to attend the training programme. There are two levels of training offered by the University, one for those without basic knowledge in beekeeping (farmers, students, etc.) and those who already have started apiaries and would like to increase their knowledge in honey beekeeping.

In addition to training beekeepers locally, the University helps in the admission of trained personnel to undergo further training in advanced countries with beekeeping industries such as Israel, U.S., Australia, etc. Those with college degrees are recommended for graduate studies and, in turn, will later on be the core of researchers in the country. The scheme below illustrates the relationship between beekeepers, University, and government agencies.

Under this scheme, the University and government agencies closely interact each other. In turn, the beekeepers are encouraged to organize into cooperatives/associations for a smoother linkage. Most often, University staff become advisers to organized beekeeping.

There are some national policies that, when implemented, are beneficial to the promotion of beekeeping.

1. Agrarian Land Reform may be needed. That requires 3-7 ha of landholding of each farmer in the Philippines. By implementation of Land Reform, the big landholdings planted to mono-crop are subdivided into parcels and new cropping patterns would emerge (e.g. multiple cropping for more intensive utilization of the land). The importance of crop pollination by honeybees needs to be looked at for better quality of seeds and increased production under such a programme.
2. In the Philippines, educational curricula have been revised. The Technical Panel of Education (TPAE) has instructed the reduction of the credit units required for the degree of Bachelor of Science in Agriculture and the deletion of Spanish subjects, but the addition of subjects that encourage entrepreneurial attitudes. Beekeeping or apiculture subjects can now replace Spanish subjects.
3. Reforestation Projects: The reforestation of denuded forest with plant species is not only good for lumber but also for bee forage and helps promote beekeeping into the future.

A creation of an organization to coordinate all agencies at the national level and to promote beekeeping has been suggested for many apicultural development programmes. Such an agency should be under the Department of Agriculture and could be named the National Beekeeping Board (NBB) whose members would come from the University, government agencies, and beekeepers (Fig. 2).

This board should have the power to administer laws and regulations for the operation and promotion of the industry. In addition, it should have the responsibility to look for funds for research and training programmes proposed by Universities and other agencies as well as private beekeepers' associations.

The University, on the other hand, should carry on/continue its programme of research. The research activity should answer the problems of the beekeeping industry. In constant dialogue with beekeepers, the programme could be prioritized according to the needs of the industry. Some priority research topics identified are the following:

1. Management technology on *A. cerana*.
2. Predation and disease control.
3. Pesticide problem.
4. Breeding and selection.
5. Biometrical studies.
6. Hive equipment and its construction.
7. Queen rearing
8. Pollination of crops.
9. Pollen and nectar sources.

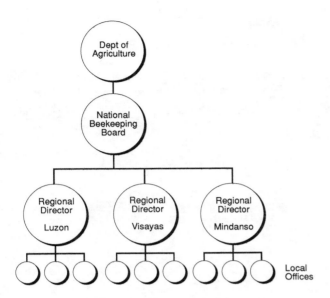

FIGURE 2. Proposed structure for a National Beekeeping Board (NBB).

RECOMMENDATIONS

I wish to conclude with the following recommendations:

1. In view of the importance of beekeeping to the
   livelihood programmes and its development as
   an industry, it deserves the all-out encouragement and support by the government. Apiculture
   research should be one of the national priority
   commodities to generate the much needed
   technology appropriate for the region.
2. Agriculture schools and colleges should include
   in their curriculum courses of apiculture, or at
   least subjects about beekeeping to develop more
   manpower for research and extension work.
3. A government agency, likely the Department of
   Science and Technology (DOST), should be
   given the task and authorized to oversee,
   coordinate and regulate beekeeping activities
   throughout the country.
4. The development of beekeeping should go hand-
   in-hand with reforestation projects to increase
   the plant species for nectar and pollen.
5. A cooperative association on a national level
   should be formed under a government agency to
   handle the manufacture or importation of much-
   needed beekeeping supplies and equipment.
   The head office should be in Manila, with regional branches located where there are
   concentrations of beekeepers.

REFERENCES

Cadapan, E.P. 1985. Philippine Apiculture: status,
needs and future prospects. Inaugural professional lecture delivered on October 24, 1985,
Plant Pathology Auditorium, UPLB, College,
Laguna.

Cadapan, E.P., H.B. Tubelleja and H. Cores. 1982.
The native honeybee (*Apis indica*): its biology,
ecology, distribution and production in the
Philippines. A progress report to NRCP. June
1981-May 1982.

Cunanan, H.C. 1982. Beekeeping in the Philippines:
an industry. MBA thesis. Asian Institute of
Management. Makati, MM. p. 210.

Delfinado, M.D. 1963. Mites of the honeybee in
Southeast Asia. Journal of Apicultural Research,
2(2): 113-114.

Doliente, W.A. 1987. Pollination of cucumber by
honeybees (*Apis cerana indica* (F)). CLSU
Unpublished B.S. Thesis. Crop Protection
Department, Muñoz, Nueva Ecija.

Duatin, M. and E.P. Cadapan. 1984. Chemical
control of *Varroa jacobsonii* Oudemans attacking
Apis mellifera L. (A research paper submitted by
the senior author as a partial requirement for his
M.S. degree).

Dumaguing, G.P. 1985. Screening of botanical
plants against the honeybee mites. CLSU
Unpublished B.S. Thesis. Crop Protection
Department, CLSU, Muñoz, Nueva Ecija.

Eckert, J.J. 1942. The pollen required by a colony
of honeybees. Journal of Economic Entomology,
35: 309-311.

Eroles, D.C. 1972. Establishment of native honeybee (*Apis indica*) for honey production. UCPA.
Unpublished B.S. Thesis, Entomology Department, UPLB.

Gabriel, B.P. 1981. Prospect for industrial entomology in the Philippines. Philippine Entomology,
4(6): 525-534.

Laigo, F.M. 1973. The ecological competitors of the
imported honeybee, *Apis mellifera* L. in the
Philippines. Progress Report, NRCP Bulletin
20(1): 115-119.

Malabuyoc, L.A. 1972. Studies of the source of
infestation and control of bee mites, *Varroa
jacobsonii* and *Tropilaelaps clareae*. Unpublished B.S. Thesis, UPLB Department of Entomology, College of Agriculture, UPLB.

Mataac, R. 1984. Queen rearing of the native bee
Apis cerana indica Fab. during rainy season.
CLSU Technical Journal.

Morse, R.A. and F.M. Laigo. 1968a Beekeeping in
the Philippines. Farm Bulletin 27, U.P. College

of Agriculture, 56 pp.

Morse, R.A. and F.M. Laigo. 1968b. Honeybees in the Philippines. Philippine Biota, 3(1):3-4.

Morse, R.A. and F.M. Laigo. 1968c. The mite *Tropilaelaps clareae* in *Apis dorsata* colonies in the Philippines. Bee World, 49: 116-118.

Morse, R.A. and F.M. Laigo. 1969a. Control of the bee mites, *Varroa jacobsonii* Oudemans and *Tropilaelaps clareae* Delfinado and Baker with chlorobenzylate. Philippine Entomologist, 1(2): 144-148.

Morse, R.A. and F.M. Laigo. 1969b. The potential and problems of beekeeping in the Philippines. Bee World, 50(1): 9-14.

Otanes, F.Q. 1950. Beekeeping in the Philippines. Plant Industry Digest, 13(12): 2-8.

Otanes, F.Q. 1952. The control of plant pests and diseases in the Philippines. *In*: Half Century of Philippine Agricultures, pp. 10-32. Published for the Bureau of Agriculture, Golden Jubilee by Graphica House, Manila.

Pangga, G.A. 1973. Beekeeping in the Philippines. *In*: Beekeeping Workshop-Seminar. Published by Central Luzon State University, Muñoz, Nueva Ecija.

Payawal, P.C. 1984. Pollen and nectar sources of Italian honeybees (*A. mellifera* L.) in the Philippines. 1. Analyses of pollen pellets from Debuena and Mayumo Apiaries, Metro Manila. The Philippine Bee Journal, 1: 28-34.

Quiniones, A.C. 1981. Artificial production of honeybee queen by grafting. CLSU Technical Journal, 1: 25-27.

Rabanal, J.C. 1982. Observation of brood temperature of *Apis indica* F. in Central Luzon State University. Unpublished B.S. Thesis. Crop Protection Department, CLSU, Muñoz, Nueva Ecija.

Summataro, D. and A. Avitable. 1978. The Beekeepers Handbook. Dexter, Michigan, USA, Peach Mountain Press, 131 pp, from IBRA.

Sevilla V.J. 1963. Observations on the life history and habits of the three new acarine pests of honeybees in the Philippines. Unpublished undergraduate thesis, UPLB, Department of Entomology, College of Agriculture, UPLB.

Vitales, F.O. 1984. Foraging activity of honeybees (*Apis indica* (Fab.)) on three varieties of mungo. CLSU. Unpublished B.S. Thesis. Crop Protection Department, CLSU, Muñoz, Nueva Ecija.

CHAPTER 37

DEVELOPING AGENCIES FUNDING
AND INTERINSTITUTIONAL COOPERATION

NICOLA BRADBEAR and K. MACKAY

INTRODUCTION

People with few resources are most likely to accept beekeeping as a worthwhile activity if easily-managed bees and well-proven beekeeping techniques and materials are available. Within Asia, beekeeping with the native *Apis cerana* is being developed in two ways, firstly by beekeeping programmes which seek to promote and improve beekeeping with *A. cerana*, and secondly by research into the biology and behaviour of *A. cerana*, carried out at various institutes. Extension and research are not necessarily separate activities and many development programmes and institutes undertake both. The purpose of this chapter is to provide a summary of the current situation in the development of beekeeping with *A. cerana*. Part A describes the programmes under way since 1981 and the reports and other information they have generated. Part B details institutes reporting *A. cerana* research, and Part C gives details of the information sources available on *A. cerana* beekeeping. The objective is that by grouping this information together, it may further stimulate liaison between the various organizations involved, provide a useful source of reference for *A. cerana*, and reveal possible areas where further research and extension effort are required.

The authors accept that there may be various inaccuracies and omissions, and welcome any further data to add to this chapter.

DISTRIBUTION OF *APIS CERANA*

The distribution of *A. cerana* extends from North East Iran eastward to Japan, and from the USSR and China in the North to Indonesia and mainland Papua New Guinea in the South. A list of the countries in which *A. cerana* is found is given below.

Traditional beekeeping with *A. cerana* has at some time been practised in almost all of these countries, and is still practised in most of them. Some of those listed have well developed beekeeping industries, but in most cases this is based on the use of introduced *Apis mellifera* rather than *A. cerana*. One important exception is China where *A. cerana* is widely used and relatively sophisticated

Afghanistan (Central	North Korea
& the Eastern districts,	Laos
Kunar, Ningrahar and	Republic of Korea
Paktya)	Macao
Bangladesh	Malaysia
Bhutan	Nepal
Brunei	Pakistan
Burma	Papua New Guinea
China	(mainland, introduced
Hong Kong	from Java)
India, including the	Philippines
Nicobar and Andaman	Singapore
Islands	Sri Lanka
Indonesia (Sumatra, Java,	Taiwan
Borneo)	Thailand
Iran (North East region)	Vietnam
Japan (not in Hokkaido)	USSR
Kampuchea	

techniques for its management have been developed.

A. BEEKEEPING DEVELOPMENT PROJECTS UNDER WAY AND FEASIBILITY STUDIES COMPLETED DURING THE PERIOD 1981-1988 IN COUNTRIES WHERE *APIS CERANA* IS PRESENT

A.1 Introduction

Listed here are programmes organized to develop beekeeping, funded by international or local aid agencies.

For each country, information on projects and feasibility studies undertaken since 1981 is given.

For information prior to this, please see Technical Co-operation Activities: Beekeeping, A Directory and Guide (details section C.2.5).

In countries where more than one project or feasibility study has taken place, these are numbered in order of starting date. Data are given under the following categories:

> Aid agency, Counterpart agency, Project title, Inputs, Total funds, Objectives, and Outcome. Not all of these data are available for every project.

The species of hive bee, *A. cerana* or *A. mellifera*, which the project seeks to promote is given in brackets: { }.

Reports relating to the programmes, or papers specifically discussing the status of beekeeping development within the country are cited in chronological order at the end of each country entry. For references to other aspects of beekeeping in each country, please see parts B and C of this chapter.

The information presented here is compiled from files held at the International Bee Research Association.

A.2 List of Countries

Afghanistan

Project 1 {*A. mellifera*}
Aid agency: FAO
Dates: 1983/84
Project title: Apiculture development Technical Cooperation Programme/AFG/2201
Inputs: Consultancy services, equipment and training
Total funds: US $100,000+
Objectives: Establish a training and demonstration apiary at an agricultural research station.
                 Prepare a second-phase follow-up project designed to spread modern beekeeping practises.
Reports: **Beekeeping in Afghanistan** by J. Woyke. *In* Proceedings of the expert consultation on beekeeping with *Apis mellifera* in tropical and sub-tropical Asia, Bangkok/Chiang Mai, Thailand, 9-14 April 1984, Rome, Italy: FAO

Bangladesh

Project 1 (locally organized) {*A. cerana*}
Aid agency: PROSHIKA
Dates: Ongoing

Objectives: Proshika apiculture scheme runs some 600 colonies of bees

Project 2 (locally organized) {*A. cerana*}
Aid agency: Oxfam and other agencies
Inputs: Funded various aspects of beekeeping development

Feasibility Study 1
Aid agency: FAO
Project title: Development planning for the sundarbans and other coastal forest areas
Inputs: Consultancy services, equipment and training
Objectives: Introduction of apiculture to fully utilize the production potential.
Action: Unknown

Feasibility Study 2
Aid agency: CIDA
Date: 1983
Project title: The potential for beekeeping in Bangladesh by P.K. Kevan
Inputs: Funded Bangladesh Institute of Apiculture three times for short intervals

Feasibility Study 3
Aid agency: CARE
Date: 1986
Action: Not funding beekeeping at present
Reports: **Beekeeping in Bangladesh** by W.T. Nash and D.C. Murrell (1982). American Bee Journal 121(5).
                 Apiculture in Bangladesh by S.M. Abdul Latif Dewan. *In* Proceedings of the expert consultation on beekeeping with *Apis mellifera* in tropical and sub-tropical Asia, Bangkok/Chiang Mai, Thailand, 9-14 April 1984, Rome, Italy: FAO.
                 Economic impact of beekeeping: A case study of Bangladesh by Ali Mohammad. *In* Proceedings of the expert consultation on beekeeping with *Apis mellifera* in tropical and sub-tropical Asia, Bangkok/Chiang Mai, Thailand, 9-14 April 1984, Rome, Italy: FAO.
                 Beekeeping technology in Bangladesh by B. Svensson (1987). Bikonsult HB, Sala, Sweden.
                 Beekeeping - means of income generation for rural poor by B. Svensson (1987). Bikonsult HB, Sala, Sweden.

Bhutan

Aid agency: UNICEF
Dates: 1981-1982
Inputs: Distribution of hives and equipment to beekeepers in southern Bhutan
Report: Report prepared by N. Bradbear in 1986.

Burma

Project 1 {*A. cerana* and *A. mellifera*}
Aid agency: FAO/UNDP
Counterpart agency: Ministry of Agriculture and Forests
Project title: Beekeeping for cottage industry BUR/78/013
Dates: 1980-1983
Inputs: Consultancy services, training, equipment and facilities
Total funds: US $400,000+
Objectives: Multiply by 3 each year the number of colonies.
                Operate queen rearing on a domestic, commercial basis.
                Develop processing of honey and other products.
                Product prototype honey extractors.
                Extend the capability for providing extension services to farmers and rural communities.
Project now finished
Reports: **Bee disease consultancy in Burma** by R. Morse, on behalf of FAO, March 1982.
                Evaluation of honey plans in Burma by C. Zmarlicki. FAO Field Document, 1983.
                Beekeeping with *Apis mellifera* and mite control in Burma by C. Zmarlicki. *In* Proceedings of the expert consultation on beekeeping with *Apis mellifera* in tropical and sub-tropical Asia, Bangkok/Chiang Mai, Thailand, 9-14 April 1984, Rome, Italy: FAO.
                Study on traditional method of keeping Indian honeybees in Burma and keeping with modern method. *In* Seminar, Bureau of Life Science, Burma Research Association (1984), Beekeeping Division, Rangoon, Burma.

China

No information on aid-agency funded projects.
Reports: **The present status and development plan of keeping European bees (*Apis mellifera*) in tropical and sub-tropical regions of China** by Fang Yue-Zhen. *In* Proceedings of the expert consultation on beekeeping with *Apis mellifera* in tropical and sub-tropical Asia, Bangkok/Chiang Mai, Thailand, 9-14 April 1984, Rome, Italy: FAO.
                Advancing Chinese apiculture by Liu Xianshu. *In* Proceedings of the Third International Conference on Apiculture in Tropical Climates, Nairobi, Kenya, 5-9 November 1984, IBRA, London, 1985.

India

Project 1 {*A. cerana*}
Aid agency: GTZ
Counterpart agency: Forestry Department, Himachal Pradesh
Location: Dhauladhar, Himachal Pradesh
Dates: 1981-?
Project 2 (locally organized) {*A. cerana*}
Organizer: Igor Rosegger
Dates: 1982 onwards
Location: Auroville, Tamil Nadu
Inputs: Technical assistance
Objectives: Beekeeping development in Auroville areas. Working solely with *A. cerana* at present.

Other locally organized projects
Aid agencies: Oxfam, YMCA, CARE-India, Action-Aid, SIDA, (in cooperation with SAI-culture)
Reports: **Patterns of assistance under beekeeping programme of the Khadi and Village Industries Commission** by The Indian Bee Journal (1980). Indian Bee Journal 42(3).
                Beekeeping in northern India: Major Constraints and Potentials by L.R. Verma. *In* Proceedings of the expert consultation on beekeeping with *Apis mellifera* in tropical and sub-tropical Asia, Bangkok/Chiang Mai, Thailand, 9-14 April 1984, Rome, Italy: FAO.

Indonesia

Project 1 {*A. cerana*}

Donor organizations:	PT Caltex Pacific Indonesia, Chevron Research Company
Counterpart agency:	Indonesian Government
Project title:	Honeybee Research Development Project
Location:	Riau province
Dates:	1982-1985
Objectives:	Developing techniques for modern management of indigenous honeybees.
	Processing local honey and wax to a level competitive with imports.
	Marketing high quality, local honey.

Project 2 {*A. cerana*}

Aid agency:	FAO/UNDP
Project title:	Beekeeping for rural development
Dates:	1986-1989
Inputs:	Consultancies and services, external and local training, equipment and material
Objectives:	To establish a research, training and demonstration centre, a local industry for the production of beekeeping equipment and wax foundation, and two queen rearing stations.
	To develop cooperative marketing of honey and other bee products.

Project 3 (locally organized)

Aid agency:	Oxfam
Location:	Central Java
Date:	1987
Inputs:	Training, fees, equipment, food and transport for courses
Funds:	£4,741

Feasibility Study 1

Aid agency:	FAO
Inputs:	Consultancy
Date:	1983
Total funds:	US $19,000
Objectives:	To establish the potential for beekeeping development and to prepare a project document for international assistance.
Outcome:	Project started in 1986 (see above)

Feasibility Study 2

Inputs:	Consultancy by Dr. A. ten Houten
Date:	1984
Outcome:	Unknown
Reports:	**Beekeeping as an activity in forest community development in**

Java by A. Soekiman (1976). *In* Apiculture in Tropical Climates, editor E. Crane, London, UK, International Bee Research Association.
Country report on beekeeping in Indonesia by B. Sukartiko (1981). *In* Proceedings of the XXVIIth International Congress of Apiculture, Acapulco, 1981. Bucharest, Romania; Apimondia Publishing House.
[Fundamental concept for beekeeping development [Indonesia]] by B. Yuadji (1982). Jutta Rimba 8(55).
Beekeeping for rural community development in Indonesia by B. Sukartiko (1985). *In* Proceedings of the XXIXth International Congress of Apiculture, Budapest, 1983. Bucharest, Romania; Apimondia Publishing House.
Beekeeping in Indonesia by R. Soerjono. *In* Proceedings of the expert consultation on beekeeping with *Apis mellifera* in tropical and sub-tropical Asia, Bangkok/Chiang Mai, Thailand, 9-14 April 1984, Rome, Italy: FAO.

Iran

Project 1 {*A. mellifera*}

Aid agency:	FAO
Project title:	Queen rearing
Inputs:	Consultancy services
Objectives:	Training in queen rearing.

Republic of Korea

Project 1 {*A. cerana* and *A. mellifera*}

Aid agency:	FAO
Project title:	Apiculture Development Laboratory and Training Centre
Dates:	1986-1987 (12 months)
Inputs:	Consultancies and services, external and local training, equipment and materials
Objectives:	To establish an experimental and demonstration apiary.
	To initiate applied research and extension programmes.
Reports:	**Beekeeping in Korea** by Sang Kun Lee. *In* Proceedings of the XXVIIth

International Congress of Apiculture, Acapulco, 1981. Bucharest, Romania; Apimondia Publishing House. pp. 193-196.

Brief report on the status of Korean beekeeping by Seung Yoon Choi. *In* Proceedings of the expert consultation on beekeeping with *Apis mellifera* in tropical and sub-tropical Asia, Bangkok/Chiang Mai, Thailand, 9-14 April 1984, Rome, Italy: FAO.

Malaysia

Project 1 {*A. cerana*}
Aid agency: IDRC
Counterpart   Universiti Pertanian, Selangor;
agency: Malaysian Agricultural Research and Development Institute (MARDI); Rubber Research Institute of Malaysia (RRIM); Department of Agriculture
Project title: Beekeeping
Dates: 1981, ongoing
Objectives: Research, training and development.

Feasibility Study 1
Date: 1982
Project title: Apiculture development potential in Malaysia by P.G. Kevan
Reports: **Honeybees in Malaysia** by L.C. Kang (1980). Nature Malasiana 5(3).
                 A preliminary report on the status of beekeeping in peninsular Malaysia by Chan Han Hoe and Azizol Md Alias. A report presented at the M F Meeting in Kuala Lumpur in April, 1982.
                 Beekeeping in Malaysia by A.C.G. Phoon (1983). Pertanika 6 (Revue supplement).
                 Current status, problems, prospects and research needs of *Apis mellifera* in Malaysia by Makhdzir Mardan. *In* Proceedings of the expert consultation on beekeeping with *Apis mellifera* in tropical and sub-tropical Asia, Bangkok/Chiang Mai, Thailand, 9-14 April 1984, Rome, Italy: FAO.
                 Beekeeping: UPM IDRC Research and Development Annual Reports 1985, 1986.

Nepal

Project 1 {*A. cerana*}
Aid agency: SNV-Nepal
Counterpart   His Majesty's Government of Nepal,
agency: Department of Agriculture, Industrial Entomological Project
Project title: Beekeeping in Nepal
Location: Whole of Nepal
Dates: 1984-1987
Inputs: Technical assistance, equipment and training

Project 2 (locally organized) {*A. cerana*}
Aid agency: UNICEF
Counterpart   His Majesty's Government of Nepal,
agency: Department of Agriculture and Agricultural Development Bank [Nepal] Small Farmers' Development Project
Dates: Ongoing
Inputs: Financial support and technical help
Reports: **Beekeeping in Nepal** by R. Morse (1982). Gleaning in Bee Culture 110(9).
                 Report of a consultancy in Nepal to investigate bee disease on behalf of FAO by R. Morse, 1982.
                 Country status report on beekeeping in Nepal by S.K. Gautam. *In* Proceedings of the expert consultation on beekeeping with *Apis mellifera* in tropical and sub-tropical Asia, Bangkok/Chiang Mai, Thailand, 9-14 April 1984, Rome, Italy: FAO.
                 Report on beekeeping training SFDP/UNICEF/IEP by K. Speth, 1984-1985.
                 Report on evaluation of beekeeping programme in the SFDP-Project areas by K. Speth, 1986.

Pakistan

Project 1 {*A. mellifera*}
Aid agency: UNHCR
Project title: Beekeeping project for Afghan Refugees
Dates: 1983, ongoing
Inputs: Provide apiculture training for 30-70 Afghan Refugees each year, at the Agricultural Research Institute at Tarnab, Peshawar. Each refugee received 7 colonies of *Apis mellifera* (imported from Australia)

Objectives: To help Afghan Refugees to generate income and thereby reduce their dependence on foreign assistance.

Project 2 {*A. cerana* and *A. mellifera*}
Aid agency: FAO
Project title: Technical Assistance Programme for the Apicultural Research Centre
Dates: 3 years
Inputs: Consultancies and services, local training, equipment and material
Objectives: To provide technical assistance for the Pakistan Agricultural Research Council.
Assistance comprises practical training in all aspects of honeybee management.
Reports: **Country status report on beekeeping in Pakistan** by R. Ahmad. *In* Proceedings of the expert consultation on beekeeping with *Apis mellifera* in tropical and sub-tropical Asia, Bangkok/Chiang Mai, Thailand, 9-14 April 1984, Rome, Italy: FAO.
Evaluation report of Agriculture Cell Afghan Refugees for 1985, UNHCR, Peshawar, 1986.

Papua New Guinea

Project 1 {*A. mellifera*}
Aid agency: Ministry of Foreign Affairs and Ministry of Agriculture and Fisheries, New Zealand
Counterpart agency: Department of Primary Industries, Papua New Guinea
Dates: 1975-1982
Inputs: Training, equipment, workshop, honey-processing plant

Project 2 {*A. mellifera*}
Aid agency: OED
Dates: 1981 onwards
Inputs: Technical assistance.
Reports: **Beekeeping development programmes in the tropical and sub-tropical Pacific** by G.M. Walton (1976). *In* Apiculture In Tropical Climates, editor E. Crane, London, UK, International Bee Research Association.

Philippines

Project 1 {*A. cerana*}
Aid agency: SNV-Manila-Philippines
Dates: Ongoing

Project 2 (locally organized) {*A. cerana*}
Aid agency: Science and Technology Resource Agency Inc. (NGO)
Dates: 1987-1989.
Objectives: Promote and stimulate beekeeping in low income families of Cebu and neighbouring islands.

Feasibility Study 1
Aid agency: SNV-Manila-Philippines
Objectives: Feasibility study by Evert Jan Robberts in 1987.
Outcome: Project started (see above)
Reports: **Beekeeping with Apis mellifera in the Philippines** by E.P. Cadapan. *In* Proceedings of the expert consultation on beekeeping with *Apis mellifera* in tropical and sub-tropical Asia, Bangkok/Chiang Mai, Thailand, 9-14 April 1984, Rome, Italy: FAO.

Sri Lanka

Project 1 {*A. cerana*}
Aid agency: CIDA
Counterpart agency: Ministry of Agriculture and Lands, Sri Lanka
Project title: Apiculture
Location: Apiculture Development Centre, Bindunuwewa, Bandarawela
Dates: 1976, ongoing
Inputs: Financial and technical assistance
Objectives: To establish an Apiculture Section in the Ministry of Agriculture and Lands, to undertake training, extension, development and research.

Project 2 (locally organized) {*A. cerana*}
Aid agency: Mahaweli Development Programme
Counterpart agency: Sri Lanka Bee Farmers' Association
Project title: Beekeeping popularization
Dates: Ongoing
Project location: Nochiyagama

Feasibility Study 1
Aid agency: FAO
Project title: Apiculture Development
Objectives: Establish production for beekeeping development and prepare project documents for international assistance.
Outcome: No follow-up action
Reports: **The ecology of honey production in Sri Lanka** by E.F.W. Fernando (1979). *In* Beekeeping in rural development: unexploited beekeeping potential in the tropics with

particular reference to the Common-wealth, London, UK, Commonwealth Secretariat.

Beekeeping in Sri Lanka by G.A. Lanerolle. *In* Proceedings of the expert consultation on beekeeping with *Apis mellifera* in tropical and sub-tropical Asia, Bangkok/Chiang Mai, Thailand, 9-14 April 1984, Rome, Italy: FAO.

Taiwan

Reports: **A brief history of beekeeping in Taiwan** by D.F. Yen and K.K. Ho (1977). Chinese Bee Journal 1(1).
Beekeeping industry in Taiwan, Republic of China by J-M Tseng (1977). Chinese Bee Journal, 20 January.
Beekeeping in Taiwan, Republic of China by J.L. MacDonald (1977). Chinese Bee Journal 1(2).
[Economic study of the beekeeping industry in Taiwan] by S.T. Shyu (1983). Journal of Agricultural Economics, No. 33

Thailand

Project 1 {*A. cerana* and *A. mellifera*}
Aid agency: UNDP/FAO
Project title: Development of diversified forest rehabilitation in northeast Thailand - project THA/81/604
Dates: 1981-1983
Objectives: Include the introduction of apiculture to rural populations.
Reports: **Apiculture in Thailand** by M. Burgett. Report of a visit December 1981 - March 1982.
Australian cooperation with the National Agricultural Research Project, Thailand: apicultural research by F.G. Smith (1983). Western Australian Overseas Project Authority, Department of Agriculture, Perth, Western Australia.
Beekeeping industry with *Apis mellifera* in Thailand by P. Akratanakul. *In* Proceedings of the expert consultation on beekeeping with *Apis mellifera* in tropical and sub-tropical Asia, Bangkok/Chiang Mai, Thailand, 9-14 April 1984, Rome, Italy: FAO.

Beekeeping and research needs in Thailand by H.A. Sylvester and S. Wongsiri (1986). Apiacta 21(4).

Vietnam

Project 1 {*A. cerana* and *A. mellifera*}
Aid agency: FAO (Technical Cooperation Programme) VIE 4405
Project title: Assistance to Apiculture Development
Date: 1985
Inputs: Consultancy services, equipment and training
Objectives: Develop a simple and efficient control method for parasitic mites.
Provide and select more profitable strains of bees.
Modernize laboratories and beekeeping equipment of Lang Song Beekeeping Station.
Train trainers to act as extension agents to fulfil national requirements.
Train beekeeping specialists.
Project 2 {*A. cerana* and *A. mellifera*}
Aid agency: KWT
Counterpart agency: National Vietnamese Honeybee Company
Project title: Cooperation in beekeeping in Vietnam
Dates: 1987-1991
Inputs: Consultancy services and equipment
Objectives: To observe and describe the present situation.
To give advice at all levels of beekeeping.
To find short-term possibilities for cooperation activities.
To work in various activities but mainly in the field of honey quality improvement.
Reports: **[Beekeeping in Vietnam]** by I.L. Razmadze and V.A. Revenok (1980). Pchelovodstvo No. 9.
Cooperation in beekeeping in Vietnam by V. Mulder, 1987.

A.3 Further details of aid agencies

ActionAid, Hamlyn House, Archway, London N19 5PG, UK
CARE, 660 First Avenue, New York, NY 10016, USA
CIDA (Canadian International Development Agency), Place du Centre, 200 Promenade du Portage,

Hull, Quebec, K1A 0G4, Canada

EEC (Commission of the European Communities), Directorate General for Development, rue de la Loi 200, 1049 Brussels, Belgium

FAO (Food and Agriculture Organization of the United Nations), Via delle Terme di Caracalla, 00100 Rome, Italy.

GTZ (Deutsche Gesellschaft für Technische Zusammenarbeit), Dag Hammarskjöld-Weg 1, D-6236, Ischborn 1, Federal Republic of Germany.

IDRC (International Development Research Centre), P.O. Box 8500, Ottawa, Ontario, K1G 3H9, Canada.

KWT (Komitee Wetenschnap en Techniek voor Vietnam), Prinseneiland 13-15, 1013 LL Amsterdam, The Netherlands.

Mahaweli Development Programme, c/o Sri Lanka Bee Farmers' Association, 41 Flower Road, Colombo 7, Sri Lanka.

Ministry of Foreign Affairs, Private Bag, Auckland, New Zealand.

OED (Österreichischer Entwicklungsdienst), Turkenstr 3/III, A-1020, Vienna, Austria.

Oxfam, 274 Banbury Road, Oxford OX2 7DZ, UK.

PROSHIKA, GPO Box No 3149, Ramna, Dhaka, Bangladesh.

SIDA (Swedish International Development Authority), 105 25 Stockholm, Sweden.

SNV (Netherlands Development Organization), Postbus 20061, 2500 EB, The Hague, The Netherlands.

SNV-Nepal, P.O. Box 1966, Kathmandu, Nepal.

STRAIN (Science and Technology Resource Agency Inc), 30 Legaspi Street, Cebu City 6401, Philippines.

UNDP (United Nations Development Programme), 1 United Nations Plaza, New York, NY 10017, USA.

UNHCR (United Nations High Commission for Refugees), 1 United Nations Plaza, New York, NY 10017, USA.

UNICEF (United Nations Children's Fund), 855 United Nations Plaza, 6th Floor, New York, NY 10017, USA.

YMCA, National Council of YMCAs in India, P.O. Box 14, Jai Singh Road, New Delhi 110 001, India.

B. INSTITUTES REPORTING *APIS CERANA* RESEARCH

B.1 Asian institutes reporting *Apis cerana* research

The following list has been compiled from publi-cations on *A. cerana* research cited in Apicultural Abstracts during the ten-year period of 1978-1987. The address of each institute is given, followed by the names of the researchers, examples of their most recent papers reported in Apicultural Abstracts, the principal subject areas of papers published, and Apicultural Abstract reference numbers of these papers. The addresses of other institutes undertaking honeybee research are also given for each country.

Bangladesh

Department of Botany
University of Dhaka
Dhaka
BANGLADESH

Researchers: Khan, M.R.
                 Razzaque, M.A.

Recent paper: A microbiological approach to the causes of migration of honeybees from their hives AA 112/83.

Other institutes in Bangladesh involved with honeybee research

Bangladesh Honeybee Research Project, 135 Santi Nagar, Dhaka **(Nessa, Z.)**

Bangladesh Institute of Apiculture, House No 8, Street No 1, Shyamoli, Dhaka 7 **(Dewan, A.L.)**

Bangladesh Small and Cottage Industry Corp, 137/138 Motjheel Commercial Area, Dhaka 2 **(Chowdhury, M.R.)**

Burma

Bee House
United Nations Development Program
Rangoon
BURMA

Researchers: Maung Maung Nyein

Recent papers: Control of mites in European bees in Burma AA 275/84
                 Study on traditional method of keeping Indian honeybees in Burma and keeping with modern method AA 67/87

China

Department of Biology
Beijing University
Beijing
CHINA

Researchers: Du, Z.L.
                 Li Shao-Wen

Zhang, Z.B.

Recent papers: [An electron microscopical observation on the hypopharyngeal glands of the worker honeybee *Apis cerana*] AA 1155/87

[Ultrastructural change in the hypopharyngeal glands of worker honeybees (*Apis cerana*) infected with sacbrood virus] AA 1156/87

Apicultural Abstracts
reference numbers: 419/83

Fujian Agricultural College
Jingtong
Sanming
Fujian
CHINA

Researchers: Gong, Y.F.

Recent paper: The natural beekeeping conditions and honeybee races in China AA 156/85

Institute of Apicultural Research
The Chinese Academy of Agricultural Sciences
Xiang Shan
Beijing
CHINA

Researchers: Ma De-Feng   Li, G.X.
Chen, D.H.   Liu, Y.W.
Fang, W.A.   Shi, B.L.
Fang, Y.Z.   Xiao, H.L.
Lai, D.   Xu, S.Y.

Recent papers: [Studies of tissue culture of sacbrood virus from *Apis cerana sinensis*] AA 816/83

[The distribution and geographical variation of *Apis cerana sinensis* in China (Part 1)] AA 1150/83

Research areas: Geographical variation of *Apis cerana sinensis*
Management of *Apis cerana*
Study of bee diseases

Apicultural Abstracts
reference numbers: 788/82, 789/82, 1166/82, 1167/82, 815/83

Medicinal Materials Company
Shazhou County
Jiangsu
CHINA

Researchers: Qian, Z.

Recent paper: [The cause of gnawing combs by Chinese honeybees, and prevention measures] AA 814/83

Native Products Company

Huiyang Prefecture
Guangdong
CHINA

Researchers: Luo, M.S.
Ye, K.

Recent paper: [A method of producing comb honey using Chinese honeybees] AA 813/83

Other institutes in China involved with honeybee research

Institute of Beekeeping, No 15 Beizheng Street, Changan, Linxiang, Hunan, **(Li Zhong-pu)**

India

Central Bee Research Institute
Khadi & Village Industries Commission
1153 Ganeshkhind Road
Shivajinagar
Pune 411 016
INDIA

Researchers: Chandran, K.   Rajan, P.
Chauhan, R.M.   Ranade, D.R.
Desai, D.B.   Rao, G.M.
Divan, V.V.   Salvi, S.R.
Joseph, D.   Seethalakshmi, V.S.
Kshirsagar, K.K.   Shelar, D.G.
Lazar, M.   Suryanarayana, M.C.
Mahindre, D.B.   Wakhle, D.M.
Mittal, M.C.

Recent papers: Morphometric studies on the Indian hive bee *Apis cerana indica* F. 1. Morphometric characters useful in identification of intraspecific taxa AA 792/85

Seasonal fluctuations in the incidence of acarine disease in bees and colony losses in India AA 800/85

Research agency: Diseases
Foraging behaviour
Honey analysis
Indian *Streptococcus pluton*
Morphometry
Nosema apis
Pollination

Apicultural Abstracts
reference numbers: 785/78, 783L/78, 1119/78, 1123/78, 738/82, 284/82, 286L/82, 424/83, 1147/83, 416/83, 144/85, 778/85, 779/85, 782/85

Department of Biophysics
Punjab University
Chandigarh

INDIA

Researchers: Bawa, S.R.
                Marwaha, R.K.
Recent paper: Apical cells in the testis of the honeybee, *Apis cerana indica* AA 815/80

Department of Entomology & Apiculture
College of Agriculture
Himachal Pradesh Agricultural University
Chambaghat-Solan
173 230 Himachal Pradesh
INDIA

Researchers: Adlakha, R.L.   Mishra, R.C.
                Bhalla, O.P.   Nath, A.
                Dhaliwal, H.S.   Sharma, D.C.
                Dinabandhoo, C.L. Sharma, I.D.
                Dogra, G.S.   Sharma, P.L.
                Gupta, P.R.   Srivastava, S.
                Kakkar, K.L.   Verma, A.K.
                Kumar, J.
Recent papers: The pyemotoids (Acarina: Pyemotidae) and their significance in apiculture AA 72/87
                Metabolism of endosulfan in the Indian honeybee AA 78/87
Research   Disease
areas: Insecticide toxicity
                Morphometry
                Pollination studies
                Post-embryonic development of *Apis cerana*

Apicultural Abstracts
reference numbers: 1125/78,   127/80,   247/81, 813/81, 816/81, 442/85, 788/85, 789/85, 794/85, 795/85, 801/85, 802/85, 1147/85, 1150/85

Department of Entomology
College of Agriculture
Punjab Agricultural University
Ludhiana
INDIA

Researchers: Goyal, N.P.
                Atwal, A.S.
                Jhajj, H.S.
                Tanda, A.S.
Recent papers: Morphological and behavioural characteristics of honeybees. Workers reared in combs with larger cells AA 791/85
                Floral biology, pollen dispersal, and foraging behaviour of honeybees in okra (*Abelmoschus esculentus*) AA 1039/86
Research   Effect of insecticides

areas: Foraging behaviour
                Pollination studies
Apicultural Abstracts
reference numbers: 115/78,   482/78,   1518/79, 179/80, 442/80, 814/80, 1165/80, 1267/80, 129/81, 130/81, 109/83, 800/84

Department of Entomology
University of Agriculture and Technology
Kanpur
INDIA

Researchers: Pandey, R.S.
Recent paper: Behaviour of the Indian honeybee in double brood chamber hives AA 1115/78

Department of Entomology & Department of Microbiology
University of Agricultural Sciences
Hebbal
Bangalore 560 024
INDIA

Researchers: Basavanna, G.P.C. Rajashek-
                Devaiah, M.A.   harappa, B.J.
                Panchabhavi, K.S. Siddappaji, C.
Recent papers: Influence of brood on the attraction and mobility of worker honeybees (*Apis cerana*) AA 422/83
                Role of honeybees in the pollination of cardamom *Elettaria cardamomum* (L.) Maton AA 805/85
Research   Colony life cycle and behaviour
areas: Pollination
                Queen rearing
Apicultural Abstracts
reference numbers: 1116/78,   1117/78,   445/80, 126/81, 471/81, 473/81, 421/83

Department of Zoology
School of Life Sciences
North-Eastern Hill University
Shillong 703 014
INDIA

Researchers: Dey, S.
                Varman, A.R.
Recent papers: Ascorbic acid in the compound eye of the honeybee *Apis cerana indica* AA 822/86
                Occurrence of resilin in the lens-cuticle of the honey bee, *Apis cerana indica* AA 823/86

Department of Zoology
University of Delhi

Delhi 110 007
INDIA
Researchers: Agrawal, H.C.
Joshi, M.
Recent paper: Site of cholesterol absorption in some insects AA 96/79

Government Beekeeping Station
Jeolikote, Dist: Nainital
Uttar Pradesh
INDIA
Researchers: Singh, Y.
Verma, S.K.
Recent papers: *Apis* iridescent virus AA 787L/82
Studies on the effect of water soluble vitamin 'C' on brood rearing and comb building activities of worker honeybees (*Apis cerana indica* F.) AA 790/85
Apicultural Abstracts
reference numbers: 817/81, 785L/82

Haryana Agricultural University
Department of Zoology & Entomology
Hissar
Haryana 125 004
INDIA
Researchers: Kapil, R.P.
Lamba, D.P.S.
Recent paper: Toxicity of some important insecticides to *Apis cerana* AA 116/78

Horticultural Experimental & Training Centre
Saharanpur
INDIA
Researchers: Singh, Y.P.
Recent paper: Studies on pollen gathering activity of Indian honeybee (*Apis cerana indica*) under Saharanpur condition AA 812/83

Indian Agricultural Research Institute
Division of Entomology
IARI
New Delhi 110 012
INDIA
Researchers: Mehrotra, K.N.   Phadke, K.G.
Bisht, D.D.   Phokela, A.
Dale, D.   Sinha, R.B.P.
Naim, M.   Tiwari, L.D.
Recent papers: Physiological studies on the cholinesterase enzyme from the Indian honeybee *Apis cerana indica* AA 797/85
Haemolymph protein pattern of drones and workers of the Indian

honeybee AA 799/85
Research Bee flora
areas: Foraging behaviour
Haemolymph protein pattern
Hive design
Honeybee cholinesterase
Apicultural Abstracts
reference numbers: 776/78, 778/86, 1121/78, 1126/78, 126/80, 439/84, 146/85, 147/85, 777/85

Indian Cardamom Research Institute
Myladumpara
Kailasandu PO
Kerala 685 553
INDIA
Researchers: Dandin, S.B.
Madhusoodanan, K.J.
Recent paper: Flower biology of cardamom (*Elettaria cardamomum*) in relation to the foraging behaviour of honeybees (*Apis* sp.) AA 423/83

Regional Bee Research Centre
KVIC
Pathankot
Punjab
INDIA
Researchers: Chaudhary, R.K.
Recent paper: Floral fidelity in the Indian honeybee (*Apis cerana indica* F.) AA 131/81

Regional Bee Research Centre
Nagrota Bagwan
Dist: Kangra
Himachal Pradesh 176 047
INDIA
Researchers: Garg, R.
Salvi, S.R.
Sharma, O.P.
Thakur, A.K.
Recent papers: Vertebrate enemies of bees and their control in Dhahladhar mountains (Himachal Pradesh, India) AA 425/83
Beekeeping in the Kangra valley AA 446L/83
Apicultural Abstracts
reference numbers: AA 1122/78

Shah Beekeepers
Kursu
Rajbagh
Srinagar
Kashmir 190 008

INDIA

Researchers: Shah, F.A.
                 Shah, T.A.

Recent papers: Egg-laying capacity of Kashmir *Apis cerana* AA 426/82
                 The role of Kashmir bee in exploiting beekeeping potential in India AA 75/87

Research areas: Flora
                 Life cycle of Kashmir *Apis cerana*

Apicultural Abstracts
reference numbers: 128/80, 811/81, 70/82, 71L/82

Systematic Laboratory
Department of Botany
Garhwal University
Srinagar
INDIA

Researchers: Gaur, R.D.

Recent paper: Resource development through bee farming in the Garhwal Himalaya AA 1169/87

University of Bangalore
Bee Division
Department of Zoology
Bangalore
Karnataka 560 056
INDIA

Researchers: Reddy, C.C.
                 Bai, A.R.K.

Recent papers: Effect of insecticides on the activities of digestive amylase and protease of honeybee *Apis cerana indica* AA 815/81
                 Foraging index of Indian honeybee *Apis cerana indica* F. AA 803/85

Research areas: Foraging
                 Insecticide poisoning

Apicultural Abstracts
reference numbers: 777/78, 779/78, 1120/78, 443/80

University of Himachal Pradesh
Simla 171 005
INDIA

Researchers: Verma, L.R.   Rana, B.S.
                 Mahajan, U.   Sharma, N.
                 Mattu, V.K.

Recent papers: Seasonal incidence of *Apis* iridescent virus in *Apis cerana indica* F. in Uttar Pradesh, India AA 74L/87
                 [Biological and economic characters of *Apis cerana indica* F.] AA 817/87

Research areas: Behavioural studies
                 Disease incidence

Honey analysis
Morphometry
Pollen analysis

Apicultural Abstracts
reference numbers: 88/84, 1160/84, 784/85, 785/85, 787/85, 793/85, 1245/85, 1360/85, 69/87, 71/87

University of Lucknow
Department of Zoology
Lucknow
Uttar Pradesh 226 007
INDIA

Researchers: Saxena, P.
                 Banerjee, A.

Recent paper: Digestive enzymes in the alimentary canal and associated glands of foragers of *Apis cerana indica* AA 796/85

Other institutes in Indian involved with honeybee research

All India Co-ordinated Project on Honeybee, Research & Training, Haryana Agricultural University, Hissar, Haryana 125 004 **(Mishra, R.C.)**

Government Bee Breeding Farm, Department of Agriculture, Dist: PO Gurdaspur, Punjab 143 521 **(Chief Agricultural Officer)**

Government Post Graduate College, Department of Botany, Gopeshwar, Chamoli, Uttar Pradesh 246 401 **(Sah, V.K.)**

Kerala Forest Research Institute, Division of Entomology, Peechi, Dist: Trichur, Kerala 680 653 **(Padmanabhan, P.)**

Khadi & Village Industries Commission, 3 Irla Road, Vile Parle (West), Bombay 400 056 **(Phadke, R.P.)**

Tamil Nadu Agricultural University, Lawley Road Post, Coimbatore, Tamil Nadu 641 003 **(Sundara Babu, P.C.)**

University of Shinaji, Kolhapur, Maharashtra 416 004 **(Chaubali, P.D.)**

Indonesia

University Gadja Mada
INDONESIA

Researchers: Bhikuningputro, W.
                 Santianawaty
                 Woelaningsih, S.

Recent paper: Pollen collected by *Apis cerana* AA 1242L/78

Other institutes in Indonesia involved with honeybee research

Honeybee Research & Development Project, Tromol

Pos 4/ Bkn, Bangkinang 28402, Riau, Sumatra **(Soesilawati Hadisoesilo)**

Perum Perhutani, Jalan Gatot Subroto 17-18, Karkarta **(Sukiman Atmosudaryo)**

Perum Perhutani, Unit 1, J1 Pawlawan 151, Semarang **(Pramoedibyo, I.S.)**

Iran

Apicultural Institute
University of Isfahan
Isfahan
IRAN

Researchers: Gassparian, S.
                          Pourasghar, D.

Recent papers: Studies of *Apis cerana* in the eastern part of Iran AA 782L/82
Investigations on morphological characteristics of Iranian native honeybees AA 890/83

Apicultural Abstracts
reference numbers: AA 1127/78

Japan

Institute of Honeybee Science
Faculty of Agriculture
Tamagawa University
Machida-shi
Tokyo 194
JAPAN

Researcher: Okada, I.   Matsuka, M.
                        Hara, A.   Nakamura, C.
                        Hoshiba, H.   Ono, M.
                        Kubota, A.   Sato, M.
                        Kurihara, T.   Shimomaki, S.

Recent papers: [Comparison of pollen plants foraged by Japanese and European bees] AA 1148/85
G-banding analysis of male chromosomes in *Apis cerana* and *Apis mellifera ligustica* AA 70/87

Apicultural Abstracts
reference numbers: 1349/80, 73L/82, 76/82, 94L/82, 435/82, 87/84, 481/85, 932/85 1149/85

Sumiyoshi Experimental Farm
Faculty of Agriculture
Miyazaki University
Miyazaki-shi 880 01
JAPAN

Researchers: Hamakawa, H.
Recent paper: [Foraging behaviour of honeybees (*Apis cerana* and *Apis mellifera*) and *Vespula flaviceps* visiting flowers of buckwheat] AA 1113/86

Other institutes in Japan involved with honeybee research
Daito Bunka University, Dai-Ichi High School, Itabashi, Tokyo 175 **(Hoshiba, H; Okada, I.)**

South Korea

Institute of Korea Beekeeping Science
College of Agriculture
Seoul National University
Suwou
SOUTH KOREA

Researchers: Choi, S.Y.
                          Lee, M.L.

Recent paper: [Biometrical studies on the variation of some morphometrical characters in Korean honeybees] AA 510/87

Other institutes in South Korea involved with honeybee research
Korea Beekeeping Research Institute, SPO Box 175, Seoul **(Lee, S.K.)**

Korean Entomological Institute, Korea University, Anam-Dong, Seoul **(Lee, J.O.)**

Malaysia

Department of Food Science
Universiti Pertanian Malaysia
Serdang
Selangor
MALAYSIA

Researchers: Ghazali, H.M.
                          Sin, M.K.

Recent paper: Coconut honey: the effect of storage temperature on some of its physio-chemical properties   AA 324/87

University Pertanian Malaysia
Serdang
Selangor
43400
MALAYSIA

Researchers: Mardan, M.   Ibrahim, R.
                         Azhar Phoon, C.G. Kiew, R.
                         Ghazali, H.   Muid, M.

Recent papers: Flowering periods of plants visited by honeybees in two areas of Malaysia AA 190/86
Effect of the presence of *Apis cerana* colonies on cashew fruit set AA 104/86

Research   *Apis dorsata*
areas: Botany

Honey analysis
Management
Nutrition
Pests and disease
Apicultural Abstracts
reference numbers: 103/86, 1138/86

Other institutes in Malaysia involved with honey-bee research

Institut Pertanian, Ayer Hitam, Kluang, Johor (Boon Hean Lim)
MARDI, Bag Berkunci No 202, Pejabat Pos Universiti Pertanian, Serdang, Selangor

Nepal

Lumle Agricultural Centre
c/o British Embassy
Lainchaur
PO Box 106
Kathmandu
NEPAL
Researchers: Garrod, G.
                  Budathoki, K.
Recent paper: Pollination trail in Chinese cabbage
                  AA 418/83

Other institutes in Nepal involved with honeybee research

Industrial Entomology Centre, PO Box 436, Kathmandu, NEPAL (Kafle, G.P.)

Pakistan

Pakistan Agricultural Research Council
Honeybee Research Programme
National Agricultural Research Centre
PO National Institute of Health
Islamabad
PAKISTAN
Researchers: Ahmad, R.
                  Ali, Q.
                  Muzaffar, N.
Recent paper: Biological control of the wax moths
                  Achroia grisella (F.) and Galleria
                  mellonella (L.) (Lep., Galleridae) by
                  augmentation of the parasite Apan-
                  teles galleriae Wilk. (Hym., Bracon-
                  idae) in Pakistan AA 443/85

Other institutes in Pakistan involved with honey-bee research

Beekeeping Research Station, Nowshera, District Khushab (Uban-ul-Haque)
Beekeeping Research Station, Shamsabad, Rawa-

pindi (Siddique Chohon, M.)
Pakistan Forest Institute, Peshawar (The Director of Entomology)

Philippines

Institutes in the Philippines involved with honey-bee research

Bicolandia Bee Raisers Association Inc., 255 Oro Site, Legaspi City (Barrameda, R.G.)
Honeybee Research & Experimental Farm, PO Box 1474, MCC, Makati, Metro Manila (Velasco, E.M.)
Philippines Bee Research, Alaminos, Laguna 3724 (Shippey, D.R.)
Twin Rivers Research Center, Technical Services & Extension Division, PO Box 305, Davao City, 9501 (Flores, T.B.; Grande, R.A.)

Sri Lanka

Apiculture Development Centre
Bindunuwewa
Bandarawela
SRI LANKA
Researchers: Baptist, B.A.
                  Lanerolle, G.
                  Punchihewa, R.K.W.
Recent paper: A preliminary analysis of the princi-
                  pal factors which will affect honey
                  production in Sri Lanka AA 833/85

Department of Zoology
Vidyalankara Campus
University of Sri Lanka
Kelaniya
SRI LANKA
Researchers: Fernando, E.F.W.
Recent papers: Studies on apiculture in Sri Lanka.
                  Characteristics of some honeys AA
                  1329/78
                  Some biometrical features of Apis
                  cerana (F.) from Sri Lanka AA
                  814/81

Taiwan

Address unknown
Researchers: Kang-Chen, L.
                  Ron-Su, C.
Recent paper: The preliminary investigation on bee
                  mites in Taiwan AA 946L/78

Thailand

Bee Biology Research Unit
Faculty of Science
Chulalongkorn University
Bangkok
THAILAND

Researchers: Wongsiri, S.
                 Lai, Y.S.
                 Liu, Z.S.
Recent papers: Beekeeping in the Guangdong Province of China and some observations on the Chinese honeybee *Apis cerana cerana* and the European honeybee *Apis mellifera ligustica* AA 815/87
                 Apis cerana F. beekeeping in Thailand: problems and research needs AA 1154/87

Other institutes in Thailand involved with honeybee research

Apiculture Research Section, Ministry of Agriculture & Cooperatives, Bangkok **(Boongird, S.; Buranapawang, S.; Polnurak, P.)**

King Mongut's Institute of Technology, The Faculty of Agricultural Technology, Ladkrabang Campus, Bangkok **(Chantrasom, W.)**

University of Chiang Mai, Department of Entomology, Faculty of Agriculture, Chiang Mai 50002 **(Budharugsa, S.)**

University of Kasetsart, Bee Research Laboratory, Entomology Department, Kam Phaeng Saen Campus, Nakorn Pathom **(Akratanakul, P.)**

University of Khon Kaen, Bee Division, Faculty of Agriculture, Khon Kaen 40002 **(Waikakul, Y.)**

University of Prince of Songkla, Faculty of Natural Resources, Haadyai, Songkla, PO Box 6, Kohongo, 90110 **(Kritsaneephaiboon, S.)**

B.2 Institutes outside Asia reporting *Apis cerana* research

Federal Republic of Germany

Institute Bienenkunde
University of Frankfurt
Im Rothkopf 5
6730 Oberusel/Ts
FEDERAL REPUBLIC OF GERMANY

Researchers: Koeniger, N.   Maul, V.
                 Hanel, H.   Ruttner, F.
                 Koeniger, G.   Vorwohl, G.

                 Maschwitz, U.   Weiss, J.
Recent papers: Experimental analysis of reproduction interspecies isolation of *Apis mellifera ligustica* and *Apis cerana* F. AA 786/85
                 The origin of the pore in the drone cell capping of *Apis cerana* Fabr. AA 68/87

Apicultural Abstracts
reference numbers: 124/80, 1239/81, 72/82, 439/85

Poland

Bee Culture Division
Agricultural University of Warsaw
Warsaw 12
Ursynó
POLAND

Researchers: Woyke, J.
Recent papers: Biology of reproduction and genetics of the honeybee AA 163/80
                 Evidence and action of cannibalism substance in *Apis cerana indica* AA 472/81

UK

International Bee Research Association
18 North Road
Cardiff CFI 3DY
UK

Researcher: Bradbear, N.J.
Recent papers: World distribution of major honeybee diseases and pests 1256/88
                 Honeybees in Bhutan 777L/90

Rothamsted Experimental Station
Harpenden
Herts AL5 2JQ
UK

Researchers: Carpenter, J.M.   Williams, I.H.
                 Bailey, L.   Wood, R.D.
                 Ball, B.V.
Recent papers: A strain of sacbrood virus from *Apis cerana* AA 1149/83
                 The pollination of pigeon pea (*Cajanus cajan*) in India AA 781/85

Apicultural Abstracts
reference numbers: 125/80, 1165/82

USA

Bioenvironmental Bee Laboratory

USDA-SEA
Beltsville
MD 20705
USA
Researchers: Baker, E.W.
                Delfinado-Baker, M.
Recent papers: Infestations of *Apis cerana indica* by
                Acarapis woodi and *Varroa jacob-*
                soni AA 817/83
                A new species of *Neocypholaelaps*
                (Acavi: Ameroseiidae) from brood
                combs of the Indian honeybee AA
                801/84
Apicultural Abstracts
reference numbers: 402L/83, 427/83

Department of Entomology
University of California
Davis
California 95616
USA
Researchers: Fang, Y.
                Peng, Y.S.
Recent paper: The resistance mechanism of the
                Asian honeybee, *Apis cerana* F., to
                an ectoparasitic mite, *Varroa jacob-*
                soni Oudemans AA ?/88

C. SOURCES OF INFORMATION ON *APIS CER-*
ANA

C.1 Recent text books referring to beekeeping in specific countries in Asia

Publications are in English unless stated other-
wise. For publications prior to 1978, please see the
Bibliography of Tropical Apiculture (details page
C.2.3).

BANGLADESH
A beekeeping guide to Bangladesh by H.D.A.
Attfield (1980), Dhaka, Bangladesh Agricultural
Research Council. 45 pages.

CHINA
[Manual of beekeeping] by Kiangsia Province
Beekeeping Research Institute (1975), Peking, China,
Agricultural Publishing House. 480 pages (in Chin-
ese). This is a comprehensive text book for the
Chinese Peoples' Republic. It relates mostly to
keeping *Apis mellifera* in Langstroth hives, but
includes *Apis cerana*, and the use of traditional box
and basket hives.
[Beekeeping] (1980), Peking Agricultural Research
Institute, Peking, China. 94 pages (in Chinese)

[New methods in beekeeping] (1979), Yuen-nan
Peoples' Press, Chinese Peoples' Republic. 56
pages (in Chinese). Simple illustrated account of
methods used in the Chinese Peoples' Republic.

INDIA
[Beekeeping questions and answers] by B.S.
Rawat (1978), Rawat Apiaries, Ranikhet, India (in
Hindi). 146 pages
[Elementary beekeeping] by B.S. Rawat (1981),
Rawat Apiaries, Ranikhet, India (in Hindi). 63 pages
Bee farming in India by B.S. Rawat (1982), Rawat
Apiaries, Ranikhet, India. 258 pages, paperback.
Published in English, this book provides a useful text
for *Apis cerana* beekeeping - dimensions of all the
hive types commonly found in India are given, and
methods of *Apis cerana* management. Also gives
lists of bee plants found in North India. Lists 7
beekeeping books in Hindi and 4 in Urdu.
Fundamentals of beekeeping by F.A. Shah (1983),
Shah Beekeepers, India. 60 pages, paperback.
Shah beekeepers are based in Kashmir and the book
contains information on how to over-winter *Apis
cerana*, and a useful calendar showing the sources
of pollen and nectar available throughout the year,
fluctuations in bee numbers with the seasons and
appropriate management techniques.
Beekeeping in India by S. Singh, Indian Council of
Agricultural Research, Delhi, India (first published
1962, reprinted 1982). 214 pages, paperback. A
clearly printed, comprehensive guide to beekeeping.
Management technique for both *Apis cerana* and
Apis mellifera are discussed.

INDONESIA
[Guide to beekeeping] by S. Hadiwiyoto (1980),
Jakarta, Indonesia; Pradnya Paramita. 125 pages (in
Indonesian).
[Building and developing beekeeping in Indon-
esia] by K. Patra and S. Santosa (1980), Bandung,
Indonesia; Karya Inti Nusantara. 92 pages (in
Indonesian).
[Establishing the beekeeping industry of *Apis*
***mellifera*]** by S. Soerodjotanojo and Kardjono (1980),
Jarkarta, Indonesia; Balai Pustaka. 57 pages (in
Indonesian).
[Modern beekeeping] by R.M. Sumoprastowo and
R.A. Suprapto (1980), Jakarta, Indonesia; Bhratara
Karya Aksara. 217 pages (in Indonesian)

NEPAL
[Practical knowledge in beekeeping] by K. Buda-
thoki (1982), Pokhara, Gandaki Anchal, Nepal; Lumle
Agricultural Centre. 88 pages (in Nepáli)
[Modern beekeeping] by G.P. Kafle (1979), Kath-
mandu, Nepal, Rypayan Press. 269 pages (in Nepáli)

Beekeeping: an introduction to modern beekeeping in Nepal by Br. Saubolle and A. Bachmann (1979), Kathmandu; Sahoyogi Prakashan

PAKISTAN

[Rearing honeybees] by R. Ahmad (1979), Pakistan Agricultural Research Council. 15 pages (in Urdu)

[Beekeeping] by R. Ahmad (1980), Pakistan Agricultural Council. 20 pages (in Urdu)

[Modern beekeeping] by R. Ahmad and N. Muzaffar (1984), Pakistan Agricultural Research Council, Islamabad, Pakistan. 350 page (in Urdu)

PHILIPPINES

Beekeeping modules 1-5 by Technology Resource Centre Foundation Inc. (1982), Metro Manila, Philippines, Technology Resource Centre Foundation in cooperation with University of Life Correspondence School. The 5 booklets form the official handbook of the Apiculture and Development Programme of TRCF.

THAILAND

[On bees and beekeeping] by P. Akratanakul (1983). 182 pages (in Thai)

C.2 More general text books referring to beekeeping with *Apis cerana*

Publications are in English unless stated otherwise and most are available from IBRA.

2.1 Honeybee diseases and enemies in Asia: a practical guide by P. Akratanakul, FAO Agricultural Services Bulletin, 68/5 (1987), FAO, Rome, Italy. 51 pages, paperback, ISBN 92-5-102519-3. This publication describes concisely the various diseases, parasites, and predators which face honeybees in Asia.

2.2 Beekeeping in Asia by P. Akratanakul, FAO Agricultural Services Bulletin, 68/4, (1987), FAO, Rome, Italy.

2.3 Bibliography of Tropical Apiculture by Dr. Eva Crane (1978), IBRA, London, UK. 380 pages (Preparation funded by the IDRC, Ottawa, Canada). The Bibliography is subdivided into 24 parts, available separately. Parts relevant to *Apis cerana* beekeeping are listed below.

3. Beekeeping in the Indian sub-continent (with Afghanistan and Iran)
4. Beekeeping in Asia east of India
7. Beekeeping in the Pacific area
15. Bee forage in the tropics
16. Beekeeping management and equipment in the tropics
17. Indigenous materials, methods and knowledge relating to the exploitation of bees in the tropics
18. Bee diseases, enemies and poisoning in the tropics
19. Honey in the tropics
20. Beeswax and other hive products in the tropics
21. Descriptions of pollen grains in tropical honeys
22. Bees for pollination in the tropics
S/28 Beekeeping and bee research in India
S/32 *Apis cerana*: laboratory studies
S/34 Bee forage in specific regions of the tropics
S/35 Bee diseases and pests in specific regions of the tropics
S/36 Honeys of specific region of the tropics
S/38 Bee pollination in specific regions of the tropics

2.4 Beekeeping: Some tools for agriculture introduced by Eva Crane (1987), Intermediate Technology Publications. 22 pages, paperback, ISBN 0-946688-88-5. In 1985 Intermediate Technology published "Tools for agriculture: a buyer's guide to appropriate equipment", a source of information about equipment available for farming on a small scale and where it can be purchased. Chapter 12: "Beekeeping" has been reproduced as a single volume with the above title.

2.5 Technical co-operation activities: beekeeping, a directory and guide by Prof. W. Drescher and Dr. Eva Crane (1982), German Aid Agency, GTZ, Eschborn, Federal Republic of Germany. 172 pages. Directory of past and present beekeeping programmes in developing countries, with guidelines for carrying out such programmes and feasibility studies. Briefly describes *Apis cerana* morphology, behaviour and distribution.

2.6 Proceedings of the expert consultation on beekeeping with *Apis mellifera* in tropical and subtropical Asia (1984), FAO, Rome. 252 pages.

2.7 Tropical and sub-tropical apiculture, FAO Agricultural Services Bulletin No 68 (1986), FAO, Rome, Italy. 283 pages, paperback, ISBN 92-5-102444-8. A general introduction to the beekeeping encountered in developing countries. Technical information found in standard beekeeping manuals is not repeated in this book, which instead concentrates on the particular points which create problems for beekeepers in the tropics.

2.8 Apiculture in Tropical Climates. Full report on the First International Conference on Apiculture in Tropical Climates, London 1976. IBRA, London, UK. 220 pages, reprinted 1981, 1983. Papers described *Apis cerana* beekeeping development in India, Sri Lanka, and Indonesia.

2.9 Proceedings of the Second International Con-

ference on Apiculture in Tropical Climates, New Delhi, India, 1980 (1983). Indian Agricultural Research Institute, New Delhi, India. 728 pages. Photographs and diagrams. Descriptions of research, training and development programmes in India, Sri Lanka, Bangladesh, Thailand, Malaysia. Morphometric and biochemical studies on *Apis cerana* and pollination experiments.

2.10 Proceedings of the Third International Conference on Apiculture in Tropical Climates, Nairobi, Kenya, 1984 (1985). IBRA, London, UK. Apiculture in tropical Asia, pollination studies in Malaysia and India.

2.11 Beekeeping in rural development: unexploited beekeeping potential in the tropics, with particular reference to the Commonwealth, edited by Commonwealth Secretariat and IBRA (1979). Commonwealth Secretariat, London, UK. 196 pages. Photographs. Beekeeping development programmes in India, Sri Lanka and the Pacific (articles reprinted from (2.8) above).

C.3 Beekeeping journals published in Asia

CHINA
Zhongguo Yangfeng Chinese Academy of Agricultural Science, Xiang Shan, Beijing. (Chinese) 6/year.

INDIA
Indian Bee Journal All India Beekeepers' Association, 817 Sadashiv Peth, Pune 411 030. (English) 4/year.
Indian Honey Indian Institute of Honey, Martandam, Kuzhithurai, 629 163, Dist: Kanyakumari, Tamil Nadu. (English, Tamil, Malayalam) 4/year.
Madhu Prapancha D K Beekeepers' Cooperative Society Ltd., No L 386, Puttur 574 201, DK. (Kannada) 4/year.
Patrika Uttar Pradesh, Mannapal Sangh, PO Jeolikote, Dist: Mainital, UP. (Hindi) Irregular.

INDONESIA
Beekeeping Notes The Irian Jaya Joint Development Foundation, Jalan Percetakan 4-6, PO Box 410, Jayapura, Irian Jaya. (English, Bahasa) Irregular.

JAPAN
Honeybee Science Institute of Honeybee Science, Tamagawa University, Machida-shi, Tokyo 194. 4/year.

SOUTH KOREA
Korean Journal of Apiculture Apicultural Society of Korea, Institute of Korea Beekeeping Science, Department of Agricultural Biology, College of Agriculture, Seoul National University, Suwon 170. 2/year.

C.4 Other sources of information on Asian beekeeping
International Bee Research Association, 18 North Road, Cardiff CF1 3DY, UK.

IBRA houses one of the world's largest apicultural libraries and holds data on all aspects of bees and beekeeping. Files are maintained on the beekeeping development programmes in every country and with permission as necessary, IBRA seeks to make this information widely available. IBRA is a non-profit making charity: where possible, services are provided free of charge to beekeepers in developing countries, under funding from ODA.

The IBRA journals published quarterly (**Bee World, Journal of Apicultural Research, Apicultural Abstracts** and **The Newsletter for beekeepers in tropical and subtropical countries**) are all available on subscription and selected publications (including Bee World) are available at no cost, or at a reduced rate, to Members of the Association. Institutes in Asian Commonwealth countries may be eligible to receive Apicultural Abstracts free of charge by contacting the Commonwealth Advisory Bureau Liaison Officer at their British High Commission.

The Newsletter carries information on low-technology beekeeping and provides an opportunity for news of projects and developments to be circulated.

IBRA has two branch libraries in Asia:

Tropical Asia: Central Bee Research Institute, Khadi & Village Industries Commission, 1153 Ganeshkhind Road, Shivajinagar, Pune 411 016, INDIA

Eastern Asia: Institute of Honeybee Science, Tamagawa University, Machida-shi, Tokyo 194, JAPAN

C.5 Centres for beekeeping training with *Apis cerana*

Many of the programmes and research institutes listed in parts A and B offer training and extension in beekeeping. The Institutes listed below offer training and research facilities to both local and foreign, suitably qualified candidates. For other training centres (teaching *Apis mellifera* beekeeping) see Source Materials for Apiculture Leaflet 4, published by IBRA.

INDIA
Central Bee Research Institute, Khadi & Village Industries Commission, 1153 Ganeshkhind Road, Shivajinagar, Pune 411 016, INDIA
Director: Dr. R.P. Phadke
CBRI gives training from beginner-beekeeper to

post-graduate level. Various specialized courses are arranged, and the institute is recognized by the University of Pune as a centre for post-graduate research. Overseas students are accepted and course are taught in English.

JAPAN
Institute of Honeybee Science, Tamagawa University, Machida-shi, Tokyo 194, JAPAN.
Director: Professor T. Sakai
Six-month courses in beekeeping taught in English and Japanese: although *Apis cerana* is still found in Japan and colonies are kept at the Institute, almost all Japanese beekeeping is with *Apis mellifera*.

MALAYSIA
University Pertanian Malaysia, Serdang, Selangor, MALAYSIA
Beekeeping project leader: Makhdzir Mardan
Various courses, from one week to longer periods, teaching advanced beekeeping techniques. Graduate and honours students undertake apicultural research. Overseas students are accepted and course are taught in English.

CONCLUSION: FURTHER DEVELOPMENT OF BEEKEEPING WITH *APIS CERANA*

The data presented in this chapter summarize the current state of beekeeping with *Apis cerana*.

Of the 25 projects in Asia listed in Part A, 9 are internationally-funded programmes, currently under way and promoting beekeeping with *A. cerana*. Despite this level of funding and interest, there are still developing countries where *A. cerana* is present but beekeeping with this species is not being promoted. In some of these countries, funding is concentrated on the use of introduced *A. mellifera*.

There are strong arguments in favour of *A. mellifera* beekeeping, and many profitable beekeeping enterprises in Asia are based on the use of this species. However, the level of technology and technical skill required to manage European *A. mellifera* efficiently in the tropics preclude this type of beekeeping for the rural poor. It is these people who stand to benefit most from the low-input type of beekeeping possible with *A. cerana*. The promotion and extension of *A. cerana* beekeeping can be a slow process, but it provides a worthwhile activity for those living at subsistence level, and once understood and adopted by them, is likely to be continued as a source of free food. This contrasts with *A. mellifera* beekeeping which, in tropical Asia, is often taken up by those who have finances available to initiate such a venture as long as beekeeping provides a worth-

while financial return, but who may quickly turn to other activities should markets for bee products fall.

It is evident that research on *A. cerana* is under way at many institutes throughout Asia (Part B), but India stands alone in having 20 institutes reporting such research. With so many different organizations interested in honeybee research, India is a good example of networking, with the recent establishment of the *All India Coordinated Project on Honeybee Research and Training*, to coordinate work at the 11 agricultural universities which undertake apicultural research.

Development programmes and research institutes generate information about *A. cerana* and its management, and references to these reports and research papers can be found in Parts A and B. Part C of this paper reported other information sources such as the text books specifically prepared for some countries, further information and training.

The compilation of all this data makes it possible to identify areas where further effort is required:

Information on the biology of *Apis cerana*: The lists of research reveal that morphology, foraging behaviour, pesticide effect and disease are relatively well documented aspects of *A. cerana* biology. Much further study is required before the level of knowledge of *A. cerana* approaches that of *A. mellifera*. Examples of necessary research are the identification of the stimuli which trigger swarming and absconding, and the identification and use of *A. cerana* pheromones. One recent event which may encourage further research on *A. cerana* is the spread of *Varroa jacobsoni* throughout *A. mellifera* colonies in much of the rest of the world. The realization that *A. cerana* (the original host species of *V. jacobsoni*) has evolved with *Varroa* and survives successfully in its presence, has led to the study of *A. cerana*'s behaviour in combating the mite. This feature of *A. cerana*'s biology is an important attribute: a major problem with maintaining stocks of *A. mellifera* in tropical Asia is the constant skilled management and chemical treatment required to maintain strong colonies in the presence of *V. jacobsoni* and *Tropilaelaps clareae*.

Information on hives for *Apis cerana*: Clear information on hives appropriate for *A. cerana* and how to build them is severely lacking. This is true both for frame hives and top-bar hives.

A variety of different frame hives for *A. cerana* are used throughout Asia. In India alone, at least 6 sizes of hive are now in use and elsewhere various other sizes of movable frame hives are found - for example, in China a relatively large-sized, 10-frame hive is used, and in Japan *A. cerana* are successfully housed in Langstroth hives. One reason for these different hives is the variation in size of races of *A.*

cerana - for example, in Northern India *A. cerana* approach *A. mellifera* in size, and Langstroth and British Standard hives are appropriate. The tiny Newton hive is still very widely used in the Indian subcontinent even though this was the first design of frame hive to be introduced to Asia. Another problem facing Asian beekeepers is the supply of suitable wax foundation for these frame hives, which are commonly used in areas where such foundation is not available.

Promotion of beekeeping depends upon people with few resources being able to obtain appropriate hives. Most development programmes have to start at the beginning, designing a suitable hives, and this search for low-cost but efficient equipment has produced various designs of top-bar hives for *A. cerana*. The lack of knowledge of management techniques for *A. cerana* is reflected in the fact that most hives are small versions of hives originally developed for use with *A. mellifera*. In Nepal, a scaled-down version of a Kenya top-bar hive has been developed, and also the top-bar-log hive, which is an attempt to improve the traditional log hive by inserting a series of top-bars along its length. Quite independently, the very similar "Gelodok" hives have been developed in Malaysia.

There is an immediate need for well-prepared plans for constructing hives for *A. cerana*. Parameters such as optimum hive volume, entrance positioning, and size must be determined and a method devised to explain to the beginner how to relate size of bee to size of bee space allocated.

Information on the management of *A. cerana*: Knowledge of management techniques for *A. cerana* must be widened. The lack of research in this field may be because experiments on management are difficult to conduct, requiring identical test and control colonies, maintained under identical conditions.

One of the major problems with *A. cerana* is the tendency for colonies to abscond or swarm frequently. A common way of coping with this is the use of queen gates to prevent the queen leaving the hive. Queen gates provide an example of the necessity for co-operation between beekeepers; they have been widely used throughout the Indian subcontinent for many years, but were unknown in Malaysia until their recent introduction by the project here. However, the use of queen gates does not solve the problem of why *A. cerana* have such a high tendency to abscond. If this is a feature of *A. cerana*'s strategy for survival in a tropical environment, then selection programmes for bees which do not show this trait become a necessity and methods must be promoted for the multiplication and distribution of colonies of bees from selected stock. An alternative suggestion is that much absconding is caused by unfavourable

hive conditions, particularly wax moth infestation, and if this is the case, improved management practices must be encouraged. In addition, traditional beekeeping in which empty hives are sited until they attract a passing swarm will tend to select for bees which abscond or swarm frequently.

Information on the production of honey and beeswax by *A. cerana* and their marketing: Little information has been published on *A. cerana* honey, beeswax and other hive products. A common problem is the harvesting of *A. cerana* honey with a high water content, and many projects addressing the marketing of honey in Asia (both *A. cerana* and *A. dorsata*) request details of equipment to remove water from honey. To date, there is no satisfactory, low-technology method to achieve this without harming honey quality.

The physical properties of beeswax produced by *A. cerana* have been documented by Indian researchers, but information on harvesting and marketing this product in Asia is not available.

Information for extension: Beekeeping projects and government departments often prepare valuable extension material - but this is commonly in a local language and is not widely available. For would-be beekeepers in countries where there is no promotion of *A. cerana* beekeeping, it can be very difficult to obtain appropriate, practical information. The International Bee Research Association will help as far as possible in providing information to those who request it, but we in turn depend upon bee experts in Asia to keep us informed of new techniques and ideas.

IN SUMMARY

The people attending this course represent research workers, practical beekeepers, extension and aid agency personnel. All of these people have a different view of what is important in the development of *A. cerana* beekeeping but my message is that if *A. cerana* research is to be directed towards improved management techniques suitable for developing countries, then the problems mentioned above must be addressed. In short, these problems are of hive design and the management of *A. cerana*. For future research on *A. cerana* to be most effective, the various interested organizations must cooperate with one another to ensure that research is not unnecessarily repeated, and new findings are quickly made available throughout Asia. Opportunities for liaison are becoming more common: in addition to this course, Apimondia now has a Standing Commission for Beekeeping in Developing Countries, and at the Apimondia Congress in Poland last year, a special session on the biology of *A. cerana* was held. The

4th International Conference on Apiculture in Tropical Climates will provide a further venue for discussion devoted to *A. cerana*. IDRC recently arranged an opportunity for Thai beekeepers to meet and discuss strategy for the future: IDRC and other aid agencies (listed in part A3) may well be interested in backing future such ventures.

CHAPTER 38

THE ROLE OF FAO IN APICULTURE DEVELOPMENT
FAO APICULTURE PROJECTS IN OPERATION
(BIENNIUM 1986-87)

G. PALTRINIERI

INTRODUCTION

Beekeeping is an agricultural activity which is particularly suited to developing countries. In developing countries beekeeping is either historically non-existent or uses unproductive traditional methods. Modern beekeeping with movable frame hives adapted to local needs can be practiced anywhere.

Almost all developing countries have very good agro-climatic conditions for the development of apiculture. The development of apiculture has a number of positive aspects:

1. It can provide part or full-time rural employment, increase rural income, raise nutritional levels and increase agricultural productivity through crop pollination.
2. It requires little space and can be practiced on very small plots of land or even by landless people.
3. It requires small investment and a minimum of imported equipment.
4. It is complementary rather than competitive to other agricultural activities.
5. Honey, beeswax and other by-products are highly prized commodities.
6. Bees contribute to environmental preservation.

Apiculture is particularly suited to women because, in addition to the above:

1. It can be a part-time activity which can be carried out near the home without interfering with other household activities, and simultaneously improving the farmers' nutrition level.
2. It can generate independent income for women, with a consequent rise in social status.
3. It can stimulate rural craftsmanship based on beeswax, in which women are traditionally predominant.

It is in light of the above that the Agricultural Services Division of FAO has expanded the programme of beekeeping development in the last few years (Fig. 1). To promote apiculture among rural communities in developing countries, FAO is putting particular emphasis on:

1. Training of nationals at all levels.
2. Use of appropriate technology, bees and processing methods.

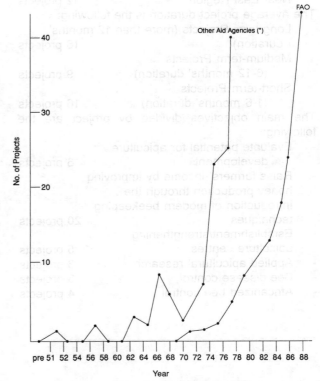

FIGURE 1. Number of beekeeping projects in operation worldwide.

3. Establishment of beekeeping centres with scientific extension staff and demonstration, research and teaching facilities.
4. Creation of groups of apiculturists in rural areas.
5. Local production of modern beekeeping equipment.
6. Control of bee diseases.
7. Integration of women into beekeeping activities.
8. Organization of regional activities in subjects of specific or regional relevance to apiculture.

FAO assists developing countries in using the appropriate techniques through direct support and advice to Member Nation as on promoting apiculture policy and planning, project identification, formulation and implementation.

A list of FAO beekeeping projects under implementation during the biennium 1986/87 is given in Appendix I. The regional distribution of projects is the following:

Africa Region	16 projects
Asia and the Pacific Region	8 projects
Latin America and the Caribbean Region	5 projects
Near East Region	12 projects

The average project duration is the following:

Long-term Projects (more than 12 months' duration)	16 projects
Medium-term Projects (6-12 months' duration)	9 projects
Short-term Projects (1-6 months' duration)	16 projects

The main objectives divided by project are the following:

- Evaluate potential for apiculture development	6 projects
- Raise farmers' income by improving honey production through the introduction of modern beekeeping techniques	20 projects
- Establishment/strengthening apiculture centres	5 projects
- Applied apicultural research	3 projects
- Bee disease control	3 projects
- Africanized bee control	4 projects

APPENDIX I. List of FAO beekeeping projects under implementation during 1986/87.

COUNTRY	TITLE AND PROJECT SYMBOL	DURATION	OBJECTIVES OF ASSISTANCE	INPUTS PROVIDED BY FAO
Africa Region				
Burkina Faso	Apiculture Development TCP/BKF/4510	22 months	To improve honey production and standards of living of the rural population and to establish a National Central of Apiculture.	Advisory service, consultancy services, external and local training, equipment and material.
	Apiculture Development at the Farm Level TCP/BKF/5760	4,5 months	To improve honey production at farm level.	Consultancy services, local training.
	Intensification of Apiculture at the Farm Level BKF/87/016	30 months	To increase the income of 200 farmers each year from the 2nd year of life of the project, particularly the women, and to improve their level of occupation.	Advisory service, consultancy services, external and local training, equipment and material.
Cape Verde	Reafforestation (Apiculture Component) GCP/CVI/015/BEL	5 years (1 month)	To assist the national forestry service to prepare and carry out a reafforestation programme and to evaluate potential for beekeeping development.	Consultancy services.
Ethiopia	Land Potential of Coffee and Oil Crops (Apiculture Component) TCP/ETH/4521	12 months (1 month)	To make a preliminary assessment of the suitability of the western forest of Kaffa for the production of crops other than coffee.	Consultancy services, local training, equipment and material.
	Assistance in Apiculture Development TCP/ETH/6763	18 months	To increase the production of honey in the country through introduction of new beekeeping techniques.	Consultancy services, external and local training, equipment and material.
Gabon	Apiculture Development TCP/GAB/6752	1 month	To evaluate the feasibility of an apiculture programme.	Consultancy services.
Ghana	Apiculture Promotion TCP/GHA/4505	12 months	To improve the standards of living of rural families through beekeeping activities, to extend the Apiculture Promotion Unit training activities to a wider rural area and to improve the quality of the training programme.	Consultancy services, external and local training.
Guinea	Integrated Rural Development in Fouta Djallon (Apiculture Component) GUI/86/004	36 months (1 month)	To evaluate potential for apiculture development in the project area.	Consultancy services.
Guinea Bissau	Apiculture Development	1 month	To evaluate potential for beekeeping development in the country.	Consultancy services.
Madagascar	Apiculture Development TCP/MAG/4507	12 months	To increase honey production through modern methods of production.	Consultancy services, external and local training, equipment and material.
	Apiculture Development in Ambositra Province MAG/608/MUL		To increase apiculture development in the area by providing modern beekeeping equipment.	Equipment and material.

APPENDIX I - continued

COUNTRY	TITLE AND PROJECT SYMBOL	DURATION	OBJECTIVES OF ASSISTANCE	INPUTS PROVIDED BY FAO
Mali	Apiculture Development MLI/85/003	24 months	To consolidate and organize the National Centre of Apiculture of Bamako which has the responsibility of training, technical assistance and research. To prepare and initiate applied research programmes. To consolidate rural apiculture activities.	Advisory service, consultancy services, external and local training, equipment and material.
Mauritius	Assistance to the Agricultural Sector (Apiculture Component: Queens for Sale to Beekeepers) MAR/86/002	12 months (2 months)	To increase honey production through better queen rearing methods and supply more prolific queens to beekeepers.	Consultancy services, local training, equipment and services.
Mozambique	Apiculture Development in Manica Province TCP/MOZ/6756	18 months	To increase the production and marketing of honey and beeswax in the Manica Province through the introduction of modern techniques and improved beehives, using the existing resources and popularizing the activity at all community levels so that it can more fully contribute to the improvement of the population's diet and raising of rural incomes and employment.	Consultancy services, local training, equipment and material.
Sao Tome	Apiculture Development TCP/STP/4504	12 months	To establish a scientific base for modern apiculture. To train local staff to promote apiculture. To promote the creation of beekeepers' cooperatives and associations.	Consultancy services, external and local training, equipment and material.

Asia and the Pacific Region

Afghanistan	Apiculture Development AFG/85/028	27 months	To provide advisory services and technical assistance to the existing Apiculture Centre in Kabul for upgrading its staff and facilities to undertake research, training and extension in apiculture.	Advisory service, external and local training, equipment and material.
India	Centre of Advanced Studies for Post-Graduate Phase III: Agricultural Education (Apiculture Component) IND/78/020	7,5 years (1 month)	To increase and strengthen facilities for post-graduate studies and research in apiculture.	Consultancy services, local training, equipment and material.
Indonesia	Beekeeping for Rural Development INS/85/008	36 months	To establish a research, training and demonstration centre. To establish a local industry for production of beekeeping equipment and bee foundation, and two queen rearing stations.	Advisory service, consultancy services, external and local training, equipment and material.

APPENDIX I - continued

COUNTRY	TITLE AND PROJECT SYMBOL	DURATION	OBJECTIVES OF ASSISTANCE	INPUTS PROVIDED BY FAO
Maldives	Advisory Services and Fellowship in Agriculture, Fisheries, Livestock, and Forestry (Apiculture Component) RAS/79/123	24 months (1 month)	To evaluate potential for bee pollination development in cocoa plantation.	Consultancy services.
Pakistan	Technical Assistance Programme for the Pakistan Agricultural Research Centre (Apiculture Component) UTF/PAK/072	36 months (3 months)	To provide technical assistance to the Pakistan Agricultural Research Council. Assistance comprises practical training for queen rearing and honeybee management, delivery of lectures on selective breeding of honeybees, queen rearing, pollen, and royal jelly production.	Consultancy services, local training.
Republic of Korea	Apiculture Development Laboratory and Training Centre TCP/ROK/6651	18 months	To establish an experimental and demonstration apiary to initiate applied research and extension programmes.	Consultancy services, external and local training, equipment and material.
Vanuatu	Beekeeping Training and Demonstration Programme TCP/VAN/6651	18 months	To establish and optimize European honeybees and to establish a trained cadre of extension beekeeping specialists.	Advisory service, external and local training, equipment and material.
Vietnam	Assistance to Apiculture Development TCP/VIE/4405	24 months	To increase honey production in the country by providing assistance to the Beekeeping Company in developing methods of parasitic mites control, provision and selection of strains of bees, modernization of laboratory and beekeeping equipment, training of technicians and beekeepers.	Consultancy services, external and local training, equipment and material.

Latin America and the Caribbean

Brazil	Apiculture Development in the State of Bahia TCP/BRA/6653	12 months	To stimulate the expansion of beekeeping in regions with a good potential for apiculture development, but where until today hunting has been the only method used to collect honey. To preserve stingless bees useful for pollination, introducing new techniques for handling them, adapted to different regional realities. To improve the Africanized bees, mainly through the selection of queen bees, in order to increase their productivity and to reduce their aggressivity.	Consultancy services, external and local training, equipment and material.
El Salvador	Assistance to the African Bee Prevention and Control Programme (TCP/ELS/4503	12 months	To cooperate in establishing a national programme of African bee control. To train technicians and beekeepers. To establish model hives.	Consultancy services, external and local training, equipment and material.

APPENDIX I - continued

COUNTRY	TITLE AND PROJECT SYMBOL	DURATION	OBJECTIVES OF ASSISTANCE	INPUTS PROVIDED BY FAO
Guyana	Development of the Bee Industry TCP/GUY/6651	12 months	The general objective of the project is to improve the economy of rural families through a wider use of beekeeping as primary and secondary sources of family income, as well as to reach local self-sufficiency and export of honey. The specific purpose of the project is to assist the Ministry of Agriculture to establish a pilot scale commercial honey production unit and to prepare a feasibility study for the large scale production of honey to meet local and export needs.	Consultancy services, local training, equipment and material.
Honduras	Assistance to the African Bee Control Programme TCP/HON/4507	12 months	To prepare a programme for the control of the Africanized bees. To train technicians and beekeepers.	Consultancy services, external and local training, equipment and material.
Mexico	Assistance to African Bee Prevention and National Control Programme TCP/MEX/4505	24 months	To establish a national documentation centre for apiculture, to produce didactic material for beekeepers and to establish experimental stations to control Africanized bees in Chiapas and Yucatan.	Consultancy services, external and local training, equipment and material.
Near East Region				
Algeria	Formation and Divulgation (Apiculture Component) ALG/83/002	12 months (2 months)	To contribute to the establishment and consolidation of the national extension service, and of a national extension programme concentrating on the development needs of the agricultural sector.	Local training.
Djibouti	Apiculture Development TCP/DJI/6651	1 month	To evaluate potential for apiculture development in the country.	Consultancy services.
Egypt	Honey Improvement TCP/EGY/4509	12 months	To improve honey production through the introduction of improved management, integrated programme of diseases and pest control, and upgrading of local bee breeds through better queen rearing and artificial insemination techniques.	Consultancy services, external and local training, equipment and material.
Iraq	Apiculture Development TCP/IRQ/6651	24 months	To contribute to the development of the beekeeping industry on a modern basis and to increase the income of farmers through the part-time activity.	Consultancy services, local training, equipment and material.
Lebanon	Programme against *Varroa* Mite TCP/LEB/6653	8 months	To assist the government and the beekeepers in the control of *Varroa* mites.	External training, equipment and material.

APPENDIX I - continued

COUNTRY	TITLE AND PROJECT SYMBOL	DURATION	OBJECTIVES OF ASSISTANCE	INPUTS PROVIDED BY FAO
Libya	Strengthening of the Agricultural Research Centre (Apiculture Component) UTF/LIB/006/LIB	5 years (1 month)	To assist in the preparation of applied apicultural research programmes and to strengthen their efficiency.	Consultancy services, local training.
Morocco	Assistance to Women's Beekeeping Cooperatives TCP/MOR/6653	18 months	To establish 4 demonstration apiaries and to provide training to women for the development of women's apiculture cooperatives.	Consultancy services, local training, equipment and material.
Turkey	Assistance to Apiculture Development in Erzurum Province TCP/TUR/4505	12 months	To improve apiculture production through better management techniques and *Varroa* mite control.	Consultancy services, local training.
	Forestry and Livestock Training in the Near East Region (Apiculture Component) TCP/TUR/6651	19 months	To promote technical cooperation among the countries of the Near East Region with training courses in apiculture.	Local training, material.
	Erzurum Rural Development Project (Apiculture Component) UTF/TUR/028	45 months (4 months)	To increase the production of honey in Erzurum Province. To train local beekeepers in management and *Varroa* control.	Consultancy services, local training, equipment and material.
Regional	Improvement of Technical Capabilities in Apiculture Production RAB/84/003	3 years	To improve apiculture production and the standard of living of the rural population by introducing modern methods of production and to establish a framework to train local technicians.	Consultancy services, local training.

ADDRESSES OF CONTRIBUTORS

AHMAD, R. Honeybee Research Laboratory, National Agricultural Research Centre, P.O. NARC, Islamabad, Pakistan

ANDERSON, D.L. CSIRO, Division of Entomology, P.O. Box 1700, Canberra A.C.T. 2601, Australia

APPANAH, S. Forest Research Institute Malaysia, Kepong, 52109 Kuala Lumpur, Malaysia

BRADBEAR, N. International Bee Research Association, 18 North Road, Cardiff CFI 3DY, UK

CHAUDHRY, M.I. Director of Entomology, Pakistan Forest Institute, Peshawar, Pakistan

CRANE, E. International Bee Research Association, Woodside House, Woodside Hill, Gerrards Cross, Bucks SL9 9TE UK

DEWAN, S.M.A.L. Bee Research Unit, School of Applied and Pure Biology, University of Wales College of Cardiff, Cardiff CF1 3TL, U.K.

FANG, Y.Z. Institute of Apicultural Research, Chinese Academy of Agriculture Sciences, Beijing, China

GRECO, C.F. Department of Environmental Biology, University of Guelph, Guelph, Ontario N1G 2W1 Canada

HADISOESILO, S. Jl. Rawa Bambu No. 9, Pasar Minggu, Jakarta Selatan, Indonesia

IBRAHIM, R. Plant Protection Department, Universiti Pertanian Malaysia, Serdang, Selangor, Malaysia

KEVAN, P.G. Department of Environmental Biology, University of Guelph, Guelph, Ontario N1G 2W1 Canada

KHAN, B.M. Associate Professor, Dept. of Entomology, NWFP Agricultural University, Peshawar, Pakistan

KIEW, R. Department of Biology, Universiti Pertanian Malaysia, 43400 Serdang, Selangor, Malaysia

KOENIGER, N. Institut für Bienenkunde (Polytechnische Gesellschaft), Fachbereich Biologie der Universität Frankfurt/M., Karl-von-Frisch-Weg 2, D 6370 Oberursel, West Germany

KWANG, C.J. Crop Protection Branch, Department of Agriculture, Kuala Lumpur

MACKAY, K. Director, ICLARM, MC PO Box 1501, Makati, Metro Manila, 1299, Philippines

MATSUKA, M. Institute of Honeybee Science, Tamagawa University, Machida-shi, Tokyo 194 Japan

MISHRA, R.C. All India Co-ordinated Research Project on Honeybee Research and Training, Haryana Agricultural University, Hisar - 125 004, India

ONO, M. Institute of Honeybee Science, Tamagawa University, Machida, Tokyo, 194 Japan

PALTRINIERI, G. Food Industries Officer, Food and Agricultural Industries Service, Agricultural Services Division, Food and Agricultural Organization of the United Nations, Viale delle Terme di Caracalla, 00100 Rome, Italy

PAXTON, R.J. Bee Research Unit, School of Applied and Pure Biology, University of Wales College of Cardiff, Cardiff CF1 3TL, U.K.

PUNCHIHEWA, R.W.K. Honeybee Research Facility, Sri Lanka Department of Agriculture, Horticulture Research and Development Institute, Division of Apiculture, Horticulture Station, Kananwila, Horana, Sri Lanka

QUINIONES, A.C. Professor and Director for Research, Central Luzon State University, Muñoz, Nueva Ecija, Philippines

REDDY, C.C. Department of Zoology, Bangalore University, Bangalore, India

RINDERER, T.E. Honey-Bee Breeding, Genetics, and Physiology Laboratory, United States Department of Agriculture, Agriculture Research Service, 1157 Ben Hur Road, Baton Rouge, Louisiana 70820 USA

SASAKI, M. Institute of Honeybee Science, Tamagawa University, Machida-shi, Tokyo 194 Japan

SIHAG, R.C. All India Co-ordinated Research Project on Honeybee Research and Training, Haryana Agricultural University, Hisar - 125 004, India

SVENSSON, B. Box 5034, S-733 92 Sala, Sweden

SYLVESTER, H.A. Honey-Bee Breeding, Genetics, and Physiology Laboratory, United States Department of Agriculture, Agricultural Research Service, 1157 Ben Hur Road, Baton Rouge, Louisiana 70820 USA

TSURUTA, T. Institute of Honeybee Science, Tamagawa University, Machida-shi, Tokyo 194 Japan

VERMA, L.R. Department of Bio-Sciences, Himachal Pradesh University, Shimla - 171 005, Himachal Pradesh, India[1]

WILSON, G.D. Toronto, Ontario, Canada.

WONGSIRI, S. Bee Biology Research Unit, Department of Biology, Chulalongkorn University, Bangkok, Thailand

YAMAZAKI. S. Institute of Honeybee Science, Tamagawa University, Machida-shi, Tokyo 194, Japan

YOSHIDA, T. Institute of Honeybee Science, Tamagawa University, Machida-shi, Tokyo 194, Japan

YUSOF, M.R. Central Research Laboratories, Malaysian Agricultural Research and Development Inst., Serdang, Selangor, Malaysia

Hiratsuka, 17
Hirst, 181, 182
hive
    box, 15, 236
    Kenya top-bar, 251, 290
    log, 4, 9, 10, 12, 13, 19, 41, 61, 177, 209, 290
    Newton, 290
Ho, 277
hoarding, 50, 59, 117, 225
Hocking, 19, 26
Honduras, 298
Hong Kong, 189, 271
Hornitzky, 161, 162, 164-166, 169
Hoshiba, 82, 83, 85, 93, 105, 283
Howard, 138, 139, 147, 149, 151, 152
Huang, 17
Hubbell, 24-26
Huffaker, 178, 179, 199, 203, 205, 223, 227
Hussain, 42, 51
hypopharyngeal gland, 32, 33, 164, 279
Hyptis suaveolems (see suag-kabayo), 265
Ibrahim, 283
Ifantidis, 171, 173, 174
Illicium, 266
Illingworth, 181, 182
importation, 48, 81, 188, 193-195, 263, 269
India, 3-6, 9, 13, 14, 35-37, 41-48, 50, 101, 117, 129,
    131, 135-137, 143, 145, 166, 181, 189, 193, 194, 200,
    209, 212, 213, 214, 271, 273, 279, 286, 288, 290, 296
Indian ball (see *Aegle marmelos*)
indigo
    Java (see *Indigofera arrecta*), 137
    Sumatrana (see *Indigofera tinctoria*), 137
Indigofera arrecta (see indigo - Java), 137
Indigofera tinctoria tinctoria (see indigo - Sumatrana), 138
Indonesia, 6, 14, 271, 274, 282, 286, 288, 296
Inoue, 75, 77
insecticide, 13, 19, 26, 118, 145, 179, 188, 199-201,
    203-205, 212, 264, 280, 282
instrumental insemination, 31, 39, 41, 51, 81-83, 85, 86,
    101, 103, 106, 107, 109, 211
integrated pest management, 199, 204, 205
Ipomoea batates (see potato - sweet), 130
Iran, 6, 9, 30, 32, 271, 274, 283
Iraq, 298
iridovirus, 166, 169, 188
Ito, 39, 52
jackfruit (see *Artocarpus*), 130
Jackson, 204
Jadhav, 136, 139
Jamaica, 119, 121, 131
jambolan (see *Syzygium cumini*), 130
jambu (*Syzygium* spp.), 130
Jammu, 211
Jander, 24, 26
Japan, 6, 9, 11-14, 30, 34-37, 42, 45, 55, 59, 107, 166,
    171, 189, 271, 283, 288, 289
Jasinski, 101, 106
Java, 42, 45, 131, 132, 271
Jay, 125-127, 199, 203
Jeffree, 181, 182
Jeffrey, 204

Jhajj, 138, 139, 280
Jitendra Mohan, 137, 139
Johansen, 19, 26, 200, 201, 203, 204
Johansson, 24, 26, 101, 105, 210, 212, 215
Johnson, 24-26, 153, 157, 223, 227
Jones, 26, 201, 204, 232, 237, 239, 242
Jordan, 83, 85
Jørgensen, 13, 17
Joseph, 139, 279
Joshi, 13, 17, 136, 141, 209, 215, 281
jujube, 129, 135
    Chinese (see *Ziziphus jujuba*), 135
    Indian (see *Ziziphus mauritiana*), 129, 261
Justicia genederusa, 261
jute
    congo (*Corchorus* spp.), 137
    tussa (see *Corchorus olitorius*, 137
    white (see *Corchorus capsularis*), 137
Kafle, 284
Kaissling, 31, 39
kakawate (see *Gliceridia sepium*), 265
Kakkar, 136, 139, 140, 280
Kaloyereas, 241, 242
Kamal, 131, 133
Kampuchea, 6, 14, 271
Kang, 275
Kang-Chen, 284
Kapil, 42, 51, 57, 139, 141, 174, 201, 203, 204, 281
kapok (see *Ceiba pentandra*), 132
Kardjono, 286
Karnataka, 45, 46, 211
Kashmir, 5-9, 13, 43-45, 50, 145, 162, 166, 177, 211
Kaufield, 149
Kauhausen, 39
Kellogg, 42, 51
kempas (see *Koompasia malaccensis*)
kenaf (see *Hibiscus cannabinus*), 132
Kerala, 45, 46, 211
Kerr, 22, 26
Kevan, 1, vi, 19, 24, 26, 38, 77, 113, 116, 125-127, 129,
    140, 153, 156, 157, 193, 195, 199, 200, 204, 223, 225,
    227, 228, 229, 232, 251, 254, 255, 260, 262, 272, 275,
    301
Khan, 42, 51, 147, 149, 151, 181, 182, 278, 301
Khawja, 182
Khurana, 52
Kiew, 25, 26, 117, 118, 122, 123, 283, 301
Kigatiira, 223, 227
Killion, 235, 242
Kimmel, 88, 90
Kitagawa, 126, 127
kitembilla (see *Doryalis* spp.), 130
kiwi (see *Actinidia* spp.), 130
Klassen, 199, 204
Kloft, 9, 17, 34, 39
Koeniger, 29, 34-39, 42, 48, 51, 77, 85, 105, 116, 127,
    140, 171, 174, 223, 227, 228, 285, 301
Koompasia malaccensis (kempas), 22
Korea, 6, 9, 12, 13, 240, 271, 274, 283, 288, 297
Kouta, 75, 78
Koutensky, 147, 149, 150
Kozin, 199, 204